FRACTURE FEMINISM

SUNY series, Studies in the Long Nineteenth Century
———————
Pamela K. Gilbert, editor

FRACTURE FEMINISM

The Politics of Impossible Time
in British Romanticism

DAVID SIGLER

Cover art: *Mary Shelley in Italy*, by Louisa Amelia Albani, mixed media.

Published by State University of New York Press, Albany

© 2021 State University of New York

All rights reserved

Printed in the United States of America

No part of this book may be used or reproduced in any manner whatsoever without written permission. No part of this book may be stored in a retrieval system or transmitted in any form or by any means including electronic, electrostatic, magnetic tape, mechanical, photocopying, recording, or otherwise without the prior permission in writing of the publisher.

For information, contact State University of New York Press, Albany, NY
www.sunypress.edu

Library of Congress Cataloging-in-Publication Data

Name: Sigler, David, author
Title: Fracture feminism : the politics of impossible time in British romanticism / David Sigler, author.
Description: Albany : State University of New York Press, [2021] | Series: SUNY series, studies in the long nineteenth century | Includes bibliographical references and index.
Identifiers: ISBN 9781438484853 (hardcover : alk. paper) | ISBN 9781438484860 (pbk. : alk. paper) | ISBN 9781438484877 (ebook)
Library of Congress Control Number: 2021939443

10 9 8 7 6 5 4 3 2 1

Contents

Acknowledgments   vii

Introduction   1

Chapter 1   The Uses of History in Wollstonecraft's Afterlives   23

Chapter 2   Adoptive Siblings across Oceans of Futurity: *Paul and Virginia* and *The Victim of Prejudice*   65

Chapter 3   Della Cruscan Time   115

Chapter 4   Future Poetry: Clock Time Misses Barbauld, Smith, Richardson, and Hemans   155

Chapter 5   *Gulzara* and *The Last Man*: Worldwide-izing the *Roman à Clef*   203

Conclusion   241

Notes   251

Works Cited   275

Index   301

Acknowledgments

This research was funded by an Insight Grant from the Social Sciences and Humanities Research Council of Canada (Agency Reference Number 435-2017-0037). The book would never have been possible without the grant, so I'm extremely thankful for it. Several of the ideas in this book were set in motion at the NEH Summer Seminar on "Reassessing Romanticism" held in 2013 at the University of Nebraska, led by Stephen C. Behrendt. I remain grateful for that opportunity and Dr. Behrendt's mentorship. A portion of chapter 2 appeared in an earlier form as an article entitled " 'The Ocean of Futurity, Which Has No Boundaries': The Deconstructive Politics of Helen Maria Williams's Translation of *Paul and Virginia*," in *European Romantic Review* vol. 23, no. 5, pp. 575–592. The article was published on October 1, 2012, and is reprinted here by permission of the publisher, Taylor & Francis Ltd., http://www.tandfonline.com.

I would like to thank everyone at SUNY Press who helped bring this manuscript through the publication process. I especially thank Rebecca Colesworthy, the acquisitions editor, for her enthusiasm for this project and astonishing gumption, as well as James Peltz, the Press's associate director and editor-in-chief, who seamlessly covered for Rebecca as necessary along the way. I am grateful to have had anonymous peer reviewers who took such care and showed such great intellectual generosity with this manuscript. They gave truly expert advice. I also thank editorial coordinator Catherine Blackwell for her care with the details.

I have received tremendous support, intellectual and material, from the University of Calgary. I would especially like to acknowledge Richard Sigurdson, Dean of the Faculty of Arts, and Jacqueline Jenkins, Head of English, as they have been enormously supportive. Startup funds, departmental travel funds, and a developmental SSHRC-funded grant internally administered by the Faculty of Arts helped get me started on this project; a well-timed Research and Scholarship Leave enabled the project's completion. My more immediate colleagues have given me a strong research community in which to develop my thinking. I want to recognize for special thanks Karen Bourrier, Susan Cahill, Anthony Camara, Michael Tavel Clarke, Donna Coates, Faye Halpern, Larissa Lai, Derritt Mason, Christian Olbey, Michael Ullyot, Martin Wagner, and Jason Wiens, all of whom offered me good advice along the way. I am grateful to those in the Faculty of Arts who helped me develop my grant proposal—most of all Kinga Olszewska, whose judgment I have learned always to trust, and also Robert Oxoby and Penny Pexman, during their terms as Associate Deans (Research). Finally, I would like to thank University of Calgary Research Services and the librarians at University of Calgary Libraries and Cultural Resources, particularly Melanie Boyd.

I have worked with a superb graduate research assistant over the last several years, Isabelle Michalski, who along the way became my research collaborator on a separate essay. I have also appreciated the chance to work collaboratively with Celiese Lypka on two articles that, although distinct from this book project, informed my thinking for it. Isabelle and Celiese have been important interlocutors for me over the last few years. Less formally, discussions with graduate students John MacPhereson, Bobby Sze Chun Ng, and Neil Surkan have sustained me in this work.

Many extramural colleagues have been hugely supportive, both as mentors and friends, throughout this project. They have given me opportunities to develop this work, read pieces of work in progress, offered advice on new directions, alerted me when things appeared to be spiraling into futility, or suggested the perfect next thing to read. In the process, through a blend of attentiveness, praise, and what often seemed to be open hostility, they pushed me into better arguments. The most vital of these allies have been Suzanne Barnett, Stephen Behrendt, Colin Carman, David Clark, David Collings, Ashley Cross, Kellie Donovan-Condron, Joel Faflak, Cassandra Falke, Michelle Faubert, Elizabeth Fay, Daniela Garofalo, Michael Genovese, Erin Goss, Shoshannah Bryn Jones Square, Michael Kramp, Devoney Looser, Nowell Marshall, Anne McCarthy, Grace Moore, Lucy Morrison, Jonathan Mulrooney, Christopher Nagle, Jean-Michel Rabaté, Brian Rejack, Marlon Ross, Richard Sha, Anna Shajirat, Kate Singer, Orianne Smith, Michele Speitz, Michael Theune, Crystal Veronie, Orrin Wang, Chris Washington, and Gary Williams. Much could (and ought to) be said about the intellectual generosity of each of these people, the opportunities they have opened for me, and the mark they have left on this work, but I will simply express my deepest thanks without inelegantly gushing.

Most of all, I am in awe of my unfaltering partner, Dawn Hamilton, who unsuspectingly serves as a model of intelligence, love, feminism, and work ethic for me. It has not escaped me how often the fracture feminists wrote enthusiastically of "dawn," and I believe it is apt. I wish to thank Ms. Hamilton for not murdering me while we sheltered in place to avoid the coronavirus. I reserve similar supreme thanks for my parents, Judy and Murray Sigler, who have been, as ever, the picture of love, support, and encouragement.

Introduction

In the British Romantic period, feminist literary writers would often question the meaning of time, rather than directly champion rights for women. Perceiving time to be a system of social control, they pried open its linearity to display what we might think of as a fracture within; they placed themselves, rhetorically speaking, within that fracture as a way of discussing current events. I call this tradition "fracture feminism." By occupying a fracture in time, these writers could seize the space and authority to assess the immediate political world. The fracture feminists resisted the demands of clock and calendar, the obligatory patriotism that often came along with such demands, and the prevailing narratives of English history. They seemed to have knowledge from the future, or at least a strange disregard for chronology. By keeping a foothold in the future while remaining focused on the present, their writing was incompletely subject to the demands of time.

To give an example: in June of 1809, the fifteen-year-old Felicia Dorothea Browne, later to be known as Felicia Hemans, was writing "her first mature poem," an ambitious work of over 800 lines, entitled "War and Peace."[1] The poem would eventually become part of Browne's third collection, *The Domestic Affections*, which would establish her literary stardom in 1812. Browne was a patriotic child from a military family, and so, perhaps inevitably, she thought of the United Kingdom as a massive war machine. Her country had been at war her entire life, having assembled, through the eighteenth century, its standing army and enormous military apparatus.[2] The family's correspondences reveal that Browne thought of the army as an essential attribute of Britishness generally, even as "she was aware that this [interest of hers] was not wholly appropriate for a young woman."[3] Caught between a national war effort with which

1

she was fascinated and the domestic realm that was supposed to be her station—a tension captured by the poem's very presence in a volume of that title and theme—Browne appealed to the future as a way to navigate the impasse. The poem begins:

> Thou, bright Futurity! whose prospect beams,
> In dawning radiance on our day-light dreams;
> Whose lambent meteors and ethereal forms
> Gild the dark clouds, and glitter thro' the storms;
> . . .
> Thou bright Futurity! whose morning-star
> Still beams unveil'd, unclouded, from afar;
> Whose lovely vista smiling Hope surveys,
> Thro' the dim twilight of the silvery haze[.][4]

Two obvious questions arise from this passage. The first is a question of rhetorical authority: how did a teenager, especially one who felt strictly beholden to normative codes of female behavior and thought, begin to feel emboldened to intervene in matters of foreign policy? Let us keep in mind that Browne was, at this time, aspiring to write "around the pressure and expectations of what a woman poet 'should' write" and would go on to become "the central Romantic-era poet of feminine domesticity."[5] The second question arises from the *non sequitur* of "bright Futurity": what does "bright Futurity" have to do with contemporary matters of "War and Peace"? Or, put differently, why would "Futurity" be the proper addressee of a girl's political commentary, given that the politics in question were playing out here and now? The two questions may seem unrelated, but this book will suggest that they are intertwined in complex ways. Browne, I will suggest, gained authority by drawing upon a specific tradition of feminist writing, one less than twice as old as Browne herself, which used an orientation to the future to make space for political commentary by women. Browne's appeal to "futurity" was, in this way, a decidedly gendered response to questions of national security.

Early pioneers of that women's writing tradition included the Della Cruscan poetic circle, Catherine Macaulay, Mary Wollstonecraft, Anna Letitia Barbauld, and Helen Maria Williams. They, in turn, would inspire the feminist novels of Mary Hays, the late-career poetry of Charlotte Smith, the post-Waterloo poetry of Charlotte Caroline Richardson, the ambiguously dark lyricism of Felicia Hemans (as Browne would come

INTRODUCTION   3

to be known), and the science fiction pioneer Mary Shelley, each of whom extended this atemporal mode of cultural critique in new literary directions. Collectively, their work can be said to form what Stephen C. Behrendt would call a "pattern of overt reference" spanning several genres.[6] The fracture feminists would respond to contemporary politics as if they were visitors from the future, and in this way participated in, and even deconstructed, political discussions that would otherwise have disregarded a woman's perspective. The "future histories of man" that they were writing—to borrow an oxymoron from Macaulay—exploited a fracture in the dominant political discussions of their era.[7]

During the late eighteenth and early nineteenth centuries, the nation of Great Britain, then becoming the United Kingdom, was broadly instilling a new collective sense of regularized time. Time, and the subjects' obligations to uphold it, was being used as an ideological cudgel for the purposes of social control. In defiance of that mandate, a host of feminist writers, mostly women, sought ways, in their novels, poetry, and nonfiction, to deactivate both clock and calendar. These were the fracture feminists. The consequences of their efforts were, in a way, negligible, in the sense that speaking from the future seems so unimaginable that it will often resonate silently or meaninglessly. Yet the work was also profound, because a writer who can meddle with the system of time will always be at least partially exempt from the immediate now, which is, in a way, an optimal perspective from which to examine a culture. Their work, seen in this light, amounts to an experimental and even sometimes utopian feminist tradition. The fracture feminists would respond to political events by prematurely historicizing them or expressing nostalgia for the future. By looking at the world from the future, they learned how to affirm womanhood as an asynchronous experience, never contemporary with its own times. The movement was associated with the emergent figure of what was called "the female philosopher," a term claimed by feminist thinkers like Macaulay, Wollstonecraft, Robinson, and Hays, and that found iteration, with adaptations, through the Regency.[8] Their work is sometimes hard to recognize as fracture feminism because temporal ruptures can be subtle and ambiguous. Fracture feminism refuses to assert a positive identity, which means it does not always easily register as feminism to us. Instead, it positively asserts the negative space of the fracture itself, and thus establishes many of the protocols of what today we would call psychoanalysis and deconstruction.

There has recently been a tremendous amount of exciting work within British Romantic studies, theorizing time. This makes sense, given how, as we are better and better appreciating, this was an important period for the development of clock time as a national and global system.[9] Some scholars have emphasized how women could participate in the Romantic era's culture of prophecy and prediction.[10] Others have highlighted a tendency for Romantic writers to speculate about what the future might be like.[11] These phenomena are separate from, though adjacent to, fracture feminism. To make a prediction or to historicize one's own moment does not call chronology into question; rather, it asserts one's mastery of the timeline, while leaving the timeline intact. The fracture feminists were describing the world immediately around them; they were not making predictions, nor trying to be prophets. It was as if they, having by happenstance fallen into a temporal abyss, possessed knowledge from the future that might be relevant to people up above who were still stuck living in the now. In an attempt to convey the paradoxes of the situation, I shall call the time of such writing "the contemporary future," an oxymoron that suggests that these writers imagined the future to be already present. The contemporary future is the peculiar temporality of the fracture.

To write from the contemporary future is different from recognizing that the present will one day be someone else's past; it is to assert that the future is already here, rather than something to be awaited. When Mary Shelley claimed, in her journal of 1822, that "I am future waste paper,"[12] she was not predicting that she or her writings would one day be thrown away; she was declaring herself to be, already, the waste paper of the future. To assert one's existence as waste paper is to identify with deterioration and circumscription; it is to "be" the support and backing of an excess of writing which, if it is to remain waste paper, can never be incinerated.[13] Waste paper, which, by its very nature, is an archive of that which has been deemed regrettable or unnecessary, here becomes an archive of the future, and Shelley claims to *be* this, emphatically, in the present tense. There was a growing sense, into and across the nineteenth century, that the present was somehow excessive and would, for some time, flummox attempts to write its history.[14] Shelley claimed to be, rather than just to understand, that excess. The integrity of time collapses, I shall argue, when future waste paper offers commentary on something immediate and current.

Today, we are so accustomed to thinking of sex as a positive identity category—something that someone "is"—that it can be hard even to recognize a feminist writing tradition like this one. How can one claim to be a future excess of writing, rather than an author or subject? The

INTRODUCTION 5

fracture feminists were not, in such moments, fully asserting themselves as contributors to national conversations about politics, and neither were they writing as people excluded from those conversations. They were not developing an alternative woman's viewpoint on the politics of time; rather, they would inhabit contradictions *in* the era's emergent discourses of time, and then document, accentuate, and exploit those contradictions. It is a very different concept-metaphor from being "marginalized"; it was a mode of intimate cultural analysis that today we would call deconstructive. To occupy and embody the fracture was a dangerous rhetorical gambit for a woman writer: on the one hand, the idea of the contemporary future gave feminist writers a foothold into conversations in which they would otherwise have been excluded. In the course of those conversations, they may seek, for instance, to expand parliamentary representation, or protest a war, or challenge patriarchy, or intervene in debates around the rights of women or citizens, or chip away at the cultural prestige of banks, the army, or the empire. Exploiting the fracture in time was a way of dislocating the normative temporalities that were propping up those institutions. Yet, on the other hand, to write from the contemporary future ensured that their views would never fully "count" in an era in which many of the central political questions (including the institution of the national census in 1801) depended on counting, being counted, or being held to account.[15] It was a way of recognizing that, if contemporary political discourse were fractured along gender lines, this fracture was not of women's making, but was rather the symptom of a longstanding problem, namely, patriarchy, which displaced British women from the present through the pressure of the past. To acknowledge the temporal fracture was a way of marking the problem of women's unmaking in the present, much as Wollstonecraft so clearly diagnosed. Women, prevented from inhabiting a viable space in the contemporary moment, and thereby disincentivized from partaking in the many optimisms of the early nineteenth century, developed an alternate mode of futurity that might prove hospitable for justice, taken as an impossible event, even if this mode did not lead the way to reconciliation or belonging.

Jacques Lacan, the twentieth-century psychoanalyst, saw this ontological predicament as particular to women's experience. Women, he controversially asserts, are "pas-tout," which has been variously translated as "not-whole" or "not all."[16] Using Lacan's terminology, one would say that fracture feminists are writers who, despite being "there in full," recognize that "there is something more," a supplement—that is, the contemporary future—that ensures that they "can but be excluded."[17] In order to find avenues of resistance to the phallocratic temporalities closing in on them, they refused to register as completely current. There would remain a part of them that would be heterogenous to the contemporary, a part that could negotiate with the controls of time directly. Protesting the normative force of time, the fracture feminists claimed immediate knowledge of the future as a direct contrast to ongoing analyses of the present, which, as we see for instance in the example of Edmund Burke's *Reflections on the Revolution in France*, would often appeal to tradition and history.

Fracture feminism was an early form of what Alenka Zupančič calls "ontologically determinative negativity," which Zupančič hopes, today, could be the possible basis of an emancipatory politics. Such writing, says Zupančič, exploits a "capacity to inscribe the problem of division and difference into the world," which is "what makes it political, and politically explosive."[18] It may seem strange to say that Romantic-era writers were employing poststructuralist, psychoanalytic political strategies a century before Freud, yet British Romanticism was, it would seem, a crucial site for the early development of psychoanalytic thought,[19] much as it was for deconstructive interpretive practices.[20] Especially with regard to its sexual culture and its understanding of sexual difference, the Romantic period depended on a cultural logic of new ideas that today we would call "Lacanian"[21]—and the fracture feminists were an important if underappreciated part of this history of ideas. They commit to a sexual nonrelation and to the active maintenance of that nonrelation, as opposed to the simple absence of a relation. Their strategy of inhabiting the fracture, perfectly devised for the phallocentric culture that was then becoming dominant, had powerful political ramifications, many of them temporal. They were, to draw from Jacques Rancière, "putting two worlds in one and the same world," thus ensuring that the gap they had discovered in contemporary rights discourse could not be ignored.[22] The fracture feminists were undoing any attempt to make the political moment coherent or "one" with itself. To acknowledge their strategy for what it is—that is, an early instance of poststructuralist thought—is not an exercise in presentism, but rather a way to see the implications of a temporal fracture that had been pried open during its own literary-historical moment. Yet that very fracture would ensure that the Romantic literary-historical moment could never become completely "its own."

Literary work is the wellspring of this way of thinking, given its capacity to construct a special kind of history from impossible temporalities. As Cathy Caruth maintains, literature has the power to build such timelines because its stock in trade is "a text that, *itself*, has no single referent, a text that can *figure* what it cannot *think*."[23] I especially try to highlight the political intervention at work in this atemporal strategy. Here, I am seeking to heed the provocations of Judith Butler, who, some years ago, said that: "One of the points . . . that became most salient for me is the reintroduction of temporality and, indeed, of futurity into the thinking of social formations."[24] My project, following from that inducement, presents futurity as a factor in the politics of British Romanticism—an especially important task given how chronology was then becoming a social formation unto itself.

Time does not always seem especially political—if anything, it can be cruelly inflexible and disinterested. Yet toward the end of the eighteenth century in Britain and into the Regency, the very uniformity of time was being politicized. Our currently prevailing sense of time came into being, scholars say, between approximately 1770 and 1830.[25] These were the early years of the Industrial Revolution, in which "time is now currency: it is not passed but spent"—a change, as E.P. Thompson notes, that led to a vast expansion in the sale and ownership of clocks in Britain.[26] There were several reasons for this: people were then being forced, by the enclosure of lands and economic necessity, into cities and industrial labor, which would change their relationship to the measured hour; Republican France had decimalized the clock and calendar; aspects of military culture, including its rigid timekeeping, were seeping into civilian life; colonial administrators were developing their own temporal rationale. The fixedness of time was increasingly being treated as a matter of national security, until "time [was] no longer out of joint, but rather articulated within a universalizing temporal and spatial grid."[27]

As Reinhard Koselleck explains, Britons were then being encouraged to think of their own moment as potentially historic, and to adopt a "temporal perspective within which . . . time, past and future must be relocated with respect to each other."[28] Koselleck shows how, during these decades, "time altered layer by layer its everyday sense of flowing and the natural circulation within which histories took place. Time itself could now be interpreted as something new, since the future brought with it something else, sooner than had ever before seemed possible."[29] There was, as Christopher M. Bundock submits, a "growing anxiety about the stability of historical life and what it means to be historical."[30] Literary works were now considerably more specific about dates, even while the timelines they were tracing were, largely as a result of developments in the natural sciences, much broader.[31] Governments, increasingly biopolitical in orientation, were initiating an "economy of time" characterized by state investments in "the time of life."[32] The experience of time, understood as "modernity," was now supposed to be a distinctly European affordance.[33] Meanwhile, the era's sexual culture, newly restrictive, was embracing clock time in the service of a general chrononormativity.[34] In all of these ways, "the nineteenth century began to believe that time, itself, brings change and should require political action," as Mary Mullen's work shows.[35]

Clock time was inculcated in the military, imperial administration, factories, parliament, and academe—that is, in areas of culture dominated by men. For women, this meant being excluded from, yet subsumed under, the new national mania for timekeeping and historicization. "It is clear," says Marcus Tomalin, that, when it came to wearing watches, "the rituals of usage were markedly different for the two sexes," leading to an eighteenth-century stereotype that "women (specifically) disregarded the practicalities of time telling."[36] Because the regularization of time had been a distinctly gendered experience, the concept of the future was especially central in feminist writings. John Krapp argues that because time was experienced so unequally by women and men during these decades, the period's literature distinctly highlights "the asynchronous perspectives between male and female romantic poets precisely on the subject of historical time and the human individual's place in it."[37] Even Jane Austen—a writer arguably obsessed with the scrupulous observance of cultural rules—was, Michael S. Paulson suggests, "examining the ways in which the time of capitalist modernity, in practice, tends to fall profoundly out of joint."[38] What it meant to be contemporary was a highly gendered negotiation.

One cannot not participate in time. When certain well-known Romantic texts, such as William Wordsworth's "Ode: Intimations of Immortality," fantasize about it, they also lament that it cannot be done. Which is to say that the fracture feminists were effectively achieving the impossible. "Impossible," as Zupančič stresses, simply means that something cannot subsist *at present*; Derrida goes so far as to say that: "only the impossible *can* arrive," because that which is not deemed impossible would be, in a sense, already here.[39] The fracture feminists, invested in a similar internal outside to time, were not completely contemporary with their own historical moment, and instead interacted directly with the purported controls of the system of time.

INTRODUCTION 9

It is not exactly clear what ultimately controls the system of time, or where those controls reside. In 1847–1848, needing to coordinate the global efforts of a maritime nation, Britain was the first country to adopt Greenwich mean time as a national standard, placing itself at the center of the timekeeping world. GMT would be assured by lunar measurements and the rotation of the Earth, which are supposed to guarantee time's regularity. Yet if, through "polar fracking" or the like,[40] the rotation of the planet were to speed up or slow down, we could still measure that change—meaning that there must be an external authority to which the rotation is referred. So too with the Earth's orbit and calendars. When confronted with competing calendar systems (as was happening quite often during these years, given the Revolution in France and the establishment of the opium trade with China), people could make reliable conversions between them, because the relationship between the calendars was fixed and stable. Such stability is possible because, we imagine, time is somewhere regulated in intervals that are archived and indexed. These ultimate if ineffable "controls of the system" would be a good example of what Lacan would call the big Other—that is, an authoritative but make-believe site that we treat as the governor of a symbolic system. Everyone must collectively imagine that a guarantee for time exists, and accept the universal force of that guarantee, for time to have any meaning at all. Everyone must be subject to the same standard; no one gets to renegotiate the standard. The fact that this arbiter does not exist anywhere other than in our desire is the source of its authoritativeness.

The fracture feminists split open the symbolic field of time and rhetorically inhabited it, so as to take up a direct relationship with that big Other. This is the gesture that makes them "fracture" feminists, as I will use the term. It gained them access to a reverse side of public political discourse. Any such feat, Alain Badiou recognizes, would "herald a new time" insofar as it "maintains that a cut in the spatial torsion will dispense with all rules of time"; it would achieve the "undoing" of time where one would normally get "temporalization."[41] The time of such writing is impossible; the fracture feminists' ideas can be "demonstrated" rather than, say, known or not known.[42] Such writing occurs when signifiers, through their halting and fitful refusal to cohere, impinge upon chronology and crack it open. Badiou calls this process "the undoing of the showing," and suggests that it could happen only in and through acts of writing.[43] Writing from within the fracture produces something of a different order than knowledge, yet not something entirely outside of the symbolic order;

it is rather located, as I have suggested, on its other side. That cut or fracture, written yet nonexistent, is the hallmark of this women's writing tradition. The Lacanian theorist Colette Soler advises that "what does not exist can, nevertheless, be spoken of," by which she means written; she calls that form of writing, "woman."[44]

The fracture feminists work in just such a way, exempting themselves, at strategic moments, from the dictates of chronology, to suggest that they are living in the future already. The ideological power of time, as a system, rested on its coherence—an attribute of thought that women were seldom acknowledged to share. When feminist writing was able to flip those associations on their head, it was uniquely poised to challenge those powerful institutions, just by scrambling the logics of clock and calendar. These writers do not imagine the future as something yet to come. The future is internal to their present moment, something they are already experiencing. These are writers not contemporary with their own times; they are not really writers "of" the Romantic period. Nor would I say that they were ahead of or behind the times: rather, they selectively dispensed with the whole notion of a timeline by accepting its authority only incompletely and negotiating a different relationship to the meaning of the future. For these writers and in these texts, to speak of the future was not a prediction; they were speaking from the future now.

To understand the significance of this, we can return to the example of Browne's "War and Peace." Let us note that the poem apostrophizes "futurity," rather than "the future," and seems to make an implicit distinction between the two. "The future," as Browne describes it, would seem to be an indistinct, imaginary construct, through which we might imagine something yet to come as an elaboration of our present moment. The future would be the domain of prophecy, wishes, or predictions. "Futurity" for Browne is something else, somewhat accessible, and embedded within the present. Futurity, in "War and Peace," is an *arrivant* already here, glittering and beaming through the clouds of war.[45] The speaker calls it her muse and addresses it as such. It is something with which the speaker is already working, not something that she awaits: futurity is happening "*Now, while* the sounds of martial wrath assail, / *While* the red banner floats upon the gale."[46] Futurity has been happening "while" war has been happening; it "still beams unveil'd" today. Browne, then, is not predicting anything. Rather, she seizes hold of an alternate temporality that is breaking through the regular time of the present. The "years" are "unmeasur'd."[47] Hope, in Browne's poem, surveys futurity to make a map

INTRODUCTION   11

of it: futurity is, then, a place rather than a time, and its place is here. Behind the clouds, it is radiating; it radiates.

Thus Browne maintains an impossible political perspective lodged between temporality and spatiality, which Derrida might call "world-wide-izing."[48] The title "War and Peace" is not, it turns out, specifying a set of alternatives (e.g., peace here but war there, or war now but peace later); nor is war, for Browne, the continuation of peace by other means.[49] Peace, in "War and Peace," is not the alternative to war or the cessation of it, nor a miracle, nor a brute form of politics; rather, it is a property of a future that is already here, with which Browne is well familiar, and that can be claimed already, as a supplement to the nation's seemingly righteous bellicosity. The "age of bliss" to be awaited comes in "our day," like dawn, "e'er," all of the time and already.[50] Yet it is a politics that can be realized only at the level of literary language, through ornate metaphors of stars and dawn, and through the assurances of regular, predictable rhyme. These are couplets, not the austere blank verse of the national record.

Although I have described futurity as an *arrivant*, we are not exactly in the realm of deconstruction here. Or rather, the concept of the contemporary future activates an unfamiliar form of deconstruction, one just as close to psychoanalysis. It is certainly a form of what Derrida calls "contretemporality," a simultaneity of two separate times through which "time exits from time."[51] Yet Derrida distinguishes between the future called *avenir* and the future called *futur*, privileging the former: "I prefer saying this with the to-come of the *avenir* rather than the *future* so as to point toward the coming of an event rather than toward some future present," he indicates.[52] For Derrida, "the messianic future is not a future-present," as John D. Caputo explains, but rather a recognition that the present cannot be delimited.[53] By contrast, for Browne and her fracture-seeking Romantic ilk, the future is indeed a future present. Browne, like Derrida, eschews prediction, but enacts precisely a present future in "War and Peace"—and this is the element that Derrida avoids privileging. Her *arrivant* is already here, apparent to her, and accessible in language. To claim it, though, she must disappear into a fracture in the national political discourse. To address "futurity" directly is immediately to intervene, on the one hand, in the politics of the nation, but, on the other, to reserve a line of direct access to a higher authority. Browne, still a teenager, is imagining politics in the mode of the "not-whole," from the side of the "not being there"—a Lacanian formulation to which we will return shortly.[54] I have coined the deliberately silly term "contretempopia" to indicate the utopian thinking that may arise from such arrangements, meaning utopia imagined as a time rather than a place in a future happening now.

Derrida takes care to distinguish the present tense from the future perfect, favoring the latter. Such a distinction occludes the possibility of a third perspective: the present future. The present future, I would suggest, is precisely the wellspring of Browne's appeal to futurity and this Romantic women's discourse more broadly. It is not a future that may one day arrive, or that we should await, or that we will have made possible, but a future that is currently happening, here and now. Its politics exist in and through the national political discourse without interrupting that discourse; it is a crack in the present moment. To speak from within this fracture would mean not to register as inside or outside the contemporary moment. In this sense, the "woman writer" of this literary tradition does not exist, even as her provocations cannot stop being written. Browne, as a "contemporary" writer, becomes the aporia of her own poetic discourse. It is Browne's own vantage point that must be awaited. Even her eventual death would be mourned as "an event which has cast a shadow of gloom through the sunshiny fields of contemporary literature"—that is, as a negative presence interrupting the contemporariness of her "field," having been the consequence of the very "sunshine" that was making the contemporary contemporary.[55] Thus Browne herself, rather than peace or justice, as Derrida would have it, becomes the impossible, inaccessible thing crucial for, but unthinkable within, the political order. That is why, despite Browne's deconstructive tendencies, her vision of peace is no "democracy to come." The deconstructionist thinkers we know best, such as Gayatri Chakravorty Spivak and Jacques Derrida, can tend to sanctify the future perfect tense, fixating on events that *will have happened*. To speak of the contemporary future is sort of the opposite approach: its interest is more in what *was will happening* in the aftermath of the French Revolution and its long Napoleonic wake. The grammatical awkwardness of that phrase indicates the impossibility of the fracture feminist's voice. It is a form of expression slightly different from, though clearly related to, the phenomenon tracked by Emily Rohrbach in *Modernity's Mist*, according to which Romantic writers, radically uncertain of the future, engage with "what *might will have been*."[56] The fracture feminists, unlike their more misty contemporaries, were not trying to factor in the uncertainty of a number of unknowable futures into their engagement with the present. For them, the future part is the more stable and certain aspect of temporality, while the contemporary is what gets dislocated through a fracture in its symbolic field. It is effectively the same disarming experience of time as Rohrbach describes, but viewed from the reverse side. That minimal shift in perspective, though, is substantial, because it is what enables the fracture feminists to intervene in the immediate political arena, rather than to speculate about how the future may be written. Fracture feminism is, in effect, the intimate deconstruction of a "poetics of anticipation," arising from within that discourse, pursuing what Derrida would call an "abyssal divergence of the truth" under the banner "woman."[57] It is in this sense that the fracture feminists were writing as women, for women.

Anne C. McCarthy has recently attempted a critical "experiment in a discontinuous historicism," as a way to think about poems that "generate their own, often non-linear, temporalities" through the "lyric suspension of narrative time."[58] I would like to think about my project as continuing her particular mode of historicism, pushing it across a range of genres and into more openly feminist contexts. The field of British Romantic studies continues to be dominated by historicist approaches, of the un-discontinuous sort. It is an approach that has particularly enabled the recovery of women's writing from the period, which was once, decades ago, a subordinate part of the field. Yet let us keep in mind Edward W. Said's reminder, that "what today we call historicism is an eighteenth-century idea," and a politically motivated one at that.[59] A historicist approach to fracture feminist writing, I would suggest, is not necessarily counter-ideological, and may necessarily end up being normative and masculinist, albeit unintentionally, because the fracture feminists were specifically seeking to deconstruct the founding assumptions of historicism. I am not trying to imply that every text should be read in its own preferred way. Rather, I would suggest that a gesture of humility in the face of complex texts may serve us well for material that is purposefully paradoxical and vexing, lest we reclaim texts into a canon or context by learning not to see how they counteract that very gesture. My point is that the shift toward inclusion is not enough, because some texts cannot simply be welcomed into a list of prevailing texts. The very aspiration of these feminist works is to destroy the idea of being "fully part" of their literary-political moment, so to deny them this capacity, merely in the name of austere opposition to Romantic ideology, may inadvertently exert a kind of gender surveillance.

As an alternative methodology, intensive close-reading techniques are at the heart of this work. Part of my rationale for proceeding this way is because, as feminist scholarship has shown, women's writing during the period tended to work through an accumulation of details instead of summary and overview.[60] Such texts respond especially well to deconstructive and psychoanalytic reading practices, which exert pressure on seemingly ancillary particulars. The temporal aporias I am tracking occur in seemingly mistaken or throwaway sentences or in acts of figuration that, in unexpected ways, deliberately miss their mark. I am interested especially in questions of desire as they begin to shape feminist responses to clock time and analyses of the immediate political moment. I scrutinize terms like "hope," "fancy," "to come," and "echo," which, within this tradition, come to indicate the fracture in chronology. I pay particular attention to sentences and passages where chronology seems to fold in upon itself, either in narratological terms, through figural language, or through verb tenses. The close readings, taken as a whole, draw attention to the futurity organizing these texts, and to the paradoxical ways that the future was finding its place within the Romantic era.

Sigmund Freud, in the wildly experimental phase that concluded his career, distinguished between "historical truth" and "material truth." Material truth fills in the gaps in knowledge, while historical truth reveals only the cancellation of the subject, bringing to light a perspectival disjointedness rather than more knowledge.[61] This is the sort of epistemology that is claimed in Browne's poem, and in the writings of the fracture feminists more broadly. Psychoanalysis has long recognized the feminist potential of such a capacity. Freud once claimed, strangely and gallingly, that although a woman is certainly a sexual being, she may be human in other respects, too![62] That is obviously a deeply creepy thing to say, and yet it captures the truth of the situation for Romantic-era feminist writers who enacted a certain temporal resistance to national hegemony in their work: the woman, as such, does not exist except partially and conditionally; yet her writing inscribes a jouissance, playing out throughout the very pathways of literary figuration, that can access something altogether Other. Freud refuses to elaborate on this, saying, in effect, *don't ask me, I'm just a psychoanalyst!* If you want to learn more about women's knowledge, he advises, we must: "enquire from your own experiences of life, or turn to the poets, or wait until science can give you deeper and more coherent information."[63] For Freud, as with Browne's "War and Peace," the category of "woman" is the aporia that cannot exist in the here and now; "woman" is the name of an episteme belonging either to poetry or the future. When occasional (and thus present-oriented) poetry adopts the perspective of the future, it voices the Freudian aporia that is "woman." Which is also to say that poetry is the repository of women's knowledge already here

INTRODUCTION   15

from the future, a mode of knowledge that can hollow out contemporary "experiences of life," and so forfeits any claim to the contemporary. Woman, in this way of thinking, is the name for "futurity" writing itself excessively, beyond the limits of signification or the boundaries of political possibility, in the present, as future waste paper.

This is not to say that women writers were alone in embracing futurity: Jerome Christensen finds that Romanticism in general had a special relationship to anachronism,[64] and Bundock that ideas about the future began to seem "completely unlike . . . the futures of the past" in this period.[65] One especially thinks of Percy Bysshe Shelley's aspiration that poetry serve as "the mirrors of the gigantic shadows which futurity casts upon the present," presenting a kind of temporal verso to the development, by Walter Scott and others, of the historical novel during these years.[66] Yet women were experimenting with literary futurity especially often, and were finding a very specific way to do so: by inhabiting the fracture in time. They wrote about the future as if they were already experiencing it, and their literary efforts are the subject of this book.

Behrendt's research helps us to understand the immediate political context for this tradition of writing. In the 1790s, public political commentary became more difficult for women in Britain, as the cultural establishment "began to erect new barriers to prevent women from contributing to the public discourse and to resuscitate some of the old ones."[67] Women, who were neither permitted to participate in nor ignore masculinist discussions of public policy, had to adapt those rhetorics if they wished their writing to register publicly.[68] They could do this most effectively in the genres of poetry and fiction, because women still had relatively easy access to publication in those genres and they were genres with adequate public cachet.[69] Consequently, the writing of the contemporary future employs rhetorical strategies that today we associate with deconstruction: the work is highly playful, extremely precise in its diction, self-consciously literary; it tends toward matters of justice as an experience of the impossible; it gets there by speaking from within, rather than directly challenging, the discourses of powerful men. (This is, in a perhaps unnecessarily generous reading, what Freud may have implied when he said that women have "little sense of justice" *of their own*.)[70] It is negotiation, in the deconstructive sense, as a "technique of liberation."[71] As Helen Maria Williams translates an influential novel by Jacques-Henri Bernardin de Saint-Pierre, she pulls apart the timelines that support patriarchal concepts like "tradition," "nature," "science," "citizenship," "labour," "sonnet," and "love"; Hays, too, rewrites Bernardin, mashing up *Paul et Virginie* with the horrific fictional patri-opticon of Richardson's *Clarissa*. Hemans and Shelley, in "A Spirit's Return" and *The Last Man*, each commandeer the legacy of Lord Byron as a way of thinking about posthumous existence. Fracture feminism, then, is not separate or separable from masculinist writing during the period; it often duplicates hegemonic discourse so faithfully that it exposes the internal contradictions of patriarchal politics. And of course, there is nothing biological about this gender division: there were male writers and publishers, such as Robert Merry, John Bell, Bernardin, and John Souter, who participated in this tradition and helped to build its publication networks. Yet the networks they were building aspired to promote women's writing specifically, and, even in their own work, they remained positively committed to a sexual nonrelation. Whereas most writers of the era (of both sexes) thought of themselves as part of their current moment (as one generally does), the fracture feminists (of both sexes) would "not allow for any universality," as Lacan would say, and so their writing, awaited but already here, "will be a not-whole, insofar as it has the choice of positing itself . . . [on the side of] not being there."[72] It is, then, an experiment in occluded *Dasein*. Speaking of and through the institutions that were regularizing time, the fracture feminists reserved a channel of direct access to its Other. It is in that sense that the fracture feminists are, symbolically speaking, "women writers."[73]

Lacan would have called such writing "a camber . . . which produces the break or a discontinuity" in temporal discourse.[74] Academic historians, Lacan alleges in *Seminar X*, naively imagine that events have "causes," and thus can only see events at the symbolic level, settling for the ability to trace a signifying chain without seeing its relations to the imaginary and real.[75] Just as the object *a*, for Lacan, becomes the "cause of desire" for a subject, so too does it become, when considered as a historiographic factor, "the meaning of history," its "primordial cause" and "the substance of this function of cause." Thus, instead of historians, he urges, we should seek writers of the *après-coup* who can teach us how not to fill in "the gap between cause and effect."[76] This is exactly the blankness and atemporality that characterizes the work of the fracture feminists. They were cultivating a very specific form of relation to temporality and the future, which would serve as, as Krapp suggests, "a structural form of intervention into the sphere of political commentary dominated by men."[77] Central among their concerns was what it meant to live, or not live, in one's own times. Fracture feminists were deeply concerned with the political events of their

INTRODUCTION   17

respective present moments, from the Siege of Gibraltar to the French
Revolution to the Napoleonic Wars and the victory at Waterloo; plantation
slavery and the monarchy; women's rights and the push for parliamentary
reform. Yet instead of commenting on these matters directly, these feminist
writers were responding *as historians* to the contemporary moment, as
if they themselves were not fully subject to the demands of chronology.

The temporal aporia may be glimpsed from either a psychoanalytic
or deconstructive point of view—indeed, it is the duration-without-du-
ration that the two discourses, despite their constant squabbling, share.
Karen Hadley stresses that "time is, and should be acknowledged as,
a key factor in understanding the deconstructive conception of text,
because the rupturing of time is what prevents concepts from closing in
on themselves, from totalizing."[78] In studying fracture feminism, then, we
find ourselves in the zone held in common between psychoanalysis and
deconstruction—two ways of close reading that, despite their intimacy,
have often mistrusted one another.

Derrida worried that history, as an epistemology and discipline,
had yet to accommodate the temporal and technological paradoxes of
psychoanalysis.[79] And psychoanalysis, for its part, understands history to
be an impossible field of knowledge, insofar as "each event seems to be
overdetermined."[80] Following these prompts, *Fracture Feminism* attempts to
think about feminist literary history as a psychoanalytic intervention into
the very concept of history, through the collective project of disaffiliating
history from chronology. We are within the intellectual wheelhouse of
what Derrida calls "a psychoanalyst historian" (as opposed to "an ordinary historian"),[81] whose temporality would be "Freuderridian time."[82]
To proceed by such a method, Hélène Cixous suggests, would be to raise
such questions as: To whom does time belong? Who "has" time? What
and whose time can be said to be "ours"?[83] In the Romantic period, it was
the feminist poets and novelists who were asking these questions. Cixous
suspects that one can respond to such questions only by developing a
mode of psychoanalysis infused with deconstructive impulses, beyond
Freudian dictates. "One must imagine, then, another analysis," she says,
one that she calls, addressing the late Derrida, "your philanalysis."[84] She
predicts the rise of "your philanalysis" as a quasi-Derridean methodology
and field of theoretical study: "One day people will study Derridanalysis."[85]
The fracture feminists were not only "female philosophers" but female
philanalysts. Yet the texts discussed here, I suggest, generally eschew
a Cixousian language of prediction and move directly into performing

18   FRACTURE FEMINISM

the awaited Derridanalysis. They explore the intellectual space between deconstruction and psychoanalysis as a collective strategy for upending the hegemonies of clock and calendar, as well as the hegemonies sustained by clock and calendar.

To write in such a register depends upon maintaining the gap between "time" and "temporality," as we saw Browne doing in "War and Peace." Time, as I suggested above, is a system of measure that depends on everyone's collective acceptance of it. It must appear to be something objective to have any meaning. Temporality, meanwhile, might refer to a person's sense of time passing, or their experience of time. One term is meant to be objective, the other subjective. Romanticism often deals with the gap between these registers: famous examples might include Wordsworth's immortality ode and Austen's *Persuasion*, both of which dwell on a person's peculiar affective relation to the standardized ticking of the clock, figuratively speaking. Such a gap, this study will suggest, could be exploited rhetorically as a form of literary activism. In psychoanalysis, this predicament of being caught between objective and subjective chronologies is known as "logical time," after an essay by Lacan in which the solution to a puzzle has to be explained twice, once each in subjective and objective registers, in order to make sense.[86] Women writers of the Romantic period would likewise emphasize the disjuncture between time and temporality, in an attempt to hold open the gap between objective and subjective chronologies and thus deconstruct the era's prevailing political discourses. Their philanalysis announced an ex-sistence that was sustainable, if still conceptually impossible, for feminist writing. It was not an opposing discourse to mainstream political-temporal sensibilities, in the sense that it could not be totalized into a system of its own; rather, it highlighted the contradictions in hegemonic discourses and asserted itself within those contradictions in a way that could never become participation. Hence, from the perspective of the culture at large, their work described the impossible, that is, something that could not happen in that time or place, and yet was ambiguously *there*.

Chapter 1, "The Uses of History in Wollstonecraft's Afterlives," establishes Wollstonecraft's centrality to fracture feminism, and suggests how certain later texts, written in the wake of her death, pushed that fracture in new directions. The later texts are "Ithuriel," a short story recently discovered in an archive, which inducts the recently deceased Wollstonecraft into a cosmic feminist hall of fame that interrupts an all-male assembly of speakers; *A Letter to the Women of England*, by Mary Robinson (writing

INTRODUCTION 19

under the pseudonym Mary Anne Randall), which institutionalizes Wollstonecraft's call for improved female education with the proposal for an
all-female university to be established now, but in the future; and finally
Anna Letitia Barbauld's essay "On the Uses of History," which I read in
concert with her poem *Eighteen Hundred and Eleven* and Mary Shelley's
"Valerius, or the Reanimated Roman." These texts, taken together, suggest
that the fracture that Wollstonecraft had impossibly ventriloquized could,
if approached strategically, become the basis for a worldwide-ized feminist historiography. These writers saw Wollstonecraft as someone "whose
death has not been sufficiently lamented, but to whose genius posterity
will render justice."[87]

Chapter 2, "Adoptive Siblings across Oceans of Futurity," brings
together a pair of feminist novels: *Paul and Virginia* as translated by Helen
Maria Williams, and *The Victim of Prejudice* by Mary Hays. Both use sexual
relations between adoptive siblings as a way to discuss the contemporary future and the rights of woman in a worldwide-ized context. In my
analysis of *Paul and Virginia*, I show how Bernardin's French colonialist
fantasy was adapted, through an elaborate system of narrative frames, for
an ambivalent negotiation of chattel slavery rooted in a creolizing politics
of the contemporary future. I then turn to *The Victim of Prejudice*, a
novel inspired both by Wollstonecraft's thought and Williams's translation
of Bernardin, which presents women's rights as exclusively a matter for
the future. Hays's protagonist learns to claim rights only through their
perpetual deferment, in a form of justice only ever to come yet available
already to be written. She achieves this less exploitative future through an
elaborate and highly idealized depiction of father-daughter incest, which
in *The Victim of Prejudice* offers an alternative to the tragic pastoral bliss
of *Paul and Virginia*–style yearnings. In so doing, Hays vindicates the
right of the Oedipus complex in ways that psychoanalytic theory is still
catching up to, today, in the recently published texts of Lacan.

Chapter 3, "Della Cruscan Time," discusses poems by Robinson,
Robert Merry, and Hannah Cowley—playful poets who, in the 1780s
and '90s, were publishing ornate erotic verse in the newspaper. Their
poetry would overload its diction with sexual enjoyment beyond the usual
capacity of language, to create a fracture in time. They used that temporal
fracture to upend norms of monogamy, which in turn enabled them to
develop atemporal responses to major international political events, such
as the French Revolution and the Siege of Gibraltar. I focus especially
on Robinson's tribute to Merry in *Ainsi va le Monde*, which becomes a

detailed commentary on the fractured queer temporality of the French Revolution; on Merry's "Ode to Folly," which attaches geological timeframes to the Siege of Gibraltar as a way of counteracting British nationalism and militarism; on the lush prosody of Merry's "The Adieu and Recall to Love," which opens up a proto-Wollstonecraftian jouissance of the future; and on a couple of Cowley's poems dedicated to Della Crusca, which use expressions of jealousy to expose the Della Cruscan poetic exchange to further temporal disruption.

Chapter 4, "Future Poetry," considers poems by Anna Letitia Barbauld, Charlotte Smith, Charlotte Caroline Richardson, and Felicia Hemans in the context of Wollstonecraft's remarks about poetry. In a pair of poems by Barbauld, time gets either allegorized as a military incursion or reconstituted as a memory from the future. Smith's *Beachy Head* reckons with the figural power of "Hope" and "Fancy's hand" as it deconstructs the timelines of triumphal nationalism through the figure of a hermit. Richardson's post-Waterloo poem of jubilee, *Harvest: A Poem*, upends national celebrations of victory through an ethos of hospitality and a healthy dose of Oedipal preoccupation. Hemans's experiments with time, ghosts, and the future in "A Spirit's Return" establish the contemporary future as a possible conduit for desire. Hemans would continue this line of thought in "An Evening Prayer at a Girls' School," in which the reader, psychotically prevented from having any separation from the subjects of the poem, is asked to experience the future already. Taken together, these poetic experiments in contretemporality develop utopias of lack but not limitation; they show us (as Wollstonecraft had) that utopia can be a time rather than a place—an impossible future that had already arrived. This is what I am calling "contretempopia," the utopia of the contemporary future.

Chapter 5, "*Gulzara* and *The Last Man*: The Worldwide-ization of the *Roman à Clef*," brings together two *romans à clef* that refuse to be fully *romans à clef* by virtue of their orientation toward the contemporary future. Both novels acknowledge the future as an aspect of the present by insistently crossing narrative frames and switching genres midstream. Both novels reckon with what it would mean to "count" oneself in a culture where one must remain forever, like Echo of ancient Roman myth, not-whole.

In the book's Conclusion, I consider the question of whether "fracture feminism," which seems to depend on the idea of setting oneself apart from others, would have political purchase in a world in which political movements tend to be associated with collectives. I take up questions posed by the philosophers Giorgio Agamben, who asks "of whom and of

INTRODUCTION   21

what are we contemporaries?," and Julia Kristeva, who asks how feminine
genius can make a political impact if it is rooted in the singularity of an
individual mind. I respond to and challenge both Agamben and Kristeva
in light of insights gleaned from the Romantic fracture feminist tradition.

Fracture Feminism finds that feminist writers could use their very
sociopolitical exclusion as a basis for a new kind of authority. I build in
some ways on Crystal B. Lake's view, that the very experience of being
"encouraged to read and sympathize with a history that marginalized them
in myriad ways, while they were being discouraged from writing it themselves, engendered unique opportunities for women to intervene creatively
in historiography . . . through fiction, poetry, and drama."[88] Yet, as I have
suggested above, marginalization is not exactly the right concept-metaphor for this sort of writing, given how the fracture feminists exploited a
gap internal to, rather than on the edges of, the realm of British politics.
Although women were generally to be excluded from political debates,
the fracture feminists devised a way to embed an excluded vantage point
inside the field of politics, so as to distort the debates from within. They
became part of the political debates of their day, writing from and for the
present moment, by displaying knowledge that could never be assimilated
into the "now" of that moment. Their experiments with time thwarted
existing political conversations and emergent national ideologies. As
Zupančič warns, excluded jouissance has a tendency to reappear where
it is not expected nor wanted, and this can disrupt timelines.[89]

Futurity, contemporariness, and access to literary authority were
powerfully connected in the fracture feminist tradition. Embroiled in the
cultural conversation yet never fully part of the moment, they maintained
a perspective that simply could not exist—that is, it does not make sense—
and yet, there it unfailingly was.[90] They teach us how to think of utopia
as a time rather than a place, how to think of Britain as a worldwide-ized
project of womanly genius separate from but intrinsic to the nation, and
how to picture the future as something embedded in the present.

Chapter 1

The Uses of History in Wollstonecraft's Afterlives

Sonia Hofkosh lauds Mary Wollstonecraft for "her orientation towards a future time," seeing the feminist philosopher as someone who is, in effect, "contemporary" with us.[1] It is true, I think, that Wollstonecraft was oriented toward the future, and I would agree that her writing can seem stunningly modern. Yet it was Wollstonecraft's refusal to be contemporary—with her own generation or with anyone—that I value most. Wollstonecraft offers no assurance that we, as readers and feminists today, will be the cohort she was awaiting. I see her in a more deconstructive vein, a person writing about the present in the midst of "a future radically *to come*, which is to say indeterminate, determined only by this opening of the future to come." She is not one of us; she stages, rather, in her own present, what Jacques Derrida would recognize as "indetermination *en abyme*."[2] If, as Julie A. Carlson finds, "at the heart of Wollstonecraft's novel writing, and of those multiple-staged scenes of writing in her novels, is the belief that eyes will eventually emerge that are capable of apprehending words written before their time," then this, I would suggest, is a present-oriented feature in her work, a reckoning, in her current moment, with atemporality itself, rather than a prophecy or prediction.[3]

Wollstonecraft's inclination to explore havens safe from time made her intensely compelling to other feminist thinkers of her era. But negotiating Wollstonecraft's legacy became more difficult after her death in 1797. Her work, which was well known and well received in her lifetime (bearing in mind its radical content), fell into disrepute in 1798 once William Godwin published her *Posthumous Works* and his own devastating, if well intentioned, *Memoirs of the Author of the Vindication of the Rights of Woman*. Wollstonecraft's unusual reception history helps us question the assumption that she was writing for the future. She was, I would rather say, writing *from* the future. Readers during her lifetime responded well, with either encomia or vicious *ad feminam* attacks, according to their political affiliations; this was what it meant to be taken seriously, and to make an impact, as a public thinker in an era of partisan reviewing. She cemented whole categories of public thought, such as the "female philosopher," to which other writers then flocked.[4] Her overtures from the future seem to have landed with her immediate contemporaries, and her death offered an occasion for them to affirm the presence of that future as an invisible, occluding element already manifest in the late eighteenth century, and even into the nineteenth.

This chapter discusses three feminist responses to Wollstonecraft's legacy: the anonymously written short story "Ithuriel," written six months after Wollstonecraft's passing; Mary Robinson's polemic *A Letter to the Women of England*, written in 1799 as a defiant act of mourning for the disgraced feminist hero; and Anna Letitia Barbauld's "On the Uses of History," a late-career essay by one of Wollstonecraft's contemporaries, published posthumously in 1826, which doesn't mention Wollstonecraft directly but builds on her intellectual framework and aspires to Wollstonecraftian ends. All three texts treat Wollstonecraft as the voice of a posthumous future that can reorganize the political world.

Even Barbauld's text does this. At one time, scholars would cite Barbauld's poem "The Rights of Woman," also published posthumously, as evidence that she and Wollstonecraft were enemies or that Barbauld was an antifeminist. Wollstonecraft even accuses Barbauld, in the *Vindication*, of writing in "the language of men."[5] I, however, side with those who have seen in Barbauld's work a "highly complex" relationship to Wollstonecraft's legacy, rooted in a high degree of mutual agreement and a shared basis in the Dissenting tradition, as well as "a complex engagement with the rhetoric of rights which emerged from this framework."[6] Scholarship of the twenty-first century has revealed Barbauld to be a thinker whose supposed antifeminism was constructed posthumously by her more conservative (yet still feminist) niece and editor Lucy Aikin. If Barbauld could sometimes react oddly to feminist projects, including Wollstonecraft's, it was, stresses William McCarthy, "not because she embraced gender convention, but precisely because she feared and hated it."[7] Wollstonecraft did once praise Barbauld's essay writing, as E.J. Clery notes; ironically, that was specifically with regard to Barbauld's opinion that one should not expect the impossible (i.e., from book reviewers).[8] Yet a tendency to write the impossible, from when it least can be expected, is Barbauld's greatest debt to Wollstonecraft.

Lacan writes ~~Woman~~ with a "slanted line" to indicate that "she is not-whole," in the sense that her "supplementary jouissance" ensures that she "can but be excluded."[9] Each of the texts discussed in this chapter vindicates the jouissance of ~~Woman~~, written as barred, as the mechanism that can open the question of rights from a moment internal to, yet held apart from, clock time. Lacan warns, however cryptically, that the asymmetry of sexual difference, with regard to systems of signification, can lead, through subtle shifts of negation, to "a time [however illusory] during which things are suspended."[10] That space, I will suggest, is the fracture of fracture feminism. The texts discussed in this chapter activate Wollstonecraft's legacy, sometimes in unexpected directions, to dilate the duration of the present, as if one could extend the time of a current instant into a distant future, for the benefit of womankind and humanity. I have tried to keep in mind Ashley Cross's observation that "Wollstonecraft's reception functioned as a hotspot that would determine the longevity of women's writing—her own as well as that of other contemporary women writers."[11] The specific question of the longevity of women's thought looms large throughout these texts, despite such thought being presented as an impossible thing, a promise fulfillable, paradoxically, only in death. If, as Scott Juengel suggests, "to think of the future is thus already to think of death," then part of our task will be to theorize how and why these texts engage with death, through its affiliations with deferment and the future, to announce feminist uprisings in present.[12]

A Dead Feminists' Society, Differently Constituted

Before we get to "Ithuriel," *A Letter to the Women of England*, and "On the Uses of History," I should briefly outline how Wollstonecraft's most important text, *A Vindication of the Rights of Woman*, situates itself in the contemporary future through "indetermination *en abyme*." My commentary is not meant to be an exhaustive or definitive reading of this endlessly generative text. I aim simply to highlight some of its best-known features, to indicate why later writers would affix themselves to this text, or text to come, despite the risks of being associated with its suddenly controversial author. These concerns move beyond the question of female education, bourgeois gender codes, and the social function of marriage, into analyses of the exclusivity of public debate, the fantasmatic structure of historiography, and the inexhaustibility of women's writing. That is because, as Hofkosh rightly emphasizes, Wollstonecraft's feminist "argument was pitched as part of a much larger set of concerns: the 'revolution in female manners' for which she calls in *A Vindication of the Rights of Woman* was integral to a wider call 'to reform the world.' "[13] Yet such reform, as I will suggest below, was understood to be impossible, and even undesirable, by Wollstonecraft. A more radical act is needed, according to which "a justice that may never be realized on the stage of history," to borrow David Collings's words, could be stitched, through acts of remembering the dead, into the present moment.[14] It is on this basis, as fracture feminists of the Real, that Robinson, Barbauld, and the author of "Ithuriel" take up Wollstonecraft's legacy.

The problem with the contemporary marriage state, argues Wollstonecraft in *Rights of Woman*, is that "a future state of existence is scarcely taken into the reckoning when only negative virtues are cultivated" (VRW 141). By this, she means that the afterlife is too often disregarded when it comes to evaluating female morality. She uses this warrant to present women as always already immortal—that is, as only incompletely subject to the demands of time, even during their lives. This statement also implies that woman currently exists only as lack—that is, as not independent, not strong, not educated, and so forth—but that she can attain a kind of perfection in embodying this vortex of negation. Is not that women are uneducated, exactly, but that they are the culmination of a perverse education: they excel in a system designed to render its charges either "romantic and inconsistent" or "vain and mean" (VRW 143). This binds women to the present, in an unsustainable kind of negative subjectivity: they wither away because "virtue" gets measured only in terms of its immediate utility, and "the mind is left to rust" (VRW 145). Women as they currently exist have no relation to the future. They are "degraded by the same propensity to enjoy the present moment" (VRW 121). As a consequence, they are "reduced to a mere cypher," such that the idea of "a man and his wife" is "an absurd unit" (VRW 215). There is no such thing as marriage, it would seem, because the woman does not exist. Wollstonecraft thus puts the fracture that is sexual nonrelation at the core of contemporary gender politics.

THE USES OF HISTORY IN WOLLSTONECRAFT'S AFTERLIVES   27

What is to be done?[15] Wollstonecraft offers us no encouragement in this regard. She says: "In the present state of society, this evil can scarcely be remedied, I am afraid, in the slightest degree; should a more laudable ambition ever gain ground, they may be brought nearer to nature and reason" (VRW 143). Note how women, in this account, are not naturally natural; they must be made natural artificially. This, however, cannot happen yet: "Still there are some loop-holes out of which a man may creep, and dare to think and act for himself; but for a woman it is a herculean task, because she has difficulties peculiar to her sex to overcome, which require almost super-human power" (VRW 215). The project of justice, then, requires not merely allowing a woman to be a human being, so that she may enjoy the "rights of men," but of building something "super-human" and titanic in scale.

Wollstonecraft, even as much as Marx, thinks in terms of an economic base and an ideological superstructure. She recognizes that even if sexual difference is only a social construction, that doesn't mean that it will have been easy to reconfigure. "Men and women must be educated, in a great degree, by the opinions and manners of the society they live in," she says: "It may then fairly be inferred, that, till society be differently constituted, much cannot be expected from education" (VRW 90). If women are to change, education will first have needed to change; yet education only reflects the interests of the ruling class, meaning that if education is to change, the underpinnings of society will first have needed to change. Is it conceivable to change those underpinnings? One would think that current events would have made it thinkable to Wollstonecraft. The second *Vindication* is a text, after all, written during the French Revolution, by a historian of that Revolution, who is calling for "a revolution in female manners" (VRW 114). Nevertheless, she says: "But for this epoch we must wait" (VRW 91). Women are simply too weak and pleasure oriented to rise up, "according to the present modification of society"; the revolution "may be impossible" (VRW 124, 90). "In the present state of society this evil can scarcely be remedied, I am afraid, in the slightest degree," she matter-of-factly says, a statement that rules out even incremental change (VRW 143). Women will be worthy of rights only in the future, a future that seems far away and, from the present vantage, impossible: "These may be termed Utopian dreams" (VRW 105). It is not, then, a matter of reforming the education system and developing professional opportunities for women. The revolution can have been only a wishful act of supposition:

"Supposing, however, that women were, in some future revolution of time, to become, what I sincerely wish them to be, even love would acquire more serious dignity, and be purified in its own fires" (VRW 188–189). It is not that women currently exist, but are oppressed; women cannot exist except as a radical act of imagining the impossible, and if there is to be a revolution, it will need to be a "revolution of time."

How far away is this revolution, in Wollstonecraft's estimation? The word "some" in "some future revolution" suggests that nothing is ready to hand. In her travel writings, she hazards an estimate of "a million or two of years." Even then, there will be, of course, a catch. By then, the world would also surely be overpopulated. In a kind of proto-Malthusian nightmare, Wollstonecraft warns that "the earth would perhaps be so perfectly cultivated, and so completely peopled, as to render it necessary to inhabit every spot; . . . I really became distressed for these fellow creatures, yet unborn. The images fastened on me, and the world appeared a vast prison."[16] Accordingly, she will not entertain even the fantasy of a far, far distant future in which progress has been made. Even then, reform would be, in Wollstonecraft's estimation, inescapably tied to the compromises and horrors of market capitalism, which, as Angela Keane has remarked, creates a ghastly double bind.[17]

Therefore, literally nothing is to be done. Women (i.e., "nothing") should find a mode of present existence ("is") at once lodged in the future ("to be") and past ("done"). Rather than asserting themselves as a positive entity, women must learn to "ex-sist" as ~~Woman~~ rather than continuing to exist in negated form. It would involve finding a distant future that can also be contemporary. Hence, we hear "for this epoch we must wait," from someone who is obviously there already—even beyond it, as the negation can only be made to ex-sist once it has been remembered. Only this combination of impossible temporalities, we are assured, would make possible the arrival of a female philosopher, or even philanalyst, that is, the author of the second *Vindication*. To mark the impossibility of the revolution *is* a, or "some," revolution in time, just as queer time, according to Elizabeth Freeman, has been made out of "the shrapnel of failed revolutions," for these are "moments when an established temporal order gets interrupted and new encounters consequently take place."[18]

Wollstonecraft herself embodies such an ex-sistence, but, with characteristic humility, identifies Catherine Macaulay as the prototype. If Macaulay is to be admired, Wollstonecraft says, it will only be in times to come (e.g., "posterity, however, will be more just"), despite the fact that

THE USES OF HISTORY IN WOLLSTONECRAFT'S AFTERLIVES   29

Wollstonecraft, writing in the present "as a philosopher," is doing justice to her legacy right now (VRW 175, 103). Wollstonecraft remembers Macaulay, the recently deceased fracture feminist pioneer, as a woman from the future who must, in the future, be remembered: "Remember that Catharine Macaulay was an example of intellectual acquirements supposed to be incompatible with the weakness of her sex. In her style of writing, indeed, no sex appears, for it is like the sense it conveys, strong and clear. I will not call hers a masculine understanding" (VRW 175). This is no proto-Woolfian call for literary androgyny.[19] It is a demand to write the retroactive history of the present, not in a proto-Foucauldian genealogical style,[20] but rather from the vantage of the not-all: it lionizes the voice of "no sex," the sex that does not exist, not-feminine, not-masculine, impossible, and *après coup*. The past tense pertaining to Macaulay's person ("was an example") clashes with a present tense reserved for her texts ("appears," "conveys") and a future tense reserved for Wollstonecraft's current act of writing, which is expressed through the negative ("I will not"). It is an imperative that Derrida would associate with the divine: "in the future, remember to remember the future."[21]

Sexual difference, argues Wollstonecraft, arises out of differential relations to signification, through the pathways of free association. These are mental habits formed, "like the lightning's flash," without anyone's conscious input:

> The association of our ideas is either habitual or instantaneous; and the latter mode seems rather to depend on the original temperature of the mind than on the will. . . . Over those instantaneous associations we have little power; . . . the raw materials will, in some degree, arrange themselves. (VRW 185)

The unconscious pathways of these associations are what "give a sexual character to the mind" (VRW 186). One can easily see why critics like Laura Mandell have seen Wollstonecraft as a central figure in the history of psychoanalysis.[22] This is a fully developed theory of sexuation.

Being a fracture feminist, according to this Wollstonecraftian model, means being lack rather than having lack. Once one can speak the voice of lack itself, rather than about what is lacking, one can eke out a direct relation to whatever authority can be said to govern the symbolic systems of patriarchy, time included. That is, extraordinary women should find refuge in an ex-sistence which would give them the possibility of a direct

30   FRACTURE FEMINISM

relationship to the Other of time, given time's apparent inescapabilty as a
symbolic system. They would then no longer be creatures of the present,
nor condemned to the prison of the overpopulated future. The superhu-
man hero that we need, it would appear, is the voice of *nothingness*, a
voice of "vital heat" from the future, someone who, like Macaulay, must
be reconstructed, in "disappointed hope," after her death, and brought "to
my remembrance."[23] Such a writer would be "the woman of the greatest
abilities, undoubtedly, that this country has ever produced."[24] Once Wollstonecraft herself passed, some six years later, others would try to cultivate
this sort of relationship to her future pastness. Their engagement with this
aspect of her thought, which would now reach into new directions as it
was developed by ambiguously present others operating anonymously,
pseudonymously, posthumously, or only in manuscript, became, unto
itself, a revolution in time.

Dead Feminists' Society II: "Ithuriel"

Devoney Looser discovered a remarkable manuscript while working through
the papers of Jane Porter at the Kenneth Spencer Research Library at the
University of Kansas. It was the manuscript of a fictional short story, entitled "Ithuriel," apparently written in 1798 and never before published. Its
authorship remains unknown, but there are extensive editorial marks in
Porter's hand. The text, with Looser's commentary, was published for the
first time in a 2016 issue of *Tulsa Studies in Women's Literature*. A ghost
story with a brief vampire interlude, "Ithuriel" imagines a cacophonous
conflict between two groups, pitting an all-male School of Eloquence,
engaged in its usual practice of debating public issues, against an Assembly of female apparitions, effectively an all-star team of feminist thinkers
from European history. The ghosts of Lady Jane Grey, Boudica, Sappho,
Xanthippe, and Mary Wollstonecraft barge into the School of Eloquence
and cause a stir: "Speakers were interrupted, arguments broken in upon,
sentences deranged, and, finally, the company separated disappointed and
mortified."[25] It is a tale of Assemblies disassembled, a personification of
deconstruction, and a fantasy of ghostly feminist intervention urgently
needed in our own depressing times. Wollstonecraft, at the time of
"Ithuriel"'s apparent composition, was barely six months dead, meaning
exactly as dead as Macaulay had seemed to Wollstonecraft when *Rights
of Woman* was published in January 1792.

Looser notes of "Ithuriel" that "its use of time is remarkable," especially in the "long view of time past and time to come" that the story grants the spectral Wollstonecraft.[26] Looser presents "Ithuriel" as part of a literary tradition, spanning from Richard Polwhele to Virginia Woolf and beyond, which has imagined Wollstonecraft as a ghost. By granting Wollstonecraft, who had just recently died, a long view of the past and future, and by situating her within a chorus of feminist figures spanning the centuries, the text oddly, notes Looser, "occludes the immediacy of the past it describes."[27] I will suggest that the paradoxical timelines running through "Ithuriel" place it firmly within our tradition of fracture feminist writings. "Ithuriel," plainly inspired by Wollstonecraft, well understands the political work that the future could do for contemporary women writers, including the departed Wollstonecraft, in the revolutionary 1790s.

The key to understanding the strange temporality of "Ithuriel" is to avoid plotting past, present, and future along a timeline, but instead to see these terms as naming fractures in the present, co-implicated together. At the foot of the text is a date both precise and not-whole: it says "Solar System (according to the calculations of mortals) Thursday 21st March 1798" (I 90). The date would seem to call the text contemporary—an artifact of its immediate moment—yet it acknowledges something immortal, atemporal, and incalculable within that date as well. Derrida distinguishes between "three actual presents, which would be the past present, the present present, and the future present."[28] "Ithuriel," I suggest, situates its women within the past present and its men within the present present, and uses the nonrelation between these moments as a mechanism by which to harness the futurity of the future present. We see this, for instance, when the ghost of Wollstonecraft acknowledges that "slow is the progress of truth:—like the rising sun, at first its influence is but dimly felt" (I 85–86). This is more than an appeal to patience: it suggests that progress can belong to the future and the present simultaneously, as part of the future present that is never coterminous with the present present. Wollstonecraft is plotting her colleagues' current assembly "in relation to the future as such, and to hold one's identity, reflect it, declare it, announce it to oneself, only out of what comes from the future to come," as Derrida would have it.[29] Yet this experience of one's present as an orientation to the future demands a reconfiguration of what is meant by an historical personage.

In pinning its hopes on a constellation of outstanding historical women, "Ithuriel" would seem to epitomize a mode of historiography, common in the eighteenth century, that presents history as a procession of transformative figures. This is a conservative tendency that Jacques Rancière has termed "memorial-history."[30] It extols examples rather than events, holding them out for the reader's possible emulation, and thus produces something "empty."[31] "Ithuriel," despite using the dispensations of memorial-history, has a more egalitarian, inclusive, and asynchronous way of imagining history. Pastness, in "Ithuriel," is a way of being contemporary, one which, as Rancière puts it, willingly defines "tasks of the moment and promises of the future, but also threats for anyone who gets the sequence of conditions and promises wrong."[32] "Ithuriel" avails itself of these promises and threats, as we will see, as a mechanism for feminist moral judgment. For Rancière this is the most inclusive mode of historiography, marking "the time where anyone and anything at all make history and bear witness to history, . . . as the living principle of the equality of every subject under the sun."[33] In "Ithuriel," though, the principle of equality is more alive than those who principally espouse it.

Although Wollstonecraft had only recently died, "Ithuriel" presumes her to be just as dead as her legendary colleagues—someone whose impact on history is already assured. Like the real Wollstonecraft, the Wollstonecraft of "Ithuriel" is radically attuned to posterity and the experience of the future present. Taking stock of her writing career and expressing regret for her life decisions, the fictional Wollstonecraft of "Ithuriel" says:

> In warring with the prejudices, and follies, of mankind, I foresaw the resistance which my arguments would meet with: but, true benevolence embraces, not only the present, but future generations. Therefore, careless of the ridicule, or censure, of unenlightened minds, I darted with an eye of eager solicitude towards the happiness in reserve for posterity. (I 86)

Yet she also brings this happiness to come into the here and now of the text, saying: "already, behold the fruits of my exertions" (I 86). This paradox, according to which the desired result is both deferred and already present, and which the actual Wollstonecraft herself indulged frequently, is what I would call spectral time. Under its auspices, an undead female philosopher can reasonably await the present as the future of our contemporary moment. The encounter with women's thought, "Ithuriel" seems to suggest, will have the structure of a haunting, to the extent that "thought is jouissance," just as Lacan once warned.[34] Lacan urges us to read "certain serious authors, like women," for it is "they who possess men," he explains,

THE USES OF HISTORY IN WOLLSTONECRAFT'S AFTERLIVES   33

not the other way around.[35] "Ithuriel" basically literalizes this idea and in this sense allegorizes women's jouissance.

The women of "Ithuriel" are not excluded from the contemporary, but the effect of a gap, internal to the present of the School of Eloquence, which opens women's experience toward the future. Lady Jane Grey makes two speeches in this text, both praising two men of the assembly, Thomas Rees and Charles Andrews, for their excellent thoughtfulness. She reports that, as Rees was addressing the Assembly, she was "penetrating into the recesses of his mind" to find what "he would have told," and thus discovered his unspoken arguments in favor of "softness of heart" and "the union of love," expressed internally in "manly accents" (I 83, 87). Listening to Andrews is even more erotic: "my heart heaved with pleasure as I ran over the bright-tablet of his thoughts," confesses Lady Jane Grey (I 87). In real life, Rees was Jane Porter's publisher; Andrews was a botanical artist with ties to the Porter family as well.[36] Lady Jane Grey's favorable assessments of Rees and Andrews are met with "bursts of rapturous applause" and "the peals of applauding millions" (I 89, 83).

To reward Rees and Andrews for their thoughtfulness, Grey proposes that "Two females are now born who shall render happy, by their tenderness, the long existence of Thomas Rees, and Charles Andrews. These women I enrich with the possession of Beauty, Learning, Sweetness, and Philanthropy" (I 89). I want to highlight the strange temporality of this blessing: the men, already adults, are to find happiness with adult women who are just "now born"; Rees and Andrews are to take their share of enjoyment from the future: their "long existence," already having had happened, "shall [be] render[ed] happy." It is not the men who will be happy, but their "long existence"—we are, it seems, at the beginning of a long duration, at the end of which might be called "happy" retroactively. (Warns Geoffrey Bennington: "Unhappy he who claims to be his own contemporary."[37]) The future sexual enjoyment of these men derives from women blessed, or "enriched," with virtues already: it is as if the women are living in the present, but the men find their enjoyment deferred, and on the basis of the missed encounter between them, they find harmonious coexistence. Hence the ambiguity surrounding cause and effect in this declaration: it's unclear if Grey is rewarding these promising men with fine women, or morally enriching the women to make them the more worthy of these fine men. A chicken-and-egg dilemma emerges where the two sexes, never coexisting in the same moment, become rewards for each other in the future of the present or the present of a "long existence" to come. Because

34   FRACTURE FEMINISM

the reward at stake is precisely sexual enjoyment, the question of "which came first" is all-important, yet impossible, to penetrate.

The converse side of this arrangement comes from Xanthippe, wife of Socrates, who violently punishes a man for speaking too pompously, and for too long, at the School of Eloquence. The orator is John Hughes—presumably not the 1980s film director, but one cannot be sure in this future-oriented text, because his real-life analogue has not been identified.[38] As Hughes addresses the Assembly, the narrator recoils from his reflexive sexism: he "so contrived to oppress the hearts, and confuse the heads of those who intended to have exerted their talents in the defence of a long injured sex, that I cease to wonder that woman had so few champions" (I 88). The women take their revenge on Hughes by seducing him:

> [A purple cloud suddenly hovered over his head] I trembled with compassion when, looking into this interior chamber [on this shadow] of futurity—to whose opening wonders I suddenly raised my eye—I beheld a young maid advance, [she was] cloathed in the attractive garb of beauty and dazzling amidst . . . the splendor of her accomplishments, which gave a meteor radiance to and [*sic*] unideaed mind. She danced, she sang, and, rolling her eye about in tender languishments seemed to solicit Hughes to approach. (I 88)

As Hughes approaches the woman, she "suddenly dart[s] her fair fingers into his bosom." The fingers then somehow turn to fangs, which "tore and rent his heart in sunder." The vampire maiden turns out to be "the furious Xanthippe," in disguise, irascible as ever. The next speaker, John Wilkes, falls silent in shock, and "the assembly dispersed" (I 88–89). It is as if Xanthippe were the future of the present, and her revenge on "the misguided Hughes" seems to inaugurate a new mode of being in time—these are, after all, merely "opening wonders" as part of a longer operation, which is itself merely a "bold prelude" of a feminist politics to come (I 89, 90). The men seem to exist merely in the present, while the women, partaking of spectral time, exert "this shadow of futurity," even when they are from Ancient Greece.

The respective fates of Rees, Andrews, and Hughes, in confrontations each thoroughly shot through with phallic and feminine jouissance, indicate a system of rewards and punishments for their ability or inability to open themselves to the feminist future. The historical personages who adjudicate this system do not sit outside of time; they are there in the room, as representatives of a future present detached from, but weighing upon, the present present. The ghostly personages of "Ithuriel" encourage those living merely the present to remake the contemporary world through an insurrection of pastness to come. Here pastness is not the opposite of futurity but one of its constituent elements. Similarly, as we have seen, the ghost of Wollstonecraft can address "future generations" at one and the same time as "the present"—she appeals to "not only [one] . . . but" also the other, rather than holding her thoughts in abeyance until a later, more suitable time. She speaks of the future as an aspect of the present, and as a way of letting someone dead and unremembered speak again. That is, she performs an act of archivization through scattering, rather than binding together. In Derrida's account of ghosts and archives, repetition is the engine by which "the future to come . . . can . . . posit itself," with the result that the future is made out of an encounter with pastness. Thus, he advises, the death drive is central to our experience of time, and "in any case, there would be no future without repetition."[39] This is the archive drive of "Ithuriel" and the basis of its temporal disruptiveness.

For Derrida, the death drive enables the future to posit itself already. For Lacan, the death drive enables ~~Woman~~ to interfere with Schools of Eloquence. "Ithuriel," I am suggesting, combines these two insights, which are really the same insight, to indicate an often-unnoticed temporal aspect of women's jouissance. Lacan charts his sexuation graphs in spatial terms; there doesn't appear to be a temporal component. But we should recall Lacan's discussion of Achilles and the tortoise, as adapted from Zeno. If we read the tale spatially and as an allegory of heterosexual relations, Zeno's paradox would suggest that men and women can never quite intersect. Read temporally, however, as if the contest were tracked along a timeline instead of a map, Achilles and the tortoise could be said to exist in the same space but never at the same moment.[40] This is exactly the situation in "Ithuriel," where men speak only to other men, and women to women, even as they find ways to interact and intervene into each other's debates without ever coexisting temporally.

The sexual nonrelation happens, Lacan explains, because the death drive pulls apart any "one" that founds a common moment.[41] Women, he offers with characteristic charm, cannot help but be excluded from this "one," by virtue of their "supplementary jouissance"—there is "something extra" that prevents women from integrating into any system that would focus sexual enjoyment around the phallus or vagina. "A woman can but be excluded," Lacan sheepishly explains, even as "she is there in full"; she is "*not* not at all there," presiding over "something more."[42] The relationship between the sexes is thus supplementary, not complementary—there is no "one" being aspired toward.

The spectral time of "Ithuriel" finds, within but not included in the time of assembly, something intrinsic to the meeting space but not-whole. It quickly becomes a matter of possession, in every sense of that term. Time, in this way of thinking, is not inexorable; "future generations," consequently, are somehow already exorable. Spectral time, as "Ithuriel" presents it, is the making not-whole of chronology: it measures an occluded part not apparent in the present present. It resides in that fractures and names the fracture. This is what aligns the time of "Ithuriel" with women's jouissance: these ghostly luminaries, far from protesting their marginalization within patriarchal systems of control and focalization, ex-sist in the gaps and folds of that symbolic system and from there take their revenge—just as Wollstonecraft had recommended.

Dead Feminists' Society III:
A Letter to the Women of *A Letter to the Women of England*

A Letter to the Women of England is a feminist polemic by Mary Robinson, published under the pseudonym Anne Frances Randall in February 1799, and then re-published under her own name that December. It offers another instructive case in point, because it directly considers the relation and nonrelation that contemporary British women writers have to the present, and offers, as Ashley Cross explains, "a vindication of the contemporary writing women as the locus of social change."[43] Basically, it takes the spectral time explored in "Ithuriel" and begins to think about the ways that institutions and canons can be built around that fracture. "Ithuriel," as we have seen, works by and through repetition, elevated to a semi-autonomous drive. Robinson, in her sonnet cycle *Sappho and Phaon*, as Kate Singer has argued, warns against this sort of autonomous drive, seeing it as the basis of a stultifying oblivion that can trap women within prevailing gender ideologies.[44] *A Letter*, written three years later, looks to the contemporary future for other possible strategies.

A Letter has at times been read as an act of feminist self-assertion, in which Robinson seeks to save women's writing from erasure and irrelevance.[45] That is a not unreasonable interpretation: the text actually begins

THE USES OF HISTORY IN WOLLSTONECRAFT'S AFTERLIVES   37

with an epigraph calling, through litotes, for female self-assertion, and goes on to argue that women can perform as well as men in all fields of public and moral life. Yet the strange temporality of its argument complicates its attempts at self-assertion. *A Letter* does not, in the end, make space for women, too, within the field of the present. Rather, Robinson aims to locate in women, and especially in eighteenth-century women's writing, an oblique relation to the present. She does not declare that women's writing can or should count, but rather that it has the capacity to unsettle any count, timeline, or purported totality. Women's writing, in Robinson's view, arrives into the present as a supplement, to diagnose but not resolve what Giorgio Agamben calls the "broken vertebrae" of the present.[46] Robinson, drawing on techniques learned from Macaulay, Helen Maria Williams, Wollstonecraft, Barbauld, and Mary Hays, and extrapolating from her own Della Cruscan experiments with Robert Merry and Hannah Cowley, examines the future as an aspect of the present in *A Letter to the Women of England*. Her analysis of contemporary women's writing, which is dependent on what Agamben calls the "dys-chrony" of noncoincident events, shows contemporariness itself to be impossible but necessary.[47]

Robinson's commentary on Marie Antoinette demonstrates this dys-chrony succinctly. Robinson (controversially, given the year 1799) mentions the former French Queen as an example of female excellence: "Let the strength of her mind, the intrepidity of her soul, put to shame the vaunted superiority of man; and at the same time place the female character in a point of view, at once favourable to nature, and worthy of example."[48] Note how two separate things are happening "at the same time": one, in which Antoinette is already an example of female excellence, and the other, in which she may come to exemplify female conduct. That is, Robinson emphasizes how men and women would look at Robinson from separate "point[s] of view," concurrent but not synthesizable. This is what Slavoj Žižek would call a "parallax gap," meaning "the confrontation of two closely linked perspectives between which no neutral common ground is possible."[49] Sexual difference is, for Robinson, that insurmountable gap. Robinson's very next sentence indicates the fractured temporality that is strewn across that gap: "France has, amidst its recent tumultuous scenes, exhibited WOMEN whose names will be the glory of posterity" (L 28). What women have done recently, in their own time, becomes, as it crosses over into the androcentric historical record, a matter for the future (i.e., "posterity"), and even the future's future ("will be"). This parallax gap, along with its concurrent but independent temporalities, is the heart of

A Letter to the Women of England. The only link between women and men, and consequently between official state time and women's time, is the lack of a link between them.

Much of the scholarly interest in the *Letter* has focused on its appendix, in which Robinson lists, in alphabetical order, forty-four eighteenth-century female authors worth reading. It is Robinson's attempt to update *De Philologia*, a Dutch seventeenth-century scholarly text by Gerardus Joannes Vossius, written in Latin, which calls a roll of accomplished intellectual European women through the centuries.[50] Robinson includes, in her version, an ample array of our fracture feminists: Barbauld, Cowley, "Hayes" [*sic*], Macaulay, Williams, "Wolstonecraft" [*sic*], and, indeed, herself (L 99–104). Cross-historical rosters of women could be extended, in the Romantic-era contemporary future, to include very recently deceased personages such as Wollstonecraft. Wollstonecraft had done something similar herself in *A Vindication of the Rights of Woman*, recommending Macaulay and Joanna Baillie to her readers. "Ithuriel" is another clear example of this. *A Letter to the Women of England* in general attempts to present itself as an updating of Wollstonecraft and Hays's work; in particular Robinson is "intent on entwining her identity with Wollstonecraft's."[51] Robinson's innovation lies in her decision to include herself in this list: "Robinson, Mrs. --- Poems, Romances, Novels, a Tragedy, Satires, &c. &c." (L 102). The gesture amounts to Robinson's attempt to think about her own place in relation the present, and within a tradition of women's writing that presents itself as contemporary—a move complicated by the fact that the "I" of the implied author was (for the first edition) hidden behind the pseudonym Anne Frances Randall. Robinson is archiving her own polemic as a monument to the contemporary at and through the scene of its writing. She offers, along with her own name, a list of genres in which she writes, ending it with an enigmatic "&c. &c." This is more than a confession that this text is her own. It appends to the list the sign of its own inability to close the set, as with (as Žižek claims) the + in LGBTQIA+.[52] The &c. &c. is not just an indication that the list of genres could go on, *ad infinitum*, but a sign for an excess to genre itself, the Real of feminist writing as such.

What Robinson's list of women writers means has been the matter of some scholarly debate. I would suggest that Robinson is not especially seeking to grant women access to the social order controlled by powerful men, and nor is she trying to "integrate the women into a patriarchal framework."[53] Rather, she demands a social order founded on lack, that

THE USES OF HISTORY IN WOLLSTONECRAFT'S AFTERLIVES   39

would include both sexes in and through the fracture that is the contemporary future—that is, through the very nonrelation of the sexes. To
put things in Kristevan terms, literature, for Robinson, and particularly
women's writing, can serve as a "symbolic denominator" to tie together
a class of people that does not exist: the "women of England." Thus, as
Kristeva warns, the people belonging to this class become subject to strange
temporalities of the "future perfect," in which modernity and pastness
find themselves adjacent.[54] Robinson writes them a letter, knowing that
they do not exist and that a letter can only spell lack, but also seemingly
knowing that a letter always arrives at its destination.[55]

Robinson uses this strategy because, as she sees it, the women of
contemporary England are caught in a vicious double bind, a problem for
which "she [i.e., the woman] has no remedy" (L 7). She needs to be wary
of the world of men *and* not accept her exclusion from it. Men—even
friendly men—are, in Robinson's view: "the most subtle and unrelenting
enemy she has to encounter: yet, if she determines on a life of celibacy and
secludes herself wholly from his society, she becomes an object of universal
ridicule" (L 26). Women in this text seem unable to find solidarity. In
contrast to predecessors like Wollstonecraft and Hays, Robinson tends to
imagine women as a constellation of individuals, each separately excluded
from the social world.[56] Yet she also tends to avoid first-person pronouns,
preferring to present her arguments as commonly held.[57] The combination
enables her to refrain from referring women to the "all" of a social/sexual
relation, a gesture that would be, as Joan Copjec explains, a "heterosexist
assumption."[58] For Copjec, "a universe of men and women is inconceivable;
one category does not complete the other, make up for what is lacking
in the other."[59] Robinson similarly implies that it may not be possible to
make general statements in a feminist vein about the status or rights of
women. Robinson's collective "we" is an appeal to the future, interpellating
in the present the reasonable beings who will form the collectivities to
come. It is part of Robinson's larger rhetorical strategy, according to which
she can place woman at once inside and outside of hegemonic time. It is
effectively the strategy that Lacan would call "ex-sistence," in reference to
things that are neither there or not there, and "are not in their place."[60]
To ex-sist is to present oneself multiply and contradictorily, subject to the
multiplicity of the drive and alive to the unconscious. It is to acknowledge
the Real as a factor in the carrying on of things, &c. &c.; it is to allow, as
Lacan puts it, that "an empty bag is still a bag," even if it does not always
get to assert itself as "one."[61] Robinson, too, teaches us to see women as

a vacancy held together by the Real, neither included nor excluded from a set, positioned inside the social space controlled by men but extimate to it. In this way one can survive, and even flourish, as a contemporary.

Robinson's list of contemporary women writers formalizes that overall strategy. Although it is often today discussed as a semi-autonomous appendix, Robinson presents it as the culmination of a broader, future-oriented task of institution building. Within the text, it immediately follows Robinson's proposal to establish a university for women, and is offered as an elaboration of that broader plan. Robinson's imagined university is focused on reason to an unusual extent: women would enroll there to learn the rigorous practice of reason specifically. Robinson adopts Wollstonecraft's call to consider, here and now, a "future state," but what separates her proposal from, say, that of *A Vindication of the Rights of Woman* or, say, *A Room of One's Own*, is its unusual use of the term "reason." Quoting Cicero as an authority, she uses the term to mean the process by which "we are taught intuitively to hope for a future state" (L 16). "Reason" is by Robinson's definition the learned act of hoping; it is, one might say, the very opposite of logical deduction. Through this odd definition, Robinson activates a basic paradox that will, by the end of the text, form the cornerstone of her proposed university: can reason be intuitive, or, conversely, can intuition be taught? And in what sense would such knowledge qualify as "reason," given how "intuition" has been defined since the seventeenth century as knowledge gained "without the intervention of any reasoning process"?[62] There is a syntactical ambiguity, as well, by which it is unclear whether the curriculum is supposed to activate the students' existing intuition, or if intuition can itself be a method of teaching—it depends on whether "we are taught intuitively" or if we are taught "intuitively to hope." "Intuitively to hope" suggests a university pointed both in the direction of intuition, that is, the *immediate* grasping of knowledge, and deferral.

Robinson's university is an impossibility. Its curriculum entirely consists of knowledge from the future, and it looks to the future, as well, to recruit the faculty who would teach its students. As Robinson explains:

> In half a century there would be a sufficient number of learned women to fill all the departments of the university, and those who excelled in an eminent degree should receive honorary medals, which they should wear as an ORDER of LITERARY

MERIT. O! my unenlightened country-women! read, and profit, by the admonition of Reason. Shake off the trifling, glittering shackles, which debase you. (L 93, emphasis Robinson's)

The university would have to *create* the very women who would "fill all the departments" and thus train its own faculty. It would take "half a century" to "fill" this university with its various constituent departments. Yet that university would need to be teaching its future faculty already, in order for the faculty to be trained into their disciplines. The undergraduate students are thus understood to have already become its professors, despite the fact that staffing the university requires fifty years of concerted pedagogy. Moreover, "all the departments" seem to be "literary": no mention is made of the study of, say, mathematics or physics. A literary education, or, perhaps more broadly, a humanities education, seems to be its sole purpose. Such a program would "give them [i.e., women] that genuine glow of conscious virtue which will grace them to posterity"—which means that learning to hope, from teachers from the future, would have benefits that would themselves arise through, and be subject to, endless deferral (L 94–95). Robinson layers futurity upon futurity in an impossible present tense, in order to mount a curriculum that would teach women, intuitively, intuitively to hope. The "order of literary merit" that Robinson enshrines ex-sists only as a confrontation with various futurities in the present. And in this context specifically she presents her celebrated list of eighteenth-century women writers.

The study of literature and the maintenance of literary canons are themselves acts of futurity. Christina Lupton argues that "The duration that comes with books of classic status, whose relevance can be both still to come and already there," introduces a "duration" into the present that exists "in anticipation of its audience, toward things still to come."[63] This is exactly the case in Robinson's handling of classic women's texts throughout the *Letter*. But Robinson goes one step further, conferring this "classic status" upon herself and her fellow fracture feminists in advance. Immediately upon proposing a women's university for the study of reason by way of literature, she inducts her feminist contemporaries into what is literally an "order of literary merit." Her "LIST OF BRITISH *FEMALE LITERARY CHARACTERS* Living in the Eighteenth Century" creates a literary history of the present, one that speaks of the literary present (and recent past) as if they were the objects of "hope" for people living in the future (L 99, emphasis Robinson's). By listing women writers of the present and recent past, she refuses them their ability to function *in* the present; they are perceptible to the present but not part of it. Robinson thus carves out a certain ex-sistence for these writers, including herself. One is reminded of a thought of Stéphane Mallarmé's, to which Lacan approvingly alludes: literature provides an "exception" to communication, a form of silence that will pull apart "talk," and thus present a point of interference within "everything among the different kinds of contemporary."[64] Robinson similarly places her hopes in literary studies as a repository of hopes to come. She recognizes women who have been courageous enough to work as contemporaries, within the field of literature, under sexist conditions; she would seem to agree with Agamben's assessment that "contemporaries are rare," because "to be contemporary is, first and foremost, a question of courage."[65]

Robinson evinces what Derrida would call "faith in the university and, within the university, faith in the Humanities of tomorrow."[66] A university worthy of those principles, Derrida needlessly reminds us, has never existed.[67] Yet imagined as an article of faith, or even by an authorizing fiction, it would stand for the "principal right to say everything, even if it be under the heading of fiction," and, moreover, the unlimited "right to deconstruction." These are the commitments that orient the university toward the future and that "fundamentally links the university . . . to what is called literature, in the European and modern sense of the term."[68] Robinson shares this vision of a university to come, with a faculty to come teaching a knowledge to come in the mode of *as if*—with fiction at the heart of the curriculum. And she places her own call for such a university within its future curriculum, as if *A Letter* were performatively enacting the future in the English now.

The list, which includes every one of our female fracture feminists from before the year 1799, would seem to connect contemporary women's writing to the future. It undermines the homogeneity of the present by operating in multiple temporalities at once. "Of their several claims to the wreath of Fame, the Public and the critics are left to decide," explains Robinson: "Most of them have been highly distinguished at the tribunal of literature" (L 104). Robinson compiles the list in the present, as an act of female canon-making and recovery. She speaks of the authors' recognition as an event yet to come, still "left to decide." Yet she speaks of their literary accomplishments in the passive voice and present perfect tense, suggesting that the recognition has already happened, but with some indeterminacy

THE USES OF HISTORY IN WOLLSTONECRAFT'S AFTERLIVES   43

about when and by whom the women were recognized. The women *are being listed*, they *shall be evaluated*, and they *have been distinguished*. The important thing to note here is how, through the inconsistent verb tenses, Robinson ensures that the "tribunal of literature" is different and separate from "the Public and the critics." These are separate procedures happening at different times. Contemporary women writers, she suggests, were not writing in the present, but will have already been read from the future. Robinson's *Letter* will have created the very audience capable of recognizing its significance, which, in a kind of *après coup* movement, retroactively will have certified its critical judgments as worthy—incidentally, the same kind of paradox of time that Lupton has traced in Godwin's work.[69] To present such a text is to write the future into the present. It is as if the women of England are receiving a letter from their future selves—which is to say that women are, at present, absent from the *Letter*. Derrida maintains that a letter always presupposes the absence of the addressee.[70] Like any written text, it depends, for its meaning, upon iterability—meaning that it must be "structurally legible . . . beyond the death of the addressee."[71] The author, too, must be ready to disappear,[72] in the sense that she would be subject to the same demands for iterability as the "women of England." Well, disappear she does. Robinson, signing her text "Anne Frances Randall," claims a judgment from posterity for her own act of writing, upon an author who, in 1799, was never there. If *A Letter to the Women of England* is supposed to be among the works of "Mrs. Robinson," it is only so as a supplement, and as a name for the cut in the very system of literary writing: "&c. &c."

The gesture has been interpreted as Robinson's attempt to remain pseudonymous, to place herself among the leading feminist minds of the century, or to recognize herself as part of an alternative, woman-centered literary canon.[73] Yet, as we will see in our discussion of *The Last Man* in chapter 5, a female author's decision to include herself in her own account, lest she be erased from history, produces a certain dys-chronicity. It is an act of evasion: as Robinson explains in her preface to the second edition, her self-references were "merely inserted with a view to mislead the reader respecting the REAL AUTHOR of the Pamphlet" (L, n.p., "Robinson's advertisement to the second edition"). She is, in effect, hiding in plain sight by enacting a quarter-turn, according to which she is not the signatory of the text but the object of its critical judgment. It is not a matter of extending the field of "contemporary women's writing" to include one's own name, as if women's writing were a homogenous plane in need of

44   FRACTURE FEMINISM

wider boundaries; rather, Robinson is including an absence—herself—in a curated set that is already in contact with the future. To count oneself in one's own tally is, perhaps, to make a naïve error (e.g., the example from Lacan, which we will explore further in chapter 5, of "I have three brothers, Paul, Ernest, and me"),[74] but the "error" only seems erroneous because it has activated multiple, incompatible timelines that would otherwise be repressed as the subject learns to classify things properly. Robinson has refused to learn not to include herself in her own count. Writing her own name as a way of not signing her text, Robinson shifts her own work, including the work still being written, into the recent past. It is the same paradox that Derrida sneaks into *Archive Fever* when he says, "I wrote these pages some ten days ago": in stating that the present is his own recent past, he makes the reader wonder in what time the sentence could have been typed.[75]

Robinson's era, also being the era of Rousseau, is said to have invented the "modern signature," which depends on implicit claims about the presence and life of a singular writing subject, a connection between author and text, and certain formal properties of language.[76] In general, the author's "I" and signature, argues Derrida, "marks and retains this having-been present in a past now, which will remain a future now, and therefore in a now in general, in the transcendental form of nowness." A text is "stapled to present punctuality . . . in the form of the signature."[77] Robinson counteracts this effect by shifting the name "Mrs. Robinson" onto the list—making her, so to speak, an "eighteenth-century" author instead of a *fin-de-siècle* author, and giving her a place in her own paratext but not in what seems to be the "main text" of the letter. Through the bending of this parergon, Randall assigns "Robinson" to the past, to be judged in the future, and "Randall" to the future, to be judged in the present. Which is to say that the feminist *argument* of the *Letter*—sometimes taken to be "a homogenous element across which the unity and integrity of meaning is not affected in an essential way"[78]—is postponed by a parasitic, supplementary element *in* and *outside* the letter, named "Mrs. Robinson," which makes the text unreadable except in times to come. She opens a semantic field to "nonsemantic movements," to create a "passageway or opening" in time.[79]

The gesture requires the author's ex-sistence, and thus her thoroughgoing reckoning with the unconscious, through the simultaneous operation of multiple temporalities. Robinson's self-including gesture in *A Letter* provides the template for Lionel Verney's narratorial effort in Shelley's *The*

THE USES OF HISTORY IN WOLLSTONECRAFT'S AFTERLIVES   45

Last Man, as we shall see, holding open the question of what it means to count oneself in one's own narrative. (It is perhaps noteworthy that Lionel Verney's sister, in that novel, is named Perdita—a Shakespearean nickname which Robinson, a generation earlier, had made thoroughly her own, and that had often been used in media attempts to pillory her for her sexual activity.) Through the radical act of counting oneself under a fictional name, Mary Shelley (as Lionel Verney) and Mary Robinson (as Anne Frances Randall) affirm the atemporal, counter-chronological vectors of ex-sistence, offering the unconscious as a path to the contemporary future.

The postscript that Robinson includes to her *Letter*—as if it were an actual letter to the ~~women~~ of England—makes this plain:

> P.S. Should this Letter be the means of influencing the minds of those to whom it is addressed, so far as to benefit the rising generation, my end and aim will be accomplished. I am well assured, that it will meet with little serious attention from the MALE disciples of MODERN PHILOSOPHY. The critics, though they have liberally patronized the works of British women, will perhaps condemn that doctrine. (L 97, emphasis Robinson's)

Much as we saw in "Ithuriel," Robinson's imagined male critics are, plainly, living in the present, and thus have little chance of giving the *Letter* "serious attention." Yet its "end and aim will be accomplished"—in the future tense—because the "rising generation" is "to whom it is addressed." That is, it will have already influenced the minds of the readers of the future, even while its present readership neglects it. In this sense, I am not sure that I would agree with Cross that Robinson's *Letter* aims "to create a history of women writers—the phalanx—that would counter an otherwise dire future."[80] Rather, I would say that it counters a dire present with a future that is already here—which is why she is able to include her own name, for writing that was still in that moment underway, in a catalogue of notable eighteenth-century women writers. The history of women's writing, for Robinson, is about memorializing the future in the present. "Of their learning we have certain monuments," she writes, meaning the writing itself (L 39). Writing, in this model, is a form of preserving, even archiving: if women write so their thought can be remembered in times to come, rather than to make an intervention into their "own" historical moment, it is likely because, as Robinson implies, they can never have been said to "own" the present. Women today, explains Robinson, have no impact on the political discourse: "in modern Britain women are scarcely allowed to express any opinions at all!," she exclaims (L 89n.). Still, fracture feminism will have been a monument to the future within "modern Britain" but inassimilable to it.

On the Uses of History in "On the Uses of History"

In his seminar of 1969–1970, under the title *The Other Side of Psychoanalysis*, Lacan began to theorize four discourses and their relation to "the social link." Responding ambivalently to the student movements of 1968, he was proposing something literally "revolutionary": a way of putting knowledge through a series of quarter-turns, so as to reorganize the power structures that sustain it.[81] As the four elements of his schema (i.e., the split subject, the master signifier, knowledge, and the cause of desire) rotate through four fixed positions (to pinpoint the agent, addressee, secret truth, and product of the discourse), Lacan sought to reveal why attempts at political resistance so often self-destruct, and how psychoanalysis might be uniquely equipped to stage a more meaningful, if politically noncommittal, insurrection. Lacan was seeking to understand what would happen to an episteme if its aims, motivations, and objects were switched. He outlines a master's discourse, derived from Hegel but familiar to us from modern capitalism, neoliberalism, and fascism; a hysteric's discourse, in which the wounded subject probes the knowledge of the master subversively; a university discourse, in which the accumulation of knowledge, seemingly objective, is shown to hide a latent authoritarianism; and an analyst's discourse, the category in which Lacan places his own enigmatic utterances.[82] In the analyst's discourse, an unbearable lack or void (i.e., object *a*) begins to "speak," addressing a cut in the subject ($), and thereby produces a master signifier of its own (S1). As it does so, another form of knowledge (S2), one detached from the master's aspirations, operates secretly underneath.

A similar psychoanalytic "revolution" is underway in Anna Letitia Barbauld's essay "On the Uses of History," which anchored a posthumous edition of her otherwise unpublished pedagogical writings entitled *A Legacy for Young Ladies* (1826). It is implicitly Barbauld's attempt to solve many of the methodological problems that Wollstonecraft had raised in *Rights of Woman* and *An Historical and Moral View of the French Revolution*. Barbauld's essay, often discussed as if it were a guide to Barbauld's poem

Eighteen Hundred and Eleven, has been important for scholarship on relationships to time and history in the Romantic period, especially as these topics pertain to women.[83] The essay, comprised of four letters to Barbauld's real-life charge Lydia Rickards, advises the reader not to develop histories that rely upon the concept of time. To achieve this unusual aim, Barbauld must separate history from any notion of a timeline: "unfortunately there are many gaps and chasms in history," she observes to Rickards, and so we cannot achieve "a regular chronology."[84] Dates are particularly unhelpful when thinking about history, Barbauld argues, because each nation's history develops on an independent scale. Wisely refusing to "confuse synchrony with simultaneity,"[85] but with no consistent measuring stick by which to think internationally, Barbauld finds that historical events "mock all power of calculation" (U 398). This, then, is the very picture of the excess of a symbolic system (object *a*) coming back to "speak" directly to someone ($) about how to construct a master signifier for historical knowledge, in the face of the realization that existing systems of historiography are lacking. History, as conventionally understood, is often anchored in an arbitrary and meaningless signifier (e.g., the birth of Christ; the rise and fall of a nation), fears Barbauld; she proposes instead to let the excess to that system—its "gaps and chasms"—address the field of all knowledge. In her account, then, History itself becomes a sublime master signifier—something precisely without "uses." Historical thinking, Barbauld holds, is all the more potent for being "founded upon conjecture and clouded with uncertainty," but to harness its power the student of history must become vulnerable to its uncertain procedures (U 422).

Such an attitude distinguishes Barbauld from other historians of her era. Jacques Rancière identifies four modes of historical writing in the European tradition: traditionally, says Rancière, we have had "memorial-history," which proffers examples of great personages worthy of our imitation; secondarily, especially in the nineteenth century, we had history as an illustrative story or fable; third, we can see history as the story of time itself, which crushes all personages under the weight of constant catastrophe, as "the unrepresentable lays down the law"; and fourth—which Rancière sees as the most emancipatory—we have the aesthetic shift that happens with modernism as "history puts itself on show," and finds new ways to inhabit, look at, and enjoy natural and built spaces.[86] It is clear that Barbauld, in her resistance to time and dates, is recommending none of these options. Or rather, she incompletely and provisionally inhabits these historiographical registers but, in doing so, fractures them. She crosses the first three categories, for instance, in encouraging Rickards to construct a "line of life"—which in her account is anything but linear—to better understand how "distinguished characters . . . touch each other"; this would mean constructing a visual network of concurrent but asynchronous international timelines, rather than seeing "distinguished characters" individually (U 425). Put in Lacanian terms, we might say that "On the Uses of History" performs a quarter-turn on the university discourse of history, in an attempt to construct historical authority (S1) apart from symbolic systems such as dates (S2), time (S2), or "distinguished characters" (S1, but as the agent, not the product, of the discourse). In so doing, Barbauld's essay overturns the fundamental premises of historical writing, as it develops new and different relations to contemporary life that depend on knowledge from the future. Whether this Barbauldian discourse can be said to be "historical" is very much an open question, given its outright rejection of pastness and its orientation toward the future.

It is, I will suggest, a psychoanalytic form of historical thought, indebted to Wollstonecraft's own. To determine whether such a reading can be sustained, and to better understand the stakes of Barbauld's divorcing history from time, we would first have to determine what psychoanalysis is. Lacan's essay on that subject is "Variations on the Standard Treatment," in which he asks: what constitutes psychoanalysis? With so many competing schools and strands of post-Freudian thought, what can we say is the core idea that makes a clinical practice psychoanalytic? Disturbingly, he finds that there is not one. There is no idea of Freud's that has not been challenged in the name of psychoanalytic progress; analysts of every stripe seek to improve on Freud all the time, often in the pursuit of a cure. Lacan is suspicious of such endeavors: a cure, in such circumstances, may be helpful to the patient, but can the procedure still be called psychoanalysis? One cannot, after all, be cured of the unconscious. Lacan's proposal to this impasse is surprising, not least for the ways that it anticipates Jacques Derrida's vision of a "geopsychoanalysis": any psychoanalysis worthy of the name will disperse, like shrapnel, globally, says Lacan.[87] Psychoanalysis is at root a "movement" that "spreads"; it is characterized by "dispersion," and this tendency, being "internal" to it, is its only core.[88] We can only know psychoanalysis by its "temporal foundation," the dialectical play of logical time that we encounter in the transference, and that, says Lacan, is inherited directly from Freud.[89] Yet this "temporal foundation" has only an "external coherence": it becomes apparent only through a dialectical play of misrecognition.[90] Barbauld's text, I argue, prepares Lydia Rickards

THE USES OF HISTORY IN WOLLSTONECRAFT'S AFTERLIVES   49

for such an externalized relationship to temporality, and does so by carrying history through its global dispersion. In so doing, "On the Uses of History" reorganizes the relationship between history, contemporariness, and time into a decentered and multimodal "line of life."

In making these arguments, Barbauld was pushing back against patriarchal modes of historiography and developing a feminist alternative to Wollstonecraft's feminist alternative. Barbauld was advising Rickards in a historical moment when "more eighteenth-century girls were being encouraged to *read* history" and the genre was "taking on a powerful conduct book force," as Looser explains—a spirit that *A Legacy for Young Ladies* definitely aspires to achieve.[91] Generally, though, there was a concomitant concern that "too much history reading could be detrimental to women"—a concern that Barbauld does not seem to share.[92] Barbauld understands history as a lesson in self-control, which "makes it particularly proper that *ladies* who interest themselves in the events of public life should have their minds cultivated by an acquaintance with history, without which they are apt to let the whole warmth of their natures flow out" in a manner "more zealous than candid" (U 403, emphasis Barbauld's). Here, we are well outside of any of Rancière's categories for historical representation. The study of history, argues Barbauld, can be an important check on a woman's zealous ardor, and yet in accepting this cut to her enjoyment, she opens a pathway into "the events of public life." This, then, is the crucial temporal paradox of Barbauld's historical thinking: women are those who study contemporary public life as "history," experiencing the pastness of the present in the mode of a public participation to come. "On the Uses of History" locates the uses of history not outside of patriarchal norms, as in the fantasy of recovering a "herstory," but on the other side (as with a Moebius strip) of standard male historiographies: it is the voice of that other side.

The feminist content of the essay resides primarily in Barbauld's teaching Rickards how to think asynchronously, implicitly as Wollstonecraft had urged, without undue emphasis on dates. Ultimately, these are lessons in how not to be contemporary, how not to think of oneself as the outcome of history, and how to unsettle nationalist grand narratives of progress and perfectibility. "Although I recommend to you a constant attention to chronology, I do not think it desirable to load your memory with a great number of specific dates," she advises (U 422). Is there such thing as "constant attention to chronology" without recourse to dates, we might wonder? For Barbauld, the answer is yes—whatever that might mean. Yet it is also apparently true that one cannot study chronology without already having have mastered history, and "digested" it: "chronology can never be fully possessed till after history has been long studied and carefully digested," Barbauld says in signing off (U 426). Chronology needs to be studied alongside history, and instead of history, but without reference to too many dates; yet one must already have mastered history before one can learn chronology. That is why the study of history is, in a radical sense, prerequisite: one can only study history now, but can only study chronology from the future. When Barbauld asks "when did the historian live?," she asks a trick question (U 416).

The essay's eagerness to disregard dates can be understood as Barbauld's response to John Wilson Croker, who viciously reviewed *Eighteen Hundred and Eleven* for *The Quarterly Review*. In general, the poem was "harshly reviewed for its lack of patriotism" and for "breaching the faultline between literary and political public spheres."[93] Croker, seizing upon the title of the poem, mocks Barbauld for her supposed failure, in a work about English history, to understand the meaning and use of dates. James Chandler was the first to read Barbauld's essay as an elaborate retort to Croker: in his account, Barbauld's essay "makes explicit some of the tacit assumptions that underlay this predominantly male enterprise" and acknowledges "the gender barriers to be overcome."[94] Since Chandler, there has been a critical tendency to overstate the significance of Croker's review for Barbauld's subsequent career, something which Clery's book on Barbauld attempts to rectify.[95] I would add that Barbauld does not seem to aspire to join Croker in the masculinist world of historiography; rather, she seems eager to show the ways that a belief in the integrity of dates would be misplaced. Barbauld does not seem to think that accuracy in dating is something necessarily unbearable, and nor does she see it as a privilege from which she has been barred on the basis of her sex. Rather, our ability or inability to arrive at accurate dates serves, for Barbauld, as an index of our own contemporariness with the events in question. That is why, "as we come nearer to our own times, dates must be more exact," in her view (U 425). For Barbauld, the contemporary world is more "historical" than the past is.

Derrida says that "there would, without the future, be no more history, . . . but there would also be no future, no future as such, no novelty at all, without some sort of historical link, memory, retention or tradition, thus without some sort of synthesis."[96] Barbauld seems to seek such synthesis in "On the Uses of History," much as she does in *Eighteen*

Hundred and Eleven, which I will briefly discuss below before returning to Barbauld's essay. An ambitious poem like that, with its capacity to fold deep historical pasts and depopulated futures into a present moment, puts Derrida's expectations to the test.

Eighteen Hundred and Eleven seems to understand chronology geographically rather than temporally. The poem's present already contains the deep past (of the Roman Empire) and distant future (of a depopulated London visited by American tourists), and so the poem can measure time through geographical movement, from Rome to England to America. The poem encourages the reader to recognize, through the project of historicizing England's present moment, that England is not the culmination of history, that its greatness is contingent, fragile, and has already been eclipsed. Lacan proposes that "the present is contingent, just as the past is futile. It is to the future that we must hold," because "tomorrow's unknown conqueror is already in command today."[97] Lacan's statement essentially rehearses the argument of *Eighteen Hundred and Eleven*, which grasps the relative powerlessness of Britain in the face of both the nation's own deep history of being conquered and the ascent of an American superpower to come. This becomes the basis for the geo-psychoanalyzing impulses of "On the Uses of History."

The poem's status as a poem is crucial to its historiography: poetry, explains Barbauld in her essay, is the truest form of history writing, as it "impresses both geography and history in a most agreeable manner," which is why "we take our ideas from Shakespeare more than History" U 425–426). Barbauld here exploits the phenomenon that Jane Gallop calls "the temporality of book writing, the temporality of authorship."[98] If History proves problematic in its pretensions to systematicity, one can simply study History without History: the literary tradition of any nation compensates for the gaps and incoherencies in history proper, building connections across culture to thatch an adequately stable history for the nation (U 424). This is akin to what Robinson was doing, implicitly, in *A Letter to the Women of England*. Yet Barbauld, unlike Robinson, stresses how History, being real, can offer a "counterbalance" to the "privileges" of fiction (U 404).

In some ways, and as Chandler suggests, "On the Uses of History" offers a defense of *Eighteen Hundred and Eleven*, and continues along that poem's trajectory: "It would be a pleasing speculation to see how the arbitrary divisions of kingdoms and provinces vary, and become obsolete, and large towns flourish and fall again into ruins," Barbauld warns Rickards, in apparent reference to her controversial poem (U 409). In other ways, it can seem like "On the Uses of History" attempts to atone for Barbauld's radical poetic past. Letter II, for instance, largely understands History as the study of a single nation-state—invariably one's own—as it transforms and develops over time: "The Englishman conversant in history has long been acquainted with his country[,] . . . he has traced her gradual improvement through many a dark and turbulent period, many a storm of civil warfare, to the fair reign of her liberty and law, to the fulness of her prosperity and the amplitude of her fame" (U 401). Such a study of history, which is said to qualify as a form of patriotism, is especially well adapted to a Whig model of political reform: England, each day, gets progressively more liberal, more just, and more prosperous, and history is the study of that trajectory. It is the form of historical writing that Wollstonecraft models in *An Historical and Moral View of the French Revolution*. Yet in the face of this unbroken chain of improvements, Barbauld, like Wollstonecraft, asks us to confront, and take seriously, a fracture in history. Barbauld's exploration of that fracture carries her essay into its most intimate contact with *Eighteen Hundred and Eleven*. The fracture asserts itself once we start to read history comparatively, in a worldwide-ized way.

Recent research suggests that "globalization," in the neoliberal sense that we mean that term today, has been underway for four or five centuries.[99] It can sometimes seem inescapable, as if an economic law. The very term "globalization" helps to produce the sense of its inevitability, argues Derrida, given how fantasies of a globe (as opposed to, say, a "world") tend to naturalize the expansion of European hegemony.[100] Western metaphysics play an important part in that ideological project, because "reason" itself is often the thing that is violently globalizing.[101] To untie the knot between globalization, empire, and metaphysics, says Derrida, would require new ways of thinking, and of evaluating arguments—far from easy tasks, given how "reason," being global or universal from the start, would seem to admit of no useful outside. To this end, Derrida proposes an alternative form of thinking, one he calls *mondialisation*, which could reveal the complicity between "reason" so-called and the centuries of violence done in its name. (With deliberate awkwardness, "worldwide-ization" has become the standard English translation of Derrida's preferred term, so I will use that here.) Yet Ryan Gustafson rightly points out that "for Derrida *mondialisation* does not so much call for an abandonment of what has been called reason as it is a matter of thinking the conditions for the possibility of another *mise en jeu* of reason."[102] It is not an alternative to European

THE USES OF HISTORY IN WOLLSTONECRAFT'S AFTERLIVES   53

traditions of thought, but an exploration of the way that those traditions collapse under their own expectations. Such a mode of thought would belong to the future, which Derrida was awaiting.

To better illustrate this, I will beg the reader's indulgence as I briefly discuss a key passage from Barbauld's poem *Eighteen Hundred and Eleven*, the insights from which I plan then to bring back over to "On the Uses of History." The poem presents contemporary London, then the world's largest city at 1.3 million, as a marvel of cultural and religious diversity: it is where "the turban'd Moslem, bearded Jew, / And woolly Afric, met the brown Hindu."[103] The city is a nexus for a global network of commercial and cultural energies, a gateway perpetually open for the flows of deterritorialized capital and desire that might be called a body without organs.[104] Thus it is unexpected when Barbauld pauses to imagine a future in which American tourists visit London, now in ruins, to experience its "faded glories."[105] The visitors find London emptied of its human population, seeking to wander amidst the "still, untrodden street; / Or of some crumbling turret, mined by time."[106] The encounter with what had been London leads the tourists to consider their own place in the world: they understand that the America they love was once, in the distant past of the poem's projected future, a British colony, and thus find their own Americanness defamiliarized. The city of their refuge becomes, then, a testing ground for a democracy to come already here.[107]

Jonathan Sachs marks how Barbauld's "examples [in this passage] underscore the connection between concerns over decline and changes in how Romantic subjects perceived their relationship to time and, especially, to the future."[108] Yet that temporal axis is crisscrossed with a worldwide-izing pull. That element, as it plays out through a fracture in the present, is how Barbauld goes further than simply the realization, so often noted in this period's writing, that history is that which persists into the future.[109] It is rather the reverse realization, that the future, *qua* future, and not simply as a present yet to come, has a history separate from what we are living in now.[110] Time, effectively, is refracted worldwide, as Barbauld illustrates through the American tourists of the future. They cannot perceive the racial and cultural diversity that had characterized the London of 1811, because they apprehend only the archaeological London, "those shades that ruled the realms of mind." That is why they wrongly experience the deserted city as the ancestor of their own, now-dominant American culture, the wellspring of their Americanness. They are, in effect, time travelers, but they cannot factor geographical range into their assessment of the city. In this sense, they are not unlike the eponymous subject of Mary Shelley's short story "Valerius, the Reanimated Roman," who comes back after millennia dead, seeking the descendants of his Roman contemporaries, but learns, with "bitter disdain," that Italy now houses only "wretched Italians."[111] Barbauld's future Americans are, similarly, time travelers in search of justice; they, too, would have to teach their thoughts to "pause in their course" if they were to understand what had happened to the civilization in ruins before them.[112]

The pause is provided by the arrival into the poem of what seems to be a magic word. As the Americans, Valerius-like, try to reckon with what has happened in their absence, Barbauld's poem begins to speak of "justice," presenting as "just" the impossible experience of examining one's current moment from the distant future:

And when midst fallen London, they survey
The stone where Alexander's ashes lay,
Shall own with humbled pride the lesson just
By Time's slow finger written in the dust.[113]

Meanwhile, the British reader of 1812 gets the opportunity to look at their own city through the eyes of a future American, and not to recognize it. The British reader is led to realize two things about modern London: first, that European hegemony will not be permanent and is already not even actually dominant, even in the metropolis of the world's mightiest nation (which was Sachs's point); but also secondly, and equally importantly, that "Britishness"—the most valuable cultural commodity in the world at the time—is constructed retroactively, as a fantasy projected onto London from a future taking place elsewhere.

Existing scholarship tends to see Barbauld's vision of London-in-ruins as a moment of perverse reassurance. In such readings, the vision would be aimed at a British readership concerned about the American Declaration of Independence, that is, as Barbauld's way of allowing for an ongoing, if displaced, continuity of British hegemony. For Sachs, the lines provide a "view of the future that functions as a means to . . . perpetuate the value of the present"; for Jessie Reeder, they offer "a consolatory prophesy of ongoing cultural centrality"; for Emily Rohrbach, they indicate an impoverished model of "historical progress that allows nothing outside the normativity of the past into its purview; . . . a world in which a single

THE USES OF HISTORY IN WOLLSTONECRAFT'S AFTERLIVES   55

model of progress would apply to every nation or culture."[114] I see the passage a bit differently. Barbauld situates herself in the future not to make a reassuring or fatalistic prediction—an approach she says is inadvisable, also, in "On the Uses of History"—but rather, like Valerius, to gain the ability to interrogate the present archeologically. Barbauld is not offering a wishful projection of cultural continuity, because the England that survives has never existed except retroactively, in monumentalized form.

That is, the London that survives has existed only in the future and has little relationship to the London of 1811. The visitors, keen on finding archaeological monuments to a great civilization, cannot see that Barbauld's London had been "ungirt by walls," or that it had been a city where "floods of people poured itself abroad" and that built no "jealous drawbridge" to keep out foreigners.[115] Barbauld's poem, then, challenges the monumentalizing attitude, precisely by accepting, in advance, that contemporariness is an act of impossible archaeology whose object is the present. In defiance of the Americans of the future, *Eighteen Hundred and Eleven* creates an archive of British multiculturalism that, in the mode of a democracy to come, awaits its own future enactment in the present. The poem documents the living London of Barbauld's contemporary moment, the body without organs moving with flows of capital, desire, and multiethnic cacophony. The monumentalized London of the future is quite different: its "foreignness" to come arises from its being an American fantasy, such that England is perpetually displaced and fragmented into world museums and archaeological projects. The archaeological London of the future is more a measure of American fantasies of cultural dominance than an unearthing of any historical past. The crux of the problem is that the visitors don't know how to count themselves in their own fantasy: although they see themselves as visitors, they are visiting only themselves, and Barbauld seems to decry the violence and repression of such an endeavor. In opposition to this mode of future historiography, Barbauld articulates an archeological vision of the contemporary cosmopolitan city, a mode of relating to time both impossible and necessary, through which a poet might publicly comment upon the condition of not being wholly contemporary. The poem analyzes contemporary British culture from a time that is not concurrent with itself.

Contemporary English art in such a temporal vortex, including pre-sumably *Eighteen Hundred and Eleven* in a sort of mise-en-abyme, must be recognized as an artefact from someone else's future:

56   FRACTURE FEMINISM

> Oft shall the strangers turn their eager feet
> The rich remains of antient art to greet,
> The pictured walls with critic eye explore,
> And Reynolds be what Raphael was before.[116]

Contemporary art, the passage suggests, looks utterly different when encountered again in future centuries. Yet our ability to recognize this circumstance in the moment itself exerts a deforming force, as if the act of awaiting the eyes of the future demands that our artworks are always already world-historical "masterpieces." Pointedly, the future Americans will value British artworks as the culmination of their project of amassing the "spoils from every clime," and expect them to serve as their "Egyptian granites and . . . Etruscan vase" (209–210). In showing us these artworks from the future, Barbauld implies that contemporary British art and literature disclose their complicity into colonial violence and cultural plunder, to an extent yet unrecognized by her culture.

In both Barbauld texts, history is quintessentially an encounter with strangers, by which we ask them to give an account of themselves, "till at length it embraces the whole globe which we inhabit" (U 396). "On the Uses of History" explains the consequences of that worldwide-ization, to employ the Derridean term.[117] Barbauld is indeed tracking the worldwide-ization of historical discourse, which (as Lacan and Derrida each predicted of psychoanalysis) is arguably its hallmark. One might think that such an approach would be valuable for its lessons in cultural difference, but one would be wrong about that. Rather, learning the history of one's own nation is what gives one the experience of cosmopolitanism—it is a form of travel, accessible to everyone, which actually enhances one's feelings of cultural superiority by removing "those low, illiberal prejudices which adhere to the uninformed of every nation" (U 402). Yet, ironically, by becoming less like those foreign uninformed, the student of history learns to abandon "an arrogant assumption of superiority" and blindly partisan "party spirit" (U 402). In doing so, though, one comes to terms with the "permanency of human characters" (U 406). The comparative study of history, far from introducing difference into the analysis, shows "not human nature as it exists in one age or climate or particular spot of earth, but human nature under all the various circumstances by which it can be affected. . . . It shows us that man is still man, in Turkey and in Lapland, as a vassal in Russia, or a member of a wandering tribe in India" (U 396). That is, a training in comparative history teaches one to disregard cultural differences. It is history without any encounter with pastness: pastness is converted into cultural difference, which is itself immediately arrested through recourse to the *point de capiton* of "human nature."[118] In learning history, then, one learns how to approach problems in a de-historicized fashion.

Barbauld's discursive "quarter turn" destabilizes the entire enterprise of history writing, because it challenges the very association between history and the past. Instead, Barbauld presents history as a geographical movement: to learn the history of one's own nation, she argues paradoxically, is a form of affordable world travel (U 402). Though this would seem to align her with a geographizing modality of history emergent in the Enlightenment, hers was not the "conjectural" mode of writing history, which, finding global stages of supposed human "development," would "study . . . the features distinguishing both the stages typologically and the sequence of human development overall."[119] Barbauld makes, essentially, the opposite assumption. Studying history is a form of travel because there is no center to it: as each national history "exists in your mind separately, . . . you have at no time the state of the world," and so one must simply "keep one kingdom as a metre for the rest" (U 423–24). A master signifier becomes the product, rather than the agent, of Barbauld's historicism, setting her at odds with conjectural historians of her era. The study of chronology is emphatically geographical: "The young student should make it an invariable rule never to read history without a map before him" (U 410). As contemporary Turkey, Lapland, Russia, and India become examples of English pastness, history, now deprived of its pastness, enters a geopsychoanalytic register. By separating history from any possible chronology, Barbauld establishes her credentials as a fracture feminist and historian of the future. This amounts to the "worldwide-ization" of discourse, which would be a marker, in Derrida's estimation, of the psychoanalytic "revolution" to come, and suggest an intellectual movement at odds with the globalizing assumptions of conjectural history.[120]

"The association of geography and history in this way was a commonplace of post-Renaissance thought," says Charles W.J. Withers.[121] But the point is not, for Barbauld, that the two are associated, as per the conventional metaphor of looking through left and right eyes, but that one is directly the study of the other. History is, for Barbauld, the art of fixing knowledge in geographical terms: this is why one should and can study chronology constantly, without unduly worrying about dates or sequences. Once chronology becomes a form of mapping, it can cross the distance between nations, and thus provide "a common measure" between our highly personal experiences of time. Yet, paradoxically, it will only succeed as a "common measure" to the extent to which "I may compare the relater of an event with myself" (U 416). That is, one must inscribe oneself into the chronology as its necessary and only addressee ($), if a transnational master signifier (S1) may be produced. "Dates give you only the dry catalogue of accessions," Barbauld warns, "and you have at no time the whole state of the world." One can justifiably learn "a few dates," but only insofar as one agrees to use them as "landmarks"—that is, as long as they are still comfortably geographical in function—or incorporate them into "anecdotes," something perhaps approaching Rancière's second register (U 423).

This is, in part, how the essay detaches chronology from time, which Barbauld sees as relative, complex, and culturally specific. "The meaning of the *when* is not quite so obvious," explains Barbauld at the beginning of Letter IV, because "a date is a very artificial thing" and "*When* is a relative term" (U 415, emphasis Barbauld's). Chronology, done wisely, eschews considerations of before and after. Rather, it proceeds spatially, always as a form of geography: "chronology supplies this longitude and latitude, fixes every event to its precise point in the chart of universal time," she explains (U 416).

The challenge of this approach is that Barbauld had already, in Letter III, sought to distinguish the study of geography from that of chronology. These disciplines are, she says, not identical with history, but are "collateral branches of science" which are its "two eyes" (U 408). While this would seem very clearly to employ the optical metaphor so common in Enlightenment speculative historiography, Barbauld introduces a fracture into that visual field. The trick is to learn to see geography and chronology as the two vectors across which one can study history—with the understanding that one can jump, strategically, across and between those vectors at will. The map has become three-dimensional. Yet in what sense is the study of the history of one nation (i.e., what Barbauld means by "history") analogous to the comparative study of the present (i.e., what Barbauld means by "geography")? Are studies along a temporal axis exactly equivalent, and indeed interchangeable, with studies along a spatial axis? And if so, how could one be preferable to the other? This is a central question, not just for Barbauld, but for modernity, of which the ideological separation of temporal from spatial analysis has been said to be the hallmark.[122] This, despite the fact that "language expressions for spatial and temporal

THE USES OF HISTORY IN WOLLSTONECRAFT'S AFTERLIVES   59

phenomena have long been recognized as being extremely puzzling and closely interconnected," as Marija Brala Vukanović and Lovorka Gruić Grmuša have recognized.[123]

In light of these intellectual contexts, how can we understand the emphatic slippage between the geographical and temporal axes in Barbauld's text? Mary A. Favret finds, as I have, that "On the Uses of History" works by the "mutual implication of geography and chronology in the study of History." In her estimation, Barbauld is trying to achieve a "general" perspective on history that will be both "impersonal" and disembodied, much as she is said to have been doing in *Eighteen Hundred and Eleven*.[124] I read the import of Barbauld's arguments quite differently: far from aspiring to achieve a totalizing mastery over knowledge (i.e., a master's discourse), Barbauld is trying to inscribe the historian's desire *into* the historical record. This quilting point—affixed to the aporia where geography and chronology cannot be reconciled—is what gives the historian an orientation toward the future. The key, for Barbauld I think, is in learning to see oneself as the object of one's own inquiry, much as Robinson had done in her list of eighteenth-century women writers, and Shelley would do, as we shall see, in *The Last Man*. That is, the task is to make history account for one's desire as its student. That is why Barbauld conducts her historiography within the analyst's discourse, which addresses itself to the lack in the subject. Barbauld is highlighting the temporal effects of this arrangement; these are paradoxical, to say the least, but become a modality of women's resistance in an era devoted to chrononormativity.

Reinhart Koselleck has given us a history of time in the historical discourses of the European eighteenth and nineteenth centuries. The Romantic period, he argues, was pivotal for the development of standardized relations to time, and his account highlights the ways that Barbauld's arguments about the worldwide-ization of history reflect a broader cultural discourse, aligned with Empire, of histories of the world:

> the collective concept "History," coined in the eighteenth century, has a preeminent meaning. It will become apparent that it is with History experienced as a new temporality that specific dispositions and ways of assimilating experience emerge. Our modern concept of history is the outcome of Enlightenment reflection on the growing complexity of "history in general," in which the determinations of experience are increasingly removed from experience itself. This is true both of a world

history extending spatially, which contains the modern concept of history in general, and of the temporal perspective within which, since that time, past and future must be relocated with respect to each other.[125]

Barbauld's essay can be seen as such an attempt to relocate past and future across a spatialized and world-encompassing plane. The problems of cultural relativity that Barbauld was confronting posed a significant epistemological crisis in the period, as Koselleck reminds us:

Who would wish to deny that history is viewed from different perspectives, and that change in history is accompanied by alterations in historical statements about this history? The ancient trinity of place, time, and person clearly enters the work of a historical author.[126]

Barbauld's encounter with this problem is fascinating for its willingness to offer herself, *qua* historian, as the repository of this new, modern space-time. But to achieve this, she needs to be able to present the contemporary historian as an "historical author" always already. That is, just as European culture was coming to terms with the idea of regularized time, Barbauld proposed to solve that problem by making the historian exist in multiple temporal dimensions at once, so as to become the object of her own historical enquiry. This is what gives Barbauld's solution its radical, paradoxical edge and its affiliation with psychoanalytic reason. Her theory of history implicitly pursues a quintessentially Freudian question, one given voice by Derrida: "To make of psychoanalysis *one's own/its own contemporary*, is such a thing thinkable?"[127] It is here that Barbauld's thought departs from that of other early nineteenth-century thinkers, whom I hesitate to call Barbauld's contemporaries. Generally, as Mark Salber Phillips explains: "The Romantics not only deepened the desire for immediacy in some areas where sentimentalism had already prepared the way, but also brought a new demand for close engagement in places where eighteenth-century historical thought valued a greater degree of distantiation," in "an intensification of an already existing movement toward actuality and immediacy."[128] Barbauld's gestures to the worldwide, rather than the immediate or abstract-hegemonic "global," signal her arriving into "an earth of psychoanalysis" and not a globalization of comparative history.[129] History finds its "uses" dialectically, as a geopsychoanalysis to come.

THE USES OF HISTORY IN WOLLSTONECRAFT'S AFTERLIVES   61

Like Oedipus plumbing the mysteries of Thebes, Barbauld's quest for a "common measure" leads her to "herself." The historian is the one person who is never wholly inscribed into the present, and who seeks direct access to the judgments of the future; in a Lacanian sense, the historian is by definition a "woman," having chosen to maintain a direct relation to the signifier of the Other.[130] Unlike male historians who aspire to mastery, Barbauld personifies the lack in the subject. She seeks to stabilize the system of time around an element in the historical chain that has no function there. The product of her historiography having been rendered useless, Barbauld devotes some space to thinking about how historians themselves can become useful. She posits: "It is needless to insist on the uses of history to those whose situation in life gives them room to expect that their actions may one day become the objects of it" (U 405). That is, the agent of historiography—the historian—has to imagine herself as the object-lesson of that history if the history is to have any use value. History begins to be spoken by the object-cause of its own desire, as a way for "significant personages" to encounter themselves from the other side of a discursive Moebius strip.

Crucially, Barbauld associates this posture with the future: motivating the historian through "hope and fear," the historian learns to dread the future as an "incorruptible tribunal, and the severe, soul-searching inquisition of Posterity" (U 405). Here, as in Derrida, "psychoanalysis searches the states of its soul," complete with an echo of the incorruptible Robespierre: Barbauld wants us to anticipate history as a truth procedure that true historians—the objects of their own accounts—will have endured. When history takes itself as its own object, or when the object-cause of history begins to speak its surplus jouissance, history will have become a machine for inflicting suffering. "I make myself or I let myself suffer cruelly," which, says Derrida, is "one of the horizons most proper to psychoanalysis."[131] History is, for Barbauld, a combination of auto-da-fé and autobiography, a truth procedure that will have been exercised upon oneself in the present future. It invokes a Wollstonecraftian "future state" in its moral evaluations, and in so doing serves essentially a superegoic function: it is "the unseen hand" whose "indelible characters . . . will soon be held up for the judgment of the world at large" (U 406). Yet it interacts with the superego from an unusual angle, because it approaches the judgment of the Other through a process of deferment and dissemination. For Freud, the superego internalizes the judgment of "civilization," such that said judgment can be taken as one's own;[132] here, conversely, history externalizes one's hidden desires, producing a giddy jouissance derived from the hope that one will, in the future, have been judged by the Other. Through this mechanism of deferred judgment through the production of indelible biographical writing, history becomes, primarily, estrangement from contemporariness. It means recognizing oneself as a potentially "illustrious character" and seeing "illustrious characters continuing to live on in the eye of posterity, their memories still fresh" (U 406). To study history is not to study the past, but to encounter oneself from the future, and live, already, retroactively, like Valerius or the Americans in a future London. That privilege of learning to live in the future is Barbauld's vision of "justice"; it is her model for living on, beyond one's own time, as "an active agent in the world" (U 407). It is the experience of deferred self-discovery, which is why it must take the historian as its subject, and why "the more History approaches to Biography the more interest it excites" (U 404). Those who feel that history may really affect them in the future do not need to be convinced of history's benefits: already they fear the truth procedure, and so they study history diligently in self-defense. For these, the elect, one's contemporary moment is already "history" insofar as it will have been traced by "history"—and so history is the way that the future writes itself into the present. If History, as Barbauld claims, "conducts our retrospective view through the past ages" (U 400), it is only because our contemporary moment is already, to the fracture feminist, past. History is something that happens in the future; it is the name for an orientation toward the future.

History, in that sense, is the discursive summoning of a justice to come; it does this by turning its own procedures into the object of its own future study. In doing this, it alienates the historian from herself, creating a gap, called "chronology," to separate the subject of the history from the speaking historian. Because it is never present, its "unseen hand" directs ever more history; that is how the accumulation of knowledge (S2) becomes the secret truth of this discourse. It offers chronology without dates, an ex-sistence underway concurrent with the present, even though it only arises as the other's future. The fracture feminist is the person who can confront the gap, which affects all of us, between our "speech" and our "discourse," once she realizes that we are ourselves implicated into the performative work of our investigations: as Lacan explains, "This is how true discourse . . . makes the latter appear to be lying speech—since it pledges the future, which, as they say, belongs to no one—and ambiguous too in that it constantly outstrips the being it concerns."[133] That is,

THE USES OF HISTORY IN WOLLSTONECRAFT'S AFTERLIVES   63

the performative work of studying history becomes a way of giving an account of oneself from the future. History is not a way to account for the actions of great men (which would be the university discourse); it is not a new, more powerful master for our master (which would be the hysteric's discourse); it addresses itself, rather, to a hole in the master, to the lack that constitutes him ($). Barbauld's historian, like the analyst in Lacan, "makes himself the underwriter, the hostage," and even the waste product "to be eliminated from the process," once the discourse makes another quarter-turn back into mastery.[134] Yet in the here and now, history is merely the voice of that surplus enjoyment as it addresses the lack in its subject. As Barbauld explains: "From this method a regular chronology might certainly be deduced if we had the whole unbroken series; but unfortunately there are many gaps and chasms in history, and you will easily see that if any links in the chain are wanting, the whole composition is rendered imperfect" (U 417). It takes the imaginative, performative work of "pledging the future," as Lacan would have it, to distance the historian from herself and enable her to exist in and for the future alone.

Entangled in this worldwide web of *différance*, Barbauld proposes that the way out would be, precisely, a master signifier: "We want, therefore, an universal date, like a lofty obelisk seen by all the country round, from and to which every distance should be measured." Such an obelisk is the aspiration of Barbauld's historical method, which endeavors to triangulate timelines across national discrepancies until we achieve temporal standardization: facing the flow of time, "we must raise a pillar upon its banks and measure our distances from that, both up and down the stream," she urges (U 417–418). That is, history will have needed to orient itself from the future, retroactively, if it shall have any use today.

It may at first seem like Barbauld's call for a "universal date" would upend certain recent approaches to Barbauld and time. I am thinking especially of Sachs's recent work, which, in challenging Chandler's historicist approach to Barbauld, suggests that the title *Eighteen Hundred and Eleven* "serves as a marker to call our attention to a more complex, layered, and heterochronic understanding of temporality that we might understand as an affective history of the present moment."[135] Yet the "universal date" is actually what allows Barbauld to achieve heterochronicity within "On the Uses of History," and so, despite first appearances, my findings actually support Sachs's conclusions. Barbauld's work, far from providing an alternative to masculinist eighteenth-century historiographies, or a complementary second methodology, simply prevents masculinist historiographies from closing or becoming coherent. This is history being written not-whole, emerging from within the epistemologies of historical research and offer itself "to Lydia" as a supplement, not a complement, to traditional modes of history writing.[136] While this was not really a characteristic attitude for female historians of the period, Barbauld was, in the process, implicitly aligning herself with a tradition of Romantic-era women writers, including Macaulay and Wollstonecraft, who likewise voiced their ideas through supplementary. Like them, Barbauld saw herself not as an *historian* historian, but someone specifically writing the future history of "man" from the other side.

This is not to say that women writers of the Romantic period had a distinctive way of thinking about history. When Looser warns that "I do not believe that there was a characteristic women's relationship to history," she suggests that "we have a long way to go to understand history's multiple genderings."[137] Her important study reveals that "women were much more involved in the burgeoning genre of history than we have formerly thought," because "history has not been an entirely male preserve . . . [and] criticism of history's sexism is not of recent origin."[138] Barbauld's experiments in geopsychoanalytic contemporary historiography should be seen as an important part of that tradition. They build especially on earlier efforts by women, including Wollstonecraft and Macaulay, to write contemporary histories of the French Revolution, and to reveal how revolutionary, in a discursive sense, such projects could be. Although the master's historical discourse endeavors to hide its "impediment, failure, split," we find, in work such as this chapter has traced, that "a loss emerges from this trajectory."[139] That lost object is the object *a*, which Barbauld, like Macaulay, Wollstonecraft, Robinson, and the author of "Ithuriel," will have learned to make speak. Writing future histories from beyond the grave, they confronted chrononormativity—that is, arguably the signal ideological resource of their moment—from the analyst's side. Such writings demonstrate how a fracture in masculinist histories could take place from within, but "not-all" the way within, the temporal discursive framework of those histories.

Chapter 2

Adoptive Siblings across Oceans of Futurity

Paul and Virginia and *The Victim of Prejudice*

Jacques-Henri Bernardin de Saint-Pierre, the eighteenth-century French colonist, botanist, author, and close friend to Helen Maria Williams, was, to be sure, a contradictory figure. The "insular, 'indigenist,' incestuous world" of his *Paul et Virginie* (1788), a novel "caught up in the web of its own impossible paradoxes," would resonate across French and British Romantic literature deep into the nineteenth century.[1] As Pratima Prasad has shown, Bernardin's influence is especially felt in the raft of novels that use adoptive siblings to examine kinship structures, interracial sexuality, and incest, often in a global frame.[2] Wherever adopted children are being groomed for love and marriage to their siblings, as we see most famously, and twice over, in *Frankenstein*, we feel the influence of Bernardin's narrative. Such plots were tacitly political, explains Eric C. Walker, given "the association of adoption with France, where adoption was construed as an essential mark of revolutionary citizenship."[3] Williams would, for instance, sign into library guestbooks as "an adopted child of the French Republic," as Walker points out.[4]

This chapter will pursue two such novels, both of which appear to have influenced *Frankenstein*: Williams's experimental English translation of *Paul et Virginie*, entitled *Paul and Virginia* (1795), and Mary Hays's *The Victim of Prejudice* (1799). Analyzing these novels, I will ask: How could the eroticization of adoptive siblings, a plot itself adopted, in its pastoral splendor, from Bernardin, contribute to the feminist discourse of the contemporary future? Would there be a special temporality of love between siblings in Romantic-era writings—one thinks immediately of "Tintern Abbey" and *Manfred*—and why would this be a particular direction for feminist writing? How would the formal features of literary texts, such as narrative frames and inset poetry, affect the time of the stories narrated? What new varieties of time arise when siblings are encouraged to fall in love, and this vector of semi-taboo desire begins to interfere with, or run up against, the chronological ordering of phases normally expected, at least within a certain psychoanalytic tradition, of childhood sexual development? Jacques Lacan admired British Romanticism specifically for its capacity to help us un-think the temporality of those phases, urging his students to see the child, as represented in the literature of the period, as a "reference point, a vanishing point," and not "a foil," for adult, Oedipalized sexuality.[5] It is as if "the stream of time" first charted by Freud would open into "an ocean of futurity, which has no boundaries"—which is expressly how Williams, translating Bernardin, characterizes the feelings of an adult who is likening himself to a pair of amorous adoptive siblings.[6]

Some suggest that Romantic-era feminist authors gravitated toward narratives of adoption as a way to stress that gender roles are socially con-structed.[7] But the emphasis in such novels is very often as much erotic as it is sociological, which indicates that authors may also have been invested in finding technicalities, such as adoption, through which they might explore taboo subjects such as incest and the Oedipus complex. Some novels go out of their way to emphasize the naturalness of the adoptive bond, as when, in Susan Ferrier's *Marriage* (1818), Mrs. Douglas discovers that the "instinct of a parent's love warmed her Heart" as she holds her adopted daughter.[8] Moreover, Romantic-era texts such as *Paul and Virginia* and *The Victim of Prejudice* have a tendency to imagine brother-sister incest, whether adoptive or not, as simply an outgrowth of "the normal sibling relation," and as something to be purposefully pursued, if also sometimes punishable.[9] Existing work on Romantic-era kinship structures will sometimes assume that one can read a novel either vertically, through its Oedipal plot, or horizontally, through a dynamic of sibling rivalry, as if adopted siblings did not usually bring with them the additional issue of adoptive parents, and as if these vectors of forbidden, yet strangely socially sanctioned and parentally ordained desire, would not mutually complicate one another.[10] Psychoanalysts, meanwhile, worry about how adoption might multiply affect sibling bonds and the Oedipal situation.[11] Lacan urges psychoanalysis to find ways to study kinship horizontally, between siblings, in addition to vertically, across generations, as a way to deepen Freudian models of intrafamily identification; Prophecy Coles tries to understand how a sexual relationship between siblings, either enacted or in fantasy, may possibly bypass the Oedipus complex, yet concludes that, in the end, such relationships may instill the Oedipus complex all the more deeply.[12] This is very much the case, as we shall see, in *Paul and Virginia* and *The Victim of Prejudice*.

Late-eighteenth-century Britons were strangely prone to miss the obvious main point of *Oedipus Rex*, which is: even if you do not know you are guilty, and even if you take measures, such as adoption, specifically to shield yourself, you are still probably guilty and deserve to be thoroughly punished. Somehow, people in the Romantic period tended to see *Oedipus Rex* as a story of injustice rather than a warning about desire—they were outraged by the tragic events of the play, as they thought that Oedipus did nothing wrong.[13] Mary Wollstonecraft makes this case directly: "What moral lesson, for example, can be drawn from the story of Oedipus, the favorite subject of a number of tragedies?—The gods impel him on, and, led imperiously by blind fate, though perfectly innocent, he is fearfully punished, with all his hapless race, for a crime in which his will had no part."[14] In this reading, the incest taboo was wrongly enforced because Oedipus was not aware of the situation—an interpretation that asks us to see roadside killings and the mismanagement of a public health crisis as features of "perfect innocence." Wollstonecraft sees Oedipus as a special case, exempt from the cosmic laws governing incest as a result of his adopted upbringing. If Giorgio Agamben was right to suggest that "tragedy appears as the guilt of the just and comedy as the justification of the guilty," then we could say that Wollstonecraft was bent on turning *Oedipus Rex* into a comedy, in the sense that she leads the King of Thebes to salvation through her acts of interpretation.[15]

Lacan, intriguingly, sees Oedipus the same way—but with an important extra twist. In his seminar on ethics, he offers a stunning re-evaluation of the Oedipus complex, in light of what he saw as the metaphorical nature of paternity:

> If Oedipus is a whole man, if Oedipus doesn't have an Oedipus complex, it is because in his case there is no father at all. The person who served as father was his adoptive father. And, my good friends, that's the case with all of us.[16]

All fathers, Lacan advises, are "adoptive fathers," which makes everyone exempt from the fate that is said, by Freud, to await "all of us."[17] Jacques Derrida, in *Politics of Friendship*, analogously claims, on the horizontal vector, that all brothers are "adoptive." "The brother is always a brother of alliance" and not of "nature," he explains, because fraternity is something produced symbolically rather than biologically.[18] This chapter, taking to heart these observations, will consider *Paul and Virginia* and *The Victim of Prejudice* in deconstructive and psychoanalytic ways, in order to theorize the unique temporality of adoptive sibling love at the crossroads of the incest taboo, the exemption that Oedipus, like "all of us," perhaps enjoyed, and the worldwide-izing forces afoot that would embroil any family romance within wider political issues such as slavery, capital, and women's rights. Wollstonecraft was right about *Oedipus Rex*, even if she did not fully grasp the extra Lacanian-Derridean twist. Because everyone is exempt from the Oedipus complex, those who are not completely exempt (i.e., "not-all of us") begin an ex-sistence in relation to that universal set. Once the exemption is universally granted, it becomes the very thing that would qualify someone to be punished after all! The adopted child, it would seem, makes "no father at all" of the man—which, as Hays and later Mary Shelley would indicate, will make a young man dread to make a wife of his adopted sister. Once the love story of quasi-incestuous siblings, whose intimacy is originally encouraged, begins to intersect with the "no" of the parent or parents' social obligation and material need, and is pushed in a global and directly political direction, as a question of rights, we are left with a family romance, now Lacanianized and deconstructed, which serves as "*a moving platform* for a theory of global culture by virtue of the deconstruction it includes as its essential moment."[19] In effect, it demands the worldwide-ization of the Oedipus complex, such that this notorious Freudian concept, taken in its Romantic proto-Freudian form, reveals the contemporary future through the fracture of enforced sexual difference. This, in the context of a culture of Romanticism in which "experiences of globalization were usually felt from within the boundaries of the nation-state" and were "textually driven," as Evan Gottlieb has shown.[20]

The Ocean of Futurity: Parergonal *Paul and Virginia*

When, in 1795, Helen Maria Williams translated *Paul et Virginie* into English, the act of doing so proclaimed a republic of international friendship in

ADOPTIVE SIBLINGS ACROSS OCEANS OF FUTURITY   69

the midst of the Reign of Terror. An avowal of friendship is itself a claim to
the future.[21] In a time of reaction and war, Williams made a visible gesture
of solidarity and intimacy across battle lines. Her translation, appearing
just as Britain was plotting to overthrow the Republican government in
France, and increasing in popularity during the subsequent Napoleonic
Wars, seemed to be motivated by political questions not associated with
Bernardin's 1788 original.[22] It was the most successful, commercially and
reputationally, of some twenty English translations of *Paul and Virginie*,
and it became Williams's most popular and well-regarded work during
her lifetime.[23] Williams's translation is loose, adaptive, and experimental,
wildly revising and abridging Bernardin's text in the hopes of delivering
what "the serious and reflecting Englishman requires" (W 6). Williams
especially excises Bernardin's "general observations" and "long philosophical
reflections," replacing them with a number of her own original sonnets.
Indeed, the success of the volume would revive Williams's career as a
poet.[24] With these adaptations and in these new contexts, the translated
work, despite being a translation, was received as Williams's commentary
on the era's most pressing political questions, such as war with France
and the movement to abolish the slave trade. Female British translators
could, as Deirdre Coleman explains, often serve as "cultural mediators
in the Romantic era," bringing European ideas to British and Irish readers, and "confirm[ing] the central role of foreign literature in their own
self-definition as woman writers."[25]

Previous scholarship has shown how Williams infused *Paul and
Virginia* with a host of feminist ideas, and how the translation itself, in
its creative experimentation, brazenly undercuts the supposed passivity of
the translator's role.[26] Williams's presence as feminist translator additionally
changes the text's analysis of racial oppression, given how "women writers were at the centre of [British] eighteenth-century racial discourses."[27]
The specific content of Bernardin's text permits Williams to connect her
feminist concerns with questions of race (e.g., slavery) and kinship (e.g.,
lesbianism and sibling incest) in dislocating ways. Questions of race and
feminism were tied together, very often, in British Romanticism through
discussions of kinship, which could quickly become allegories for the
nation. Wollstonecraft, for instance, associates a "weak king" with "the
weak father of a family," in order to suggest that women, as the weak
father's "convenient slaves," "remain immured in their families groping in
the dark."[28] In such a model, to find oneself inside of the inside of power
(as a member of the bourgeois family in the seat of the Empire) is to

find oneself cast into the utter darkness and forgotten. As Kerry Sinanan explains, to speak from a position inside of hegemonic power, or presumed to be coextensive with it, often involved a certain envy for the fugitive black bodies beyond the reach of national surveillance.[29] It was possible to imagine a zone of blackness, conducive to feminist experimentation, outside of "the print's frame" and its "imposed borders."[30] That is, it was possible to treat racial difference through metaphors of parerga. Such a cultural logic of borders and frames, insides and outsides, creates opportunities to deconstruct patriarchy by triangulating gender-based oppression with racial oppression in the context of a family romance. Hence Bernardin's text, with its disquieting meditations on Black fugitivity, female desire, and incest, was an ideal source text for Williams to take up. Williams appropriates Bernardin's objectionable myth of the kindly slaveholder and ambiguously refracts it through a number of textual strategies, including frame narrators, inset poetry, and what Lacan would call fantasy, to deliver Bernardin's story into a fracture feminist framework. She breaks open the temporal foundations of Bernardin's text—that is, the times of narration and world travel—to offer feminist meditations upon the French Revolution, racialized feminist kinship structures, and the mutual deconstruction of racial and gender difference from within the contemporary future.

The story of *Paul and Virginia* is a moving one. Paul and Virginie—or "Virginia," in Williams's translation—are raised on the island of Mauritius, "that fatal soil," as siblings (W 12). They are adoptive siblings groomed to be lovers. Given what Derrida and Lacan say about adoption as a universal experience, I will not here be emphasizing the difference between biological siblings and adoptive siblings. The primary texts, too, treat the adoption as an incidental, if noteworthy, factor in the family bond, important especially to the extent that it makes possible queer kinship structures. Paul and Virginia's mothers, named Margaret and Madame de la Tour, are neighbors at first, until they resolve that "each of our children will have two mothers":

> United by the tie of similar wants, and the sympathy of similar misfortunes, they gave each other the tender names of companion, friend, sister.—They had but one will, one interest, one table. All their possessions were in common. (W 19, 18)

Williams had long been captivated by the idea of a household governed solely by women. Her 1790 novel *Julia*, for instance, disposes of its men

ADOPTIVE SIBLINGS ACROSS OCEANS OF FUTURITY   71

until the reader is left with a self-sustaining community of women; her writings from France describe her relief in joining "a family of women," too.[31] The perfect intimacy of the de la Tours lasts until Virginia is sent away to France for practical financial reasons. Paul, wholly in love with his sister, yearns for her until he receives a letter announcing her immediate return. When her return vessel is caught in a hurricane, though, Virginia drowns within sight of the Mauritian beach. Virginia's tragic death is witnessed by a crowd of onlookers, including Paul and the narrator. "Paul and I observed a profound silence," notes the narrator, while "those indolent Creoles" scramble in vain to rescue Virginia (W 96–97).

Derrida maintains that the world, over the course of several centuries, endured an epochal shift, in which political arrangements rooted in fraternity and national citizenship were unraveled by the economic forces of globalization.[32] One can see, even in the above plot summary, how *Paul and Virginia* crystallizes this world-historical tragedy in smaller scale. Williams was deeply concerned about these issues. A self-proclaimed "citizen of the world" and author of a sundry oeuvre unified by its consistent cosmopolitanism,[33] she sought a different model of being-worldwide. Bernardin's *Paul et Virginie* shares Williams's particular aesthetic in many ways, thoughtfully and poignantly investigating world travel (and, consequently, international politics) through a sentimental and Romantic narrative. It surely "triggered an identificatory response" in her.[34]

Yet Derrida warns, translating a line from Paul Celan, that "There are no worlds, there are only islands."[35] Which is to say that Mauritius lends itself well to experiments in proto-deconstructive thought, as a semi-allegorical setting for what will have become, in translation, an engagement with the contemporary future. It is fitting that the word "Creole" appears so often in Williams's *Paul and Virginia*, given how Mauritius is very likely the most creolized nation in the world.[36] Uninhabited until the seventeenth century and shaped by constant negotiations of Dutch, French, and British colonialism, Mauritius "has always been a creole island," explains Megan Vaughan, "a profoundly cosmopolitan place, . . . an island without natives."[37] As a result of the island's unique history, the term "Creole" takes on a specific meaning in the Mauritius: it refers to the condition of not being Hindu, Christian, or Muslim, Chinese, Indian, Dutch, British, or French, and of speaking only Mauritian Creole instead of several languages.[38] The term, then, names a lack of identity realized through monolingualism—a fracture in linguistic space—and as such, can be understood as, in effect, a synonym for deconstruction. Creolization is a way of reading and translating that will not, in Williams's hands, be willing to "give up the ghost" at the scene of "colonial power."[39] The Mauritian Creole must have intrigued Williams, given how the elimination, hollowing out, or traversal of linguistic and religious differences remained constantly at the heart of her concerns.

In Bernardin's text, the characters Paul and Virginia are explicitly Creole, of French descent; their racial identities are less explicit, and quite dynamic, in Williams's version.[40] The ambiguity is powerful because these were the years in which the scientific discourse of racism was emerging, a development that has been called a "deep structure" that gives "the underlying bass notes of the symphony" of Romanticism.[41] The actual island of Mauritius, called Île de France when Williams was translating, would become a British holding in 1810; the British government would restore the Dutch name Mauritius in 1814. It is significant, then, that Williams sets the story in "Mauritius" so-called, while Bernardin sets it on the "Île de France": she thus accomplishes at the literary level what the British government would achieve in actual fact some twenty years hence. It becomes, in this way, a text that belongs to the future, sustaining (colonial) hope at the level of language—and this, according to Derrida, would be a politics.[42]

In addition to the racial ambiguity, the categories of author and translator, France and Britain, are seen to be strangely indistinguishable and fluid in this novel: the translation, explains Williams in the preface, represents an attempt to reconcile those "two nations [i.e., Britain and France, which] seem to change characters" so readily" (W 6–7). Williams offers *Paul and Virginia* to her British readership as an act of friendship caught up irreducibly in a Revolutionary context that Bernardin, writing in 1788, could not have fully imagined: a previous draft of the translation, she notes, remains "mingled with revolutionary placards, motions, and harangues" in a government censorship office in Paris, the capital of "a country where arts have given place to arms" (W 6–7). The published version of the translation, she explains, "was written at Paris, amidst the horrors of Robespierre's tyranny." It is thoroughly a product of a Revolution that Bernardin had not anticipated. In its Rousseauvian commitments, the novel may be an early instance of "creolizing Rousseau," meaning the recent critical project of reading Rousseau against the grain in relation to a wider world of (often postcolonial) critical thought.[43]

Though Bernardin's novella features several enslaved characters, it was not always read, in the eighteenth and nineteenth centuries, as a story about

Black fugitivity. Its reception history is exceptionally complex, but suffice it to say that, in the long afterlife of its initial publication, as the story was abstracted from its original appearance in the third edition of Bernardin's *Studies of Nature*, *Paul et Virginie* and its translations became largely responsible for the stereotype of Mauritius as a sensual tropical utopia, a problematic fantasy about the island that has persisted into the twenty-first century.[44] Undoubtedly, Bernardin's invocation of an iron collar places his novel within an abolitionist context, as Conny Cassity has argued.[45] Yet the novel was still generally read as an exotic and sentimental love story; even today, it is "a novel famed for its childlike innocence"—even if it has been largely responsible for Mauritius's association with erotic passion in the European cultural imagination.[46] The "innocence and chastity" of the story are not put at odds with its seductive exoticism, but work alongside that exoticism to produce new "Edenic codes."[47] Although *Paul et Virginie* directly depicts the institution of slavery, it does so in the context of a "European republican fantasy" according to which, as Anna Neill puts it, "slavery is erased from the novel's colonial memory."[48]

Yet Williams's name on the title page ensured that her *Paul and Virginia* would be read, at least in part, as a condemnation of chattel slavery in a way that Bernardin's text seldom had been. Williams was a leading voice for abolition in Britain, renowned in liberal circles for her 1788 *Poem on the Bill Lately Passed for Regulating the Slave Trade*.[49] The 1790s and 1800s were "crucial decades" in Mauritian history: slavery persisted and even flourished on the Île de France even well after 1794, when slavery was legally abolished in France and its colonies.[50] Slavery was abolished in Mauritius only in 1835. Until that time, plantation owners depended upon the profitability of their operations, the island's small population and relative isolation, and, as the nineteenth century proceeded, its strategic significance as a base from which France could attack British vessels during the Napoleonic Wars, as justifications for their continuing enslavement of people. As the Mauritian plantations expanded under French jurisdiction, British experts began to worry that people of the Malabar Coast, which was under British control, would be enslaved by French colonialists to satisfy an urgent demand for labor.[51] In this way, Williams's translation necessarily engages with dynamic political realities affecting Europe and Mauritius alike, and re-opens, rather than sutures, a competitive rift between England and France at the levels of human rights, foreign interests, globalized labor, and military strategy. Through the novel's parergonal narrative structures, she turns Bernardin's

74   FRACTURE FEMINISM

problematic island utopia into a utopia of time in the present future—a
form of feminist thought that I am calling contretempopia, meaning the
utopia of the deconstructive contretemps.

In *Paul and Virginia*, though, Williams approaches slavery with
much more equivocality than in her other work: the translator cannot, or
refuses to, separate the horrors of slavery from the erotics of the setting, a
combination that interferes with the reader's attempts to sympathize with
the enslaved. Bernardin, a onetime slaveholding colonial administrator in
Mauritius, had already authored a highly conflicted series of considerations
upon plantation slavery before writing *Paul et Virginie*. In those earlier
texts, he had objected to the cruelty of slavery even while he advanced
rationalizations for its preservation and attempted to displace culpability
for its cruelties onto other nations (Dobie 57–60). Bernardin's 1773 travel
narrative *Voyage to the Île de France* expresses clear opposition to the
institution of slavery, but Bernardin seems to have "vacillated" about it in
the years and decades that followed, his concerns becoming increasingly
"diluted" over time.[52] *Paul and Virginia*, even in Williams's hands, retains
the ambiguity characteristic of Bernardin, presenting slavery as a matter
informed and enforced by an otherwise well-meaning cosmopolitan erotics. Yet as Williams adopts this problematic ethos and works through its
ambiguities, she formulates a provocative deconstructive meditation on the
contemporary future and, extending from there, international friendship.
Artifacts like the iron collar, being at once intensely personal, traumatic,
historical, phenomenological, and associated with collective labor, can
allow time to accumulate heterochronically, as Ian Baucom points out.[53]

At the beginning of *Paul and Virginia*, Margaret buys an "old Negro
slave," Domingo, "with whom she cultivated a little spot of this canton"
(W 13). The text does not seem outraged or saddened by this. Madame
de la Tour, meanwhile, enslaves Mary, a "woman-woman" from Mada-
gascar renowned for her weaving and ability to be "cleanly and, above
all, faithful" (W 16–17). Domingo, a "good old Negro," is "passionately
fond" of Mary, and they marry immediately (W 33, 16). They function as
honorary members of the family, affable, earnest, hardworking, and, like
their fellow characters, highly idealized. Through their marriage, their labor
becomes refigured as a kind of conjugal domesticity, even as it produces
and sustains the domestic ideal for Madame de la Tour and Margaret,
and by extension Paul and Virginia. The novel encourages us to see the
three couples, all cohabitating, in parallel: the love story of Domingo and
Mary doubles that of Paul and Virginia, and, to a lesser extent, that of

Madame de la Tour and Margaret. In such a way, uncompensated labor becomes coded as fruitful, domestic, and idyllic—simply another face of happiness and love. Indeed, "the indefatigable labors of the two slaves" hold together the generic and thematic strands of the story—sustaining, as it were, the entire household—and is, in a material way, the story's premise (W 16). As Neill points out, the institution of slavery "slips into the more convenient category of familial patronage" here. "Slaves have no place in this narrative," she rightly observes, "unless they are particularized, named, drawn into the family as pseudo-members (in which case they will love, rejoice, weep, and finally die just as and when their masters do)."[54] Slavery is supposedly a component of a fully functional (and lesbian) family economy, enabling everyone to live in harmony with each other and with nature. At the end of the novella, Bernardin refers to Domingue and Marie as "fidèles serviteurs"—in Williams's equally euphemistic translation, "faithful servants"—which makes their labor seem rather a matter of honor than coercion.[55] Hence we arrive into what will be the first of many narrative reduplications in the translated text: both in the story itself and by its very translation, the suffering of laborers, uncompensated workers of color rendered invisible, foments a bond of friendship between Europeans.

Somehow, the narrator claims to have learned from the story of Paul and Virginia the value of living "without wife, children, or slaves" (W 83). The lesson seems impossible to glean from the story. It completely repudiates the story's vision of domesticity—one championed by the narrator himself—in which even the wives have wives, the children plan to have children together, and the slaves, perversely, have their own slaves (as I shall discuss below). The narrator's remark can only be read as a symptom of Bernardin and Williams's combined efforts to ignore slavery through its disavowal, even (and especially) when the story would seem to foreground its horrors. For instance, in an attempt to illustrate how "the amiable disposition of those children [i.e., Paul and Virginia] unfolded itself daily," the narrator recalls how, as children, Paul and Virginia once "perceived a Negro woman beneath the plantains which shaded their habitation . . . almost wasted to a skeleton" (W 27). The episode is evidently based on an encounter that Bernardin had in Mauritius.[56] In the diluted fictionalization that Williams would translate, Paul and Virginia feed the woman before returning her, supposedly for her own benefit, to her master, the "rich planter" (W 27). Once they broker her return, they assure the fugitive woman that the master will take pity on her; Paul and Virginia feel good "from the remembrance of this benevolent action" (W 30).

The master, though, severely punishes the woman for having escaped. Paul and Virginia are shocked by the violence, as is the narrator: "But what pardon!," exclaims the narrator, exasperated. "How difficult it is to do good!," laments Virginia (W 33–34). The injury to the woman is not apparently troubling in itself; rather, Virginia is concerned that the events will compromise her own standing as a benevolent resident of the island. As if rising to address Paul and Virginia's near-crisis of reputation, a "troop of Maroon Negroes" immediately appears to thank the children for their unsuccessful efforts.[57] The Maroons, known to the French for their rebelliousness, call Paul and Virginia "good little white people" and lift them upon their shoulders, "overwhelm[ing them] with their bene-dictions" (W 34–35). Domingo joins and even leads them, of course. The display of appreciation and loyalty enables Virginia to remind Paul—and the reader—that "God never leaves a good action without reward" (W 34–35). It is a truly perverse lesson that the enslaved woman cannot have learned. Yet the novella does indeed "reward" the fully exculpated siblings for convincing an enslaved woman to return to the plantation and be tortured. More perversely yet, the supposed success of their endeavor becomes the basis of the siblings' erotic bond: years later, Virginia admits to Paul that "you are dear to me since the day when you wanted to fight the master of the slave for me" (W 54). Although there was never, in the space of the plot, any such fight aspired to, the siblings' decision to return the fugitive to her cruel master is understood to have been justified, despite its disastrous consequences for the woman in question, for the way that it adds an erotic supplement to a tender sibling attachment. Their decision to escort a woman back into degradation and bondage is remembered, as if through a screen memory, as a willingness to confront the master.

One might suspect that *Paul and Virginia* develops two perspectives on slavery, namely, slavery in innocence, as explored through Domingo and Mary, and slavery in experience, as explored through the fugitive woman. But this would not be correct. The exculpatory story of the enslaved fugitive does not illustrate a separate mode of thinking from that of the story of Domingo and Mary. Rather, each subplot is called upon to solve the problems of the other: Domingo ensures that Paul and Virginia are absolved of their contributions to the punitive violence, and the fugitive woman reminds the reader of the desirability of paternalistic arrangements. Each narrative strand is a lack that supplements the other, adding precisely nothing to the ideological fantasy of its counterpart:

"incomplete, unequal to the task, it lacks something in order for the lack to be fulfilled, it participates in the evil that it should repair."[58] Taken together, these episodes realize hypothetical displays of gallantry and model perfect domestic happiness. Even as the strands might seem to work at cross-purposes, they together quite directly establish the very conditions for erotic attraction and world travel. Slavery, that is, proves to be essential to the colonial project, which, in turn, proves essential to "love."

Love, in *Paul and Virginia*, is both domesticating and queer. It is in itself a "translation," by Derrida's analysis of that term, in the sense that it pertains to contradictions apparent in the economy of the home.[59] Breaking with Bernardin, Williams implies that Madame de la Tour and Margaret have a romantic relationship. They write love poetry for one another. Madame de la Tour "poured forth the effusions of melancholy in the language of verse" when she thinks of Margaret and their home, composing, among other poems, a "Sonnet to Love" (W 18–19). This has no basis in Bernardin's text. Yet the "Sonnet to Love" tells, in highly compressed form, the story of *Paul and Virginia*, now presented as an elaborate conceit for a lesbian household. The sonnet asserts that the love possible between women is like—figuratively speaking—the setting and plot of *Paul and Virginia*; love itself, like French colonialism, is said to travel "o'er the deep." The conceit ensures that the sonnet is an exercise in re-telling, not foreshadowing: allusive and not ominous in tone, the poem only makes sense, contextually, if the reader already knows Bernardin's novella. The speaker tells of perfect youthful days "ere yet I knew thy [i.e., Love's] fatal power," days which were like "torrid rays, / That paint the broad-leaved plantain's glossy bower." Love, receiving a narrative about itself, arrives into the sonnet like a hurricane: "Disturb'd and wild as ocean's troubled breast, / When the hoarse tempest of the night is there." The sonnet thus turns Bernardin's story itself into the vehicle of a self-reflexive act of figuration. Williams's work as translator adds another dimension to this dynamic: if, as Derrida suspected, "the world is an island whose map we do not have," then "translation was always, in me, the other face of a jealous and admiring love."[60] Through the sonnet's processes of figuration, the reader learns, on the one hand, to recognize the structural logic of love in the asymmetrical power politics of empire, and on the other, to recognize in *Paul et Virginie* the narrative structure of love. Which is to say that the figurative language cuts both ways. At one level, the exotic island becomes, in Williams's hands, the very expression of idyllic romance, while, on the other, the story of the separated lovers becomes a mere analogy through which we can grasp the depth of the relationship between Margaret and Madame de la Tour, the true subject of the sonnet. Much more than Bernardin's text, then, Williams's *Paul and Virginia* can be said to devour its own boundaries, turning against itself in search of a lesson about love: it devotes a part of itself—fourteen lines—to turning the entire plot, as inherited from Bernardin, into a metaphor for its lesbian subplot. Thus, the text gets entangled in the difficulties of ornamentation: the framed lyric is framed by the main narrative once it has become a frame for its own frame.

Through this process, we find that Williams's attempt to produce a "transnational matriarchal utopia," as Calè describes it, only goes so far.[61] The text ultimately subordinates the voices of its women to that of an old man—the narrator—wearing "the ancient garb of the island" (W 10). At the very outset, Williams's frame narrator discovers the man, genuflecting to him and calling him "Father," and solicits from him the story of Margaret, Madame de la Tour, Paul, and Virginia (W 10). Almost every paragraph of the translation begins with quotation marks attributed to the "father"—quotation marks not there in Bernardin's text. The novella thus gains a residual patriarchal presence that, it would seem, operates at a separate narrative level than the inset tale of female self-reliance. Bernardin's novella consists of these same two narrative levels—the brief narrative frame, in which a tourist narrates the discovery of the man, and then, inset, the story of Paul and Virginia, as told by the man—but without the recurring marker of his voice. Additionally, Williams nests these two stories within a yet wider frame, relating her own editorial and translating experience and situating Bernardin's fiction within the revolutionary and Anglo-French contexts of its production and dissemination. This frame, in parergonal fashion, is neither part of the story nor the outside world.

In *The Truth in Painting*, Derrida outlines the complexities of the parergon, a supplementary embellishment to a text or artwork that serves as its edge and decoration. A picture frame is the quintessential example; columns around buildings and absolutely transparent veils also qualify. "What constitutes them as *parerga*," argues Derrida, "is not simply their exteriority [to the main artwork] as a surplus, it is the internal structural link which rivets them to the lack in the interior of the *ergon*," or main artwork. We can think of these narrative ornaments in such a way. Distinguishable both from the main narrative and from the "real world," the narrative frames and supplementary poems "supposedly do not belong to the whole of the representation" yet neither are they separate from it.[62]

Although I am wary of using the term "parergon" too loosely (heeding recent warnings to that effect),[63] I find the slipperiness involved with the term is actually useful as a way to think about the supplementary features of *Paul and Virginia*, and also useful as a way to think about the contemporary future as it sits on the inside and outside of clock time and on the inside and outside of the charmed circle that is the European family.

Already employing a parergonal narrative frame, Williams processes those levels through the additional distancing effect of her irony: she introduces her translation, for instance, by explaining that the text has been adapted for British readers, who seek "in novel writing, as in the theater, a rapid succession of incidents, much bustle and stage effect, without suffering the author to appear himself" (W 6). The translation thus introduces itself through a strategic self-effacement, a gesture undercut by the frequent intrusion of sonnets into the narrative—sonnets that, according to the obituary for Williams printed in *Gentleman's Magazine*, "destroyed" "the exquisite simplicity" of the original.[64] Intrinsic to this looming destruction, and essential to the irony of it, is how Williams utterly claims the sonnets, making clear to her readers, through repeated use of the word "my," that they are resolutely her own: she speaks of "my last poetical productions," "my earlier compositions," and "my poetical taste," adding that "I can scarcely flatter myself" about them (W 6–7). These sonnets, then, being entirely "mine," encroach into Bernardin's narrative, and, by extension, the tourist's and, by further extension, the old man's, crossing several layers of narration at once. The sonnets embed themselves in the text yet further by being attributed, within the space of the story, to Madame de la Tour. We receive this one, though, from the narrating old man, who, having heard it from Madame de la Tour, recites it from memory, attributing the sonnet to de la Tour's "genuine sensibility"; meanwhile, though, in the outermost narrative frame, Williams herself cops to having introduced the sonnets from the outside and after the fact (W 18, 6). Thus, mimicking the figural work underway *inside* the "Sonnet to Love," the very *placement* of Williams's original poetry becomes framed by the main narrative, which in turn is framed by the "father," whose tale in turn is framed by the tourist, whose tale in turn is framed, in a narrative Moebius strip, by Williams-the-translator, author of the poetry, and writer who, in her accounts of Revolutionary France, had evoked "a sense of futurity not *and* but *in* the present."[65]

Things are further complicated when the male narrator himself becomes, temporarily and at strategic moments, a character in the tale, a tale that is, as we have seen, only a metaphor for the relationship between the protagonists' mothers. Much as Williams ironically implants her own compositions into the text that she translates so as to remain imperceptible to the reader, the male narrator of *Paul and Virginia* frequently locates himself within his third-person omniscient narration. This compromises its capacity to function as third-person omniscient narration. He enters the story at the beginning of the tale, to help the women become domestic partners; he joins Paul to watch Virginia drown at the end, implicating himself into his own story and forcing his narrative voice to switch into a jarring first person. Williams pulls no punches in exploiting the strangeness of this narrative style. In a paradox of temporality, for instance, the narrator has an epiphany while reading the story of Paul and Virginia in the form of a book (W 84). As it is unclear whether characters-in-translation would read in English or French, the book is perhaps Bernardin's and perhaps Williams's: he is reading either the book that he is narrating or its source text. Although he does not mention *Paul et Virginie* by name, he claims to read novels that explain why the inhabitants of Mauritius are so miserable, such that he may learn to live; these are readings which, he says, "make that world, which I have abandoned, still contribute to my satisfaction" (W 84). Yet the narrator's "abandonment" of the island is what allows him to reconstitute it narratively, making it present for a British readership for whom Mauritius might otherwise be out of mind. Such a narrator is clearly a figure for Bernardin himself, who was, in writing *Paul et Virginie*, nostalgically reconstituting his own time in Mauritius. But the narrator's description of that reading experience becomes part of what is being collected as the content of the very book he is reading. His "satisfaction" comes primarily from finding himself in the book he is reading: he reads to experience the "sort of negative happiness" that arrives as he compares "their destiny and my own" (W 84). The comparison is tautological, however, as he *is* a character in the novel he is reading—and his very commentary on negative happiness is part of the text as well. Nevertheless, and paradoxically, his persona as a narrator depends upon his complete detachment from the events he has been narrating: "Thus I pass my days far from mankind whom I wished to serve," he says: "I lead a solitary life, without wife, children, or slaves," as mentioned above (W 83). It is this detachment, it seems, defined by the privation of others' privation, that produces the "negative happiness," even as the separation must be compromised for the negatively pleasing comparison to be made. Even still, the narrator's paradoxical perspective entirely depends upon

ADOPTIVE SIBLINGS ACROSS OCEANS OF FUTURITY 81

his being directly involved in the action of the story, even as he remains completely removed from it:

> Like a man whom shipwreck has thrown upon a rock, I contemplate, from my solitude, the storms which roll over the rest of the world; and my repose seems more profound from the distant sounds of the tempest. *I suffer myself to be led calmly down the stream of time to the ocean of futurity, which has no boundaries*; while, in the contemplation of the present harmony of nature, I raise my soul towards its supreme Author. (W 84, emphasis mine)

It is a complex utterance for its multiple levels of figuration. God is like an author; a narrator is like a shipwrecked man; distant storms "roll" like an ocean and yet mark one's distance from an ocean; being distant from an ocean-like storm is like floating down a stream, which leads to an ocean. The temporal ocean has no boundaries but we calmly float into it, meaning that we are approaching it, meaning that it has boundaries. It is a fantasy of being both in the world, and passively led through it, and yet uniquely exempt from "the rest of the world"—really, a fracture-feminist vision of being the exception to the temporal order. Time collapses here, as "the present harmony" indicates an affiliation with "the ocean of futurity," which is here already. It is a vision of living in the future in the present. In describing the experience of being *outside* of the text whilst reading it as being "like a man whom shipwreck has thrown upon a rock," the old man makes his own fate analogous to Virginia's. The pointed simile suggests that on the one hand, and in a sense, he is the subject of his own narration, and is therefore by no means external to the story at hand; and on the other hand, it implies that he has been learning about the world from reading *Paul and Virginia*, or possibly *Paul et Virginie*, books which, he says, "teach me to become better" (W 84). Whether he means *better morally* or *better at narrating* remains, as a result of these parergonal layers, undecidable; perhaps these forms of improvement are inseparable or indistinguishable. In any case, "better," here, appears to mean learning to accept a metaphorical death in the name of world friendship. It is to give one's own death through seemingly unlimited narrative proliferation; the novella is, in this way, a gift of death with a narratology of the death drive. That deathliness gets imported onto the metalevel of the text's translation, as part of the text's reception, given the many perils that

Williams was facing given her public support for the Revolution.[66] The narrator is explaining the experience of being trapped within the story-worlds of Paul and Virginia, on one level, of their mothers, on another, of the tourist, on another, of Bernardin, on a fourth, and of Williams, on a fifth. When he presumes God to be the "supreme Author" of this work, he creates a sixth level of narration, presumed to exist at once inside and outside of the text. It suggests that Bernardin and Williams, and by extension himself and the tourist, and by extension Paul and Virginia and their mothers, are characters framed by a yet wider providence. It is an intensely parergonal text.

Friendship, in Derrida's estimation, accomplishes "the very work of the political" insofar as it, Virginia-like, "transports itself in death."[67] Although death and friendship may seem a surprising tandem, Derrida reminds us that Aristotle expresses a preference for friendship that "bears death in itself in bearing itself over to death."[68] Indeed, says Derrida, "it is *thanks* to death that friendship can be declared" in the name of "the literary community," especially as that community, working through the force of comparative literature as such, resists the "becoming-worldwide" of politics.[69] Such comments give us a way to understand the ambiguous tragedy of *Paul and Virginia*. A text marked by a traumatic complicity with chattel slavery, and haunted by its own privileging of (and experience with) forgiveness, Williams's version, even more than Bernardin's original, floats into a boundless ocean of futurity to formulate a cosmopolitan politics within the immobile experiences of waiting, reading, rootedness, and death.

The tragic love story of Paul and Virginia "is affecting," observes Williams as she translates Bernardin, "but what European, pursuing his way to the Indies . . . can picture happiness to his imagination amidst poverty and neglect" (W 11). In this way, the imagined "happiness" of the "European" can be achieved *only* in an idealized pastoral setting, through the international and paternalistic management of occupied lands. "Wherefore do we come to these islands?," asks the fictional governor Monsieur de la Bourdonnais, bluntly, as he attempts to convince Virginia's mother to send Virginia to France: "Is it not to acquire a fortune? And will it not be more agreeable to return and find it in your own country?" (W 62). In this way, Mauritius is offered as a more lucrative substitute for France. The equivalence that the governor claims, whereby one's global location is a matter of indifference as long as it generates wealth, is precisely the sort of abstraction that worldwide-ization seeks to unthink. Because of Williams's deconstructive engagement with Bernardin's text, the question of which country is one's "own" remains muddy in this profoundly multi-national, creolized, and cosmopolitan text—indeed, Bourdonnais poses these questions as he himself "breakfasted in the manner of the Creoles" (W 63). *Paul and Virginia* relentlessly inverts Bourdonnais's colonial logic, sending Virginia to France to collect a fortune so it can be imported back to the Mauritian homeland. Even as Paul accedes to Bourdonnais's plan, he warns Virginia that "Riches have great attractions. You will soon find in the new world [i.e., France], to which you are going, another to whom you will give the name of brother [i.e., husband], which you will bestow on me no more" (W 69). France becomes "the new world" in this text, a land of exoticism, riches, and erotic possibility, and yet one that, for Paul—through the very force of its potential for *fraternité*—seems a "barbarous country," "a land of savages" (W 71, 80).

Just as Williams's "Sonnet to Love" imagines love as a form of col-onization ("Love has all my heart possess'd"), and colonization, a metaphor for love, the text of *Paul and Virginia*, as we have seen, is willing to make analogies between chattel slavery and European cosmopolitanism (W 19). On the one hand, such analogies are outrageous. On the other hand, and more productively, such analogies, far from authorizing a kind of global humanism or world citizenship, construct interpretive aporias that the translator cannot resolve through conventional narrative means. The text, just like its translator, remains caught between two conceptions of inter-national travel, coding life abroad as both libertarian cosmopolitanism and enforced exile. The transoceanic movement of Virginia, in particular, demands to be understood in two incompatible ways. The double-coding of her movement produces, in herself and others, the complicated feeling of living in one's "own country . . . as in a foreign land" (W 49). As the foreign becomes a constitutive element of domestic life, and national belonging becomes strange to itself, the sentimental love story becomes "a nonpassage" characterized by "a not knowing where to go."[70] The text, caught between Bernardin's colonialist fantasy and Williams's echo, begins to speak the political out of that very impasse; caught between concern for enslaved Mauritians and a globalizing humanism, the English text finds no way to reconcile the situation. The undecidability is, at root, a temporal disruption, manageable only by recourse to "the ocean of futurity, which has no boundaries."

Paul and Virginia survives its double binds by making three highly unstable and ambiguous rhetorical moves. First, as we have seen, it toggles between, and even crosses, supposedly separate levels of narration, and

84   FRACTURE FEMINISM

in so doing summons the future into the fractured present of the text. Its appeal to the future seeks to reconcile the various demands made upon Paul and Virginia; the arrival of the future, described by the frame narrator as an "ocean of futurity," becomes a sort of metaphorical cosmopolitanism in its own right (W 84). The translation thus extends Williams's work on the Revolution in France by speaking the contemporary future. Interestingly, Williams is not bent upon focusing the reader's attention upon the future. In fact, she cuts from her translation several passages in which the old man considers futurity (he praises those who "lived far from the society of their contemporaries," for instance, asking Paul: "who would want to live if he knew the future?" [PV trans. Donovan 106–107]). Williams excises these provocations, removing the future from the story at the level of its explicit content and displacing it into the formal structure of the narration. It can be awaited and experienced, still, but less easily predicted.

Second, in a way entirely appropriate to the Mauritian setting, the text's "ocean of futurity" creolizes Paul and Virginia, enabling each to function in multiple and contradictory ways as the narrative requires. Again, this takes place by making racial identification less apparent in the text itself: Williams actually removes Bernardin's reference to the yellowing of Virginia's skin, focusing attention instead upon the metaphorical roles that the characters are asked to play and in the differential power relations between them.[71]

Third, it reconciles the foreign and cosmopolitan through the reading of literature: indeed, Virginia feels like a foreigner in her "own" country precisely because of her study of what is now called comparative literature, which here becomes a privileged form of cosmopolitanism. World travel, in *Paul and Virginia*, proves inseparable from the act of reading: living with her cruel aunt in France, for instance, Virginia is treated not with dignity but as "a romantic girl, whose head was turned by novels" (W 94). But her mistreatment, arising out of a cultural difference between the pastoral simplicity of Mauritian life and the supposedly more complicated life in France, causes her to experience absence from Paul as a kind of emotional and geographic "transport" (W 94). In this way, literary study comes to mediate between conflicting ways of understanding cultural difference and the global movement by which such difference becomes apparent. It is also the linchpin of its engagement with the contemporary future: time is deconstructable to the extent that it is acknowledged to be a literary device. Derrida, for instance, boasts that deconstruction will "put the hour in question, put in crisis the unit called 'hour,' " showing the hour to be a "purely fictional countable unit" and an act of figuration.[72] *Paul and Virginia* exploits the literariness of time in an attempt—ultimately failed—to move beyond a white and European "world"-view.

Literature and the Seeds of Future Enslavement

Williams uses the narrative frames to highlight the affinities between "novel writing" and "the theater"; she does so, however, by excising the most formally dramatic part of Bernardin's text—namely, the material in which the male narrator speaks with Paul. In the French text, Paul and "Le Vieillard" are introduced in this way before either speaks, and their words are reported directly, without being quoted by a narrator, as if they were characters in a play.[73] Williams's translation eliminates most of their conversation, some twelve pages of text, and brings what remains of it into conventional novelistic third-person narration, with the conversation reported in quotation marks by a narrator (W 90–93). Ironically, she claims to have done so in order to better capture the "bustle and stage effect" preferred by British readers: in effect, she is novelizing the most theatrical material in an attempt to satisfy a readership that prefers reading plays to novels. It is thus amusing that *Paul and Virginia* flourished as a comic opera at Covent Garden's Theatre Royal in 1800, in an adaptation that traded on the immense popularity of Williams's translation.[74]

We have seen how the narrator sometimes intervenes in the story as a character. He teaches Paul how to read and write, for instance. Paul, says the narrator, "till now indifferent as a Creole with respect to what was passing in the world, desired I would teach him to read and write, that he might carry on a correspondence with Virginia" (W 76). Hence Paul learns to read Virginia's words under the tutelage of the person responsible for reporting them. Yet this new skill, in repeating a childhood game, also seems to express Paul's desire to be distant from the narrator instead of Virginia, a distance that emerges only through a figural process that doubly triangulates Paul's relation to the narrator, and also to Virginia, across racial and linguistic lines (i.e., "as a Creole"). Even as children, the narrator explains, Paul and Virginia liked to sit upon a rock, called the Discovery of Friendship, and mimic with a handkerchief the nautical signals of "a vessel coming from Europe, or returning thither" (W 39). Paul and Virginia, we are told, would affix their handkerchief to a piece of bamboo, raising and lowering it to signal the presence and absence of

86   FRACTURE FEMINISM

the narrator. It is a narratological version of the Freudian *fort/da* game, albeit metaphorizing world-systems of colonial transportation rather than military deployment. Back then, the narrator, keen to teach the children the Rousseauvian association between writing and absence, saw fit to "engrav[e] an inscription upon the stalk of this reed," because, he says, there is no pleasure in the world so sweet as the "reading of well written inscription" (W 39). The inscription in Latin—intended as a signal of absence, and written upon the very signal of presence and absence, and yet, at the same time, on one of the island's indigenous plants, and modeled on the transoceanic vessels doing the work of colonial rule—signals presence instead. The inscription functions as a voice, a mark of continuous presence: "It seems to me as if a human voice issued from the stone and making itself heard through the lapse of ages, addressed man . . . and told him that I was not alone." Inscriptions, explains the narrator, can "lead the soul through infinite space . . . by showing that a thought has survived the ruins of empire" (W 40). Time and space thus collapse into each other, and become ciphers for one another, through the rehearsal of presence and absence.

Paul and Virginia achieve a kind of intimacy by studying similar curricula half a world away from each other. Virginia, like Paul, is learning about "history, geography, grammar," along with other topics, but has "so little capacity for all those sciences, that I make but small progress with my masters" (W 78). The simultaneity of their studies, and their shared distaste for the curriculum, ironically realizes a kind of world citizenship in and of itself. Paul, like Virginia, "found little satisfaction in the study of geography": he feels constrained by "its political boundaries" and learns more by "the reading of romances" (W 77). Paul devotes himself to learning European customs, and therefore Virginia's circumstances, by studying fiction: "I stood in no need of books when Virginia was here," he laments (W 82–83, 92–93). Hence, fiction, creating "an affectively charged association among distanced readers," sustains a sentimental community for Paul as a supplement to Virginia's absence.[75] It enables him to take pleasure in waiting. Virginia might soon return, he reasons, and "Virginia being rich," "we shall have a number of Negroes, who will labor for you" (W 91). Although he has not heard anything from her for some time, he learns from books that "it took so little time to come from Europe with a fair wind!," a fact which, he explains to the narrator, "was exstasy." The nature of atemporal jouissance is not straightforward. When Paul hears nothing from Virginia, he takes it as a sign that she is *en route* and very wealthy. The lack of communication from his lover enables him to love lack as such.

On the one hand, he achieves this jouissance by fantasizing about becoming (instead of, I suppose, remaining) a slaveholder. On the other hand, in order for Paul to realize his dream, his must work without pay to sustain the family. If Virginia is to have become wealthy, Paul notes, it is probably because "her aunt has married her to some great lord" (W 91). If Virginia were to marry a wealthy Frenchman, she could use that fortune, along with the eventual inheritance from her aunt, to improve the lives of her family members in Mauritius. Paul, as Virginia's brother, would stand to benefit from such a windfall, but would have become, in the process, just another unsuccessful suitor. Hence the double bind: Paul wants to remain both Virginia's lover *and* brother, yet the plot will not allow him to be both at once. Early in life, he was designated her *brother* and told to await a marriage that would happen in the future: "While they were yet in their cradle, their mothers talked of marriage" (W 19). As they grow up, though, the incest taboo, as well as prohibitions against premarital sex, stymie their urge for sexual intercourse: "Oh, Paul! Paul! you are far dearer to me than a brother!," Virginia laments, "How much it has cost me to avoid you!" (W 71). *Lover*, in this context, has become a supplement to *brother*, a futural excess that arrives into the present as a contretemps—the two moments, as Derrida would say, "summoned to appear . . . in the same present," but still happening "in two times."[76] They try to maintain this contretemps by being, quite simply, very intimate siblings, of the sort we know from later texts such as *The Victim of Prejudice* and *Frankenstein*, until Virginia moves to France. Then, the full impossibility of the contretemps comes into view, and they begin to, once again, defer the erotic aspect of the friendship: Virginia hopes that being in France will help her "resist your caresses" "till Heaven can bless our union" (W 71). But she is hoping to marry a Frenchman. Virginia is being sent to France because she is marriageable. We have an erotics that can play out through either deferment or difference, but, in Virginia's calculation, never both at once. This is a temporal problem that Paul yearns to solve.

Paul maintains his dual roles of brother and future husband by putting himself below the law. He forfeits, or will have forfeited, his privilege as a slaveholder. "In France," he daydreams at the time of Virginia's departure, "where you go in search of fortune and of grandeur, I will attend you as your slave" (W 70). A fantasy of contretemporal enslavement is his best strategy, he thinks, for remaining her brother and lover at once. Yet Paul cannot be Virginia's slave in France because the family urgently needs his labor in Mauritius, now that Domingo and Mary are old and frail. Paul worries that "I am condemned to waste my wretched life in labor, far from Virginia" (W 89). A lifespan is understood to be a geographical, rather than temporal, problem. He is prevented from fulfilling his fantasy of *pretending* to be enslaved because he has *literally*, if only technically, become enslaved: he will not have been free to leave Mauritius, as he is forced to work, unpaid, to support his mothers and their (former?) slaves. Paul, like the enslaved woman he encountered as a child, dreams of self-destruction as a pathway to freedom: "labor becomes painful, society irksome," he laments, "Would to heaven that war were declared in India! I would go there and die" (W 91–92). Yet, like Domingo, he stays and works, remembering that Virginia appreciates his labor: "It is for you I go," she assures Paul as she leaves for France, "for you, whom I see every day bent beneath the labor of sustaining two infirm families" (W 70–71). Paul maintains his impossible intimacy with Virginia through the fantasy of his own future enslavement.

What Paul's labor accomplishes, besides the survival of his family, is the creolization of the Mauritian landscape. He makes it quasi-European through agriculture. Virginia encourages this as a sort of intimacy, so that they can be, in a sense, together:

> It will give me great delight if you should one day see apple trees growing at the side of the plantain, and elms blending their foliage with cocoa trees. You will fancy yourself in Normandy, which you love so much. (W 80)

Virginia sends seeds for Paul to plant. Paul plants them, and, "with a careful hand . . . sowed the European seeds, particularly . . . the flowers . . . which seem to bear some analogy to the character and situation of Virginia, by whom they had been recommended" (W 82). This explicit analogy between the flower seeds and Virginia—both her "character" and "situation," or her spirit and body—"binds together two times in the same time."[77] The seeds are artifacts of the future, in the sense of "artifacts" introduced by Cassity—clinging to their historicity yet exceeding it too.[78]

The temporal strangeness soon becomes geographical, as, in planting a European garden in Mauritius, Paul is again reversing the directionality of colonial possession: whereas in actual fact institutions such as the Jardin des Plantes in Paris would collect Mauritian plants for display and scientific study, in the fictional space of *Paul et Virginie* European plants are sent as metonymic emissaries to Mauritius, to mark the geographical extent of Virginia's love. Bernardin knew well the colonial logic of the botanical garden: a nonscientist, he was nevertheless appointed in 1792 to be Superintendent of the Jardin des Plantes and Curator of the Natural History Collections. Interestingly, one of his "few ideas of value" in this role, according to Frank N. Egerton, was to warn people across the empire against the planting of invasive flora.[79] As early as 1784, in his *Studies of Nature*—the 1788 third edition of which was the original home of *Paul et Virginie*—Bernardin warned that "every country has those [species] peculiar to itself" and thus, to avoid inadvertently destroying local ecosystems, should be careful to avoid cultivating foreign crops, fruit and trees.[80] He made that assessment based on his experiences in Mauritius. Hence it is fortuitous that no European insects emerge from Virginia's European seeds to destroy the Mauritian ecosystem. Still, for reasons of climate and because they are metaphors, Paul's European plants grow sparsely and imperfectly in Mauritius. As he plants the seeds, Paul worries that Virginia "was upon the point of being married" or "was already married"; he "feared that the heart of Virginia was corrupted" (W 82–83). In accordance with these fears, "a very small number of them blew, and none came to perfection" (W 82). The seeds grow not in the expected European style, given how "the soil of this part of Africa is unfavorable to their growth," but are creolized (W 82). Through the associative force of the metonym, then, the future marriage is creolized, too, and rendered polyamorous.

Derrida holds that "culture is linked to agriculture" in a contradictory way. Even as agriculture ties communities to the land, these acts of settlement involve "opening oneself to another culture," and thus becoming "engaged . . . in migrations and revolutions."[81] The seeds of *Paul and Virginia* do triple figural duty, serving first as a metonym for Virginia, second as metaphor for her transoceanic travels, and third as a symbol of a future already here. They symbolically restore Virginia to Paul, in a reversal of the colonial logic of scientific collecting. They also resolve, at the level of metaphor, the double bind of Paul's matrimonial aspirations, given their performance and prospects as seeds. They remind one that the future is already here in a material way, yet they teach one to find comfort in waiting without guarantees or even the likelihood of success. Figuratively, then, Paul is, in the utmost sense, suffering himself to be led calmly down the stream of time to the ocean of futurity, which has no boundaries. There are no boundaries, in this case, because he assumes that he and Virginia are living parallel lives, intimately, across the world from one another. This in itself is a form of figural worldwide-ization. It finds its echo upon Virginia's return to Mauritius: suddenly, Paul's fantasy of lethal travel ("I would go there and die") finds its horrific expression in his beloved's experience. In a novella of impossible longing and thwarted hope, such cruelties qualify as a kind of intimacy, or at least solidarity. Paul is metaphorically enslaved, and so is Virginia; Paul is fantasmatically enslaved, and so, in a sexual sense, is Virginia; Paul is hopeful for the future, and so is Virginia; Paul learns to hate geography and love literature, as does Virginia. But, like the seeds from Europe, none of this can be realized yet, and, what is more, its fruit will no longer be recognizably European when it comes. It is for Paul a poignant kind of "negative happiness" that always might not arrive at its destination.

Such a possibility is eulogized in Williams's "Sonnet to the White Bird of the Tropic," attributed to Madame de la Tour. It apostrophizes "thou, who lov'st to stray, . . . or mark'st the bounds which torrid beams confine / By thy averted course" (W 86). Williams's aviary metaphor lends spatiality to the temporal metaphor of the seeds: we again find ourselves adrift in an "ocean of futurity," as cosmopolitanism becomes figural, futural, and immediate. The analogies in themselves effect a kind of displacement: they, too, "lov'st to stray," their course averted by the very marking of "the bounds" of Bernardin's text. The bird that is eulogized, explains Natasha Duquette, "invites readers to imagine its Trans-Atlantic migration" in the context of solidarity with a diverse array of people across the global South.[82]

Virginia's bequest yet further inverts the colonial economy of plants as epitomized by the Jardin in Paris, and the lovers manage to sustain their sibling and erotic bonds by such means. We are told, for instance, that "Virginia . . . never ate of any fruit without planting the seed or kernel in the ground. 'From this,' said she, 'trees will come, which will give their fruit to some traveler, or at least to some bird'" (W 87). One pawpaw tree thus planted, notes Paul, will become a gift from Virginia to Mauritians "more dear and useful than if she had given them a library" (W 90). The distinction is a strange one, given how, as Maria Zytaruk has stressed, libraries were often full of seeds, and seeds were transmitted textually in the eighteenth century, given the frequency with which seeds were transmitted in letters and books.[83] It is apt, then, that Paul will need a library if he is to understand the temporality of the gift: "I wish I was at least learned enough to look into futurity," he laments, clinging to the pawpaw tree: "Virginia must come back" (W 90). Given the seeds, Paul begins to treat Virginia as a revenant: she embodies a "futurity" that "begins by coming back."[84]

The tragedy of Virginia's death grimly fulfills their erotic pact. As Virginia stands on the sinking skip before "an immense crowd of people," a naked sailor "strong as Hercules" attempts to save her life. The sailor attempts to convince Virginia to disrobe for easier swimming, but Virginia, clutching her dress to her chest, "repulsed him with modesty" (W 100). Virginia prefers to die fully clothed than survive with a breast exposed to public view, and the text—both Bernardin's original and the translation—accommodates that preference. While it is easy to read this scene within a late-eighteenth-century discourse of female modesty and self-sacrifice (the sentimental conventions of which structure many of Williams's other texts), these tropes familiar to European sensibility here become a repetition of the fate of the enslaved woman. She, after all, had considered suicide by drowning; she, too, had been wearing "no other garment but a shred of course cloth" as she was rescued (W 27). As Carolyn Vellenga Berman notes, the risk of Virginia's nakedness recalls not only the escaped woman from within the story, but also invites a broader comparison with the bodies of enslaved Africans or South Asians up for auction.[85] If the grateful Maroons once helped the eponymous characters escape the ambiguities of enslavement, settlement, and reconciliation, those issues, now transmuted into metonymic form, continue to haunt the novella's tragic climax.

Spectacular death scenes in sentimental novels, of which the conclusion to *Paul and Virginia* would be the quintessential instance, would sometimes, it has been argued, ameliorate the tensions inherent in late-eighteenth-century rights discourses by establishing communities of sympathy.[86] Virginia is being returned from "liberty," a quintessentially French keyword in 1794, to a stronghold of plantation slavery (i.e., Mauritius). Thus, what could have been a poignant denouement is rendered thoroughly perverse by its inseparability from the violence and exploitation of slavery. Ethical action in this situation requires the supplement of modesty in order to conform to natural virtue, just as it does for Rousseau.[87] By clinging to her modesty at the expense of her own life, Virginia confirms, in her last moments of life, her allegiance with the masters: she differentiates herself from the enslaved woman even as she appears as her revenant. As the novella ends in sorrow and in a display of worldwide affection as Virginia's funeral is attended by "the natives of different countries," Virginia's death renders the Indian Ocean an "ocean of futurity." Once again, the frame narrative is framed by the main narrative.

One is reminded, as Virginia drowns and is mourned, of a parallel episode from the beginning of the novella, in which Madame de la Tour, alone and pregnant with Virginia, is advised by the narrator to combine her habitation with Margaret's "for the future interests of their children, and to prevent the intrusion of any other settler" (W 14). An act of friendship, even love, here calls itself "hospitality" precisely, and ironically, for its attempt to keep future comers at bay (W 14). In this way, *Paul and Virginia* enacts a politics of futurity rooted in friendship, a promise fulfilled and undone in the aftermath of the shipwreck. Virginia's gift to Mauritius, as Paul notes in relation to the paw-paw tree, cannot yet be appreciated, because it is a gift from the future. She gives the island an international gathering to come, one dependent upon a worldwide international consciousness to come; yet it is already here. It is the gift of her own arrival, even though this gift is, as Derrida says, "ma[d]e or let come . . . even if it be [in] death."[88] Love exists only in being awaited, either *in utero*, or at the plantation, or through European seeds, or at the wrecked ship; her possible arrival heralds an intimacy or cosmopolitanism that guards against its own arrival by turning ever to the future. The gift of death presents Virginia as an exception to time, as if she were somehow excused from its dictates: as Williams writes, "Time, which so rapidly destroys the proud monuments of empires, seems in this desert to spare those of friendship" (W 15). If friendship and love can defend against the march of time, still "successive sorrows crowd the space" of the novel—to borrow the final line of Williams's sonnet "To the Strawberry"—to pull apart the atemporality that the novel so laboriously constructs (W 42). Subjected to a narrative death drive, *Paul and Virginia* mourns the loss of the contemporary future in the very act of holding open the possibility.

Paul and Virginia participates vigorously in seemingly timeless discourses of globalization—for example, the obscene myths of the kindly slaveholder and the pastoral island of sexual innocence—but subjects those fantasies to bizarre strategies for making narrative meaning. "Worldwide-ization" names the figural and narratological work that happens within that process; in that sense, against all odds, it would seem that "globalization" and "worldwide-ization" are synonymous after all.[89] By insisting upon an impossible futurity already happening "now," although not "here," Williams's translation speaks the discourse of European hegemony so thoroughly and directly that Europeanness begins to outpace itself.

As its narrative and figural procedures misfire, Bernardin's globalizing discourses become prone to worldwide-ization.

Derrida surprised many in arguing that European "heritage is irreplaceable and vital for the future of the world. We must fight to hold on to it." Such a statement highlights how European literatures have, despite their complicity with a program of world domination, also been a "cradle of counter-globalisation."[90] Given the possibility of such a "cradle," it would follow that intra-European resistance to globalization is still in development, and must, for its full expression, be awaited. But *Paul and Virginia*, like *The Victim of Prejudice* (to which we will turn momentarily), cultivates a discourse of the future that operates through, rather than around, the temporal impasses of European rights discourses. The texts' figural mechanisms inhabit existing hegemonic structures so fiercely that the timelines that support that hegemony begin to pull apart, leaving the texts worldwide-ized and inverted through their recourse to the contemporary future. Hays's enthusiastic Oedipal eroticism, like Williams's ambivalent engagements with slavery, signals international solidarity through the very practice of epistemic violence. It enacts a worldwide literary process that has been "uneven, heterogeneous, discontinuous, but irreversible and tending toward the worldwide as conjoined history, once again, of literature and rights, and of the right to literature."[91] This was one of the ways that fiction of the 1790s sought to "make political theory accessible by integrating it with fiction," in the words of April London.[92] Though *Paul and Virginia*, like *The Victim of Prejudice*, is clearly wary of Enlightenment rights discourses, it finds new ways to imagine women's rights in times to come through the placement of that "conjoined history" in the fracture that is the contemporary future.

Mary Hays:
A Vindication of the Rights of the Oedipus Complex

Although Hays's *The Victim of Prejudice* does not directly mention France or the Revolution, it is usually considered to be a "Jacobin novel" for its radical communitarian politics and its frustration at the gradualness of reform in Britain. Like all of Hays's work, it is "intellectually protean, curious, persistent, creative and brilliant."[93] Hays, at the time of writing, was known for "being a Wollstonecraftian protégée" despite Wollstonecraft's outright rejection of her overtures.[94] Her first novel, *The Memoirs of Emma Courtney*, which had been developed in consultation with William Godwin, sought to fictionalize the predicament of the female philosopher.[95] With *The Victim of Prejudice*, her follow-up effort, Hays is said to have begun to write for future readers instead of direct contemporaries.[96] Yet the novel also obliterates any distinction between future readers and direct contemporaries, a scenario that complicates its approach to women's rights. "Time," Hays writes, "seemed doubled by a lively and exquisite consciousness to every instant as it passed," an uncanniness that fills the protagonist Mary Raymond with a sense of "undefineable contradiction."[97] It is a fracture feminist novel especially for the way that it theorizes rights from within the double binds of this contradiction.

Interestingly, for a novel written in tribute to Wollstonecraft's legacy, *The Victim of Prejudice* takes a cynical view of women's rights. Even as the protagonist Mary Raymond asserts a "right to exist" from her malevolent harasser and rapist Sir Peter Osborne, she finds her rights to be useless when pitted against the legal rights of men, including her suitors and stepfather (H 141). She can claim her own rights only vaguely and in some impossible future, yet she is thrown into debtors' prison and encouraged to marry Peter to satisfy the rights of men. She even begins to imagine nature itself as having and claiming sadistic rights to enjoyment: "My confidence in you is unbounded," she explains to her stepfather, "but nature will, for a time, assert her powerful rights" (H 45). In this quotation, Mary feels the contradiction between two systems of rights: the law of the father, here triply embodied by her stepfather, her roguish, late biological father, and the cruel Sir Peter, which exercises patriarchal authority over her sexuality in increasingly nightmarish ways, and the rights of "nature," which insist upon the heart's need to follow its own path, in this case Mary's continued sexual relations with her stepbrother William. Navigating this impasse becomes a temporal problem, which is why the subordinate clause "for a time" proves so crucial to her understanding of rights: caught between conflicting rights-based claims, Mary can only "wait patiently," claiming rights entirely separate from "the laws of my country" which seem designed to fail her (H 100). She learns to claim rights in abeyance, as part of a discourse of hope or of looking to the future, and thus she claims rights only as rights that she *will did have*. The novel presents this retroactive deferment as part of a complicated Oedipal situation: under urgent threat from patriarchal forces, she refracts sexual enjoyment into the past and future, especially by imagining the sufferings of her long-absent mother, even as she takes her place in the erotic plans mapped out by her stepfather's kindly if seemingly callous erotic advice. In the impasse between nature's rights and the law of the father in this novel, sexual experience plays out through and around the incest taboo. The incest taboo, in the long eighteenth century in Britain, had been closely associated with questions of property, chattel slavery, and women's rights, offering a discourse through which authors spanning from Daniel Defoe to Jane Austen could align the condition of enslaved nonwhite people with the predicament of white women.[98] Explorations of incest also had the capacity to open discursive space for women writers, given the topic's tendency to highlight crises of patriarchal authority.[99] Hays, inheriting this tradition of English writing, activates it as a way to think about rights deferred, impossible, and necessary.

Scholarship on this novel has tended to focus on Mary's problems with Sir Peter, which has led to its being described as a condensed rewriting of *Clarissa*.[100] While there is no question that Hays has Richardson firmly in mind, to overemphasize the connection requires us to discount the first fifty or so pages of the novel, in which Mary is raised by her adoptive father. The early part of the novel, in which the adoptive siblings frolic gaily in a garden paradise before being forcibly separated at a parent's command to prepare for an exogamous marriage market, is better read as an adaptation of *Paul et Virginie*, which was then popular in England thanks to Williams's celebrated translation. The echoes of Williams's translation especially ramify in the early part of Hays's novel, the erotics of which provide a template for the many horrors to follow. Hays, throughout the novel, presents the later horrors as the inevitable outgrowth of Mary's teenage experience. This is part of the novel's Godwinianism—its commitment to necessitarianism as a way of obviating personal responsibility for misfortune.[101] (Many fracture feminists metaphorize cause and effect with chain imagery, it would appear.) By yanking Mary's chain, we can identify the Oedipal echoes in the novel, learn to read them as a form of logical time, and thus begin to see how the Oedipus complex opens up a mode of feminist resistance. This form of resistance does not simply contest the expectations of the patriarchy, as Eleanor Ty has maintained of Hays's novel. In Ty's analysis, Mary is learning to resist the confines of the symbolic order.[102] I will maintain, as an alternative reading, that Mary strategically capitulates to the symbolic structures around her, horrific though they are, learning to see in them a perverse sort of right maintained by the wealthy. Yet she maintains her own erotics, rooted in the illicit desires and bent temporalities of Williams's translation of Bernardin, at the level of the imaginary. Specifically, Mary manages to sustain her defiance of the incest taboo as a right of her own—the rights, we might say, of ~~woman~~, written as barred.

It is far from customary, in psychoanalytic theory, to think about the Oedipus complex in terms of rights. Yet the subject's right to the Oedipus complex, and the father's right to impose it, are among Jacques Lacan's speculations in his fifth seminar, *The Formations of the Unconscious*, given in 1957–1958 and only recently published in English.[103] In two sessions of mid- to late January 1958, Lacan presents the Oedipus complex as a matter of rights retroactively deferred in a way that opens new possible interpretations of *The Victim of Prejudice*. The right to the Oedipus complex is one that can be claimed only in the future or from the future. Lacan explains that when we identify with the image of our father, we claim a right that doesn't yet exist.[104] Yet "the father intervenes as having rights and not as a real person," and thus becomes foundational to a person's past.[105] The result of this tension is the deferment of sexual enjoyment perpetually, along similar lines to what we saw in Williams's translation of Bernardin.[106] Lacan's unfamiliar treatment of the Oedipus complex brings us to reconsider the rights claimed by Mary Raymond. The more misfortune to which Mary is subjected—she is reprimanded, imprisoned, bartered, forgotten, insulted, and raped—the more she speaks of rights, and her appeals to rights discourse generally tend in the direction of the future and her stepfather. Lacan's innovative and only recently translated re-theorization of the Oedipus complex can help us appreciate the radical edge of this novel as it considers the asynchronous way that rights are claimed and retroactively deferred in the context of 1790s feminism.

Discussions of rights in Lacan's work usually begin and end with *Seminar VII*—such as his celebrated analyses of the rights of enjoyment in the Marquis de Sade and the rights of the dead in *Antigone*—and the related material in "Kant with Sade." But Lacan had more, and very different, things to say about rights in *Seminar V*: he speaks of a child's right to the Oedipus complex, and of the father's rights in exploiting that child's desire. The theory is a somewhat uncomfortable one, as it seems to participate in a number of sexist clichés, such as: psychic life is the gradual revelation of the father's power, and our learning to identify with it; if you don't see the totalizing power of the father, that's because you are still caught at an earlier stage; behind this power is the silent influence of a woman, who is ultimately his teammate; there is a woman behind every powerful man, manipulating him to get what she wants; women don't suffer the same sorts of anxieties that men do when it comes to sexual performance; and, as Lacan brutally asserts, "true women always have something a little lost about them."[107] The theory, then, would seem to be especially ill-suited for a novel like Hays's, which seeks to reveal the costs of totalizing patriarchal power. I should add, then, that Lacan's theory actually aspires to quite the opposite conclusion: he insists that this process shows that "insofar as he is virile, a man is always more or less his own metaphor. This is even what places this touch of ridicule, which should be mentioned all the same, upon the term 'virility.' "[108] The aspect of Lacan's thought that proves most fruitful here is the way that the Oedipus complex becomes a set of phases superadded to Freud's own three- and four-part processes for boys and girls.

Riffing on Freud's essay "The Dissolution of the Oedipus Complex," Lacan urges fresh attention on the imaginary component of the complex. He focuses especially on the child's decision to identify with the phallus as a crucial step in the Oedipus complex in boys and girls. As the child of either sex learns to identify with paternal agency, they pass through "three moments": first, in which the father's power is veiled, his patriarchal privilege marking everything in the world, where "the law of the symbol reigns," and so the paternal and maternal dynamics operate silently, "in a veiled, or not yet apparent, form"; second, in which the child comes to identify with the mother, learning to see how the mother mediates all relations to phallic power and his or her own complicity in its processes; and third, in which "the father "intervenes as real and potent" and is "internalized," meaning that the child comes to identify with the father's "having it," that is the phallus, such that patriarchal power is no longer "veiled." In this third step, the ego-ideal, or superego, is installed—the father no longer speaks for himself but as the father function, for all of culture—and the nascent subject finds his or her way out of the Oedipus complex.[109] This third stage, Lacan says, is where a gap opens up between male and female experience. The girl does not have to carry out this identification nor retain this "title to virility," because "she knows where it is, and she knows where she has to go to get it"—meaning, in a perverse way, that the world is easier to navigate for women because they are forced into an awareness of power structures stacked in the favor of men, and so are accustomed to thinking critically about issues of access and privilege.[110] Neither side really "has" the phallus, of course, but "for the girl, it is a good thing that she should recognize that she has no phallus, whereas for the boy, this would be an absolutely disastrous outcome, and it sometimes is." While these comments can seem outlandishly chauvinistic, Hays's novel reveals their feminist edge. *The Victim of Prejudice* roughly follows these Lacanian routes, and in Hays's hands, they become a roadmap for survival and resistance through the dialectical reversal of patriarchal exploitation.

The journey begins with Mary's playful gambols with William in her stepfather's garden, as she learns about pleasure and the boundaries of property; next, once Mr. Raymond intervenes with an incest prohibition, she begins to identify with the image of her late mother, fantasizing at length about her past sufferings so as to put herself in the pathway of her stepfather's desire; finally, she confronts the cruel authority of patriarchal judgment and accepts her imprisonment, claiming rights in the mode of "to come." Naturally, the novel does not exactly replicate Lacan's pathways, nor would I expect it to: Mary here desires her stepfather's gaze, not her mother directly, and the incest prohibition forbids Mary from having sex with her brother, not her mother. Yet one of the real innovations of Lacan's theory, one he adapts from Melanie Klein, is the very interchangeability of father and mother. Lacan, introducing his concept of the "paternal metaphor," insists to his seminar that "the father is a signifier substituted for another signifier," and that "the father's function in the Oedipus complex is to be a signifier substituted for the first signifier introduced into symbolization, the maternal signifier." Hence, the father as theorized in *Seminar V* merely "comes to the place of the mother," working as a kind of substitute satisfaction in the *fort-da* game of the child's maternal attachment, covering over for her absence.[111] This is an unorthodox psychoanalytic idea, and also a useful concept for a novel in which the protagonist spends pages fantasizing about her lost mother, a casualty of patriarchal violence, through her stepfather's accounts of her suffering.

A second major innovation in *Seminar V* is Lacan's invocation of an "inverted Oedipus complex."[112] "The inverted Oedipus complex" is not an alternative form of the Oedipus complex but its haunting double: it is the persistence, even in the middle of the Oedipal crisis, of a "disconcerting" love for the father and his representatives; it "is never absent from the function of the Oedipus complex."[113] Exerting a centrifugal force, which pulls together the gendered subject in "a dialectic that remains very ambiguous between love and identification" for and with the father, the inverted Oedipus complex hovers over the regular Oedipus complex as its dangerous supplement. Just as all fathers are standing in for other fathers and ultimately for the mother, hostility toward the father is haunted by love for the father. The inverted Oedipus complex works in concert with the Oedipus complex, to produce an ambivalence in our relation to "this redoubtable father who has forbidden so many things but who is otherwise quite nice," and who is standing as an obstacle to our enjoyment: "It consists in placing oneself in the right place to gain [his] favours[,] . . . that is to say, getting him to love one" despite "the threat of castration that this position entails." Through this process Lacan explains, everyone joins "the ranks of women."[114]

This ambiguity, which is also keenly felt by Mary Raymond, leads Lacan to present the Oedipus complex in terms of the child's rights: "The child has all the entitlements for being a man," he explains, "and what may be challenged in him later, at the time of puberty, is to be referred to something that has not entirely fulfilled the metaphorical identification with the image of the father, insofar as it has formed across these three moments."[115] This is very difficult syntax to understand, but I think Lacan is suggesting that the identification with the image of the father is necessarily incomplete—not necessarily a failed experiment, but an incompletely successful one. Do all children really have "all the entitlements for being a man," and from whom would one claim that entitlement? The statement disregards the very notion of rights. And how would the Oedipus complex, as Lacan presents it, cut across those rights, given its role as the culturally approved pathway for "the subject's assumption of his own sex—that is, to call things by their name, what makes it the case that a man assumes the virile type and that a woman assumes a certain feminine type, recognizes herself as a woman and identifies with her functions as a woman."[116] Is it really a meaningful "right" to be subjected to the cruel demands of the gendering process, against one's wishes? All the while, the child's right runs up against the father's, in Lacan's thought: in the second (maternal) phase of the Oedipal experience, "the father intervenes as having rights and not as a real person."[117] Rights, in Lacan's discourse, appear to be chiefly biopolitical: they valorize a set of functions over and above a person's singularity, and in doing so undo that singularity. These are exactly the kinds of rights that Derrida is especially critical of, in texts such as his second death penalty seminar.[118]

The Victim of Prejudice is a challenging test case for Lacan's theory, because of the novel's overt feminism, its commitment to women's rights, and its remarkably Oedipal plot. The risk of incest is very much at the heart of the novel as it traces its protagonist's sexual development. Although Mr. Raymond is Mary's stepfather, he is also, it is implied, at least her metaphorical father, and possibly her biological one: unbeknownst to Mary, Mr. Raymond was also her mother Mary's lover in the months before Mary Jr. was born. Mr. Raymond calls Mary Jr. "my child," and she, the narrator, calls him "my more than father," even not yet knowing her mother's tragic story (H 15). Soon after adopting Mary, Mr. Raymond takes in another child, William Pelham, whose father is too busy and wealthy to care for him. Immediately, William is pressed into service as Mr. Raymond's proxy: Mr. Raymond speaks of the pleasures of watching the two adoptive siblings at play, and encourages the siblings to form a playful and sensual bond together.

Upon William's first arrival at Mr. Raymond's house, the stepfather sends Mary to show William "our collection of botanical plants," a quintessential eighteenth-century scene of forbidden jouissance and a nod to Bernardin (H 9).[119] William, moving in and out of the gaze of his stepfather, flirts with Mary. A younger brother, Edmund Pelham, is "exhilarated by our gambols," while Mr. Raymond "perceived with pleasure the harmony which subsisted between us," and "delighted in observing" (H 11). This rhetoric of visual pleasure continues for some thirty pages, until William is nineteen, Mary seventeen, and the novel strongly suggests that the two have been playfully and experimentally having sex. Even as the two have "our usual lively affectionate intercourse," Mr. Raymond prepares his plan to separate the adoptive siblings and prepare them for their respective sexual futures (H 27). Yet, because William was, from the start, a proxy and alibi for Mr. Raymond's jouissance, it is ambiguous who is being "cut off" from Mary's affections.

Mary wants to delight in her accession to her stepfather's demands, but obedience is difficult when the demands are contradictory. He begins by prohibiting himself from her affections. Overcome by his desire for her in a way that prefigures Shelley's *Mathilda*, Mr. Raymond takes himself away from his child, despite and because of his sexual desires: "We should separate, for days, for months, perhaps for years." He puts himself off limits to her, despite enjoying "the tender attentions, caresses, and society, of my little girl." Mary reacts with an immediate flood of jouissance: "I started, trembled, shuddered; I felt a sudden revulsion of blood and spirits." Regaining her composure, she asks why she must be responsible for the father's desire: "What have I done? . . . that I must be exiled from your presence?" (H 30). This is a signal that Mary has not yet identified with the image of the father: she is still in Lacan's second phase. "I had not inquired into the nature of my sensations," she soon will admit (H

33). Mr. Raymond's response to Mary's question is exceptionally strange for the way that it brings the whole affair to the level of signification and substitution. As if correcting her, and without acknowledging the complete shift from what he had stated before, he says: "It is from *William* . . . that I think it prudent to separate you" (H 31). Just two paragraphs before, he had said it was himself: "I must, for a time, rob myself of the joy of my life" (H 30). The contradiction makes sense only if the "the joy of my life" were not Mary *per se*, but rather the visual pleasure watching of Mary with William: it has always been a scene staged for the father's enjoyment. At the level of the prohibition, much as in the Raymond household gener-ally, William is called upon to substitute for Mr. Raymond, in a defensive attempt to create a socially acceptable situation. All along, one form of incest has been standing in for another, even up to and including the sudden prohibition of this replacement incest.

Mary immediately accedes, saying: "I am prepared . . . to conform myself to your commands" (H 36). She had long believed that "my father . . . never restricts us unreasonably" (H 12). Yet Mr. Raymond is taken aback by her willingness: "*Commands*, Mary! I am no tyrant; I am unaccustomed to command" (H 36). This is a classic example of displacement, which is evident from Mr. Raymond's use of affirmational syntax to positively state a negative: "I am"; "I am." He is the voice of something lacking: "I am" and am not the voice of cultural prohibition; I am and am not the object of your desire. It only works if the father presents himself as a signifier replacing another signifier, a substitution that he can use as his alibi. The father's command makes sense only in the future, and it makes sense, currently, to him: "Yes, my child! this, at present, I own, is a subject too subtle for reasoning; *time and experience* only can evince the propriety of my conduct. . . . aware of your fortitude, I accept the sacrifice you offer" (H 36). That is, he claims the perspective of the contemporary future in order to say "yes" to Mary's affirmation of his own affirmative "no," a feat that would have been logically impossible had he not presently been in the future.

Mary, faced with the bewildering exchangeability of father, step-father, brother, and brother's father, feels "a convulsive tremor" (H 31). She is caught between the imaginary father and the name of the father. Mr. Raymond's prohibitions seek to prevent Mary from fulfilling a script that he has previously authorized: in seeking to spare Mary the shame of marrying her stepbrother, he accepts the risk of loving her as a stepfather. Mr. Raymond wavers, even within the space of a paragraph, between outlawing himself and outlawing William as the object of her desire, hinting that William has been a stand-in for the father's enjoyment. William, Mr. Raymond warns, will soon be "effaced in the riot of voluptuous gratification," once he is sent to France, as Bernardin's Virginia was (H 98), and he wants Mary to avoid longing for him as Bernardin's Paul would have done. Mary responds ambivalently as she seeks to accept, but also resist, these atemporal prohibitions. She offers to accept any sacrifice the father demands except a sacrifice of the father himself.

To stop Mary from marrying her adopted brother, Mr. Raymond bifurcates his voice, which enables him to differentiate between his own liberal views and the cruel prohibitions of culture at large. He says:

> You are now no longer children; you are too lovely and too susceptible to indulge in an intercourse, however amiable, innocent, and full of charms, which may lead to consequences that timely caution can only avert. Were it not for certain prejudices, which the world has agreed to respect and to observe, I should perceive your growing tenderness with delight . . . but I am responsible to another tribunal than that of *reason* and my own heart . . . the imperious uses of society, with a stern voice, now command us to pause. Her mandates, often irrational, are, nevertheless, always despotic: contemn them, . . . and the penalty may be tremendous. (H 31)

Mr. Raymond preserves his own pleasure by attributing his incestuous ideas to "another tribunal," that is, society at large as he imagines it, which supposedly would have very different expectations from his own. The bifurcation of his discourse establishes the parameters through which the novel can establish its two contrasting visions of rights—Mary's "right to exist" running up against the sadistic "rights of nature." Here, society, being "irrational" and "despotic," takes on the position of the superego, making further and further demands for the renunciation of Mary's enjoyment. He is articulating the gap—and temporal fracture—between his role as symbolic father and his role as imaginary father. As Mr. Raymond steps into his symbolic aspect, Mary is coaxed to see him as a signifier substituting for another set of signifiers, not as a human person but as a metaphorical function. The dead father—that is, Mary's mother's criminal partner—looms in the voice of "culture," that sadistic enjoying father; he has been replaced by a living perverse father, Mr. Raymond, who in turn

ADOPTIVE SIBLINGS ACROSS OCEANS OF FUTURITY   103

has appointed William to stand in for his experience in child-rearing for his own visual pleasure. Note, in this passage, how Mr. Raymond's diction—the language of "observe" and "perceive"—continues the visual logic of his previous jouissance: even in cutting off William from Mary, and himself from the visual pleasure of the scene, he permits himself to continue as an overseer and as a masochist, subject to "imperious," "despotic" "commands": *a child is being castrated, and I am looking on.* For Mr. Raymond, the custom of exogamy is an insane, sadistic cultural prohibition, which we observe only under threat of punishment, not because we endorse it. "Society," is the final father—a mother, or Mr. Pelham—who has "irrational" mandates that must be respected. Mary is led to wonder, "what must be the habits of society, which could give rise to such an apprehension!" (H 25).

The twist here is that the expectations of "society" exist only in the future, which sets up a clash of temporalities. If we, in general, must conform to society's expectations, the specific shape of this conformity matches William's father's, Mr. Pelham's, desire: as Mr. Raymond explains to Mary, "His [William's] father has far other views for him; views, in which, at a future period, her will probably acquiesce . . . [he will] become a *man of the world*" (H 32, emphasis in original). Exogamy is here presented as a deferment of jouissance, of placing the prospect of one's future happiness ahead of one's continuing present happiness. Here, we find Mr. Raymond outlining a normative path for William, exposed already in the here and now to "a future period": adult sexuality means that one's current pleasures must be replaced with the pleasures of the future—the very purpose, Lacan reminds us, of the Oedipus complex. This deferment, as Lacan explains, is how the father can maintain a strongly normative function despite the fact that "he himself isn't normal"[120]—that is, it is the perversity of Mr. Raymond's desire that enables him to instill the pressures of civilization on the objects of his desire.

Mary's response to her father opens the contemporary future yet further. She cries out as if to glean enjoyment from the prohibition itself—from the jouissance of castration: "Why can *I never be the wife of William Pelham*? What tyranny is this? . . . why should the heart be controlled? who will dare control it?" (H 35, emphasis in the original). The shifts in verb tense and between active and passive voice suggests that present tyranny is controlled, by some unknown power, from the future. Echoes of *Oedipus Tyrannus* and Thomas Paine come through in the word "tyranny," in this context. Mary swiftly moves from this defiant tone to a nonsensical double negative that deserves our close attention. "Yet do not misconceive me, my father; with my present views and feelings, I dare *not engage* to love William *no longer*. . . . I yield, for the present, my conduct to your directions. Mark out for me the path I should pursue" (H 37, emphasis mine). It is an especially Godwinian request, given Godwin's arguments against promises in *Political Justice* (1793). Godwin holds that, because a person is "perpetually acquiring new information as to that respecting which his [*sic*] conduct is to be decided at some future period," promises should be seen as invalid or even "evil."[121] Hays was, of course, mentored by Godwin;[122] still, her sense of the temporality of promises is quite different. Godwin's point about futurity is merely that one's knowledge is never bounded, making any closure of the present impossible. One can anticipate knowing more in the future and that this knowledge might cause one to change one's mind. Mary, contrastingly, produces a fracture of negation in the present.

There are at least eight strange aspects of her response. First: Mary is raising the unusual question of what it means to be "misconceived" by, or perhaps with, one's father—who, in the end, is not her biological relation. The hint of "misconceived by," indicating sexual actions of the past, as contradicted by "misconceive with," a phrase implying gestation and pregnancy, pits the past against the future undecidably. As Ernst Bloch warns: "nothing is stranger for an adolescent than to imagine the courtship of his parents."[123] Indeed not, for Mary! Second: the statement "I yield, for the present," effectively means its opposite, that I won't yield. To yield only for the present is effectively a promise to not yield in the future, which is not at all to yield. Unlike Godwin, Mary is content to make promises as long as they promise a negative. Third: the statement "I dare not" suggests that she does not, in fact, willingly "yield"—it suggests an action taken because of timidity or calculation, rather than deference. Fourth: to say "engage to love" in the context of discussing a wedding engagement is to offer "engage" as a performative act of love. It describes a praxis, but also makes a promise, in the future, to marry. The temporality of "engage" therefore cuts against the concession of "for the present," placing the time of the performative utterance in the future, despite this being a report specifically on Mary's "present views and feelings." Fifth: there is a vexed temporality of the strange double negative, according to which Mary dares not engage to love him "no longer." Does she mean *I do not dare to love him no longer*, which is to say that she must love him yet more? Or *I dare not stop engaging him no longer*, marks her utterance as "impossible" according to Lacan's famous maxim of feminine jouissance: "The 'doesn't stop not being written,' on the contrary, is the impossible, as I define it on the basis of the fact that it cannot in any case be written, and it is with this that I characterize the sexual relationship—the sexual relationship doesn't stop not being written," he says.[124] The meaning is again undecidable. The "no longer" suggests a past imperfect time, something that has been carrying on, and may be continued. I dare not engage (i.e., begin) to love him continued, from now on. Sixth: she qualifies the statement by saying, "with my present views and feelings," effectively announcing that these resolutions are unlikely to hold in the future, which means they are not resolutions. It is an announcement that things will likely be different in the future, when they will surely be engaged. Then, she will engage to love him and make him her husband—which is the same as announcing herself engaged right now. Seventh: there is a strange temporality at work when one says: *with my present view, and only for a while, I will not do something in the future.* She yields to her father's advice only in the present, although his advice pertains to future events, and thus binds her literally to nothing: to the gap between the present and future. It is akin to the strange phrase *was will happening* that I invoked in the Introduction. Lacan suggests that such grammar would indicate the purposefulness of one's jouissance: it reveals "the confused embrace wherein jouissance finds its cause, its last cause, which is formal—isn't it something like grammar that commands it?"[125] Eighth, and hopefully last, is her suggesting that these are "my" views and feelings—her own—when the issue at stake is that she is reacting to an external prohibition, passed from the culture at large to the father to the stepfather to the Other to me, and only in the present. Mary will soon begin to wonder whose jouissance is really at stake here: "Is it to his own passions he requires the sacrifice of mine?" (H 40).

Mr. Raymond responds in kind, presenting his daughter's possible marriage to his son as warfare happening in the present that will have been the result of an experiment having taken place in a future laboratory. It is if a scientist of the future were currently, through some experimentation to come, producing the matrimonial warfare of the present: in effect, it is "I shall be with you on your wedding-night."[126] He says:

> Human life has not unaptly been compared to a warfare: whether rendered so by nature or by civil institution, *it is for future experiments* to determine: *for the present*, we have too frequently but a *choice of evils*. . . . In a *wild and uncertain calculation of the future*, the happiness of the *present* (all that

properly can be termed our own) ought not to be trifled with:
yet there are limits, even upon this principle, that to overleap
would become insanity; the present crisis, if I mistake not,
marks the boundary. (H 37, emphasis mine)

The meaning of the current warfare—namely, a "choice of evils"—will be
decided only by scientists in times to come. What exactly does he mean
by the "choice of evils"? Mary is deciding whether to marry William and
be happy with him, or not marry him (as her father recommends) and let
him go and live as he pleases. Somehow, he understands this as a painful
forced choice, as in "your money or your life," even though both options
may be satisfactory. He emphasizes how the choice is not yet meaningful:
he is ascribing her to what Lacan would call "non-meaning," meaning the
unconscious. This is what Lacan calls the *vel* of alienation, through which
subjectivity is summoned "in the field of the Other."[127] Mr. Raymond
presents it as a choice between the present and the future, as if Mary's
mutually exclusive options were two phases of the same decision. He imagines her choosing not between yes and no, but being now or meaning to
come. If one were to follow his logic, one would commit to being happy
in the present, because meaning comes only from the future, and so is
currently unavailable. Happiness, after all, is the only thing that is "our
own"—our personal property—because the future is always in the hands of
the Other. (In essence, this logic would produce a Wollstonecraftian-type
misinterpretation of *Oedipus Rex*, if it were applied to that play). Yet he
defies his own logic, ambivalently, by stressing the issue of the "limit" of
happiness. There are limits to our adherence to the future, and this "present
crisis, if I mistake not, marks the boundary!" To commit to the present,
Mr. Raymond says, would be "insanity" in this case, because Mary's is
apparently an exceptional limit case. But we cannot know if it is a limit
case until the scientists of the future are through with their experiment.
He is urging her to act *as if* she already had knowledge from the future,
as if there were meaning in non-meaning, *as if* she were conscious of the
unconscious, but only "if I mistake not."

The Victim of Prejudice/The Children of Oedipus

The future is to be taken as part of the present in *The Victim of Prejudice*.
In a narrative structure not unlike Williams's *Paul and Virginia*, here the

narrator, who is pretending to be the author, has sent a delegate, for whom the reader serves as a second delegate, to receive her own transmission in the future. The narration of this novel, also like *Paul and Virginia*, revels in *différance* amidst a drama of messages sent and possibly received. Mary Raymond assures us, in our role as her future delegate's future delegate, that she, being her mother Mary's future delegate, is a narrator "whose unconquerable spirit . . . seeks to beguile, by the retrospect of an unsullied life, the short interval, to which will succeed a welcome and never-ending repose" (H 3). This is a strange phrase, to be sure: it describes a continuing and ongoing perspective (an "unconquerable spirit") that endeavors to beguile an interval (i.e., not to beguile *for* a short interval, but to beguile the interval itself), which is apparently prelude to something "never-ending." This interminable state of the narratorial present, standing in for the mother's future, provides the platform through which to retrospectively examine the "interval" itself, called "life." The statement combines the temporality of a Freudian screen memory with the diction from *Paul and Virginia*'s "ocean of futurity" passage (i.e., "my repose seems more profound") to establish a form of enquiry paradoxically both retrospective and interminable. From within that double temporality, her act of guile can be said to hoodwink a definite future timeframe called "the retrospect" of the character's "life," from a "never-ending repose" ever to come. Mary's narrative, told to us from the here and now of her captivity, will be constructed *après coup* but only in the future. This double encoding of the present and the future as simultaneous experiences is sustained throughout the novel as its "undefineable contradiction" and, I will argue, becomes its way of negotiating Oedipal desires and paternal prohibitions. Specifically, Hays writes the future into the present as a way to help her protagonist navigate the cruel renunciations demanded by the incest taboo. It is a structure that sustains Mary's desire within an Oedipal framework. But even as the novel anticipates a Freudian model of sexual development in girls, it also significantly complicates Freud by creating a deconstructive temporal loop. As I mentioned above, such are the aspects of British Romanticism that Lacan especially admired.

Temporality is very often the forgotten or neglected aspect of the Oedipus complex. Although Lacan, in these early years, seldom criticizes Freud, in these meetings he expresses concern that the temporality of the Oedipus complex, its "retroaction[,] . . . seems to have escaped thought. People have only thought about the demands of the temporal past." According to Lacan, when we neglect the future-oriented aspect of the

Oedipus complex, we are doomed to see perversion as the only alternative to neurosis: the Oedipus complex creates either neurotic, perverse,
or psychotic subjects through its sorting mechanisms. Yet the imaginary
register continues to cling to the Oedipal processes and fills them, retroactively, with perverse jouissance throughout.[128] In *The Victim of Prejudice*,
perverse jouissance shapes the sexual life of the protagonist, who is soon
either fed to the wolves or left to rot in prison. The ambivalence Mary
encounters, upon being denied sexual access to her stepbrother and her
stepfather, both representatives of the father's desire and embodiments of
the paternal metaphor, reflects danger and high stakes of gendering in the
late eighteenth century, the way that rights discourse could be adapted
for Oedipal situation, and the usefulness of some neglected corners of
Lacanian theory. If the "rights of woman" demand a female subject to
claim them, Lacan, like Hays, considers how the right to the Oedipus
complex, the right to defer one's jouissance into some impossible exogamous future horizon, becomes implicated into those Wollstonecraftian
claims and deconstructs them from within.

The risk of incest is very much at the heart of the novel as it traces
its protagonist's sexual development. Mary Raymond's sexual feelings in
childhood are detailed at such length because they are, as she explains,
"a material link in the chain of events, that led the subsequent incidents"
(H 6). Mary has been adopted, sometime before the age of ten, by Mr.
Raymond, a kindly and progressive man who is committed to raising
Mary in accordance with Wollstonecraftian-Godwinian dictates. Although
Mr. Raymond is Mary's stepfather, he is also, it is implied, at least her
metaphorical father, and possibly her biological one: unbeknownst to
Mary, Mr. Raymond was also her mother Mary's lover in the months
before Mary Jr. was born. Mr. Raymond calls Mary Jr. "my child," and
she, the narrator, calls him "my more than father," even not yet knowing her mother's tragic story (H 15). Mr. Raymond soon after takes in
another child, William Pelham, whose father is too busy and wealthy to
care for him. In tracing, over the first third of the novel, the idealized
love between these two adoptive siblings, Hays is responding to Jacques-
Henri Bernardin de Saint-Pierre's novella *Paul et Virginie*, which was then
popular in England thanks to Helen Maria Williams's translation.[129] Like
Paul and Virginia, William and Mary, with their names so suggestive of
an English revolution, frolic gaily under benevolent step-parenting, until
they enter their late teens and begin to experiment sexually. Mary starts
to describe William as "my lover," spurring Mr. Raymond into action: "He,

deeply regretted the painful necessity of checking a sympathy at once so natural, virtuous, and amiable" (H 48, 25). As in *Paul and Virginia*, the solution, however heartbreaking, is to send one sibling away to find a wealthy suitor elsewhere. Given the plot that follows, it is as if *The Victim of Prejudice* wants to present *Clarissa* as the action that happens "offstage," as it were, when Virginia reaches France in *Paul and Virginia*—a decidedly bleak way to fill in diegetic gaps, and an extreme case, given the length of *Clarissa*, of what Jonathan Walker calls "temporal dilation."[130] This is how *The Victim of Prejudice* gets worldwide-ized, too. As Wollstonecraft warned: "Every individual is in this respect a world in itself."[131]

Mr. Raymond's intervention is all the more complicated because of the many ways that his watching of the children has been sexualized, from the very start when her encourages them to frolic together in the "botanic garden"—a scene of eighteenth-century sexual enjoyment if ever there was one, as work by Sam George and others has clearly established—and in the multiple ways that he conscripts William to be his younger sexual proxy.[132] To avoid or make permissible the pleasures of incest, the adopted brother is offered as the substitute for the stepfather, who in turn is a substitute for the biological father, who was, in his vicious criminality, only ever a substitute for the stepfather anyway; the stepfather, back in those days, was a sympathetic stand-in for the biological father, though. This cascading chain of substitutions is what Lacan would call "the paternal metaphor," in which the father is a signifier who substitutes for another signifier. Lacan suggests that these fathers are all merely standing in for the mother—and that's certainly true in Hays's text, in which the mother's letter to her daughter reaches its destination at last, once things get really dire. This cascading wall of replacement fathers standing in for the mother, is, as Lacan says, "at the heart of the question of the Oedipus complex."[133]

Mary's desire for William is an aspect of the novel that scholars have overlooked, even when exploring how Hays presents chastity as "a maneuverable construct."[134] Mr. Raymond explains that, although the nineteen-year-old William and seventeen-year-old Mary aren't related by blood, they are siblings, making any sexual contact between them potentially scandalous. Mary explains that she has been "accustomed to love William from my childhood, to receive and to return his innocent and lively caresses," and so "had not inquired into the nature of my sensations, and I now understood them but obscurely" (H 33). In a dramatic moment, Mr. Raymond issues a prohibition across two temporalities, in the present and future simultaneously: they are to desist with their sexual contact immediately and give up any future plans for marriage. The double temporality of the prohibition matches that of the sibling relationship. "William and I bounded into each other's embraces," explains Mary, "and, in the joyous present and anticipated future, forgot the anxieties and vexations of the past" (H 25). The novel is establishing a dichotomy between the past (home of anxieties and vexations) and the "present and anticipated future," which here function together as a single temporal entity. This is especially ironic given the way that childhood, in this novel, is emphatically presented as an "Edenic idyll," as Ty observes, complete with stolen grapes, innocent sensuality, and a garden bower.[135]

Julia Kristeva, as part of her project of reclaiming figures of "feminine genius," suggests that women can sometimes use the particularities of the Oedipus complex (which, for them, is multiply-encoded, never-ending, hopeless) to mount a challenge to chronology. The psychodynamics of being raised female, Kristeva argues, instantiates a headlong "desire-unto-death" that "breaks with linear time," which is perhaps why works of feminine genius so often work "against the linear time of the realization of a destiny."[136] In just such a way, as Hays's Mary confronts paternal prohibitions, she continues to collapse timelines in a way characteristic of Oedipal attachment. As she puts it: "Enjoying the present, and anticipating the future, with the light and sanguine spirits of youth, I forgot, in the society of the son, the painful feelings inspired by the presence of the father" (H 10). Here, she articulates a double repression: the innocent pleasures of the present, as embodied in her brother William, are "enjoyed" by and through the "painful feelings" of their future prohibition. In that William is, as I mentioned, so often the proxy for Mr. Raymond's enjoyment, the distinction between present and future proves unsustainable—there can be no difference between the enjoyment of sex and the "painful feelings" of the prohibition. Indeed, Mary experiences jouissance as Mr. Raymond iterates the incest taboo: "I started, trembled, shuddered; I felt a sudden revulsion of blood and spirits" (H 30). Through the interaction and interchangeability of William and Mr. Raymond, the future and present coexist and interact in the narrative present. As we saw with "Ithuriel" in chapter 1, this is an example of spectral jouissance interfering with the meaning of the present.

In Ty's reading of *The Victim of Prejudice*, Mary pays the price for seeking "the pre-Oedipal mother-child relation" as part of her "refusal to yield to the Father's Law."[137] Yet Mary seems eager to submit to her father's prohibitions even as she is crushed to lose contact with her brother:

ADOPTIVE SIBLINGS ACROSS OCEANS OF FUTURITY   111

"Name the sacrifice you require," she begs Mr. Raymond, "Behold me, my father, resigned to your will!" (H 30). When Mary fantasizes about her mother's life, she is not seeking an alternative to the law of the father but proceeding through its usual pathways. To see this, it can help to think of the Oedipus complex in the way made possible by Lacan's *Seminar V*. Lacan there posits that the Oedipus complex, in girls and boys alike, depends upon the overlapping of the present and future. By slicing the Oedipus complex across a hitherto unnoticed temporal vector, it can become an engine for deferment and posterity: it "doesn't mean that the child is going to enter in possession of all his sexual powers and deploy them, as you well know. On the contrary."[138] The Oedipus complex works through deferment, but only by situating the future within the present. Even as the Oedipal subject is, in the present, "stripped of the exercise of the functions which had begun to awaken," nevertheless "he has in his pocket all the title-deeds for him to make use of in the future."[139]

Lacan's metaphor of "title-deeds" is cruelly ironic if applied to this novel, as Sir Peter Osborne's repeated offers to Mary of "a legal title to his hand and fortune" reveal the depth of his cruelty (H 164). Mary chooses jail instead of Sir Peter, who throughout the novel has been using his privilege to harass her. Exasperated by the way the system has scripted her abjection, Mary offers a poignant prayer: "A child of misfortune, a wretched outcast from my fellow-beings, driven with ignominy from social intercourse, cut off from human sympathy, immured in the gloomy walls of a prison, I spread my hands and lift my eyes to the Moral Governor of the Universe" (H 3). This kind of appeal to "a third party" is typical of "the normal oedipal position," explains Lacan, and is part of the novel's Wollstonecraftian inheritance.[140] The prayer seeks out an alternate system of justice beyond the law; the law, as the novel goes on to show as it traces her bleak experience, serves only the caprice of wealthy men. (Freud once observed that only "the experience of painful disappointments" can dissolve the Oedipus complex;[141] Lacan's theory of overlapping temporalities, playing one disappointment against another, is an attempt to expand on that idea.) She uses five subordinate clauses, all describing herself in the third person, before speaking of herself as "I": she is examining herself from the outside, situating herself socially to understand how she arrived in her current predicament. The syntax suggests that she has emerged as the effect of what has happened to her, and thus self-discovery involves her noticing a wide system of recursive oppressions, each operating in the context of the others like a set of Russian *matryoshka* dolls: she notes how she is

112   FRACTURE FEMINISM

contained in a cell, which is in a larger prison, and which, as Ty notes, gives "physical reality" to everything that has befallen her already;[142] the prison is, further, part of a city, and a marginal part, and her marginality in it means a further confinement from the currents of sympathy, which would be, as we know, a kind of starvation for a fictional middle-class woman in the age of sensibility. There is no opposition to be drawn here between the confinement of the prisoner and the freedom of the citizen; the cell is simply one corner of a totalizing system of oppression. Each oppression fits within the others, which suggests that the prayer to the "Moral Governor of the Universe" might be in vain; it is a "last appeal" following many others, implying that God may be yet one more level in the chain of oppressive and exclusionary apparatuses (H 3). It gives the impression of Mary's being entrapped by a sadistic set of institutions, as Jennifer Golightly has noted.[143]

The prayer hinges on the "and." Although it was to be Mary's "last appeal," the "and" extends it into the future. Having just appealed to a higher jurisdiction, it marks a second appeal, a refraction of the prayer, which works across time rather than cosmic space: "And thou, the victim of despotism, oppression, or error, tenant of a dungeon, and successor to its present devoted inhabitant, should these sheets fall into thy possession, when the hand that wrote them moulders in the dust, . . . read" (H 3). It enables Mary to imagine her future self, someone equally "the victim of despotism." There is some suggestion, from the exhortation to "read," that the reader of *The Victim of Prejudice* might be this person, which suggests metaphorically that what we take for daily life might be effectively a prison, in Hays's estimation. Pivoting mid-apostrophe from the theological to the temporal plane, Mary situates the present within the future as an ambiguously separate yet simultaneous plane of experience. Mary asks her successor to "spare from the contemplation of thy own misery one hour, and devote it to the memory of a fellow-sufferer" (H 3). This request marks a clear difference between Mary and her successor—they are not interchangeable, and Mary's suffering is the better topic for contemplation for "one hour"—yet it also asks that the future reader make an impossible leap backward, through sympathy, into Mary's current place. In the sense that the future cellmate is the reader of the novel, the reader is being warned to attend to the differences between him- or herself and the protagonist, who is also the "author" of the narrative; we are warned, by the conditional "should," that a future reader might never exist; in any case the future reader is asked to stop existing, to disregard his or her own sufferings while reading the story of Mary Raymond, and thus to become Mary Raymond through an act of sympathy and identification. The future reader *is* Mary Raymond, in a sense, as the reader will have been a version of a person whose pleasures have been deferred since childhood and whose sufferings can be considered only in the time to come. This, in a novel by Mary Hays with its protagonist, also named Mary, as its intended reader; further yet, later in the novel, Mary will learn that her mother was also called Mary and was also imprisoned unjustly, having demanded that Mr. Raymond, of all people, "disturb not my remnant of life" (H 62–3). In this sense, Mary Raymond is writing at one and the same time for the present (i.e., God) and the future (i.e., her successor in the cell), which repeats the fate of her mother, Mary. In one wish for justice, then, she activates three temporalities that must be experienced simultaneously. Yet Hays maintains a gap between Mary Raymond in the here and now and the Mary Raymond of the future, both of whom are fictional author and imagined recipient of this narrative. Mary is speaking of herself, to herself, as the object of historical memory, a remnant of the past, and as a repetition of her mother's fate. The present and future are concurrent in this novel.

For Freud, the Oedipus complex is highly contingent but thoroughly linear: there are different pathways, some neurotic and some perverse, some male and some female, some homosexual and some heterosexual, but in any eventuality the path remains clearly plotted, in that sexual maturation occurs through a series of phases that can be embraced or skirted at the subject's peril. Hays outlines similar Oedipal crossroads, but, in contradistinction to Freud, collapses several temporalities into one synchronous experience, such that the subject's present and future have to coexist in the narrative present. Essentially, she is accomplishing at the level of individual sexual development the same trick that Wollstonecraft had accomplished in *An Historical and Moral View of the French Revolution*, in which a progressivist theory of history, claimed as a positive good, undoes itself as it runs up against the atemporal fragments harbored within in. For Hays, the Oedipus complex is its own aftermath, as it overlays several life phases at once, effectively embedding the future in the present. Conceptually, it is a significant idea, as it is quite different from the way that Freud charted the Oedipus complex, through a timeline of discrete and consecutive phases, and it anticipates a neglected aspect of Lacan's work as he tried to re-theorize the Oedipus complex across and between the genders. In embedding the future within the present through a normative structure of Oedipal desire, Hays can be said to be theorizing the Oedipus complex even as she places herself into dialogue with feminist contemporaries such as Mary Robinson, Mary Wollstonecraft, and Helen Maria Williams, each of whom likewise imagined the future to be coterminous with the present in their political analyses of the revolutionary culture of the 1790s. Hays, thinking desire through multivalent temporalities in a way that reflects the feminist sensibilities of her era, devises a model of Oedipal attachment that challenges and augments one of the core concepts of psychoanalysis.

What we find in both novels, *Paul and Virginia* and *The Victim of Prejudice*, is fraternal-sororal eroticism being channeled through a patriarchal figure, either the narrator or the adoptive father. Both father-proxies deconstruct pastoral eroticism to arrive into impossible temporalities, which undo the chronologies associated with the sexual development of young people. Further, both novels use their structural features to construct time-bending and worldwide-izing parerga. Hays's novel takes the additional step of incorporating *Paul and Virginia* itself into its own narrative (much as Williams had done with Bernardin), with all of the doom that that implies for Mary Raymond and women in general. But both novels, however tragic in their outlook and cynical in their assessment of rights, maintain a space of non-meaning that gets explored only through blips of grammar and figuration, as if the contemporary future were always at hand as a feminist heterotopia, construed temporally as the experience of the impossible. If the ocean of futurity has a boundary after all, it would not be found beyond the limits of the present, as Mr. Raymond suggests, but as a fragment of the Real internal to the now of these storyworlds.

Chapter 3

Della Cruscan Time

Lyric poetry by its nature has a complex relationship to time. It pits "a timeless present" against "sequentiality, causality, time, [and] teleological meaning" in a tension which, as Anne C. McCarthy points out, inheres in its structural features.[1] When lyric poetry is published in the newspaper, it gains new dimensions of timeliness and ephemerality; when collected in an anthology, these dimensions become embroiled in questions of canonicity and the archive. Within the lyric tradition, certain experiments in language make possible even stranger temporalities. In this chapter, I consider the Della Cruscan poetic circle as a virtual community of writers who, through their formal inventiveness and willingness to experiment with sexuality and time, and their willingness to explore these matters at the levels of print media, trope, and signification, collectively bring the future into poetry as a political and sexual practice. Caught between ephemerality and the archive, playful posturing and deep political engagement, their poems quickly become subject to what Jacques Derrida calls an "anarchive drive," an "archiviolithic force [that] leaves nothing of its own behind," proceeding, through acts of "radical effacement" and the development of an "erotic simulacrum," to open up the question of the contemporary future.[2] The world-shattering future becomes present for the Della Cruscans in the form of a jouissance that serves as a cut in time. Their poetry is thus an experiment in "presentify[ing]" jouissance (as Lacan would say),[3] a jouissance immediately enacted through experiments in language even as it remains, paradoxically, deferred. This jouissance, in its cutting action, forcefully dislodges the existing elements of the petrified

115

present, a form of temporal warping and evacuation that we can detect in the Della Cruscans' overstuffed language.

Della Cruscan poetry had its beginnings in Italy, circa 1784 and 1785, with the publication of *The Arno Miscellany* and *The Florence Miscellany*. A collaborative literary project bringing together male and female, British and Italian, poets, it aspired to link poetry to friendship and restore poetic language to an imagined early modern ideal.[4] But when the movement's leader Robert Merry moved back to Britain in 1787, he began to interact with entirely new collaborators, and the project began to pursue a more experimental line of speculative feminist thought that would respond to the contemporary future. The poetry published in *The World*, a London newspaper, between 1787 and 1794 reveled in the particularly excessive features of literary language, in a technique that Lacan would call "*lalangue*" or "llanguage." Llanguage, a form of writing that Lacan associates especially with James Joyce's *Finnegans Wake*, "produces the break or discontinuity" in meaning, through which it positions literary writing (and, says Lacan, psychoanalytic discourse, as well as mathematics) within but outside the symbolic register, such that it would embody feminine jouissance.[5] In such writing, Lacan explains, "the signifier stuffs the signified" and thus pushes language beyond its communicative functions, which is what makes it "difficult to read" or, more likely, "not read at all."[6] This technique, I will suggest, anchors the Della Cruscans' more directly political poems such as "Ode to Folly" (1787) and *Ainsi va le Monde* (1790), and structures their playful erotic triangles; these aspects of the poetry are what ultimately give Della Cruscan poetry its affiliation with the contemporary future. The Della Cruscans' innovation in poetic language was, I argue, a breakthrough of llanguage in a contretemporal key, one vital for the formation of the contemporary future as a feminist literary discourse.

The new phase of Della Cruscanism began on June 29, 1787, with the newspaper publication of Merry's poem "The Adieu and Recall to Love," a poem that seems bent on packing sexual enjoyment into literary language. With it, Merry began to make an atemporal feminist intervention into the era's sexual politics. Yet, as Michael Gamer notices, it was Hannah Cowley, publishing "To Del[la] Crusca: The Pen" in the same newspaper, *The World*, on July 10, 1787, who transformed "The Adieu and Recall" into the basis of a poetic correspondence. Arguably, then, and in Gamer's assessment, "Merry's female respondents played an even greater role than he did" in the development of the Della Cruscan ethos.[7] Cowley and Mary Robinson, along with several others, maintained a poetic exchange with Merry in the pages of *The World* between 1787 and 1794. Cowley, using the moniker "Anna Matilda," Robinson, as "Laura Maria," and Merry, as "Della Crusca," wrote playful, lavish, inventive, and titillating poetry, which fashionable people hated. John Bell collected their poems in an anthology, *The Poetry of The World* (1788), which was re-titled *The British Album* starting in 1790 as it kept expanding over a number of editions. The anthologies, by privileging Merry, Cowley, and Robinson as the signal poets of Della Cruscanism, would "consolidate a fairly heterogenous group of poets . . . into a discrete 'movement.'"[8] The triumvirate, constantly responding to one another in verse, conceived of politics as the emptying out of the contemporary. They aligned poetry with the future by developing a discourse of female sexual pleasure; Cowley's first poem to Della Crusca fantasized about his penetrating her body with his pen, for instance.[9] Using their pseudonyms as elaborate "masks of seduction," as Derrida would say, they arguably invented the contemporary future as a way of responding to recent political events.[10]

To best illustrate this, I shall begin with discussion of Mary Robinson's *Ainsi va le Monde*, a poem that demonstrates with particular clarity the Della Cruscan anti-chrononormative queer style. In *Ainsi*, Robinson affirms Merry and the French Revolution in a radically aysnchronic way, which, I argue, establishes her fracture-feminist bona fides, even before she would write *A Letter to the Women of England*. The fractured temporality of the poem lends it special significance within the queer history of Romanticism. Next, I suggest how that poem's queer atemporality was part of its response to Merry's *The Laurel of Liberty*, published just three days earlier, and with which it is in continuous dialogue, and how *The Laurel of Liberty* is itself, in turn, in constant dialogue with Cowley's poetry—including Anna Matilda's stinging rebukes to Della Crusca about his flirtation with Laura Maria. In a third section of the chapter, I discuss Cowley's poetic tributes to Merry in two poems entitled "To Della Crusca," tracing the playfully jealous poetic interactions between Merry, Cowley, and Robinson, as the three mutually explore atemporal, triangular love relations in a virtual space. Next, I bring this triangulated structure of erotics back to Merry's own experiments in llanguage in "The Adieu and Recall to Love" (the inaugural poem of the sequence) and his "Ode to Tranquillity" (another early installment), to show how his particular form of homographesis skirts the era's heteronormative and implicitly chrononormative strictures at the level of prosody. Finally, I follow Merry's playful polypoetics back onto the level of official national politics by analyzing "Ode to Folly," a poem of Merry's published on September 27, 1787, which presses its water imagery into concerted resistance to the national ideologies of militarism and clock time. In sum, I hope to show how Della Cruscan poetry established many of the intellectual bases for the wider atemporal Romantic feminist discourse to come. The Della Cruscans' tacky sex poetry, I suggest, would become indispensable to the era's politics, given how, in the wider world of women's writing during these years, an abnegation of the contemporary was becoming the basis for a radical, if deliberately outmoded, vision of political resistance. Robinson, Cowley, and Merry, experimenting with mutual vulnerability and revision, and with a form of virtual quasi-collective authorship in which poems respond closely to the others' political, sexual, and temporal provocations, find themselves at or near the hollow center of a crucial, if sometimes ignored, tradition of Romantic women's writing.

From a Lacanian perspective, such a mode of writing can be considered "women's writing" for the way that it exposes meaning to the "acid-test" of llanguage, enabling these writers to chart (as Lacan remarks of his own similar path) "a difficult, ground-breaking course, whose horizon is strange."[11] Through such a course, "women's writing" moves beyond identarian categories to become a discourse of its own in the late eighteenth century, even when Merry was doing the writing. Yet even considered in identarian terms, we should note that Merry, upon his return to England, quickly found himself in league with an astonishing assembly of women writers who were already having, or would go on to have, highly influential literary careers bearing powerful feminist messages. Cowley was already then at "the forefront of contemporary playwrights," as she had been ever since the success of *The Runaway* in 1776; she was in the midst of writing a string of ten highly successful comedies, which, while often scandalizing audiences, satirized the difficulties that women face in marriage and domestic life.[12] Robinson was even more famous—she was one of the world's first modern celebrities—but was then just beginning to remake her career as a writer in the wake of a physical disability and an "image crisis" stemming from a royal sex scandal;[13] she would of course go on to write important feminist work across a wide range of genres, perhaps most crucially the novel *Walsingham*, the ballad cycle *Lyrical Tales*, the sonnet cycle *Sappho and Phaon*, and the polemic *A Letter to the Women of England*. Charlotte Dacre, their less prominent Della Cruscan colleague, would go on to write the important Gothic novels *Zofloya, or the Moor* and *The Libertine*, both of which eulogize female sexual pleasure. Their predecessor in Della Cruscanism was Hester Lynch Piozzi, a central figure in what has been called the eighteenth-century "gender revolution in authorship," who would go on to follow Catherine Macaulay in the domain of the female historian.[14] Taken together and evaluated over their entire careers, the Della Cruscans flexed an extraordinary amount of literary power for what once seemed a "minor" poetic movement.[15] Merry found himself, in short, collaborating with a roster of independently important women writers, each in the midst of making major literary contributions across a range of genres in a feminist key. Other Della Cruscan collaborators, buried under pseudonyms, have yet to be identified.

Yet the Della Cruscans were less a roster of talented individuals than "a network of writers, signatures, texts, intertexts, and media," of which publication in the newspaper was perhaps the most significant aspect.[16] "Newspaper poetry served a purpose much like that of the comics section in today's newspapers," Daniel Robinson explains, in the sense that the "poems are meant to be amusingly consumable and literally disposable."[17] Gamer agrees, calling Cowley's verse "deliberately consumable and temporary."[18] Through this ephemeral form and media, the poems would meditate upon permanence and durability, and thus activate paradoxical modes of temporality. Disseminated in contradictory media, they were scattered in the daily immediacy of *The World* but collected and preserved in *The British Album*, emblematizing at the level of print media a tension, already thematized in the poetry, between the desires for conservancy and erasure. This is what Derrida has termed "archive fever." Della Cruscan poetry aspires to document the impermanent and yet constantly remake its own archive, producing a discourse that is "cleft, divided, contradictory" and "never one with itself."[19] *The British Album* effectively institutionalized and recorded a poetic compulsion to repeat. These poems enact a form of "temporal drag," as Elizabeth Freeman has called the technique—that is, "a counter-genealogical practice of archiving culture's throwaway objects, including the outmoded masculinities and femininities from which usable pasts may be extracted."[20]

As a matter of style, Merry, Robinson, and Cowley's deliberately outmoded poetry, replete with embarrassing apostrophes, stilted rhymes, and over-formal figurations, seem to epitomize temporal drag, given their purposeful use of outmoded or unfashionable styles as a mode of sexual subversion. Such artworks, argues Freeman, not only qualify as "drag" in the sense of a deliberate campy parody meant to undermine a hegemonic (in this case temporal) norm, but also in the sense of resistance through delay.[21] It was through the eroticization of the printed word—the way that formal elements such as syntax, diction, rhyme, meter, and trope became elevated to the level of a sexual fetish, and then how those printed words were published and disseminated—that the Della Cruscans could experiment with time to situate their poetry in the future and in other asynchronous times. Their poetry offended good taste because, as Jacqueline Labbe puts it, "poetry itself was being violated, its classical purity put in the service of a pornographic emphasis on the passions."[22] It was certainly lush, playful, and erotic. In the Della Cruscan idiom, explains Labbe, "poetry and lovemaking are identical: bodily passion resides in, is communicated by, and requires poetry. The body of work takes over for the body of the beloved, and is correspondingly increasingly eroticised."[23] The poetry was, in Daniel Robinson's words, "a burlesque of Sensibility," ever "playful, full of winking allusions, dirty jokes, and considerable irony."[24] Although the Della Cruscans were often derided for their excesses, still, Merry's "histrionic" poetry proved foundational for a cohort of important women poets, who, through the very excesses of their style, would significantly shape what is now known as British Romanticism.[25] William Wordsworth, even, wrote the Preface to *Lyrical Ballads* as "a conscious critique of the Della Cruscans and the kind of writing inspired by their work," as Jerome J. McGann has argued.[26] Across this broader study, we will be able to trace their imagery into the verse of Charlotte Smith and Anna Letitia Barbauld, whose experiments with allegory, geologic time, and poetic form borrow from Della Cruscan poetics; into the work of Charlotte Caroline Richardson, who would rely upon this idea of internal difference in her analysis of English society after Waterloo; and into the world of Helen Maria Williams, whose deconstructive approach to time in the context of international politics remains in dialogue with, especially, peers such as Merry and Robinson.

As the Della Cruscans broke open the symbolic coordinates of poetry, they did indeed produce a "break or discontinuity" in time (to put things in Lacanian terms), and thereby gave rise to a feminine "not-two" ex-sisting within, yet apart from, chrononormative coordinates. Sexual difference was not, in their work, a gulf separating men from women, but a difference internal to the prevailing hegemonies of sex and politics. Through that formulation, their poetics became immediately influential for women's writing of the period, providing much of the discursive and counter-temporal framework for those who would write the contemporary future.

The Queer Asynchronies of Mary Robinson's *Ainsi va le Monde*

Robert Merry's joyous poetic encomium to the Revolution in France, *The Laurel of Liberty*, was published on November 6, 1790. It took but three days for the retired actor Mary Darby Robinson, writing under her Della Cruscan *nom de plume* Laura Maria, to publish a response poem of some 350 lines, entitled *Ainsi va le Monde*. Thus, the Della Cruscan circle of poets, known up to this point for their comically lavish style and for their habit of publishing in the newspaper, began to engage with the most pressing political event of their moment. *Ainsi* was significant, Daniel Robinson explains, for being Mary Robinson's "first truly ambitious poem, her first book publication since her juvenile works over a decade earlier, and her first foray into the British debate over the French Revolution."[27] The poem typifies the way that the Della Cruscans would resort to the future as a response to contemporary politics.

In *Time Binds*, Freeman indicates the importance of asynchronism to queer art: in a culture that often enforces heterosexuality through the insistence upon linear, monochronic time—the time that measures the passing hours, work time, leisure time, and the phases of a life supposedly well lived—any temporal disruption will inevitably be connected with sexual disruption.[28] Hegemonic sexual values, Freeman argues, are often exerted through what she terms chrononormativity, "a mode of implantation" in which "manipulations of time convert historically specific regimes of asymmetrical power into seemingly ordinary bodily tempos and routines, which in turn organize the value and meaning of time."[29] Queer artists, she suggests, have long been inclined to experiment with temporality, especially as they link sexual enjoyment to time. It is in this context that I want to consider the impossible temporalities of Robinson's response to Merry and the Revolution. Robinson has long been an important figure within queer studies in Romanticism, partly for her participation in the Della Cruscan circle, but even more for her solicitousness "to behold the lovely Marie Antoinette"[30] and for her novel of cross-dressing, *Walsingham*. *Ainsi va le Monde* has not yet been a part of that conversation, but because it imagines contemporary politics as the effect of asynchronicity, and because makes its political intervention in an erotic key, it may be a crucial text for queer Romanticism and for the broader counterdiscourse of women's writing seeking to resist the emergent culture of clock time.

The most obviously queer element of *Ainsi va le Monde* is that it stages a lesbian encounter in which the emphasis is sexual pleasure. This occurs in the last section of the poem, in which the speaker, Laura Maria, seduces "Freedom—blithe Goddess of the rainbow vest."[31] Robinson is here using a technique that Freeman calls "erotohistoriography," meaning the practice, in political writing or art, of using the pleasures of the body to hybridize the present and make it confront other times.[32] In this last section of *Ainsi va le Monde*, the erotics play out unambiguously, but only at the level of allegory: two women having sex is merely the vehicle of a metaphor, in which the emancipation of all people everywhere can be allegorized as a sex act. The disruption occurs at the allegorical level, through the excesses of the text's temporal drag, which is a technique highly typical of the Della Cruscan poetic tradition and also of the subsequent Romantic tradition of women's atemporal political writing. Allegory, Paul de Man explains, depends on repetition and therefore time to do its figural work.[33] Accordingly, as Laura Maria seduces the goddess Freedom, an orientation to the future emerges as a figural lesbian practice. Note the emphasis on women's pleasure: "I court thee from thy azure-spangled bed / Where Ether floats about thy winged head; / Where tip-toe pleasure swells the choral song, / While gales of odour waft the Cherub throng."[34] Once Freedom consents to Laura's advances, the poem becomes even more sexually explicit: "For thee the light-heel'd graces fondly twine, / To clasp thy yielding waist, a zone divine! / Venus for thee her crystal altar rears, / Deck'd with fresh myrtle."[35] As the poem reaches a climax, the allegorical level disintegrates and its jouissance spills into the wider, chrononormative political world. As Laura calls out her lover's name at the moment of orgasm, it—only because her lover is named Freedom—becomes a performative call to global revolution: "See! From her shrine electric incense rise; / Hark! 'Freedom' echoes thro' the vaulted skies."[36] Revolutionary politics comes into being, so to speak, because it was taking place through mechanisms of allegory: as language collides with jouissance, we are left, as an unintended residue, with a Mel Gibson–like call for "Freedom." Through jouissance, language is tied to the body; because of jouissance, the poem's attempts at allegory collapse and we are left to read the call for freedom at a directly political level. This is what Lacan would refer to as llanguage. As sexual enjoyment "throbs rapture thro' each palpitating vein," a politics emerges that cannot account for its own arrival and that cannot become contemporary.[37] Hence it can be considered an act of erotohistoriography.

DELLA CRUSCAN TIME   123

As the reader crosses from the allegorical level to the direct level
of rights, a delay occurs, pushing them into asynchrony: Freedom, hailed
as a lover in the immediate moment of the poem, moves into the wider
political world as an echo. That is, the "shrine electric" of the allegory
has become, effectively, the immediate past of the wider poem, such that
the French Revolution seems to be situated, temporally speaking, in the
broad aftermath of its own figuration. The echo is, as readers of Gayatri
Spivak or Ovid will know, delayed speech, an instrument of *différance*, and
an allegory in its own right meant to capture the resonance of women's
counterhegemonic discourses.[38] By imaginatively summoning the "shrine
electric," an impossible fantasy space available only at the level of figuration, where one can seduce one's own rhetorical figures, Robinson enacts
a performative politics of revolution whose effects are worldwide-ized and
immediate, yet subject to a permanent delay: in this way, and through
this perpetual deferment and displacement, "The Goddess speaks!" despite
being absent.[39]

The title of the poem is meant ironically, which in this case means
over-literally. The idiomatic French phrase "ainsi va le monde," meaning
approximately "that's just the way things are," would usually be invoked in
an attempt to naturalize hypocrisy or injustice. But Robinson, taking it too
literally and seriously and thus obviating its cynicism, maintains that the
way of progressive politics is "the way of the world," by which she means
that politics must be displaced, deferred, and worldwide-ized in order to
find a viable "way." (One also must consider that Della Cruscan poetry
was primarily published in *The World*.) The worldwide-izing gesture would
become, over the next decade, a cornerstone of the feminist discourse of
the contemporary future. Much as with *Frankenstein* in Freeman's reading
of it, the relation to history in *Ainsi* is "directly sexual."[40] The political
consequences of that are significant in the poem, because the French
Revolution, in Robinson's analysis, is not a political event, but a gap that
emerges between incompatible temporalities. As the inarticulable space that
pertains to an impossible future as a response to history and pastness, it is
a "shrine electric" unto itself. There is no contemporary France, Robinson
suggests, because the *Ancien Régime* is a world of pastness masquerading
as modernity, and this is the source of its injustices: "Where, thro' long
ages past, with watchful care, / THY TYRANTS, GALLIA, nurs'd the
witch DESPAIR."[41] She explains that "man can but reign his transitory
hour," as if to suggest that the time of revolution operates on a different

124   FRACTURE FEMINISM

scale than oppression, or that these temporalities are not coterminous.[42] Apostrophizing "ENLIGHTEN'D Gallia!" partway through, the speaker suggests that the prevailing culture of indulgence was given to France by "insidious *Art*," producing a world of luxury goods that exist "to hide pale Slavery in a mask of smiles: . . . And lead the victim in a flow'ry chain."[43] A figure for unacknowledged pastness, Louis XIV becomes "O, monstrous hypocrite!—who vainly strove / By pious fraud, to win a people's love."[44] Yet, in a dialectical movement, now that these luxuries can serve as an index of a nation's hidden oppression, that very oppression, rendered visible by a corrupt culture, begins to operate autonomously as an historical agent, which "rouses" France to revolution: "When from her Heav'n insulted *Freedom* came; / Glancing o'er earth's wide space, . . . / Wake from the torpid slumber of disgrace; / Roused by oppression, *Man* his birth-right claims."[45] The *Ancien Régime* has been training its own gravediggers.

Such an explanation for the Revolution fractures the present, turning French politics into a dispute between the past masquerading as the present and a future already here. Robinson asks: "Who shall the nat'ral Rights of Man deride, / When Freedom spreads her fost'ring banners wide? / Who shall contemn the heav'n-taught zeal that throws / The balm of comfort on a Nation's woes?"[46] Such is an unusual way of building consensus: the reader is placed between a "who" and a "when," and between the present and future, as if to suggest that Revolution is never contemporary with itself, or that it necessarily misses those who would doubt its justice. Revolution is universally celebrated, that is, because those who want it, experience it directly, right now, and those who condemn it encounter it only in the future. It becomes "universal" only by breaking apart the time of the political.

In this, Robinson may have been responding to a shift in the meaning of sovereignty underway during this period, which has been theorized by Kir Kuiken: as politics, in the wake of the revolution, began to rearrange itself around a model of sovereignty that must be "radically self-inaugurating," riddled with aporia, and constituted "retrospectively," poets would exploit the time-boundness of the imagination to expose a gap between the now of political thought and the now of politics proper.[47] David Collings, as well, discusses a sense of justice developed in this period that must remain "formally empty" and "outside of history."[48] For Robinson, such a practice relies upon a paradoxical kind of universalism because it depends on the refusal of any universal. Put in Lacanian terms, this is a politics of the not-whole.[49] Put in Derridean terms, the problem becomes

DELLA CRUSCAN TIME 125

one of delay, deferral, and dispersal. "Freedom spreads" her banners today, in the present tense, but the immediate response is something that must be deferred: "Who shall contemn" and "deride" these events, the speaker asks, even though the events are already well underway and generating a mountain of British commentary. In this sense, Revolution is something that is by its nature deferred: even when it is definitively here, it can be experienced only from the future. We are still lodged between a who and a when, and between psychoanalysis and deconstruction: as the Revolution "Wrests hidden treasure from the sordid hand, / And flings profusion o'er a famish'd land?—," it offers us an *agalma*, or "hidden treasure," that it doesn't own, and with it "flings profusion" to everyone. The treasure is a figure both for a desire that is not one and for dissemination, because the object of the search, once it has been shredded and scattered, remains the treasure that it was.[50] Such a revolution will have always been in the mode of "to come," and it will have been moving elsewhere, always, to others—it is never here yet.[51] Hence the ongoing French Revolution is not an ongoing Revolution (i.e., it will have arrived only in the future) and isn't French (i.e., it becomes what it is only in traveling worldwide, or becoming cosmopolitan). It springs from the libido and, like the libido, succeeds only by missing its aim: "Nor yet, to GALLIA are her smiles confin'd, / She opes her radiant gates to *all mankind*."[52] The status of this "all" in relation to the "nor yet" is Robinson's main concern. Even fifteen months into the Revolution, Robinson still gives us a French Revolution to come, existing only under the banner of "nor yet." *Ainsi va le Monde* thus reformulates the messianicity of deconstructive politics: the pursuit of justice would not require an attitude of vigilant patience, but would, through the unleashing of sexual enjoyment, find a democracy to come here among us already, slicing open the "all" that politics defines. The poem equally upends psychoanalytic orthodoxies, presenting jouissance as something quite attainable in queer practice, if only at the figural level. Robinson's is a worldwide revolution that will, in becoming global, retroactively become a "French" revolution. There will have been a French Revolution but there is no French Revolution. As the poem's title suggests, that is the way of the world, as Robinson sees it: only as a "world" does politics find a "way."

The poem's main image of such a politics, cosmopolitan and "nor yet," is that of Pity, an angel who goes into caves and unchains everyone: "Now snatch'd from death, the wond'ring wretch shall prove / The rapt'rous energies of social love."[53] In Pity, we see the voice of the future (e.g., "shall

126   FRACTURE FEMINISM

prove") inserted allegorically into the "now" of contemporary politics, as a figure for dissemination: Pity now shall "spread broad sun-shine in the caves of death."[54] It depends, then, on finding plenitude in the very place of negation and deprivation; the political upheaval already underway is, suggests Robinson, like sunshine in a cave—impossible.

Ainsi va le Monde writes the present as erotohistory. It unsettles the tempos and routines of political analysis, leveraging the body's jouissance to find asynchronous ways of living and surviving within relations of power. Freeman, although she is primarily interested in discussing twentieth-century examples, uses *Frankenstein* to illustrate how erotohistoriography has a longer literary history. For Freeman, Shelley's novel is erotohistoriographical because of its engagement with pastness. Robinson's poem reveals that there was also, roughly concurrently, an erotohistoriography of the future underway. *Ainsi*'s future-oriented erotohistoriography, rooted in the body by way of its jouissance and disrupting the political by way of its *différance*, may be said to challenge the orthodoxies of queer theory in a couple of important ways. First, it suggests that queer politics could arise from the literary act of taking the present to be historical, rather than, say, through acts of gender subversion or epistemologies of the closet.[55] Second, because it creates this temporal fracture by making recourse to futurity and hope, it may challenge leading queer theorists, such as Lee Edelman, who would see the future only as a normative political discourse.[56] It is not, for Robinson, the death drive versus the future, but a future opened up, and ready to be inhabited and operationalized for erotohistoriography, by the deathly, echoing, repetitive pull of annihilation.

Robinson's Merry Meets Merry's Cowley: *The Laurel of Liberty*

The above analysis treats *Ainsi va le Monde* as an independent poem, which it is not. Della Cruscan poetry generally "capitalizes on the frisson generated by the to-and-fro of the letter format," and *Ainsi* is no exception.[57] Much of its sexual play arises from its interactions with Merry's *The Laurel of Liberty*, which have been called "competitive" in nature.[58] I would characterize the relation as a more intimate one than that. *Ainsi*, as we have seen, treats Freedom as an echo-effect, but it does so precisely by speaking in echo; it does not respond to its source material, as in a dialogue, but deforms a voice internal to it. This is what makes *Ainsi* a

DELLA CRUSCAN TIME   127

clear example of fracture feminism. Laura Maria becomes, in relation to Della Crusca, "she who speaks from, and steals, the words of the other, she who takes the other at his or her word."[59] Robinson dedicates her poem to Merry, "whose liquid notes in sweet meand'rings flow," and "who deign'd to rove where twinkling glow-worms lead."[60] She presents *Ainsi* as a gift to Della Crusca, who is urged to "accept the Verse thy magic harp inspires."[61] She invokes Merry as her muse in the composition of the poem, much as Merry had himself invoked a muse—Liberty herself—for his own poetic analysis of the French Revolution. Merry, pressed into service implicitly as Liberty, seems to Robinson both sublime and stimulating: "Genius, or Muse, whate'er thou art! whose thrill / Exalts the fancy."[62] Yet Merry's capability to "exalt the fancy" must reckon with his tendency to exercise fancy indiscriminately: Merry's poem, Robinson explains, is beautiful "whether thy fancy 'pours the varying verse' / In bow'rs of bliss, or o'er the plumed hearse."[63] The alternative on offer here—that fancy will be poured either over bowers of bliss or the hearse—makes sexual enjoyment the equivalent of death. This is of course a false dichotomy, as it proves to be in the poem: each alternative is actually intrinsic to the other. Jouissance implicates the subject in the death drive (also known as archive fever) and thus into endless repetition; because the "bow'rs of bliss" pull us into "the plumed hearse," Robinson can begin to mount a challenge to the concept of history, much as Merry had done in *The Laurel*. Jouissance, as Lacan reminds us, can be discovered only at "the barrier where everything is forgotten," and ensures that sex "cannot be considered timely."[64] Robinson's sexualized tribute to Merry serves, then, as a warning and an act of deferral, as Robinson appropriates Merry and Cowley's voices to produce an echo-effect of her own.

There is no such thing as being oneself in this discourse. The cascading echo-effects "break all ipseity apart in advance."[65] Merry mentions such bowers in *The Laurel of Liberty*, when he suggests that French citizens are "sweetly pacing from her blossom'd bow'r, / [and thus] Unbound the streams . . . Who taught fair Echo in her cave serene."[66] Liberty, for Merry, according to this classical allusion, is a narcissistic entity, ready for seduction: "her zone unbound, her tresses unconfin'd."[67] Cowley then poses as (in effect) Liberty as she stages similar "bow'rs of bliss" in "To Della Crusca," a poem published in *The World* on February 26, 1789, using that pose as leverage within an erotic triangle. In that way, one of the principal aims of the French Revolution (i.e., Liberty) is introjected by a speaking subject. In that Cowley poem, which I will discuss at greater length below, Anna Matilda (i.e., Cowley) reprimands Della Crusca (i.e., Merry) for his dalliances with Laura Maria (i.e., Robinson). She reprimands him for this infidelity because Della Crusca had once resolved to "lure thee [i.e., Anna Matilda] from thy secret bow'r," because "I live for thee alone!"[68] Robinson, feeling the sting of Liberty-Anna Matilda-Cowley's rebuke, takes up this chain of echoing texts and reorganizes its network of allusions. She has Freedom echo Liberty and incorporate it. Hence Freedom incorporates a body that has already incorporated Merry's rebuke to Cowley for rebuking Robinson. The resonant secret bower, though, now becomes merely the alternative to the "plumed hearse." It nevertheless recalls Anna Matilda's acts of premature mourning for Della Crusca, in a poem from the previous June.[69] Robinson seems to be suggesting, then, that Merry's verse covers both the secret bowers of the past and the deathly echoes of the future; to continue this temporal twisting, she soon begins to appropriate Merry's Phoenix imagery from *The Laurel of Liberty*. We can see, here, how the Della Cruscan exchange begins to form a discourse through elaborate lattices of allusion and repetition, in which sexual rivalry remains ever implicit. It takes on an oppressive feeling, as if there can be nothing outside of these texts and their temporal fracture, a zone of impossible pure jouissance known as the bower of bliss. They are living inside a fracture in time, but it is unclear whether there is anything outside of that fracture—any public historical space in which that fracture inheres. In this sense, the fracture they inhabit is not only the site where an impossible temporality happens, but is itself an impossible fracture, a fracture in absence and abeyance *en abyme*.

Through Merry's debts to Cowley, voice had already been fragmented in *The Laurel of Liberty*. The splintering of ipseity through networks of classical and contemporary allusion subjects that poem's future-oriented politics to the vagaries of archive fever. Merry attributes the echo-effect to that quintessential Romantic symbol, "airy harps." Those harps are themselves an allusion to Cowley's "To Della Crusca," where Anna Matilda says (of Della Crusca's verse): "The surging aether floats across the Vale; / The Elegiac Sound, sooths my sad Ear."[70] Merry, in turn, uses *The Laurel of Liberty* to urge Anna Matilda to "wreathe round her airy harp her tim'rous joy" to sing in "her hundred tongues."[71] Merry, who had aimed in one of his poems to write such "THAT ANNA AND THAT I WERE ONE," now must confront the fact that their fusion of identities has led only to further scattering, allusion, quotation, and dissemination.[72] It is an outbreak of archive fever, and also Romanticism—if Romanticism, per Fredric Jameson, can be said to have made a political allegory out of the very unity of symbolism itself.[73] The very consistency of the imagery across the poetic sequence gives rise to a fracture of voices rather than a unification, such that the poems themselves enact the myth of Echo and Narcissus.

Merry mentions Cowley directly, and by her real name, in *The Laurel of Liberty*. He claims to be inspired by her. In olden times, he explains, poets were nothing. But his relation to Cowley is in the mode of "to come," in a way that suggests that he has been making allusions to the future:

> Nor yet, as *once*, for graceful COWLEY's brow
> He blends the laurel and the myrtle bough;
> Drinks her rich strain with extacy divine,
> Dares the bold flight, and maddens on the line,
> . . . [and so he] weaves with haste th'enthusiastic verse.
> Or should past times recur,—Tho' days of old
> Their perish'd, proudest pageantry unfold.[74]

In this passage, Merry attempts to navigate a contretemporal impasse: his *current* writing occurs "nor yet," but also in the present, given the conjugation of the verbs ("blends," "drinks," "dares," "maddens," "weaves") and the emphatic "with haste." We have two times existing within one time. The combination of so many verbs at once suggests a splintering apart of the present; these things are what Merry's persona is presently doing "nor yet" but also "as once." The alternative to this frayed temporality would be a repetition, in the present, of the past, which is also something which would seem to happen in the present: the days of old "unfold" in the here and now. To read Cowley, Merry suggests, is to break apart the meaning of the present and the very act of being oneself. He gives tribute to Cowley's ways of giving tribute to him—and for this, as we have seen, Robinson gives tribute to him for Cowley's special propensity for rejecting Merry's tributes to Robinson.

By offering tribute to Cowley, Merry suggests that a poet opens the future, but in a historical mode that connects the "now" to a global history of Europe, Africa, and Asia. That is what Cowley makes possible, in Merry's estimation: she creates the conditions for the French Revolution, which he sees as a fracture in the present. It is a break with centuries of history. This is consistent with Reinhard Koselleck's argument that "until the eighteenth century it was an almost universally accepted doctrine that one could, from the history of the past, learn lessons for the future." This changed, though, in "the decade from 1789 to 1799, [which] was experienced by the participants as the start of a future that had never yet existed."[75] In Merry's terms, we saw "the work of ages shatter'd in an hour."[76] History, all of a sudden, would have to become conscious of a gap between the singularity of an event and the structures in which the event was experienced. History would be what "shows us the boundaries of the possible otherness of our future without having to do without the structural conditions of possible repetition."[77] History as we know it, explains Merry, is "a web-work of despair, a mass of woes."[78] The Revolution in France, he argues, is not part of this history. The "hour" of the present in France is totally different from the present given to us by the past: "O how unlike Gallia at this hour."[79] Seemingly aligning the Revolution to the future by way of women's bodies and their fertility, he delights to live in "An æra, pregnant with the hopes of Man!"[80] "Man," in this formulation, has hopes only in the mode of "to come"; women like Cowley, he suggests, are *currently* living this hope-to-come as their reality. To the extent that hopes belong to men, it is only insofar as men can "fertilize the soul."[81]

Here we find the fulfillment of Slavoj Žižek's claim that "the ultimate obstacle to the sexual relationship is, of course, history itself, history at its most radical—not just a combination of narratives (stories), but the dense inertia and opacity of the Real."[82] Merry seems to take this obstacle seriously as the basis of a revolutionary politics of the not-whole. This is why Merry thinks about Cowley—who was writing *after* the start of the revolution—as the *cause* of the revolution, a force of negation that brings the future into the present and makes world history irrelevant. She is living in his future already, which is how Cowley's verse, for Merry, negates the negation at the heart of contemporary politics: "O! better were it, ever to be lost / In black Negation's sea, than reach the coast / Where naught appears but prospects dull."[83] That is, the "dull" future predicted by past history is to be disregarded in favor of a new negation. Cowley negates the nothing ("where naught appears") that had driven established world history. Merry, without guarantees of success, resolves to bet on this small sliver of futurity, despite its negative character and the long odds of it emerging from the past: "the chance is this, / One in a hundred thousand tastes of bliss!"[84]

Žižek argues that "social order," "history," and "time" are marked by particularity, a not-all that ensures that chronologies remain incomplete. Hence, "we are universal beings only in our full partial engagements."[85]

History is not a universal view of which people find themselves a part; rather, "the event of the subject derails the balance, it throws the world out of joint, but such a derailment is the universal truth of the world."[86] There is no universal absolute, merely the inability to step beyond one's own perspective.[87] Such a temporality is at the heart of Merry's endeavor. The Preface to *The Laurel of Liberty* acknowledges that the poem will be unpopular. It predicts that the British press won't welcome it, and that its future reception will be even worse, given how the French aristocracy is already planning a counterrevolution. Yet, explains Merry, "THE CAUSE OF FREEDOM IS THE CAUSE OF ALL MANKIND."[88] As we have seen, though, this "all" emerges in the poem, ironically, through its very inability to become "all." Much as we saw with Robinson's *Ainsi va le Monde*, Merry formulates the "all" of a political universal through the cut of a "nor yet," which implies both proliferation and deferral. The "cause" functions more like an instigating interruption (e.g., the object *petit a*) than a political platform: to take up a political "cause" means to affirm the excessive, negating *cause* of freedom that cuts apart the body politic and gives rise to the "all" of "all mankind." The "all" emerges in and through the minoritarian position as a cut in the historical experience. The universal is already particular given the cut given by its own excessive cause. That is how, in Žižek's terms, "our universe emerges out of its own impossibility, i.e., it is the obstacle to being which sustains being."[89]

The poem can, in this sense, be seen as something queer and utopian, in the way proposed by José Esteban Muñoz:

> [It] transports us across symbolic space, inserting us in a coterminous time when we witness new formations within the present and the future. The coterminous temporality of such performance exists within the future and the present, surpassing relegation to one temporality (the present) and insisting on the minoritarian subject's status as world-historical entity. The stage and the street, like the shop floor [and poem!], are venues for performances that allow the spectator access to minoritarian lifeworlds that exist, importantly and dialectically, within the future and the present.[90]

In this case, the minoritarian position seems to belong to British women, who uniquely provide a cut in the "aera" and render it "pregnant" with "hope." The activation, and retroactive affirmation, of this obstacle within

132 FRACTURE FEMINISM

the context of minoritarian politics is exactly what gives meaning to what otherwise might seem to be the poem's inconsistent temporality. This is the formation that I have been calling contretempopia—a utopian time only present, so to speak, within a riven now.

There is a long section of *The Laurel of Liberty* in which Liberty speaks directly to the British reader, in quotation marks even. The voice of Liberty, like the voice of Cowley earlier in the poem, speaks from the future: she has already emigrated from France to Britain, and already accomplished her revolutionary task, when she speaks to the reader. Merry, presumably, is there too, because he is able to quote Liberty directly—and so Liberty, through Merry's archiving/recording impulse, affirms that she is already here in Britain.[91] Yet Merry, in the preface, asserts that British people are largely nervous of the French Revolution, because they do not like democratic change. Liberty indicates that she had actually arrived in England in the thirteenth century, in time to sign the Magna Carta, and that everything has, against all appearances, been well ever since. But she warns that if the past ever comes back in the future, she will be ready to do what she is currently doing in France: "*Then*, shall my best beatitude conceal'd / From HER, be to new constituents reveal'd" and "So shall my meliorating mercy run."[92] Liberty here makes a prophecy about the return of England's past as the imposition of the French present in the future. Merry suggests that we are now living in the future, thanks to Cowley/ Liberty, but if the past were ever to return, the present (i.e., the future of the contemporary future) would know Liberty's merciful wrath. "SHE SPOKE, AND VANISH'D, as the vision past, / A groan of anguish murmur'd in the blast," he says, entering Liberty's prophecy into the historical record.[93] In the movement between past, future, and present, and across the English Channel, Merry achieves the queer utopian goal of "coterminous temporality" situated in the fracture of "symbolic space."

The Two Della Cruscas of Two "To Della Crusca"s

The politics of not-all explored by Merry, in *The Laurel of Liberty*, and Robinson, in *Ainsi va le Monde*, had already been long established in Della Cruscan verse. The Della Cruscans had associated queer temporality with France since even before the Revolution. Cowley would sometimes respond to Merry's erotic playfulness with complex meditations on time, in ways that open into the contemporary future. Cowley recognizes it especially in "To Della Crusca," one of her many poems of that title, published in *The World* on May 20, 1788. This iteration of "To Della Crusca" is unusual because Cowley begins to apostrophize her own avatar, Anna Matilda. The speaker, confronting the sorrow of Merry's upcoming travels to Greece, warns herself, that is, "Matilda," that "thy future *days* / [are] Lost to the Muses and to Taste," such that "Each torpid hour will joyless waste."[94] In effect, there are two Della Cruscas in "To Della Crusca," once Anna Matilda begins to interpellate herself, too, through the combined apostrophe and dedicatory title. At first, Anna Matilda is envious of Della Crusca because he soon gets to visit the land of Sappho; she wonders how she might one day experience such a thing herself. In an inventive twist of argument, she concludes that she could best accomplish this not by following him, but by traveling through France, "where thoughtless Pleasure ever reigns."[95] Her confidence that authorities in France will "ever reign" is *very* 1788. Anna Matilda advises Anna Matilda that traveling to France would enable her/me to become an English Sappho—a nickname soon to be appropriated by Mary Robinson, no less. Visiting France is treated as the best way to become fully English in one's sapphism. Cowley is excited not for the travel itself, but for the possibility of being so quickly entangled in circuits of repetition, both classical and Della Cruscan, to the extent that European travel is, for her, a journey through time rather than space. Anna Matilda, though soon to be tragically separated from her lover—whom, in any case, was only an avatar for Robert Merry, whom Cowley had never met in real life—cross-temporally reunites with him by becoming the reincarnation of the poet whose birthplace he is soon to be visiting. She aims to live in Della Crusca's future as if it were ancient literary history. This is how a poem that opens "Oh stay, oh stay! . . . Not *yet* ascend the flying deck"—which reverses the "Go, idle boy!" with which Merry had inaugurated the entire sequence of poems in "The Adieu and Recall to Love"—can so quickly settle in to a plan of international travel: the speaker's own ascent of the flying deck is experienced in the mode of "not yet."[96] It is also how a speaker who urges Della Crusca "not yet" to "ascend the flying deck" can meanwhile lament, watching his distant vessel disappear into the horizon, "Alas! Thou'rt gone."[97] In her "not yet," she is traveling through the past, which is why his present can be styled as her future, and things she predicts for herself are happening "now."[98]

No sooner does she announce this plan, than she thinks better of it: "No! Bard Belov'd," she cries out, changing her mind, and again apostrophizing both Della Cruscas: "*I* too must leave this laurel'd coast

/ . . . But not like thee, for GRECIAN shores." The paradox of "*I* too . . . but not like thee" cathects the difference at the heart of repetition. She resolves to do something different, which is to carry on with exactly the same plan as before (i.e., to go to France rather than to Greece), but to shift its meaning. Her French resolution becomes a French revolution, as the discourse through which she will have experienced her travels finds itself enduring a quarter-turn.

She has shifted into what Lacan would call the "discourse of the university."[99] Anna Matilda resolves to collect the field of all poetic knowledge (i.e., Della Crusca + Sappho + all English poetry) in order to address surplus jouissance itself: she speaks to "the boasted bliss" of "rich refulgence," which remains impossible to accommodate temporally, ex-sisting only in the time of "Ne'er." This effect she calls "Dawn," both an impossible horizon and a reliable occurrence. This orientation produces a cut in the symbolic field itself, and she emerges as a split subject, an "I" separated from "Della Crusca" through the very force of exact duplication. Having produced this impossible cut, separating her temporally from herself and from her lover, she "*will* [i.e., in the future] *greet the Dawn* where thou [i.e., Della Crusca] hast waked."[100] There are three levels of deferral here: she "hope[s]" that she "will" "greet the Dawn." This is proliferating difference produced, again, through repetition and temporal torsion—she hopes to greet the dawn "where thou hast waked" by walking "the same [French] turf where sunk thy head."[101] Yet she already can describe the resplendent colors of dawn, here a figure for a poetics to come, ever unrealizable. (Though a previous "To Della Crusca" poem had declared that, as a result of reading Merry's verse: "Day's radiance pours upon my eye. / I wake—I live!"[102]) By describing a future that she will have seen, which is here presented as both her lover's own past ("where thou has waked") and her own past ("I wake"), Cowley begins to write from a time subsequent to her own death. She thus speaks of a "lasting silence" that will have characterized her voice, a silence paradoxically enacted when she "murmurs DELLA CRUSCA's name."[103] This master signifier is the secret truth of her atemporal, erotohistoriographical discourse. It is as though they communicate over long distances by living in different eras, speaking through silence, death, and repetition.

Cowley's interest in fruitful but impossible landscapes becomes triangulated in a subsequent poem of the same title, "To Della Crusca" of February 26, 1789. Cowley, writing from Paris and again speaking as Anna Matilda, is disappointed with Merry for having written a love poem to Laura Maria, the avatar of Mary Robinson. Robinson, inspired by Merry's poetry to Anna Matilda, had written a poem to Della Crusca entitled "The Muse," published in October 1788, which bragged that her bond with Merry was intellectual rather than sexual; this led Merry, in November of that year, to develop a new avatar, "Leonardo," through which to publish a response to Laura in the newspaper; Robinson, as Laura, responded with a second poem, accusing him of being interested only in sex.[104] Thus we arrive at Cowley's response to Robinson's response to Merry's response to Robinson's response to Cowley, namely "To Della Crusca" of February 26, 1789, which accuses its addressee of infidelity and of hiding ineffectually behind his new pseudonym: "Oh! how impossible a task / To hide thy radiance in a mask!"[105] Cowley, here, directly claims the mantle of the fracture feminist as contemporary future historian.

In general, Labbe considers "the factor of time" to be "the most powerful threat to love" across the Della Cruscan poetic sequence, and "also the most inescapable, and mundane."[106] The poems seem to be plotted, loosely speaking, like a romance, Labbe argues, according to which "readers are privy to exclamations of desire, displays of sexual jealousy, the intrusion of sexual rivals."[107] All of this is on display in this "To Della Crusca." The poem warns us about the consequences of Della Crusca's sexual transgression: "never shall again his 'Golden Quill' / With magic passion every bosom thrill."[108] Cowley thus formulates the central paradox of the poem: she had been demanding monogamy from Della Crusca because she wants him to "thrill" "every bosom" "with magic passion." The poem conflates poetry with sex in manifold ways: writing poetry is understood to be a sex act just as reading poetry is shown to be a source of private erotic pleasure, as is typical across the Della Cruscan sequence.[109]

"To Della Crusca" is a poem about infidelity, disappointment, and, in a complicated way, revenge, all played out through the oxymoronic mechanism of what Cowley calls "future hist'ry."[110] Its landscape metaphors, which respond to Merry's own accounts of landscape in poems such as "Ode to Tranquillity," convert imagined space into imagined time, much as Barbauld's "On the Uses of History" and Williams's *Paul and Virginia* would do. Merry's poetry, always highly flirtatious and polyamorous, would frequently transgress the boundaries of propriety or good taste. Cowley's poem, in response, develops an admirably capacious model of poetic monogamy, which, at least as much as Merry had, challenges its era's standards of sexual decency, poetic form, and chronology. The poem depends on an unstable opposition between a forest, sometimes alternatively called the "woods" or "bower," and a plain. The speaker compares Merry's writing to agricultural efforts on a "plain" (64); the poetry is "fruit" grown by Merry's "salubrious toil."[111] This is already an unstable division, as fruit, let us admit, is as likely to be grown in a bower as on a plain. Yet Cowley's Merry, in an act of "wondrous magic," "calls food, and riches from the sterile soil."[112] The forest bower, on the other hand, is where one *reads* Merry's poetry, metaphorically speaking. This is a double entendre, as bower is also an outmoded poetic term for a woman's bedroom.[113] Although the poem encourages us to contrast the forest (i.e., the scene of reading) with the plain (i.e., the scene of writing), it also, in a kind of confusion of categories, asks us to compare the forest with the poetry itself, as both, we are told, are fruits of Merry's "CREATIVE LABOUR."[114] This crossing of categories implies that Merry's poetry is creating the conditions of its own reception, which is actually quite true. It has a paradoxical temporal structure, as does any entity that begets itself, the pleasures of the forest somehow furnishing the sunshine which then grows the poetic crops which, in turn, "drops flow'rs, and fruits, and forests o'er the land."[115]

The speaker, Anna Matilda, is trying to explain that she will be terminating her relationship with Della Crusca but not her love of his poetry. She will appreciate the poetry but not deign to inspire it, given Laura's interference. This decision of hers, we are told, is the "twilight" of the previously fecund field, a metaphor that retrofits the poem's spatial forest/plain binary for the alternative coordinates of temporality. It functions as a double metaphor: in one sense, it recites a sequence, according to which the plain must grow the poetry in the sun before those in the forest can enjoy it, activities which must all, apparently, be complete before twilight. Yet, because Anna Matilda reads in the forest and Della Crusca writes on the plain, the metaphor accentuates their physical separation and simultaneity. Hence a paradox emerges once Anna refuses to leave the forest, because that space will have depended upon the continuous productivity of the plain for it to have existed in the first place. Anna is affirming her right to remain in a place that cannot have existed, which is, once again, actually quite a perceptive thing to observe about readers of poetry in general. The irony of her *own* poetic composition, namely "To Della Crusca," remains unacknowledged, except implicitly through the meter and rhyme, which is strange for such self-referential poetry. In speaking from a future that will now no longer have happened, Anna Matilda becomes a divine arbiter of poetry. In a way, it is a suitable response to Robinson's poem "The Muse": Anna is claiming to be the muse of the muse of Robinson's muse, uniquely capable of luring "down his guardian Goddess from her throne."

Anna Matilda serves as broker between Della Crusca and his muse; without her, there will be no one to write Della Crusca's "future hist'ry," as she puts it.[116] "Future hist'ry" is an important oxymoron here, implying that the present is meaningless except as prelude to its recollection later. It is an *après coup* formation. The poem ends with a prophecy given in quotation marks, supposedly the words of the Goddess, which states, although only conditionally, that if Della Crusca should ever "sing" to "another nymph," he will lose the divine "flow" of "my fire."[117] It is a fitting phrase, further conflating Anna Matilda with the Goddess, as in both cases poetic power comes not from Merry but from a female voice inside of him, who begins to be noticed and credited only once she has withdrawn. A chicken-and-egg conundrum emerges, duplicating the logic of the self-begetting forest: if Merry's poetry is so beautiful that it alone can inspire Anna Matilda's erotic pleasure, and yet that pleasure is the only conduit to the divinity that makes such writing possible, then it is not clear how Merry's poetry could ever exist in the first place. Della Cruscan poetry is relegated to the field of the impossible, and the present is here shown to coincide with the future, in the sense that the Goddess "whilst she pour'd the richest of her store, / And charm'd his heart with bright poetic lore, / Prophetic, thus his future hist'ry read."[118] The "pouring" and "charming" are *thus* (i.e., necessarily) readings of Della Crusca's future history. The present cannot exist, except as a scene awaiting its own historicization at, and through, the very moment of poetic inspiration. Consequently, the "future hist'ry" of the poem precedes even its actual composition. Moreover, the poem meets its match in "To Della Crusca," which, in actually performing the debut reading of the prophecy in its final verse paragraph, performatively enacts the revenge that it worries it might one day predict.

Anna Matilda constructs her revenge as a fulfillment of the prophecy, treating what had been a conditional warning about the future as an accomplished fact that can justify her withdrawal from Della Crusca. As per the prophecy, Anna Matilda shows that she can distinguish between Della Crusca the poet and Della Crusca the lover, bidding "farewel," in the fifth verse paragraph, to the "FALSE Lover! [and] TRUEST Poet!" alike.[119] The distinction between poet and lover is, on its face, preposterous, mostly because Della Crusca is not a real person, but also because Cowley had had contact with Merry only through their published verse, and that the *faux pas* was Merry's writing a poem. But the poet/lover distinction is nevertheless crucial to the poem, which registers its shock by switching here from iambic tetrameter to trochaic pentameter for one line, "FALSE Lover! TRUEST Poet! now farewell," and then settling into relatively prim iambic pentameter for what remains. The permanent shift in the poem's meter, signaling irrevocable harm, marks this moment as a crisis in the poem. The stressed monosyllabic words "FALSE," and "Hark!," the former of which is completely capitalized and the latter which is superfluous to the point of becoming-Alexandrine, generate spondees that seem to herald a major reconsideration of the lovers' relationship. It is a crisis, especially, of temporality, as suggested by the performative force of "now farewell." Anna Matilda is beginning to test the now of this now.

If Della Cruscan poetry represents a "true" poet's mastery of the exquisite art of sublimating sex into poetry, then this "To Della Crusca" undoes that process, teaching its speaker to glean sexual enjoyment from poetry directly, instead of through a "false lover," before re-sublimating this practice into rhyming lines called "To Della Crusca." By cutting off Della Crusca's access to the muse, Cowley suggests a change in the forest's affective ecosystem that, however sorrowful, might generate its own alternative pleasures:

> Why sigh the winds tumultuous thro' the woods.
> Why weeps the Night in such impetuous floods?
> It is the loss of DELLA CRUSCA's Muse,
> Which thus with sorrow every plant imbues.[120]

If Merry's infidelity has produced a storm in the erotic forest, the consequent "chilling breezes" can, at a meta-level, create independent scenes of seduction:

> Soft drizzling rain, the patter'd trees confess,
> And chilling breezes on my bosom press.
> My hair, whose curls, late floated o'er my breast,
> Weighty with moisture, clings around my vest—[121]

This diction, featuring words like "confess," "bosom," "breast," "moisture," and "clings," is nearly pornographic by British late-eighteenth-century newspaper standards, and the lines, by all four rhyming, invite us to linger here twice as long as we really ought. The spondees of "soft drizzling" and "late floated" combine with the trochaic substitution in "weighty with" to suggest a dangerous pleasure developed around what the speaker calls the "am'rous touch" of the trees.[122] In that sense, the forest of reading transforms its own inclemency into a scene of solitary sexual enjoyment. If Merry's poetry can no longer be Cowley's erotic forest, the erotic forest itself can begin to serve as poetry, which is how Della Crusca can be both a "true poet" and "false lover" after all. The price of this jouissance, however, is the diachronicity of time: the Goddess's prophecy must be fulfilled before it even has been issued; the monogamy of the future finds its history in new pleasures, through the transgression of its own poetic, sexual, and ideological regulations; and the *ars erotica* of reading will take precedence, and even precede, the technical procedures of writing.

Cowley analyzes the temporal warp most directly in "To Somebody at Margate," a poem published in *The World* on September 15, 1787, and signed, backwardly, by "Matilda Anna."[123] The poem uses Della Cruscan erotic techniques to fracture clock time and summon impossible, retrospective temporalities. Matilda Anna expresses sympathy for a lover who has been incarcerated at the eponymous prison for fifteen years and counting, and who has left his watch for safekeeping with her. She is hopeful that he will soon be released—but instead of just waiting, she wishes that "Time, eager like your Watch" might "compress" hours into moments. Thus, the present time of her lover's incarceration would already be past: "And I should *retrospective* see / Those weeks, which now in prospect hover."[124] Basically, Matilda Anna is speaking from a conditional future about a nearer and more immediate future, which she identifies as "now." This is perhaps the epitome of fracture feminism, given the way that the poem pries the conditional future apart from the contemporary future. In the next two stanzas, Matilda begins to apostrophize Time directly, but seemingly to make the opposite point: she urges it first to "obey" the dictates of "this Watch" rather than lagging lazily behind, and next to "O'ertake the Watch, nor bid it stay!" She is no longer waiting primarily for the parole of her lover, but for the restoration of clock time: she anticipates a time, "one short fortnight" away, when her lover will be released from prison and the clock may "tick, tick, tick, as heretofore."[125] It is as if the speaker has sublated the fracture between subjective temporality and objective time, and is attempting to suture the relation from the other side. Her expressions of sympathy and longing jostle against the iambic tetrameter, deforming the cadence of the poem and making possible, in their play against it, a contemporary future as a function of desire. The speaker

140   FRACTURE FEMINISM

directly associates clock time with the state's apparatuses of repression, but throws that affiliation into doubt by asking Time to "be civil," as she attempts, both by direct request and through the experiments in rhythm, to decree an early parole *for time itself* through the force of her desire.[126] The watch, at once "left behind" and running "too fast," aligns its motions with the subjective temporality of desire rather than clock time, and so is rendered useless as a watch but instrumental for love. Nevertheless, because the speaker has asked Time to take on the affective qualities associated with the watch—that is, to approximate the watch's eagerness—the poem also closes the gap between them without regularizing anything. The gulf between watch and time, as dramatized by the failure of the speaker's wishes to become performative, remains impossible to discern but decisive for the experience of eroticism.

Merry's Polypoetics: An Experiment in Llanguage

Time is clearly askew throughout the flirtatious exchange in *The World*, even to the extent that, as Labbe observes, the "Della Crusca/Anna Matilda romance begins to take on the confusing aura of having pre-existed its own composition."[127] In "To Del Crusca: The Pen," Michael Gamer observes, Cowley superimposes herself onto Merry's "The Adieu and Recall to Love" "by presenting two separate events simultaneously."[128] In the above section, I have indicated the atemporal import of Cowley's responses to Merry. In this section, I will identify the source of that temporal fracture: namely, the queer erotics at work in Merry's verse as poetry taps into jouissance at the level of llanguage. Merry, I will suggest, finds a way to stuff sexual enjoyment into the signifier in a way that counteracts meaning, a technique that is then adopted, and openly admired, by Cowley and Robinson in their responses.

     To illustrate this tendency in Merry's verse, I here turn to two of his early Della Cruscan poems, "The Adieu and Recall to Love" and "Ode to Tranquillity." These poems were published in *The World* in the Summer of 1787. Although these poems (like Cowley's meditation on Margate prison, written shortly thereafter) ostensibly present love as a kind of longing or absence, an affective field subjected to a logic of confinement and deprivation, the rhyme, diction, allegory, consonance, and meter collude to reduplicate desires, turning eroticism into something multiple and provisional. Merry, in these poems, develops a polyamorous poetics: the *techne* of his verse becomes, in a Lacanian sense, "women's writing"

DELLA CRUSCAN TIME   141

as it challenges a culture of sexuality increasingly focused on monogamy and intimacy. His technique offers, in its own right, a kind of resistance to chronormativity, and would, once it gets adopted by Cowley and Robinson, become essential to Della Cruscan fracture feminism overall.

In both of these poems, Merry takes an eroticism apparently rooted in twoness—that is, in the monogamous and self-sufficient couple—and exposes it to the risk of threeness. In a sexual culture that was beginning to fixate on the monogamous couple as the basic unit of meaning for human subjectivity, it is a subversive gesture.[129] The threeness that Merry extracts from the couple-unit will, when converted into surplus jouissance, become the foundation of the three-headed entanglements that we have seen Cowley confront. The jouissance of the threeness, arising from the llangue of poetry, exposes diachronic time to the object *petit a* that is the contemporary future. Merry shows how couples and couplets already contain, or prove themselves open to, a supplementary third, and thereby versifies a polyamorous erotics in an era of sexual restriction. Style, as llangue pushes beyond meaning, begins to allegorize the flirtatious poetic triangle established in the pages of *The World*. The stylistic threeness of Merry's verse lent itself particularly well to a triangular collaboration with Cowley and Robinson, and thereby made possible a form of eroticized "women's writing" that could trouble the militarized chrononormativity of the late eighteenth century.

If I focus primarily though not exclusively on poetic form in discussing these two Merry poems, it is because Della Cruscan poetry so foregrounds its devices: as Daniel Robinson notes, "much of the poetry is about formal and metrical play."[130] Labbe goes yet further, claiming that "Della Cruscan poetry projects an erotics of form" that tests "the barrier separating romance and pornography."[131] "The Adieu and Recall to Love" has rhyming couplets in iambic tetrameter broken into two verse paragraphs; there is limited enjambment, as the poem generally tries to contain its ideas within the couplets. The couplet, I would hazard, is a sexually normative device: it reifies the couple as an atomic unit of meaning, until the world, as represented in the poetry, seems a pleasing, natural procession of couples, each self-contained. "The Adieu" might seem like a poem that aspires to coupledom, worrying as it does about "roguish leers," but it hides a polyamorous streak in its poetic language: as Merry's alliteration competes against a procession of rhyming couplets, the poem strains to usher its argument about love through multiple asymmetrical and conflicting sonic commitments.

The poem suggests that one is never really in control of one's desires. Merry's title discloses the entire plot of the poem: the speaker first asks love, apostrophized as an "idle Boy," to spare him the "roguish leer" of erotic entanglement; the speaker then changes his mind, asking love to "hasten back . . . with all thy torments."[132] The pleasure of the poem is in the *fort/da* movement of adieu and recall, which lends the poem a sense of repetition, and the poem ends with the speaker asking permission to "love again."[133] There is a hopelessness to the request, such that love would seem to come and go, never fully at one's behest. In its repetitive movement, the poem opens into the future, but cancels its own records in the process. Derrida explains this paradox best: "If repetition is thus inscribed at the heart of the future to come, one must also import there, *in the same stroke*, the death drive, the violence of forgetting, . . . in short, the possibility of putting to death the very thing, whatever its name, which *carries the law in its tradition*."[134] In much this way, as Merry seeks to establish, in newspaper poetry, a polyamorous poetics, in the course of so doing he instantiates, through his contemplation of love as a way to "love again," a loop of desire that dismantles or scatters any attempt to build its archive.

This does not appear to be a discourse of overlapping and multiple erotic opportunities, at least at first blush. The binary structure of the poem's argument makes love seem quite clear-cut: it is either here or gone, and only when it is gone is it appealing. At first, it might not seem like an especially polyamorous poem: Merry imagines love as love for a single object, either here or gone, perching in only one place at once, and especially mourned in absentia, with the agonizing jouissance and "frozen apathy" of the Petrarchan tradition.[135] Nevertheless, the poem posits that erotic experience must be mediated by an "idle Boy," who, despite being just an allegorical figure, and just a boy, and apparently quite idle to boot, must be called upon to bless any erotic experience: "But let me, let me love again," the speaker begs.[136] Love, in this formulation, very quickly exceeds its allegorical depiction, such that the personified cupid-figure takes on a jouissance of his own. There is a suggestion of erotic play in the begging, for instance, that turns any imagined erotic encounter with Louisa into *ménage à trois*. Through the apostrophe to Love, this becomes a poem in search of alternative erotic gratifications, especially the gratifications of longing and deprivation. Pleasure here is never remembered as one's own pleasure: the speaker mourns the loss of "each warm desire to please," and forswears the pursuit of "others bliss."[137] It is a poem that aims to please.

DELLA CRUSCAN TIME 143

The speaker sounds a bit bitter in recommending "Louisa's breast" to love: he misses, he says, "The Virgin of the Night." By providing a single female name as the site of "pleasures past," the speaker endorses a monogamous framework for love; by prizing her virginity above all else, he shows an investment in monopolizing and controlling his partner's sexual life.[138] Yet when someone is proclaimed a virgin specifically of the night, it implies that they have been sexually active during the day. The gesture subjects love to clock time and, from within those auspices, begins searching for loopholes. The love that is mourned here is apparently non-normative: deprived of love, the speaker resolves to walk, heretofore, "no more with devious step," implying that his love had previously been devious in some delightful way.[139] Much as we saw Cowley doing in her "To Della Crusca" poems, Merry describes, in the present tense emphatically, his own past as love's future. This is fracture feminism at work.

The formal commitments of the poem redouble this tension. On the one hand, the poem is written in couplets, and may be seen to mourn the loss of coupledom generally. The speaker resorts to couplets even to forswear love itself, as if all erotic life, even in the negation, can only and ever be organized in pairs. At the same time, the poem is quite alliterative, and this constrains the speaker in ways that cut against the competing demands of the rhyme scheme: the poem opens with a cascade of hard and soft *t* sounds: *thorn, thy, twanging, thine, tender, thrilling,* and *tear.* The variable softness and sharpness of these sounds soon gives way to a romp of consonant *f*s: *fare, free,* and *flutter,* each insinuating that words like "fuck" and "fornicate" are close at hand. The speaker escapes them only to arrive at a Charybdis of *l*s: "lave thee in thy lucid spring" links its washing, phonetically, to Louisa, mentioned soon thereafter. Next, the sensuous *w*s of "wanton wing" and "wish thee well," risk the word "woman," recalling, metonymically, Louisa's breast, which has just been remembered as a haven of abandoned delights.[140] The alliteration, then, is multiple, various, and dynamic—polyamorous, even: the speaker is committed to alliteration *per se*, but makes multiple phonetic commitments, and exercises these over and above the temporalized demands of rhyme and meter. It is llanguage: "jouissance [that] can be heard in the 'body' of language."[141] Even as the speaker is sending love away and bidding it adieu, he is staging, through alliteration, this jouissance. It signals his feminine sexuation, claiming ex-sistence in direct relation to the Other. This structure, as it intrudes into any attempt at a sexual relation, suggests Lacan, may be the ultimate and irreducible form of the *ménage à trois*.[142] The speaker may well be committed to the idea of the monogamous couple as a sacrosanct unit, as his investments in virginity and Louisa imply, and as his use of the couplet form demands; meanwhile, though, he is exploring multiple, diverse, and dynamic pleasures. These pleasures hardly disrupt the emphasis on coupledom—the couplets and remembrances carry on unabated—but nestle alongside coupledom and within coupledom, as a supplementary feature. As the poem's alliteration plays against its rhyme scheme and meter, constraining what the speaker can think and say, we find Merry playfully exploiting the possibilities of several and multiple commitments at once. After a while, one set of commitments begins to contaminate the other, or expand its range: the alliterative internal slant rhyme of "bless" and "breast," especially, dangerously supplements the end-rhymed couplet, forcing the poem to accommodate extra and other forms of rhyme and, by extension, other kinds of love.[143] As it develops this formal allegory for polyamory, the poem stalls as it attempts to articulate its argument against love. It is as if love is the name for the break or discontinuity itself—the fracture in time that attempts to make up for the lack in a sexual relationship.[144] The second verse paragraph, then, finds the speaker repeating himself unnecessarily in a kind of haplessness solved only through an expressed wish for erotic suffering. In this way, the arguably normative impulses of the rhyming couplet and iambic tetrameter meet their limits and are forced into "a frozen apathy" better adapted for nonconforming erotic encounters yet awaited.[145]

In the "Ode to Tranquillity," published just a month later, Merry dispenses with rhyme altogether, offering instead unrhymed quatrains. These too, though, imply a commitment to the couple as a unit, as the quatrains, through their meter, become grouped into twos: the first two lines of each quatrain are written in iambic pentameter, while the second two are in iambic trimeter. This gives the second part of each quatrain a jarring effect: the speaker's reflections seem, as a result of the sudden trimeter, very direct and concise. Yet sometimes these shorter lines are enjambed, which has an interesting effect. Read aloud, the lines "While in majestic Pomp's / Magnificent array," feel like an alexandrine rather than two short lines; the seemingly stable duality of the poem's structure gives way to the distinct possibility of *extra* and *excess* and *three*.[146] Merry consistently, throughout his early Della Cruscan poems, finds a way to turn couples into threes. This, I will suggest, is essential to his erotic project overall: for Merry, three-way sex is never an alternative to the logic of the couple, but a concealed part of any couple. Merry is a thinker, here again, of the dangerous supplement, an added third, that emerges alongside and within the very structure of normative sexuality, respecting its demands but always threatening to expand and destabilize it at the same time. Lacan would say that this structure is an outgrowth of the nonrelation—the fracture—that structures sexual life.

Sometimes the enjambment even connects one stanza to another, to form a freewheeling and expansive vision of eroticism. Here, for instance, we are told that Fancy "views the scene below, / Where the contending youths // Humble the yellow CERES, or gay groups / Of blushing maidens tread the verdant lawn."[147] The caesura after CERES, working in concert with the shocking "or," makes the tableau difficult to follow syntactically. To what does the "or" pertain? Is the question *what happens in this place* or *whom do the youths humble*? That is, even whilst being caught in the disarray of the enjambed stanzas, the reader must decide, despite some difficulty, if the youths can elect humble the ceres *or* the maidens, or instead, if Fancy is watching a place where two things can happen: youths can humble ceres, *or* maidens can tread the lawn. Further, the parts of speech seem in disarray, suggesting a sexual darkness: shepherd youths, conventionally the picture of humility, here "humble" as an active verb. "To humble" is quite a strange verb to place in this scene, with its suggestion of humiliation and exploitation. Here, just as adjectives bleed into the verbs, the ideas overspill their quatrain, and the syntax renders the scene undecidable, so too does the erotic spectacle overflow the vantage point: the very blushing of the maidens suggests their embarrassment at, and thus awareness of, being watched by Fancy. This too is llanguage. Through it, Merry presents an excessive sexuality that respects yet breaks open the expectations that await it. This effect is augmented as the suggestion of rhyme begins to infiltrate the generally unrhymed verse, always crossing boundaries between quatrains and connecting them: "cares" and "ear" end contiguous lines in stanzas two and three, "array" and "DAMES" do something similar in stanzas eight and nine, while "vale" and "cell" are separated by only one line, in stanzas five and six.

The situation becomes ambiguous and fluid, four lines becoming three, and pentameter giving way to trimeter and then, apparently, hexameter. Amidst this ambiguity, the speaker scrambles to recuperate lost forms of erotic pleasure from the wreckage of poetic form: "every bliss is lost," Merry warns, but "Echo sad returns."[148] It is, in effect, a meta-echo, the return of a return of the voice, the return of a return of once-discarded jouissance, as if Merry has realized that "drives are the echo in the body of a fact of

146   FRACTURE FEMINISM

saying."[149] The quest for tranquility ends only with death, and a hapless plea
not to be devoured posthumously by ravenous birds. Discarding a vision
of "the couch / Of mutual love," here Merry imagines a "maid" who can
be located only once she is lost forever, indeed one whom one can make
love to after her death through the very act of renouncing her sexually. It
reveals a "drive to figure" that becomes a manifestation of temporal drag.
To borrow again from Freeman, we have seen how the Della Cruscans
delight in "the act of plastering the body with outdated rather than just
cross-gendered accessories, whose resurrection seems to exceed the axis
of gender and begins to talk about, indeed talk back to, history."[150] The
poem narrates a personal quest for tranquility, here apostrophized as a
"modest maid." Merry's figural language folds upon itself in two similes
that undo, in their vehicle, the tenor they are meant to illustrate.

"Ode to Folly"'s Contretempopian Tropes

Merry's polyamorous poetics begin to have openly political effects as soon
as he begins to engage with questions of national security (i.e., beyond
just those of love). For Britons, the Great Siege of Gibraltar had become,
by 1787, an event saturated with patriotism. From 1779 to '83, the British
military had withstood a land and sea blockade from France and Spain,
despite high incidences of starvation and scurvy. After the British victory,
Gibraltar became a national symbol of military resilience; the courage of
the forces, as personified by commander George Augustus Eliott, became a
point of national pride badly needed as the American Revolutionary War
dragged on concurrently. Parks and streets were named after Eliott. Thus
it must have seemed unpatriotic for Merry, writing under his flamboyant
and sexually charged pseudonym, to treat the entire experience as simply
a case of folly on all sides. In "Ode to Folly," published in *The World* in
September 1787, he mocks "the loud bombastic drum / Of Patriots in,
or out of Place" and the repetitive marching of "forty thousand men."[151]
While this may be shocking enough, it is actually Merry's next step that
I find the most daring, for the poem then urges the reader to actually
stop seeing the Great Siege as an international demonstration of folly, as
if that interpretation were now a matter of course, and instead to consider
it from an unusually long historical perspective. This poem, through that
invitation, becomes particularly crucial to the history of feminist writing
about the contemporary future, given how Merry's imagery of caves, fos-

DELLA CRUSCAN TIME   147

sils, and home would be adopted by later writers in the fracture feminist tradition, such as Mary Wollstonecraft, Smith, Barbauld, and Charlotte Caroline Richardson.

Noting that "sea-shells" had been found upon "the inland mountain's height," Merry marvels that the mountains themselves may once have been the ocean's "crust."[152] The speaker asserts that "worldly symmetry, / Was hid in water long ago, / And sprang like Venus from the sea."[153] Merry describes Gibraltar as a peninsula lifted from the water, and as one of many such formations thus uplifted across Europe, each potentially embedded with fossilized reminders of their previous submarine existences. As Andrew Sargent suggests, nineteenth-century British poetry would invoke "the fossil and its citational structure" to expose "a vexed temporality" through its "radical negativity."[154] With fossils, Merry teaches the reader to see the nation's military victories from the perspective of geological time, and to see contemporary Europe as simply the long afterlife of the ocean floor. This long view of history depopulates Gibraltar more fully than the Franco-Spanish blockade ever could, enabling Merry to explore a mode of thought that we might call unexpectedly utopian despite its apocalyptic undercurrents, in the vein of what Chris Washington has called "romantic revelations."[155] If, as Labbe suggests, the Della Cruscan exchange was one "without hope," it also posits the very lack of hope as a positive presence around which to construct a political universal.[156] We have already seen him doing this, some three years later, in *The Laurel of Liberty*.

In "Ode to Folly," Merry was developing, in English sestets of iambic tetrameter, a geosyncline theory of vertical crustal movement about seventy years before the American geologists Hall and Dana would formulate the hypothesis scientifically. Through this verse, Merry would challenge the aura surrounding Eliott, whom Merry does acknowledge as "brave,"[157] and wade into his era's culture wars—and our own. The presence of fossilized shells in inland mountains remains a key talking point in today's creationist circles, which maintain, erroneously, that fossilized shells found in mountains prove that there was once a great flood of biblical proportions.[158] In the seventeenth and eighteenth centuries the phenomenon suggested the opposite conclusions. Nicolas Steno had concluded in 1667, from his analysis of fossilized shark teeth found on an Italian mountain, that fossils were of biological origin.[159] Although Steno had vastly upended religious doctrine about the age of the earth, his analysis proved persuasive in the scientific community. Alan Cutler explains that "out of these seventeenth-century ideas grew the modern concept of deep

148 FRACTURE FEMINISM

time, not to mention plate tectonics, evolution, global climate change, and dinosaurs."[160] Those long timescales would, by the Regency, become foundational to poetic engagements with history.[161]

The scientific consensus remained quite stable until the 1760s, when Voltaire proposed, with his own religious motivations, that fossilized inland shells were never underwater and may not have been organic—it was more likely, he said, that some inland travelers might have dropped some seafood as they made the mountain pass, or that limestone, being a soft rock, boasts the capacity to create inorganic land-seashells of its own.[162] Then, in the 1780s, Thomas Jefferson observed some fossilized clamshells in inland France and was moved to challenge Voltaire's conclusions. His *Notes on the State of Virginia*, first published in 1781 but republished in an expanded edition in February 1787—six months before the newspaper publication of Merry's poem—reinvigorated public debate about the inland sea-fossil phenomenon. Jefferson reviewed several possible explanations for the fossils—a global flood, the uplift of the mountains from the sea, and that fossils might not be biological material—but concluded that "the three hypotheses are equally unsatisfactory; and we must be content to acknowledge, that this great phenomenon is as yet unresolved."[163] Jefferson and Voltaire reopened for public debate a question that natural historians had, a century before, effectively settled. When "Ode to Folly" was published in the newspaper, its bold anticipation of geosyncline theory, specifically the hypothesis that mountains were pushed upward out of the ocean floor with attendant volcanic activity, Merry joined the vanguard of natural history but also founded a way thinking about temporality and politics that I would characterize as conflictingly nihilistic, contretempopian, and erotic. It is an early key text for fracture feminism. Merry is marking what Giorgio Agamben would call a "fault line" in time, which enables him "then [to] make of this fracture a meeting place, or an encounter between times and generations."[164] A poet especially associated with timeliness, having built his career on ephemeral newspaper poetry, is here finding a way to fracture the present and expose it to something radically asynchronous.

Merry begins to theorize the history of oceans, fossils, and lava in the crucial tenth through twelfth stanzas of the Ode. As the tenth stanza begins, the poem has just reached its emotional nadir, having formulated an alarmingly unpatriotic idea: that the Siege of Gibraltar, for so many a sublime spectacle "dreadful to behold," has proven to just be a colossal joke, the sly work of "Folly, with her Cap and Bells."[165] Even as fellow Britons celebrate "troops that scorn'd the thoughts of flight," Merry

DELLA CRUSCAN TIME   149

demands from those very troops "proof" that the earth's mountains were formed out of lava.[166] The demand signals Merry's scientific orientation, as well as his doubts about prevailing geological theories. Merry treats the earth itself as a repository of secret treasures that can reveal new registers of geological history representing eons of time. It also compounds the poem's nihilism, suggesting that even major political and military events deserve to be placed in extraordinarily long historical contexts that can only diminish their significance. The Siege of Gibraltar becomes a very brief episode in the longer, more important, and deadlier siege conducted by the earth itself, which seems poised eventually to destroy European civilization and even terrestrial life. This event, proceeding at the "steady pace" of geological time, shows up the lengthiness of the siege, which had seemed, to almost anyone working on a human timescale or with a modicum of sympathy, an eternity already.[167]

The speaker's bleak prediction, however, is presented as a form of scientific enquiry, the synthesis of various forms of knowledge. The speaker calls upon Folly to

> Bid many a circumstance combine,
> To make us comprehend the whole,
> And what now grows beneath the Line,
> Find petrified beneath the Pole.[168]

Merry's investigations here take on their scientific and sexual character, as geology becomes a playful gaze at the earth's metaphorical genitals. This extends the sexual character of geopolitics, as Merry perceives them, into the geological register: an earlier passage in the poem explores an international masochistic conceit, according to which Folly, the "dear Mistress," teaches France, Spain, and England to enjoy "your sway" as it binds them in chains, wounds them with darts, and catches them smiling at their wounds.[169] Suddenly again, the diction becomes embarrassingly suggestive, with Merry's use of "combine," the homophonic "whole," and his prurient interest in "what now grows beneath the Line." The entire eleventh stanza treats geology as a sexual act or as the infiltration of the earth's gonads, which makes the aforementioned "red-hot crust" of lava flow seem like the earth's ejaculate. The repetition of "beneath the line" and "beneath the Pole" suggest further and further excavations, where one might "find" the earth's organisms "petrified." The excavation of fossils in limestone, of which Gibraltar is made, is presented as a way feeling into the earth's pants—the Romanticist in me wants to breathe a pun about the Earth's "fast thick pants"—to discover the earth's erection, the petrification of its Pole. Merry continues it all the more wildly, to suggest that the fossils discovered in the limestone function as embryos of a sort: "Then strive the contr'ry to implant, / And wave your wand and we shall grant."[170] The scientific diction fuses with a rhetoric of magic and phallicism, through which Folly, which had so recently been commanded to "prove this globe was cover'd o'er" by lava, apparently compels us to grant its wishes.

The poem indicates that it will grant a magic wand's wish for the "the contr'ry" of fossils. This is very strange and inverted, as magic wands do not have desires of their own, and even if they did it is unclear what the contrary of a fossil is or what the desire for one would entail. If fossils are associated with immortal death, perhaps the wand is wishing for fleeting life, by the logic of opposites supposedly at play? Or is it wishing for the animation of nonliving things instead of the petrification of organisms? Or perhaps the wand yearns for emergent rather than residual forms of life? Only the next verse—the aforementioned and especially aquatic twelfth verse—enables us to make interpretive progress:

> With clear discussion plainly show,
> That all this worldly symmetry,
> Was hid in water long ago,
> And sprang like Venus from the sea.
> While on the inland mountain's height
> Sea-shells confirm th'opinion right.[171]

The limestone thus becomes the proof of, and not simply the repository for, fossilized seashells. The language of confirmation fulfills the speaker's own previous demand for "truth," which again here suggests a set of scientific procedures. That demand is amplified by the rhythm of the hyphenated word "sea-shells," representing the only variation to the poem's otherwise exceptionally obedient meter. This unique trochaic substitution suggests that the very term "sea-shells" is a separate, living remnant of another discourse frozen perpetually in the meter of the poem but made of different stuff. As the hyphen in "sea-shells" redoubles that suggestion, the term begins to operate as an alien body embedded in a mountain of Della Cruscan iambs—that is, the term "sea-shells" becomes, within the poem, a kind of metaphorical seashell. And so too does the rock formation emerge "like Venus," as a beautiful goddess not subject to time, and thus, it would follow, impervious to the deprivations of a siege.

DELLA CRUSCAN TIME   151

Merry hopes that the ensuing "discussion" will "plainly show" that everything—all political and sexual life, representing the *bios* and *zoe* of all terrestrial species—was once underwater. It may appear as if Merry is saying that fossils are the opposite of fossils—that the opposite of old petrified material is the idea that we will ourselves be dead and petrified one day. But it is not the fossil that finds its contrary, but our perspective on it: we discover that we ourselves are the opposite of a fossil, per the wish we will have granted to our magic wand, once we learn to take ourselves as ancient history in the making, rather than the discoverers or interpreters of geological signs. Contemporary politics is already belated in its negotiations of the future, and Merry envisions a future time when the world will have been finally been petrified. That future time, he suggests, is now.

All of this, however, turns out to be merely the vehicle of an unusually elaborate set of nested similes, as the speaker cries: "So shall I love you, ever-changing!" in the next sestet.[172] I imagine that the "you" refers primarily to Folly itself, to whom the poem is generally apostrophized, but part of the reason that "you" is "ever-changing" is because "you" also interpellates the reader, the poem's rhetorical "you"; the poem suddenly and unexpectedly, given the subject matter here, offers the reader the speaker's love. Love is offered in the future tense undyingly but yet via the threat of extinction, to a newspaper reader who can be loved specifically for her or his propensity to change. That propensity can even be demonstrated at the level of form, through our very susceptibility to enter unwittingly into the chains of substitution enacted by Merry's tropes. It is in this particular sense that we, as the beloved auditor, actually become "Folly," in the sense that we have been forced to become an allegory for the subversion, substitution, and deferment of meaning at the level of trope. Merry thus literalizes at the level of trope, if only ironically, his "Bid [to] make many a circumstance combine / To make us understand the whole": the reader is like Folly in the sense that we are dynamic and figural, much as the limestone of Eliott's Gibraltar is like the limestone of Jefferson's France and Steno's Italy, which are all like the goddess Venus, in that they arose from the sea; they are adorned with seashells, which are like the trochaic substitution "sea-shells," and which are like a magic wand, which is like a fossil, which is like a hardening penis, which is like a phallus, a signifier standing in for another signifier, and which, being discovered, gets transported, just as we have done, to the distant future, from which we will be like the contrary thing to today's fossils, meaning ourselves, emanating as we do from the distant future rather than the

152   FRACTURE FEMINISM

distant past, as Merry's "clear discussion" enables us to "plainly" grasp. The imagery is of epochal time and apocalyptic experience, as expressed through a rhetoric of fertility, virility, and scientific discovery, but the star of this show is trope itself.

Charmingly incoherent as it may be, therein lies the contretempopian impulse of the poem and its affiliation with fracture feminism. The speaker explains:

> And what is most ador'd to-day,
> From system still to system ranging,
> To-morrow shall be thrown away,
> And in the never-settled round,
> A glorious vacancy be found.[173]

This is more than the relativism it seems to be. It is true that Merry here suggests, again nihilistically, that cultural values are meaningless because they are subject to revision and renegotiation. But the temporal aspect of this claim complicates it and makes it politically redemptive: Merry is not positing the "never-settled round" as an established fact but a transition in transition. That is, the very transition "from system still to system ranging" allows those temporalities to run concurrently. "To-morrow" is the very thing getting discarded, which leaves behind "a glorious vacancy," which, like the fossilized remains of the future, "shall . . . be found." He is saying that the glorious vacancy—meaning the absence of a tomorrow, so really a term for the unknown—can be "found" already now. But the discovery will require our abandonment of any sense that tomorrow comes after today. Our cultural values exist only in abeyance, awaiting their chance to be discarded and so producing, in the here and now, "a glorious vacancy" at the heart of cultural politics. That vacancy is, in essence, a gap between two concurrent systems of time: the "system still" and "system ranging." The discarded future, in this unusual situation, is "found" to be already embedded in the present, and thus can be excavated and marveled at. This is the sort of gesture that Julia Kristeva would call "women's time," a mode of oppositional antichrononormative timekeeping that exists in the gap between clock time and what she calls (following Nietzsche) "monumental time," as that gap "englobes these supranational, sociocultural ensembles within even larger entities."[174]

Love, experienced across that temporal gap both as a system still and a system ranging, unfolds as the impossible and deferred tenor of Merry's

DELLA CRUSCAN TIME 153

interlocking water tropes, ultimately revealing an impossible eco-utopian experience founded upon lack, "a glorious vacancy" that "to-morrow shall be thrown away." The ocean, for Merry, signals both lack and excess, that our retrievable treasures of the future are really ourselves as proliferating waste. The world is an archive of prehistoric experience and a future that will never transpire except now in its own absence, establishing the dynamics of the planet's "ranging," "ever-changing," "never-settled round." The figuration becomes jouissance, opening, as Lacan predicts, a "mirage-like path" that opens in the movement between what "stops not being written" to what "doesn't stop being written."[175] That is, as we see the negation shift from the cessation of a negative to the cessation of a cessation, we can finally encounter "the drama of love" in the absence of the sexual relation, emerging as contretempopia at the level of llanguage.[176]

"Ode to Folly" is a poem about erotics and politics, or more accurately the eroticism peculiar to politics. It concerns time, sex, the siege of Gibraltar, masochism, ecological and geological transformations, and the presence of fossilized sea life on land. These interests begin to cohere at the end of the tenth stanza, in which the speaker seductively invites Folly to "O hither come . . . And prove this globe was cover'd o'er, / With red-hot crust, in days of yore."[177] This is the real turn in the poem, which had previously been discussing the Siege of Gibraltar as an act of "folly." If there is life embedded in the earth, waiting to be uncovered by magic, then the politics of the contemporary moment, its wars and sieges and parliaments, will all be underwater and/or fossilized one day. Faced with a war that had deliberately attacked civilians, and that relied on starvation as a method of warfare, the speaker proposes a magic wish for the annihilation of all terrestrial life on Earth, and with the Freudian supplement that the dead and buried material will surely someday be exposed and circulated with wonderment. This is what Chris Washington would call "an incessant and irrepressible nihilism" that offers hope through the refusal of hope in "the crucible of extinction."[178] In this way, Merry reveals at last what the contrary of a fossil would be.

What we discover in the pages of *The British Album* is a queer poetics that, as it plays some formal properties against others in subtle and disarming ways, establishes a poetic drive to destruction that somehow "belongs to the process of archivization and produces the very thing it reduces."[179] As these poems' speakers traipse through grim psychological landscapes, constantly confronting their own inadequacy and lack, the literary language generates an orientation toward the future that need not await the future's arrival. Merry, often in spite of his poems' seeming arguments, tiptoes through prosody to find fresh ways to insist upon the fruitlessness and nomadism of desire, and the intrinsic multiplicity of the sexual couple. He seems to invent, through the ironic crossing of these levels, a queer relation to the contemporary future. This becomes, in Lacanian terms, a powerfully feminine form of writing. As an instance of temporal drag, it operates through "retrogression, delay, and the pull of the past on the present," and by collecting and constantly alluding to that which a culture is bent on throwing away.[180]

I have relied here on close readings of a handful of poems, because llanguage, as considered as a function of language separate from communication, only becomes apparent through close and careful attention. Such readings might also aid in the ongoing project of reading Della Cruscan poetry through its "formal and rhetorical conventions," which, as McGann stresses, was something urgently needed just a generation ago.[181] I have hoped to show these poems' capacity for experimental temporality, how they produce a literary resistance to chrononormativity, and do so, very often, in meditations upon directly political subjects. The Della Cruscans were developing a way of thinking about politics that relied upon being not whole: they pried open contemporary poetic discourse rather than respecting its parameters; they seemed to focus on the jouissance of the signifier rather than meaning; they imagined themselves living in the future already, but made that a matter for the daily newspaper. Subsequently, *The British Album*, taken as a collective writing project, enacted and catalogued feminist temporalities in ways that would be foundational for the emergent discourse of the contemporary future. Placing themselves between the language of politics and the jouissance of llanguage, Cowley, Robinson, and Merry revealed a chasm normally hidden as the subject becomes subject to clock time, and they mined that chasm in ambiguous and destabilizing ways. In so doing, they fractured the politics of time for the revolutionary era.

Chapter 4

Future Poetry

Clock Time Misses Barbauld, Smith, Richardson, and Hemans

Mary Wollstonecraft, in a collection of aphoristic "Hints" published posthumously, discloses that "I am more and more convinced, that poetry is the first effervescence of the imagination, and the forerunner of civilization."[1] It is a remarkable statement to come from a novelist/polemicist. The woman who radicalized the act of writing from the future eschewed the genre that, in her opinion, would make that possible. She describes verse as both a point of origin and ultimate destination, "first" but already at the end. It is not simply to say that poetry has a past and future, or even, exactly, that poets are hierophants of an unapprehended inspiration.[2] Rather, she uses the present tense to assert that poetry has concurrent but separate timelines: one, pertaining to the "imagination," of which it was the first of an ongoing series, and another, yet to come, pertaining to "civilization." Poetry presently exists as the past of one thing in the future of another, but her own knowledge of this aspect of poetry is itself only gradually emerging. To know about poetry's secret affiliation with the future would be to possess knowledge from the future already, which is why it is something that one can never quite know but of which one can become "more and more convinced." To know the secret of poetry's contemporary futurity is to know only that its contemporary futurity *is* a secret. Wollstonecraft somehow recognizes it as knowledge that she herself does not have. It is knowledge that she did will have (in a matter of speaking), but never "has," "has had," or "will have had." Although we

155

do not yet know what "civilization" is, Wollstonecraft knows that poetry will have imagined it "first"; poetry is a letter without an addressee, assured of reaching its destination. It is as if "civilization" were a froth gradually accumulating through the ongoing "effervescence of the imagination"—or, as if "imagination" were the name of a future that has already happened "first," even as we continue to await the impossible event called "civilization."

Wollstonecraft's metaphor of effervescence finds an analogue in Anna Letitia Barbauld's 1797 poem "Washing Day," in which laundry suds stir childhood memories of bubble-blowing, which in turn remind the speaker of hot air balloons and, ultimately, of poetry itself and "Washing Day" in particular. Riffing on Hester Lynch Piozzi's Della Cruscan classic, "Sonnet. On an Air Balloon," published in *The World* on February 11, 1788, Barbauld implies that poetry is a form of women's work, at once nostalgic and innovative in relation to the present, but which can be plucked from the future through feats of memory. In Wollstonecraft's version of this same metaphor, "civilization" remains unrealized, while poetry, its forerunner, dwells there already. It was the first to have imagined what will have been. In this sense, poetry is a utopian genre, if we can learn to think about utopia as a time rather than a place, and one already realized, albeit hard to access, rather than proposed as a plan. It is the predominant genre of contretempopia.

Conceivably, Wollstonecraft was saying that she had detected something afoot in poetry as an evolving genre, rather than better and better appreciating poetry's eternal role. In her history of the French Revolution, Wollstonecraft had used that metaphor of effervescence to describe events already underway, though "unclocked by the national eye," as Daljit Nagra would put it.[3] Over the eighteenth century, the political subject matter of poetry had been expanding; issues that had, in the 1750s, been mostly the domain of laboring-class and otherwise less visible poets were, by 1800, being taken seriously by literary tastemakers, and poetry began more and more to concern itself with marginalized people.[4] This is to say that poetry was, over the latter half of the eighteenth century, beginning to engage imaginatively with new aspects of "civilization," just as Wollstonecraft had suspected, by way of its discontents. Literary culture was then undergoing a partition of the sensible, explains Jacques Rancière, having developed a new "landscape of signs" through which "the historical and social world becomes visible to itself."[5]

Interestingly, sexual difference—rather than class or race directly—became the "major ideological fulcrum" around which the transformation

FUTURE POETRY   157

turned, which meant that women poets featured prominently in this
aesthetic renegotiation.[6] "Aesthetic discourse often seeks, at moments of
stress, to anchor the turns of figurative language to the putative naturalness of sexual difference," as Marc Redfield posits, even to the extent
that Romantic poetry could, in its gender investments, "crumble into
an anxious . . . scene of fetishism."[7] The biggest male literary stars of
the early nineteenth century, William Wordsworth and Lord Byron, had
made their names by repackaging elements of women's writing and then
castigating their source material as effeminizing and perverse.[8] Women
poets responded, very often, by creating complex acts of mutual poetic
entanglement replete with "dark contradictions."[9] Women poets enjoyed
a "growing presence, visibility, and cultural influence" in the early nineteenth century, yet mostly while subsumed under personas such as "Mrs.
Barbauld," "Mrs. Smith," "Mrs. Richardson," and "Mrs. Hemans."[10]

I invoke these four poets not only because they were so emphatically
known by their married names, but because their work especially confirms
Wollstonecraft's growing conviction about the presence of the future in
contemporary verse. This chapter surveys the era in miniature through
a small set of close readings. I begin with an early, but posthumously
published, poem by Barbauld entitled "Love and Time," which I read
along with "Washing Day," which was written later and published sooner.
I next consider the hermit's role in Charlotte Smith's stunning *Beachy
Head* (1807), now recognized as one of the greatest poems of British
Romanticism. Moving then into the Regency, I next discuss *Harvest: A
Poem* (1818) by Charlotte Caroline Richardson, the underappreciated poet
from the Northern English mining town of Frosterly. *Harvest*, allegorizing
peacetime as harvest time in the aftermath of the Treaty of Paris, conducts
a bold poetic experiment in radical hospitality for the contemporary
future. Finally, I turn to two poems by Felicia Hemans, "Evening Prayer
at a Girls' School" (1825) and "A Spirit's Return" (1828), which in different
ways consider stillness as a form of fractural resistance to clock time. In
the former Hemans poem, the speaker flattens the symbolic hierarchies of
time, to lull the reader into what psychoanalysts today would call "ordinary
psychosis," essentially meaning a flattened way of relating to language and
signification.[11] In the latter, Hemans's speaker demands to be haunted in
a fantasy of love-after-death modeled on Byron's *Manfred*. All four poets
confront what Jonathan Culler calls "the strange time of the lyric now"
and, using the affordances of literary language, push that strangeness yet
further into truly asynchronous forms of thought.[12] I will suggest that this

158   FRACTURE FEMINISM

experiment should be considered a form of utopian thought, given the way it takes lack seriously—even, in Hemans's case, through its disavowal—as the basis of a politics. Though, much as we saw with Williams, Merry, and Barbauld, this is a utopian tradition of an impossible time already here rather than place imagined: that is, contretempopia.

Poetry ever has a complex relationship to time, in part because of meter and rhythm, the tendency of lyric to resist narrative, and a willingness to explore the world through static verbal images.[13] This quartet of poets are, even when the poems are longer than lyrics, pressing on such capacities of poetry extra firmly, so as to force open a temporal fracture. The poems discussed in this chapter employ elements of narrative to an unusual extent, without becoming narrative poems—which is a significant ambiguity because, as Paul Ricoeur suggests, "the circle of narrativity and temporality is not a vicious but a healthy circle, whose two halves mutually reinforce one another."[14] These poems have nothing invested in the "health" of that circle. They do not quite tell stories, but are still storytelling: they register images in time, for instance, the march of time across a woman's face, the slow drift of continents, the procedures of a bedtime routine, or community-building events, in series, at harvest-home. They are using the narrative strategy that Brian McHale, following Rachel Blau DuPlessis, calls "segmentivity"—that is, how poems negotiate gaps, such as matters of spacing, to create ambiguously narrative elements.[15] It is a strategy ideally suited to fracture-feminist writing. The strategy helps these poems register as events things that normally wouldn't be considered as such: seeing an unusual rock, doing the laundry, mourning one's lover, attending a dance, praying before bed.[16] Working across and against such ambiguous narrative elements, which are themselves constructed across the gaps that poetry makes possible, these poems meanwhile deform time at the figural level, through unusual uses of allegory, metaphor, or performative incantation.

By segmentally semi-narrating these semi-events, these poems display "signs from the future," as Slavoj Žižek would call them. To appreciate such signs, much as Wollstonecraft did, we would need to reconsider what "event" means in relation to "history." Žižek recommends that

> we should turn around the usual historicist perspective of understanding an event through its context and genesis. Radical emancipatory outbursts cannot be understood in this way: instead of analyzing them as part of the continuum of past and present, we should bring in the perspective of the future,

taking them as limited, distorted (sometimes even perverted) fragments of a utopian future that lies dormant in the present as its hidden potential.[17]

Moreover, he counsels that

one should learn the art of recognizing, from an engaged subjective position, elements which are here, in our space, but whose time is the emancipated future. . . . However, while we must learn to watch for such signs, we should also be aware that what we are doing now will only become readable once the future is here.[18]

These poems encourage exactly this sort of vigilance, yet the signs they offer do not seem to require retroactive interpretation. The future, they promise, is very much here and already readable, though usually unrecognized, and so they try to attune the reader to contretempopian elements present—however ghostly, silent, fanciful, and isolated—within the matrix of the fiscal-military state, its celebratory pageants and obligatory solemnities, and the clock time it superegoically demands.

Each of these poems imagines utopia as a time at work inside of, yet apart from, hegemonic discourses and structures. It is a fracture in those discourses and structures. Hence the poems work intertextually, through a logic of "intimate exteriority" that Lacan calls "extimacy."[19] These poems create spaces of exclusion underway within earlier writings by Lord Byron, Hester Mulso Chapone, Robert Merry, Mary Robinson, Helen Maria Williams, Mary Wollstonecraft, and William Wordsworth. The relation of intimate exteriority is essential to their deconstructive poetics: they voice the texts of others so intimately and faithfully as to dismember the timelines of the source material. Barbauld appropriates the voice of Chapone; Smith, Merry and Wordsworth; Richardson, Robinson; and Hemans, Byron. The intertextual engagement does not, however, tend to produce solidarity across the borders of sexual difference. Rather, it uses the act of ventriloquism to open extimate temporalities, through a kind of temporal anamorphosis built around a temporal fracture. Reading and repetition are the mechanisms that drive the technique. Because, as Christina Lupton has argued, "we read in grammatically improbable tenses not easily accommodated by descriptions of time," Barbauld, Smith, Richardson, and Hemans produce impossible temporalities through their intertextual techniques, powered by the confluence of allusion and repetition.[20] They came to inhabit the future in an era when art sought to break with the present by "incessantly stag[ing] the past,"[21] by claiming a bit of futurity lodged, like an irritant, in the present. This is how future-oriented feminist poetry performatively creates contretempopia.

Barbauld's "Love and Time" and "Washing Day"

Today, Barbauld is admired especially for *Eighteen Hundred and Eleven*, a poem that situates its poet in the contemporary future to foretell the end of British hegemony. That poem, which I discussed chapter 1 along with "On the Uses of History," is clearly central to the ethos that this book traces. Barbauld takes up similar themes in her earlier allegorical lyric, "Love and Time: To Mrs. Mulso," written in the mid-1780s and circulated in manuscript but not published until 1825.[22] In "Love and Time," Barbauld imagines a war between Love and Time on the terrain of Mary Prescott Mulso's face. Time, jealous of how much Mulso loves her husband Thomas, begins to disfigure her face "in every cell, / And every dimple" (LT, ll. 5–6). Love fights back, mocking Time for its reliance on its more powerful ally Sickness, and crowing, "But both unite, for both I here defy" (LT, l. 61). The allegory of Love's defiance of Time and Sickness depends, as I shall suggest, upon a cut within the figural work of the allegory, which tells the story of Love's resistance to military hegemony and offers a model, based on the Lacanian not-whole, for how such resistance might endure.

The poem's dedicatee, Mary Prescott Mulso, was primarily known for being Robert Prescott's sister. At the time of Barbauld's writing, Robert was famous for his role in capturing Louisbourg and Montréal from the French during the Seven Years' War, and then for his leadership during the American Revolution and in British attacks on St. Lucia. Later, he would be promoted to General in the British military, and spent crucial years as an irascible colonial governor in the West Indies and Canada.[23] "Love and Time," by way of this context, participates in the broader phenomenon of late-eighteenth-century British women poets responding forcefully and vitally, if sometimes in coded ways, to the militarization of culture and the concomitant shift into clock time.[24] Barbauld tests the ideological limits of clock time through an extended military conceit, a project possible because, in Mary A. Favret's words, "wartime in modernity . . . houses

FUTURE POETRY 161

many temporalities."[25] In many ways, the poem presages Della Cruscan uses of figural language: Merry would, shortly after, use his own military metaphors to warn Anna Matilda, the avatar of Hannah Cowley, that "Must ruthless Time's rude touch efface / Each lovely feature's varying grace."[26] In the 1780s, it seems, British women's faces were battlegrounds, where poets could stage insurgencies against clock and calendar and generate "signs from the future."

"Love and Time" is a poem about aging, as expressed through an elaborate military allegory. Time is attacking Mrs. Mulso's face, where Love has long been encamped. As Time bombards Mrs. Mulso, Love is forced to withdraw, and the battlefield—that is, Mrs. Mulso's face—is left ravaged. Love, now "entrenched in a smile" (LT, l. 11), declares its permanent resistance to Time. Time eventually allies with Sickness to overwhelm Love, leading Love to appeal to a referee, Jove, who will ensure that Love and Time continue their battle on Mrs. Mulso's face forever, in perpetual stalemate. It is a poem, then, about retaining one's desirability in one's later years, but also about learning how to defy a hegemonic power through rhetoric when one is outgunned. In that sense, it brings together two crucial aspects of Barbauld's long career, demonstrating, on the one hand, how poetry can interfere with the hegemony of the nation, and also, on the other, how it can subvert a culture's ideologies of aging and time—a topic that Devoney Looser has established as central to Barbauld's editorial practices.[27]

As we have seen throughout this study, war and time were tightly aligned, ideologically speaking, by the end of the eighteenth century. Britain had become a "fiscal military state," as John Brewer has termed it, with the ranks of the army swelling from tens of thousands of soldiers at the beginning of the eighteenth century to hundreds of thousands by the end.[28] Although Britons in this period lived in "a world almost constantly at war," the battles tended to involve "relatively small numbers of people in often far-off places," as Jeffrey Cox reminds us, which gave rise to a literary-cultural phenomenon that Favret has termed "war at a distance."[29] Favret calls attention to "the convergence between clock time and national security" in this period, reminding us that war at a distance "expresses itself most frequently and forcefully . . . through temporalities."[30] In such a context, it makes sense for Barbauld to analyze the workings of time, and the marriage of her friend, using military metaphors.

Barbauld situates Mrs. Mulso within and between military and literary realms: while the title apostrophizes "Mrs. Mulso," the sister of a war hero, the opening line situates the reader "On Stella's brow," which will serve as our battlefield. Barbauld is alluding to "To Stella," a poem by Hester Mulso Chapone, Mary's sister-in-law, which similarly apostrophizes Mary Prescott Mulso. That allegorical poem, written in 1751 and published in 1775, warns Mary Mulso that friendship is preferable to love, "Since Fate forbids that Peace should dwell with Love!"[31] Barbauld revivifies Chapone's allegory, stocking "Love and Time" poem with the same figures, but flips the allegory on its (literal figural) head. That is, while Chapone had warned Mrs. Mulso of Love's "wanton head" and "tyrant power," Barbauld sees love as a legitimate and "sovereign" power, one enduring siege from an invading army.[32] This is an especially pointed subversion, given how Robert Prescott had catapulted into national fame as a result of his participation in the Siege of Louisbourg, a turning point in the Seven Years' War, and in the British effort to quell the American Revolution. Barbauld seems to be aligning herself on the side of the besieged French and the insurgent Americans here, even as she deploys characters familiar from Chapone's allegory.

Already wedged between the literary, the martial, and the marital, Barbauld goes deeper into this morass by representing Love and Time's military actions with artistic metaphors, such as those of writing and engraving. Time, as the poem begins, with an "iron pencil" traces "crooked lines" into the "ivory tablets" of Mrs. Mulso's brow (LT, ll. 2–3). Time is seeking to replace Love as the artist who writes upon Mrs. Mulso's face, literally though figuratively de-facing her; the fact that this assault is an act of artistic expression and writing aligns the author, Barbauld, with the poem's antagonist, Time. It becomes difficult to locate any outside of this poem: as its figural work redoubles, it captures itself and its subject within its personifications and allusions.

To a remarkable extent, "Love and Time" directly enacts Paul de Man's theory of figural defacement. Any text, argues de Man, once it starts using figural language, stages a confrontation between the historical author of the text and the implied author *in* the text, given the way that figural language "deals with the giving and taking away of faces, with face and deface, figure, figuration, and disfiguration," in a process that he calls autobiography.[33] De Man outlines the process by which "the turning motion of tropes" in any text, once it confronts "the impossibility of closure and of totalization," can deliver us beyond "that [which] can be located in history."[34] The figural work, such as allegory, apostrophe, or metaphor, begins to collapse on itself: the text fails to cordon itself off

FUTURE POETRY 163

from the historical world, while the world is likewise vulnerable to the world-making capacities of the text.[35] We see this happening in "Love and Time" as the poem begins to subject itself to its own figural movements. Time, in Barbauld's account, is itself subject to time: it has been attacking Mrs. Mulso "lately," and has been "envious" (LT, l. 1). Time is "old Time," as if Time were opening a second front on its own face, to wage war against itself (LT, l. 25). Time also, though, belongs to Love: "Love's high trophies" adorn Mrs. Mulso's face, turning her face into an archive or mystic writing pad carrying traces of its past (LT, l. 4). As Time bombards Mrs. Mulso's face, it destroys those trophies, driving Love out from its "entrenchment." The language recalls the Siege of Bouchain in 1711 during the War of Spanish Succession, which innovated trench warfare with the Line of Ne Plus Ultra. Love, through this allusion, is again associated with the French military. Stella, or Mrs. Mulso, is entirely passive during this experience: her face is simply the battlefield upon which Love and Time are fighting; Love and Time are things that happen to Mrs. Mulso, not events in which she can participate. As Time blasts at the crevices of Mrs. Mulso's face to empty out her pores and dimples, we are forced to confront the confusing image of a face made out of lack, or lacking its usual lack: to empty out a dimple or a cave in the face is to empty an emptiness, or replace one emptiness with another (LT, ll. 4–6).

The image of lack blasting away at lack, or of the future using the present moment to create a fracture in the past, is at root a theory of temporality that resists the march of clock time. In this way of thinking, Time, far from simply accumulating experiences, one atop the next, registers something missing in the present and refers it to the future. Ellie Ragland and Dragan Milovanovic once penned the enigmatic Lacanian maxim: "Time is the lack that *is* desire."[36] It is a statement that I had long struggled to understand until I was engaged more deeply with Barbauld's poem. It seems to mean that time doesn't accrue, but rather carries on as lack, and ultimately serves as the lack that makes desire possible. Love, I would add, is an attempt to fill in for this lack, much as the trophies do in the recesses of Mrs. Mulso's face. Barbauld seems to operate in a similarly proto-Lacanian register, with her view that Love is the rupture that responds to this lack and situates it within symbolic coordinates.

Love, explains Lacan, is "always mutual"—not because it is reciprocated, but because it isn't.[37] "Feelings are always mutual" because a person's desire must correspond to that of the big Other, who, in intervening and interfering, is much more profoundly the object of one's affection than one's sexual partner could ever be.[38] Love, which is effectively the name of a compensatory fantasy arising in this situation, imagines itself mutual in the absence of a sexual relationship. Barbauld presents this imbalance as a matter of justice in the context of a military invasion. When Time declares that "Mine is this field, by conquest fairly won," the reader is struck with the strangeness of that oxymoron; Barbauld highlights the impossibility of a fairly won conquest in Love's response, that, "Nor was the field by conquest fairly gained" (LT, ll. 14, 56). One combatant claims legitimacy, and the other contests the claim—and yet the poem, far from presenting these competing claims as equal, elects to highlight the asymmetry between the combatants. Time, it appears, is able to invade Love's terrain, and yet "Love cannot reap his joys where Time has ploughed" (LT, l. 15). By the end of Barbauld's poem, we are caught in a loop across which Love and Time manage to address one another, despite the asymmetry between them. In face of the assault on Mrs. Mulso's face, Love responds with a repetition—for example, "nothing daunted he returned again" (LT, l. 27)—that pulls the arrangement into an endless cycle. Once Time shakes the hourglass such that "the sands would run / for many a year the strife should be maintained," the poem is locked within the repetitive pull of the death drive (LT, ll. 70–71). Love, in response, enacts a rupture in the symbolic system that turns the lack in Time, which had missed its target, into an aim in itself: "no force should Love destroy, / Nor time should quell the might of that immortal boy" (LT, ll. 72–73).

A fracture emerges in the "false unity" of the subject, which is why there can be no direct relation between Love and Time except as mediated by Jove, whose desire serves as the limit of the combatants' desire.[39] But their relation to Jove is asymmetrical, as Love has a direct line of access to Jove—meaning that Love does not meet Time on an level field of combat. Love taunts Time, saying, "Not one of them is of thy scythe in dread" (LT, l. 43). It is not simply that Love's forces are not fearful. *Not one of them*—that is, either an exception to a set, or the members of the set that are "not one"[40]—is the proper subject of Time's threat of violence. Love, in this poem, is precisely "not one of them": he is a party to the battle yet situates himself outside of the set of combatants, such that he can lament: "Ah me, that gentle Love such foes should meet!" (LT, l. 26). Love has failed to count himself as one of the "foes," as if Love were, on the one hand, through the force of allegory, collected into a Lacanian "false unity" that can act as a subject, and yet on the other hand, through the nonrelation with Time, cease counting as one of the belligerent foes.

FUTURE POETRY   165

Love's role, among this Other jouissance, is to fracture the rhetorical and
military battlefield by "sharpening smooth discourse," ensuring that the
poem "doesn't stop being written" even as Time endeavors to stop it from
not being written.[41]

This sort of cut—that is, the displacement of a negation such that a
contingent encounter becomes a necessity—qualifies as a form of political
resistance. Lacan called such an action "courage" and saw it, conveniently
enough, as the effect of love.[42] The very incompleteness of this process—
first, at the level of subjectivity, as Lacan posits, and then at the level of
allegorical closure, as de Man does—pushes clock time, through poetic
language, toward the infinite as a mode of political and military resistance.
(This makes the de Manian element quite ironic, when you think about
it.) Barbauld finds in clock time a fracture that leads to infinity, enabling
her to imagine love as the practice of an impossible temporality, which
defers every act of political resistance into the present.

The cut from "Love and Time" reappears in "Washing Day," a better-known poem of Barbauld's from 1797, though there it is rechristened
"not thou" instead of "not one."[43] Instead of revealing it through an asymmetry built into the allegory, as we saw in "Love and Time," Barbauld in
"Washing Day" simply draws the reader, through free association, *into*
the cut itself, and thus the time of the contemporary future. Later in this
chapter, we will see Hemans make a similar gesture in "Evening Prayer."
In "Washing Day," ~~Woman~~ (written as barred) is not being bombarded,
but rather pressed into work. The work of the laundry is oppressive not
only because it is physically hard and impossible to balance with the "hospitable rites" expected by men, but also on account of the repetitiveness,
inevitability, and ceaselessness of the task (WD, l. 48). That is, washing
becomes oppressive when it becomes a "day," regularized and made to
seem natural by the calendar. The speaker resents the gendered domestic
chores, "Which week, smooth sliding after week, brings on / Too soon"
(WD, l. 28). Yet her lament also points the way out, given how it highlights
the gap between objective measures of time (e.g., "smooth sliding") and
a woman's discordant experience of time (e.g., "too soon"). "Too soon"
suggests that women, despite being held to the calendar by norms of
domestic management, never completely inhabit the calendar's demands.
Then, through memory, the speaker invites the reader into that gap—an
impossible future embedded in the now. Claire Colebrook writes of the
"delay" that can arise when "a body perceives the world through memory,
with a halo of images."[44] Barbauld intuits this as well, and exploits that

166   FRACTURE FEMINISM

delay, through its imagistic world-unmaking powers, to activate a kind of
women's liberation through the fracture enacted by poetry.

"Washing Day" is a well-known poem, so I will focus just on its
conclusion. The poem reaches the future through its reference to the
brothers Montgolfier and their hot air balloon, which was, at the time,
known as an astonishing scientific achievement and a marvel to behold.
The balloon, first publicly demonstrated in 1783, was by 1797 a cultural
phenomenon.[45] Given its associations with both the French military and
the sublime spectacle of the French Revolution, it had dangerous connotations.[46] For the speaker of "Washing Day," the balloon becomes a figure
both of the future (i.e., something incredible, still yet to be imagined) and
the present (i.e., the exclusionary domain of male scientific research). The
poem, then, uses a figure of the present future to imagine, effervescently,
an alternative time of female subject-formation.

The speaker's chain of associations is essentially a timeline, moving
from early childhood play (i.e., blowing bubbles) to memories of the last
decade or so (i.e., Montgolfier), to poetry in general (perhaps situated
in the exact present) and then *this* poem, which is presumably (because
not yet complete) an object from the future. Yet the timeline is also not a
timeline, because the speaker is showing the reader how to experience the
images all at once, and associating that aptitude with women specifically. It
is strange, yet critical, that the speaker mentions Montgolfier only through
memories of memories, which then can be said not to have included any
notion of Montgolfier: the speaker specifically says that the balloon is not
part of her childhood memory (which makes sense, as that would have
been anachronistic). She does not even quite say that she remembers
blowing bubbles as a child. Rather, she remembers that she remembered
blowing bubbles as a child. The double movement of memory summons a
disavowed anachronistic memory that was not remembered, as if Barbauld
were a nineteenth-century Christopher Nolan. The whole thing pivots
around an anchoring point, a vocal master signifier that emerges slowly,
tentatively, in the passive voice, in relation to the speaker's recollections,
deep from the past: "my mother's voice was heard" (WD, l. 74).

As nested memories and non-memories (i.e., screen memories) build
an atemporal structure around the oppressive chrononormativity of washing
day, gradually an "I" emerges: "Then would I sit me down" (WD, l. 78).
The lyric "I" is held in contradistinction to an objective "me," in a process
that Lacan would call alienation.[47] This "altered I," arrived at through the
"quotidian tones" of domestic labor, is something that Stuart Curran says

FUTURE POETRY   167

is common in woman-authored poetry of the Romantic period.[48] Once
the speaker manages to say "I," she no longer has any need to satirize,
through mock-heroic playful tones, the crushing work of washing day. The
poem thenceforth devotes itself to constructing its elaborately nested set
of impossible and disavowed memories. The "me" works all day, but gets
forcibly sat down; the "I" will have "ponder[ed] much" about that work.
The fraught "I" never fits into the "smooth sliding" of "me." The speaker
guards maternal lack, as a precious *agalma mater*, within the "I."

   "My mother's voice was heard" is a peculiar use of the passive voice, in
the sense that "my mother's" implies something intimate, claimed personally.
Barbauld is going out of her way to defer the lyric "I," which is still, in
line 74, in formation, even while the voice can already be validated as "my
mother's." The combination introduces a void into the poem, a lack that is
desire. It is, I am saying, following Ragland and Milovanovic, effectively a
figure for time. It is a voice that Lacan would call an object voice, "distinct
from sonorities," that "is reflected back only by echoes in the real," and
that constitutes a void.[49] Barbauld immediately associates the voice with
a tube—a "hollow bole"—through which she remembers blowing bubbles,
whimsically, in childhood (WD, l. 79). Lost in the memory, the speaker
manages to shift into the active voice by using a collective pronoun: "we
blew, and sent aloft / The floating bubbles" (WD, ll. 80–81). Yet, in the
same sentence, she uses a gerund (i.e., "little dreaming then") to suture
the impossible future—Montgolfier and the scientific marvel that is and
was the hot air balloon—into a collective past that can include "me" and
"we" but never fully "I." It is not an "I" that directly ponders, but that,
in the conditional, "would . . . ponder." She remembers not being able
to remember the future, which is a present moment shared with Montgolfier. No sooner has the "I" that would ponder been remembered than
it disintegrates into a yet more distant scene of memory, in a temporal
double movement: the speaker, currently busy with the wash, remembers
having heard a maternal voice that had once led her to remember blowing
bubbles as a yet younger child. The "I" has had to be reconstructed in
the conditional through the memory of the voice; that "I" can then give
rise to a "we," which can give way to a "this," emphatically "this most of
all"—the poem itself, which (unlike the speaker, who *cannot* have imagined
the balloons) asserts that impossible past future in the present moment
of its enunciation (WD, l. 86).

   Being reminded of one's memories of one's own poem, which is still
in the process of being written, is the sort of temporal feat that comes

168 FRACTURE FEMINISM

up surprisingly often in the feminist writing of the Romantic period. It is akin to Mary Robinson including her own name in a list of historical women writers (as discussed in chapter 1), characters in a translated novel who seem to have read the original novel in which they are living as translations (as discussed in chapter 2), or Mary Shelley resolving to override her own narrator and include herself in her fictional narrative (to be discussed in chapter 5). To what aesthetic regime might such writing belong, if, for Rancière, the nineteenth century was all about attention to small details in service of literary realism? Well, Ernst Bloch maintains that artworks can contain the future, and that this should be understood to be part of its "realism":

> every great work of art, besides its manifest essence, is also carried towards a *latency of its coming side*, that is: towards the contents of the future which had not yet appeared in its time, in fact ultimately towards the contents of an as yet unknown final state. . . . Realistic works of art do not become less realistic through the notation of latency, through the space—however blank—of the Absolute, but more realistic; since everything real mingles with the Not-Yet within that space. Significant daydream imaginative creations do not blow soap-bubbles, they open windows.[50]

In light of this study, I would suggest that, basically, Bloch gets it right—except, of course, when the creations *do* blow soap-bubbles as an expression of latency, or use soap-bubbles as a figure for latency. *That* particular feat, which happens in verse apparently all the time (as Wollstonecraft came to realize), should register as an extimate world-historical aesthetic event.

The Hermitage of *Beachy Head*

The hermit, a complicated figure in Charlotte Smith's final poem *Beachy Head*, experiences isolation, sorrow, and the futility of his largely invisible efforts. Yet he is also a devotee of hope: "it seem'd as if young Hope / Her flattering pencil gave to Fancy's hand," the speaker says, a circumstance that has enabled the hermit to live within "ideal bowers of pleasure."[51] What is the aspiration of this Hope? It is not easy to describe *Beachy Head* as a hopeful or optimistic poem: the speaker, awaiting a French invasion,

FUTURE POETRY   169

recounts centuries of foreign domination in England, implies a grim end
to the British Empire, and concludes with the story of the lovelorn hermit
fishing corpses from the ocean before having his own corpse discovered,
long after death, by visiting shepherds. Yet, as the speaker relates this
unending bleakness, Smith seems to pin her hopes on the hermit, given
his capacity to find new ways of experiencing time. Kate Singer percep-
tively calls Smith's hermit "a figure for impossible receptivity," because he
functions as an aporia in the text, activating a set of irresolvable conflicts.[52]
That is exactly right, I think. I want to move the analysis in a different
direction from Singer's, though, away from the issue of taste and toward
a different aesthetic and figural relationship, namely, the interplay between
"young Hope," "Fancy's hand," and the mysterious gift of the "flattering
pencil." Through this small figural exchange, the poem develops a miniature allegory that becomes atemporal, in much the way that the allegory
of "Love and Time" did for Barbauld.

   Hope, as the song goes, is a dangerous thing for a woman like Smith
to have. It is a word that, in Romantic-era literature, was sometimes seen
as "morally dubious," "deceptive," and alienating; Wordsworth associated
it with "near-quietism" and scorned it a "punishable offense"; in the era's
apocalyptic writings, it would arise, paradoxically, only through hopelessness and ruin.[53] But Smith uses the word in an unusual way, by the
standards of her era's poetry, to situate herself in the future as an aspect
of the here and now. It is much closer to the way that, say, Ernst Bloch
would use the term, as a signal for the impossible utopia of the Not-Yet,
than as mere aspiration, or the "minoritarian" future-in-the-present hailed
by José Esteban Muñoz.[54] To hope is not the same as to anticipate or to
predict: the emphasis is instead on the waiting, the readiness, rather than
the outcome. Smith's Hope is precarious, something that can sustain one
through sorrow, and even transform one's currently existing despair into a
state "not indeed unhappy," because of implication into the future: "Some
future blessings he may yet enjoy" (S, l. 666). Just because the hermit does
not ever actually enjoy these blessings—he dies before the "future blessings"
are delivered—does not mean that his current circumstances will not have
been mitigated by the contretempopian "ideal bliss" that Hope provided.

   Beachy Head is, in this way, a utopian poem, but with two unexpected
twists: first, Smith imagines utopia as a gap between times, rather than
as an imaginary place, which is quite unusual in the history of utopian
thought; second, she locates that utopia in the here and now, amidst the
despair and isolation of national crisis but irreducible to it. This formation

170   FRACTURE FEMINISM

is what I have been calling contretempopia. Hope, in such a regime, is not sustainable and it cannot improve our circumstances, but it does permit a better future to be a part of contemporary experience. History, for Smith, depends upon our learning to see how the present contains glimmers of utopian futurity in the process of its own becoming, even as the very iteration of such futurity ensures its ruin, our ruin, and the nation's ruin.

By saying "it seem'd as if," Smith uses the past perfect subjunctive to introduce the allegorical abstractions Hope and Fancy, emphasizing the unreality of the situation. The bowers of pleasure, which are experienced as an impossibility by the hermit, offer a supplementary orientation, in the poem and of the poem, toward the future. In order for the hermit to inhabit "ideal bowers of pleasure," Hope seems to have needed to lend Fancy's hand a "flattering pencil." The word "flattering" suggests that the portrait is at least to some degree inaccurate: it is certainly not the product of a disinterested critical assessment. We can see it in contrast to the "faithful pencil" wielded by Memory (S, ll. 291–92), as if to suggest that the future belongs to those who would deform the present, while the past belongs to those who value accuracy. Yet it is the pencil itself that is said to be "flattering," not the image, suggesting perhaps that the swerve away from what's possible will have seemed to happen through repeated representational practices.

Fancy, in this period, was often considered "wayward, deadening, and outmoded," even if this was sometimes part of its allure for writers like the Shelleys.[55] For Smith, it seems to be duly fanciful, or at least "seem'd" to be, meaning that fancy is ready to swerve, in accordance to the customs of Hope, away from the military cadences of clock time. In Smith's usage, it invokes multiple and overlapping timeframes beyond historical time. In this, she follows Wollstonecraft, author of "The Cave of Fancy"—a posthumously published story about a hermit—who saw fancy as the nothing that makes poetry happen, in all of its effervescent orientation toward the future. "The generality of people cannot see or feel poetically, they want fancy," Wollstonecraft claims, with the idea that the fancy opens access to an immanent but latent reality.[56] The atemporal aspects of Fancy, for Smith, encourage us to question an emerging scholarly consensus, seen in important essays by Kevis Goodman and Theresa Kelley, that Beachy Head looks backward.[57] The poem thinks about time and history, but from the future. It begins with the assurance that Fancy will "represent the strange and awful hour / Of vast concussion" (S, ll. 5–6). The "hour" is strange and awful in part because it is positioned vaguely in the future, even as it refers to wars still ongoing. As Smith's speaker gazes into the water from her prospect on Beachy Head, the present must be awaited, yet the future is already happening. The line break at "awful hour" graphically separates that hour from the "vast concussion," yet its unsettling violence also makes possible the remediating continuity of the lines' enjambment. We have two examples, then—one from the start of the poem, and another as Smith describes the hermit's habitation—of Smith using the term "Fancy" to indicate alarming fractures in time but also our ability to manage and even thrive under such conditions. The poem uses this fracture as an aspect of its markedly belated temporality and even late style, given how it was composed long after Smith's literary star had faded, and published posthumously.

For a poem so devoted to ecology and nature, *Beachy Head* is eager to test the world-making power of literary language. The hermit's bower is a poetical space, especially partaking of Della Cruscan sensibilities, which the poem presents as a viable alternative to masculinist scientific episte- mologies, such as earth sciences. To endure life in wartime, Smith mentally places herself in the imaginary future of the distant past, a speculative wake of both the Roman Empire and continental drift. Goodman, tracing *Beachy Head*'s engagement with deep time, has urged us to see Smith's "revisionary understanding of the *nature* in natural history as a part of an overall historical process that includes human history no less than any other," meaning that human affairs, such as war and empire, are part of what constitutes natural space.[58] Yet even as Smith shows us how to read "nature" as an index of human history, she deploys "nature" to invite the future into the present in ways that undermine that history or render it impossible, and identifies it as the ground upon which sexual difference is demarcated. The praise of "Fancy," along with the secret bower itself, mark Smith's affiliation with the Della Cruscans. The bower is Smith's proposed remedy for the long history of continental drift, which "from the continent / Eternally divided this green isle" (S, ll. 9–10). Robert Merry, as we have seen in chapter 3, had explored this same question—treating it as a political and conceptual, rather than geological, problem—in "Ode to Folly," while Hannah Cowley had presented the secret poetic bower as a fracture in time and a site of world-making powers.

Arguably, "Ode to Folly" had recommended geological time as an alternative to military clock time. Smith is more ambivalent about rocks, electing to aestheticize fossils rather than reserving them for scientific assessment.[59] In Smith's version, eternity is an ongoing event that has already happened, and it shapes the ground from which one might contemplate a nation at war. The poem thus becomes "a critique of beauty that acknowledges and condemns the violence of global processes," as Walt Hunter observes.[60] The temporal gap introduced and enforced by Fancy explains England's very existence as an island. The nation is, by way of deep time, a hermit among the landmass of Europe. The poem, as Mark Canuel argues, follows contradictory impulses both hospitable and protectionist, effectively walling off the nation from invaders by imagining its openness.[61] The gap that opens between this double hermitage—that is, between the time of the hermit's bower and that of the nation it metaphorically represents—becomes, in its excessive lack, the wellspring of what Smith sees as Englishness. To the extent that Hope *seems to* lend her pencil to Fancy, or rather Fancy's hand, Smith would appear to have established a future within a contemporary national political world already fractured by asynchronous rates of pastness, and the "opposition between acceleration and slowness."[62] *Beachy Head* proves that texts can develop alternatives to "the precise timings of military incursions, perhaps the nation's most explicit form of synching up bodies and time," much as Elizabeth Freeman asserts.[63]

"Fancy's hand" is a strange image, given how Fancy, being the name for a property of thought, would seem not really to have hands. Yet Jacques Derrida reminds us that "thinking is not cerebral or disincarnate."[64] Hands have a contradictory "double vocation," explains Derrida, to grip and hold but also bequeath and extend. They are figures both of poetic craft (i.e., handiwork) and singularity (i.e., handwriting), simultaneously a part of the body and autonomous.[65] A hand, says Derrida on the one hand, is the gift that makes a gift of itself in being offered.[66] Smith, on the other hand, reverses that arrangement—one thinks of Plato holding forth behind Socrates, as depicted on Derrida's favorite postcard[67]—by having Fancy's hand stretch out to receive a gift from Hope. Although one would usually hope to receive a gift, here, "Hope" gives the gift, by effectively taking the hoped-for object (that is, the pencil—a figure for hope) away from Fancy's outstretched (because described as if autonomous) hand. Hope is the one said to be "young," as if youth were in the habit of giving pencils to their fanciful elders. The time of the gift, then, is multiply subverted, even while the hand imagery (as such) embroils the allegory in the literary present. As Peter Capuano explains: "between the eighteenth and nineteenth centuries there was a sudden but sustained spike in representations of hands in British fiction and in English culture

more generally," a phenomenon that suggests a complicated cultural renegotiation of the relation between hands, embodiment, labor, and writing
in the period.[68] The hermit is receiving an impossible gift from the hands
of nonexistent entities, or perhaps a loan from an imaginary donor that
could have been received only in a counterfactual alternative history. In
receiving it, he models a stance of openness toward the future through
an allegory of an allegory, here dubbed Hope. In this sense, I concur with
Jacqueline M. Labbe, who says that Smith "explores a palette characterized
by mutability and held together by an overriding interest in (re)writing
narratives," especially "narratives of history."[69]

Bloch's work is useful for showing us how being "lost among the
deepening gloom," as Smith puts it, to the extent of building one's home
out of foliage, can qualify as utopianism (S, l. 580). For Bloch, as for
Goodman, a utopian bower is connected to nature through grim historical meditations: "Finally manifested nature lies just the same as finally
manifested history in the horizon of the future," he says, because "nature
is not bygone, but the building site which has not yet been cleared at all,
the building material which does not yet adequately exist at all for the
human house which does not yet adequately exist at all."[70] Seen in this
light, Smith's similar emphasis on a natural habitation and its nonexis-
tence—its conditional life as Not-Yet but as always already illusory—reveals
the utopian aspect of her work rather than its bleakness. Nature, for
Smith, is not only a space untouched by human history but also a time
carved out within a national politics. Through Hope, Smith stitches the
future into the present instead of awaiting it. As we see in the separation
of the hermit from his lover Amanda in the past and future, and from
the maidens in the present, that utopian time is a question not only of
national security—of borders and empires—but also of sexual difference,
a question that structures the hermit's daydreams. And yet Smith urges us
to leave the hermit alone: "let him cherish his ideal bliss—/ For what is
life, when Hope has ceas'd to strew / Her fragile flowers along its thorny
way? / And sad and gloomy are his days, who lives / Of hope abandon'd!"
(S, ll. 675–679). Hope, in this analysis, is a figure for something lacking—
specifically, of hope lacking.

Smith connects Hope to dreams and, in a further Freudian key, to
unacknowledged wishes. The hermit of *Beachy Head* is a dreamer, and
Smith even includes transcriptions of his dreams. The hermit's dreams are
given in sextillas rather than the poem's predominant blank verse, which
gives them an otherworldly quality and marks the dream-thoughts as a

174   FRACTURE FEMINISM

separate plane of experience made of "love-songs and scatter'd rhymes, / Unfinished sentences or half erased" rhapsodies (S, ll. 582–583). In his daydream and in the subsequent nocturnal dream, the hermit explores topics of forgetfulness and intimacy. This diverges sharply from the tone of the previous 500 lines, which had featured feats of deep collective remembrance. The dreams are not themselves hopeful—indeed, they mournfully reconstruct what might have been in a scattered and fragmentary way half under erasure—yet they are composed, or it is as if they were composed, with a pencil borrowed from Hope. The hermit's dream-thoughts cannot be assimilated, in meter, rhyme, stanza, syntax, or content, into any of the historical timeframes of the poem.

Hermits are perhaps always wishful, as Bloch suggests in arguing that the "introverted ground" of a deliberately chosen solitude is "an *authentic wishful image*, namely of *freedom from disturbance*."[71] The speaker of *Beachy Head* wishes to be a hermit who is wishing not to have been a hermit. The hermit's daydream in *Beachy Head* is presented wishfully and only conditionally: "Were I a Shepherd on the hill / And ever as the mists withdrew . . . Where once I walk'd with you" (S, ll. 539, 543). Syntactically, this makes no sense. An "if" without a "then," it grafts a completed pastness onto a continuing eternal future: if I had been X and ever while Y, once long ago. This is apparently how a hermit dreams of human connection. The statement mimics the temporality of a dream. While the wishes that dreams encode are timeless (which is why, according to Freud, dreams cannot be read as narratives), the dreams themselves partake of contradictory temporalities. Dreams, says Freud, have multiple and overlapping instances of "simultaneity in time" across different registers of psychic experience, such that they develop in substrates. These are arranged like geological layers among the strata of the psyche, each wishfully aspiring to the future as it hopes to address intractable crises of the irretrievable past. Freud, ever eager to conserve time, warns that, "it would of course be a waste of time to try to put the psychical significance of a system of this kind into words"—but that is exactly what Smith has done.[72]

Immersed in dreams and therefore wishes, the hermit opens up multiple temporalities, each oriented toward the future, in the present. It is not that his wishes are forgotten, buried in the substrate of the dream's structure; rather, he dreams specifically of becoming the forgotten material *in* the substrate: "And then, by all but you forgot, / Sleep, where the turf that clothes the spot / May claim some pitying tears" (S, ll. 556–558). In ventriloquizing a hermit's wish to "be a Shepherd on the hill," Smith

FUTURE POETRY 175

aligns her hermit, and her speaker, with the shepherds and village farmers who, earlier in the poem, had the luxury of "unheeding such [historical and scientific] inquiry" (S, ll. 400–401). Yet, in wishing herself out of knowledge and out of herself, the poem manages to articulate an "I" for the first time, an "I" who wishes, conditionally, to walk alongside a "you," bound together intimately, though committed at the same time to absolute solitude. It echoes the way that Barbauld's "Washing Day" produces a lyric "I" through a process of alienation and disavowal.

As the hermit dreams of reuniting with Amanda, his dreadful forest enclaves become "ideal bowers of pleasure" premised upon his nostalgia for erotic fulfillment yet to come; yet that same nostalgia actually eliminates the possibility of its fulfillment, as the decision to be a hermit in this "little space" by definition separates him from the rest of humanity, even while the "village maidens" linger near enough to hear his songs and become curious (S, ll. 533, 527). Although his rustic residence is made out of hope, its construction ensures that the hermit's hope will never be fulfilled, and so, with "plaintive sounds," "complaining of his fate, . . . to the murmuring wind, of cold neglect / And baffled hope he told" (S, ll. 534–536). Hope, far from being an investment in possibilities yet to come, guarantees its own bafflement. It fulfills wishes in the here and now but never in the future—calling into question its very qualifications as "hope." The paradox arises from the collision of two incommensurate temporalities—Hope, in *Beachy Head*, terminates any happy future but enables one to be "enamour'd" of its termination (S, l. 568). This is not optimism or a "limited utopia," such as Anahid Nersessian has theorized.[73] Neither is it an "atopia" of "saturated immanence," as Frédéric Neyrat envisions, which would imaginatively subsume the boundaries of meaning in that which is "out of place."[74] Instead, Smith, like Barbauld before her, embeds a fragment of the future in the now, to create utopia out of "woodlands wild" (S, l. 585)—a utopia of the deconstructive contretemps.

Smith's thought defies the tradition of utopian thought because she envisions a utopian time, rather than a place. This is a source of pessimism in *Beachy Head*, because the time of temporal fracture is impossible. Through the visiting shepherds who find the hermit's corpse, or the village maidens who never meet their neighbor, Smith reveals that these future sanctums are always visited too late, in a future present that is already past: "The high meridian of the day is past" (S, l. 29). Grimly, Smith's hermit digs a grave for a corpse that has washed ashore, echoing both Williams's *Paul and Virginia* and Wollstonecraft's "The Cave of Fancy," until his body, through the work of digging, comes to match the chalk earth in its paleness: "the pale recluse / Dug in the chalk a sepulchre" (S, ll. 722–723). The act repeats the speaker's activity from earlier in the poem (which is later in the diegetic space of the poem, given how the speaker is speaking in the present): she had dug through the chalk to identify mysterious fossilized snail-shells, ground into a chalk of their own and thus impossible to identify, belonging ambiguously to a terrestrial present and/or a distant aquatic past (S, ll. 378–380). The imagery activates echoes of Merry's "Ode to Folly" and its contretempopian vision of deep time. No sooner does the hermit—whose sequestered dwelling makes him, in effect, a human snail—dig through the chalk than we find, immediately in the next verse paragraph, that the already-sepulchral hermit is already dead too, and his corpse is discovered by shepherds. His story is like an inverted version of *Antigone* in which he becomes reintegrated into the civic structure through a life not "between" but after two deaths, yet living "at a limit that is not accounted for by their solitude relative to others."[75] He has died, it would seem, without ever dying: the time of his death was always past and to come. The poem ends with the burial of the hermit's corpse near his old home in the city (S, ll. 733–740), as if he cannot even be a hermit in the present, but only in a future that has passed. Being a hermit is something that one had hoped for, and even fancied, but never is.

Smith warns that "All, with the lapse of Time, have passed away" (S, l. 440). Yet who and what qualifies as a member of the "all" is precisely the question that the hermit's burial raises. At the root of this difficulty is the poem's ambivalent attitude toward happiness, which quickly, in the poem, becomes a matter of sexual difference. Smith is dubious of happiness: "Ah! who *is* happy?," she asks, "Happiness! a word / That like false fire, from marsh effluvia born, / Misleads the wanderer" (S, ll. 258–260). Just as Hope is Smith's name for the lack in hope, so too is happiness known only through its tendency to produce unhappiness. The term "Misleads," though, like happiness itself, has normative implications. In a fascinating digression, Smith considers how, although both boys and girls can be fleetingly happy, they must arrive into happiness differently. The boy finds happiness by being, essentially, William Wordsworth: when climbing a tree or playing in the river, a boy displays mastery and so "is for a moment happy," and "of his prowess proud" (S, ll. 270–271). Adolescent dominance over nature, when combined with ignorance of death, is Smith's recommended pathway to masculine happiness (S, ll. 264–266). Contrastingly, "the village girl is happy" when outfitted "with bonnet newly purchas'd" (S, ll. 273–276). She is happy to look pretty and to look pretty for boys. Yet

FUTURE POETRY

"her happiness is vanish'd," Smith observes, when her brother his "mimic drum / Beats, till he drowns her rural lovers' oaths / Of constant faith, and still increasing love" (S, ll. 277–281). It is not the girl who is disillusioned here—we are told she only ever half-believed the vows, anyway—but the loudness of the drum prevents her vows from registering at the level of the big Other. They don't "count." Ironically, the boy forfeits "his freedom, and his happiness together," in the act of destroying the girl's (S, ll. 283–285). For Smith, the sexes are mutually constitutive—one's place in the world is conferred, it would seem, by compulsory heterosexuality—yet in interpellating each other asymmetrically as boy and girl they destroy their own "freedom."

Labbe argues that Smith treats gender norms as layered and multiple, akin the Lacanian structure of the Imaginary and Symbolic.[76] I would suggest that the space between those layers is, as with Smith's preferred metaphor of sedimentation, the very link that ties them together (i.e., what Lacan would call a sinthome). Smith's goal is to register "Woman," or rather, to borrow a Lacanian strategy, ~~Woman~~, as a disruptive force in that arrangement, by ensuring that Woman remains not-whole. As I have indicated earlier in this study, Lacan writing ~~The Woman~~ in strikethrough indicates that "Woman" as such is not available as a universal category, given the demands of a patriarchal society. As he explains:

> when any speaking being whatsoever situates itself under the banner "women," it is on the basis of the following—that it grounds itself as being not-whole in situating itself in the phallic function. This is what defines what? Woman precisely, except that Woman can only be written with a bar through it. There's no such thing as Woman, Woman with a capital W indicating the universal. There's no such thing as Woman because, in her essence, . . . she is not-whole.[77]

The girl's path is relayed through the boy's desire, not for the sake of their complementarity, but as a spur to her transformation. As Bloch says (whose gender biases are always, admittedly, very questionable): "We have in us what we could become. . . . It includes the girl who adorns herself for the special boy she does not know."[78] I believe this is the function of the girl's bonnet in *Beachy Head*, despite the bleak tone of Smith's analysis.

Human flourishing, Smith suggests, entails an appreciation of the deep history of things, but also total ignorance of that history; it requires an openness to the future that can only come from the heartbreaking

178   FRACTURE FEMINISM

separation of the sexes. That is how seemingly disparate questions such as, Is happiness for girls different than it is for boys?, and, How is it possible that elephant fossils were discovered on the British Isles?, and, Why am I finding fossilized seashells inland?, and, How can someone know if the particulate matter of this sand was originally a snail's shell?, become all part of the same unified meditation taking place from within a fracture in time.

Even as *Beachy Head* shows us how to place contemporary military crises within extremely long historical contexts, it seeks to incorporate the future into contemporary politics, an achievement that positions Smith as a forerunner to modern utopian thinkers of wartime such as Bloch and Judith Butler. In *Frames of War*, Butler stresses that

> the way in which debates within sexual politics are framed is already imbued with the problem of time, and of progress in particular, and with certain notions of what it means to unfold a future of freedom in time. That there is no one time, that the question of what time this is, already divides us, has to do with what histories have turned out to be formative, how they intersect—or fail to intersect—with other histories, and so with a question of how temporality is organized along spatial lines.[79]

Butler's comments help us to see how Smith is imagining temporality along spatial lines, so that the nation is a set of asymptotic timelines as a way, alternative to "homogenous, empty" clock time, of enduring the difficulties of war.[80] If clocks offered time as a remedy for crises of space, Smith develops vastly concussed hours that build contretempopian bowers, even as the concussions have produced, and continue to shape, the very landmass that clock time asks us to defend. Yet for Smith as for Butler, the question of sexual difference refracts these temporalities, complicating any notion of political space, or of national sovereignty, in the process. In doing so, it creates an alternate form of collectivity around the impossible category "woman." In so doing, Smith seems to acknowledge the risk that her poem's very utopian impulses would themselves perform ideological work. She recognizes and de-activates the familiar trap, so capably described by Fredric Jameson, in which utopian cultural texts misapprehend their own ideological work by thinking of their means and ends as strictly separate.[81] The fracture that she discovers in time, a gift from Fancy's hand, creates a contretempopian time, rather than utopian space, and embeds it in the present.

Richardson: The Hospitality of Harvest-Home

There were two British poets named Charlotte Caroline Richardson active during the Regency. The better-known one, a widowed schoolteacher and author of religious verse, hailed from York. Little is known about the other one, the author of *Harvest: A Poem* (1818), who seems to have hailed from the remote mining town of Frosterly, in County Durham in Northern England.[82] The Frosterly Richardson, though still quite obscure, has begun to attract critical attention for the subtle ways that her work, which she paid to have published, critically interrogates national political, military, and literary hegemonies. Stephen C. Behrendt has written admiringly of her, reserving special praise for *Harvest*. Some forty pages long, the poem celebrates the end of war with France by allegorizing peacetime as harvest time.[83] It develops "harvest-home" (i.e., the end of the harvest season) as a metonym for England generally at the conclusion of the Napoleonic Wars. Richardson's previous poetry collection, *Waterloo: A Poem, on the Late Victory* (1815), had celebrated Napoleon's defeat; *Harvest* deals more directly with the state of England, especially rural England, in the relatively peaceful years that followed.

Richardson appears to be particularly indebted to Mary Robinson's georgic poem "Harvest Home" (1800)—as perhaps was John Keats, who borrowed the phrase "viewless wings" from Robinson, and who follows her template in "To Autumn."[84] The poem, says Ashley Cross, was "Robinson's attempt to distance herself from her Della Cruscan past."[85] Alternating between descriptions of male bodies at work and lush, sensual description, Robinson suggests that the laborers' "blithe song" would "Echo" through the valleys of agriculture to generate "delights unspeakable."[86] The echo-effect unleashed by the workers' song creates a fragile last refuge for "your [lusty] sons" and "blooming daughters," considered separately, in a contretempopian moment "beyond the dreams / Of visionary skeptics" at the "death of Summer."[87] Robinson uses harvest time to imagine "the neighborhood of peace," which seems to be a function of sexual difference.[88] This becomes a direct influence on Richardson, it appears.

Richardson, echoing Robinson's echo, writes that "The hills, the groves, the echoing vales resound / The joyful uproar. Now, again it shakes / The list'ning woods: Again, and louder still, / Th'exulting shout proclaims the Harvest-Home!"[89] I am interested in how and why the "echoing vales" become "louder still" with each repetition. In an opposite movement to Smith's *Beachy Head*, the echoes in Richardson's *Harvest* effectively transform a time into a place. They do this primarily by repurposing the meaning of "home" in the phrase "harvest-home." "Harvest-home" would normally denote the end of the harvest season. It refers to an activity—bringing the last of the harvest home—rather than a dwelling. When Richardson makes the post-Waterloo era into an imaginary "home" called "harvest-home," she creates the effect of time flowing in reverse. A domestic space is "proclaimed" into being through the echoing speech acts of the citizenry and, by extension, the poet, as if to imply that the future has already happened, and continues to resonate now. Comparably, the citizenry, via the poet who tells their story, can summon Harvest-Home performatively because "the joyful uproar" remains the same with each new "exulting shout," making the echoes indistinguishable from the fresh recitations. The effect is not coherence or national unity, but rather dissemination or scattering: the song is "exulting" rather than "exalting." As the poem proceeds, the voices become refracted into "wild Discordance" as song "echoes round" the mansion walls (H, ll. 2.44–46)—a figure for *différance*. Repetition pulls the voices into disorder and chaos, implying the haunting presence of an anarchive drive that turns times into "places, a habitation, and always a haunted house."[90] We are back in the register of spectral time, previously glimpsed in "Ithuriel."

As an extended metaphor for postwar Britain, Harvest-Home becomes in Richardson's text an absorbing and contradictory space, combining, as the name implies, agricultural labor and domestic sociability, memories of preparedness for the future that has now arrived, after Waterloo, as Richardson's contemporary moment. The figure connects Richardson to Wollstonecraft, who, as Catherine Packham observes, would often invoke small farms as a way of presenting alternatives to exploitative economic systems,[91] and Smith, who had imagined a "lone farm . . . with granaries and sheds" as a contretempopian alternative to war with France, and whose hermit had dreamed of building "some little space" among the firs (S, ll. 174–175, 533). As with Wollstonecraft and Smith (as well as Robinson), Richardson's Harvest-Home becomes a place for theorizing gender at the limits of the British community. At first glance it would appear as if Richardson were presenting hospitality, as epitomized and exemplified by Harvest-Home, as the opposite condition to hostility between nations: the celebrations at Harvest-Home can begin once hostilities have ceased. Yet, as Derrida has famously observed, even though "hospitality" would seem to name the opposite of opposition itself, it is nevertheless "a word which carries its own contradiction incorporated into it, a . . . word which allows itself to be parasitized by its opposite, 'hostility.' "[92] The contradictions inherent to hospitality engender strange temporalities in Richardson's *Harvest*, raising what Derrida calls the "questions at once timeless, archaic, modern, current, and future [*à venir*] that the single word 'hospitality' magnetizes."[93]

Harvest-Home, taken as a space rather than an event, "magnetizes" unconditional and unlimited hospitality for Richardson: "This night the Farmer's hospitable doors / Are open'd wide, to welcome ev'ry guest: / This night shall Pleasure reign beneath his roof, / And Mirth, that knows no bounds save innocence" (H, ll. 2.32–36). The emphasis is on unconditional inclusiveness that "knows no bounds" and applies to "ev'ry guest." Yet the reign of pleasure is no sooner awaited than it is already delimited, six times over. First, the promised jouissance of the scene, its "reign of pleasure," will be mediated, as we have already seen, by the echo-effect which truncates and transmits it. It is to be awaited—it is not here yet—but we have already confronted a second, temporal, limitation: "this night" suggests a temporary suspension of the usual rules, which will be back in force tomorrow. "This night" is in the future, it seems. Third, the syntax implies a distinction between Pleasure and Mirth, and thus boundaries to each type of enjoyment. Fourth, Mirth is further regulated by "innocence," which is explicitly presented as a control on it. The moral and religious term "innocence" recalls the lines just above, the passage in which Richardson explains that "to enjoy is to obey" God's will (H, ll. 2.21). Hence, what had seemed to be riotous and untrammeled enjoyment becomes an obscene superegoic incitement to enjoy. That seems especially true because of the ambiguity of the syntax, which seems to suggest that Pleasure actually reigns over Mirth instead of existing as its syntactical equal, and which refuses to state whether Mirth is reserved for the innocent or denied to them, given Pleasure's ranking authority here. All we know for certain is that innocence is the positive or negative condition of a supposedly unbounded Mirth; we might assume that Mirth is reserved for the innocent, despite all of our experiences the contrary, but the poem does not actually indicate on which side of the innocence-boundary we should stand if we are to celebrate at Harvest-Home. We do know that innocence is a condition placed upon a hospitality "open'd wide, to welcome ev'ry guest." The provision renders illusory the text's promises of genuine hospitality. Fifth, we note that the "hospitable doors" remain "the Farmer's": in his act of supposed hospitality, the Farmer never jeopardizes his ownership or control of the space, which is how his "doors" become the regulatory threshold for patriotic celebration. It is the classic

Derridean paradox: "for there to be hospitality, there must be a door. But if there is a door, there is no longer hospitality."[94] The farmer never risks losing control of the threshold. Finally, Richardson acknowledges the reader as a sixth delimitation on the reign of Pleasure, urging the reader not "To scorn these ruder tones; and O! accept / The warm, the mutual concord of the heart" (H, ll. 2.48–49). Here again, it is unclear whether the "not" applies to the scorning *and* the accepting, or just the scorning—and thus we cannot know whether the speaker is urging us *to accept* the heart's concord or *not to accept* it, just as we have agreed not to scorn the ruder tones. Unmistakably, though, the speaker calls upon the reader to accept more pleasure, to accept absolutely anything, and thus the poem interpellates us as gatekeepers to the scene, whose approval or forgiveness must be sought. The irony is that the reader is lauded for her capacity for independent judgment at the very moment where she is incorporated into the poem. She provides a layer of possible acceptance or forgiveness supplementary to those of God, the Farmer, and the moral code, but subject to the instructions of the speaker, thus suggesting the insufficiency of each and suggesting that even God *qua* big Other has a check or two on His jouissance. If to enjoy at Harvest-Home is to obey God, it is also to subject God to the reader's authority and the reader to the speaker's. God's desire is the desire of the Other, and the Other is only a signifier standing in for another signifier, and thus not God, structurally speaking, at all.

Peter Melville and David Simpson are the scholars who have analyzed Romantic literary hospitality the most fully. Simpson suggests that the greeting of strangers within British Romanticism leads, generally speaking, to the exploration of multiple and conflicting temporalities.[95] Melville suggests that Romantic-era texts tend to conscript the reader into acts of hospitality, much as we have seen *Harvest* doing. Although Romantic texts "impose a certain violence on the others that they welcome or exclude," he argues, "they nevertheless situate themselves in an 'ethical' space that renders each scene of reading . . . an experience of responsibility."[96] In *Harvest*, however, the reader redoubles the abdication of the promised bounty, turning the Farmer's generosity into just one step in a multilayered process of deferred approvals and a labyrinth of delimitations. The very conditions of unlimited hospitality, then, are overwhelmingly conditional and policed into compliance by Richardson's syntax. It is only on these conditions that the Farmer can ensure that "the full sparkling bowl / Gives its inspiring warmth to ev'ry heart" (H, ll. 2.38–39). Richardson uses Harvest-Home delve into (as if a fracture in time) the paradoxes of hospitality, which, she understands, must be both unconditional (to qualify as hospitality) and regulated to the point where it becomes indistinguishable from hostility. It makes sense, then, that Harvest-Home has to be performatively "proclaimed," as it is literally no-place, an impossible space built out of time, constructed between the seams of the nationalist discourse. The metaphor of Harvest-Home finds meaning within the context of the enclosure of English farmland. By 1818, the actual country homes of England had been rendered uncanny by the Enclosure Acts of the previous century: they are both familiar and new, traditional and modernized, tied to the land and to labor. These double valences generate a raft of contradictions in Richardson's text.

Everyone is invited to Harvest-Home, but the genders must be invited separately:

> Come then, ye Swains;
> Ye smiling Maidens, come—all who have shar'd
> The toils of Harvest; freely now partake
> The joys of Harvest-Home!
> > Nor you alone (H, ll. 2.29–32)

The "Nor you alone," set apart as an internal line break within line 32, issues an invitation to someone else, neither swain nor maiden, who is a supplementary celebrant at this scene. It specifically refers to the figure of "The Stranger," who is, we are admonished, to be received at the Harvest-Home with all hospitality. By suggesting an alliance between "A Maid," whose sighing disrupts the festivities, and "The Stranger," who is both invited and not invited, welcomed but with a measure of reservation (as suggested, for instance, by that internal line break), Richardson subtly suggests the broken structure governing the patriotism of her political moment.

As "the guest becomes the host's host," warns Derrida, we find the emergence of "the simultaneity, the 'at the same time' of two incompatible hypotheses."[97] The text attempts to forestall this inversion, but ultimately cannot. Such is the mechanism of the echo-effect, which, as we have seen, gets louder as it proceeds precisely by eliminating any difference between before and after. As Richardson's celebration of Harvest-Home exposes the poem to the antinomies of hospitality, it generates alternative temporalities that arguably offer a way out of the "homogenous, empty

184   Fracture Feminism

time" that was becoming hegemonic during the early nineteenth century, finding ways to experience the future as an aspect of the present. Even as Harvest-Home becomes a figural mechanism for Richardson to muse about peacetime, its invocation of and exposure to the double binds of hospitality enable the poem to unsettle the telos of time itself. The poem awaits a "lovely morn" in which sexual difference becomes inflected by national politics, domestic affections, and sexual enjoyment in a "joyful uproar." In this way, Richardson comes to defer the national celebrations through a difference intrinsic to them, exposing the steady patriotic march to the delays of différance. Such is Richardson's "newly-won power over space and time," as Freud would say. Like many of Richardson's poems, *Harvest* is a complicated meditation about gender, ideology, and temporality in the context of a national political and military culture defined, over the decades previous, by "war at a distance" and its attendant ideology of "clock time."

"Nor you alone" is actually the third figure to be greeted as a Stranger in this poem. I am tracing them in the order in which they appear as echoes, meaning, with the latest coming first. The second Stranger of the poem is Frederick, who, as "A youthful Stranger, to his native plains / Was just returning from the dang'rous Seas, / Laden with wealth and honour" (H, ll. 1.176–178). By odd coincidence, he shares his name, occupation, and eagerness to reconcile with his past with Captain Wentworth of Austen's *Persuasion*, published just a few months earlier.[98] Richardson's Frederick meets an old couple, buried in grief for their son Frederick, who had been killed in the war. Frederick, somehow not recognizing his parents by their appearance, does recognize his father's voice and informs his grieving parents that their son is not only not dead, but right here in front of them. Through this strange reversal of the plot of *Oedipus Rex*, peacetime in Britain becomes characterized as a reunion of families and the end to grief. But if peace is the condition of hospitality, and thus of family, it is only that way because Peace itself had already been welcomed into the poem.

The anti-Oedipal story of Richardson's Frederick, who accidentally stumbled across his parents and thus rediscovered his own life and restored theirs, suggests that interminable mourning for deaths abroad is counterproductive and possibly unnecessary. In Derrida's analysis of *Oedipus at Colonus*, he suggests that deaths abroad must be grieved, but that alternative temporalities emerge when that grieving is forcibly fore-shortened: "in doing so he [Oedipus] also offers them [his daughters], simultaneously, a limitless respite, a sort of infinite time."[99] The opening 300 lines of *Harvest*, I would maintain, forcibly delimit the mourning for those killed in the war by placing them firmly in the past: "be comforted," the speaker enjoins, as "The shock is past. Yet, like a dream of terror, / It leaves its frightful image on the mind. / 'Tis past!" (H, ll. 1.19). The repeated insistence on the events' pastness and their insistent return as "a dream of terror" opens multiple concurrent temporalities and even, simultaneously, the "limitless respite" that Derrida would seek.

This is especially true because the first of the "Strangers" to appear in the poem is Peace itself: "Hail, gentle Peace! celestial Stranger, hail!" (H, l. 1.150). Presenting Peace as a foreign visitor who must be recognized and welcomed, Richardson suggests, on the one hand, that peace is the precondition for any hospitality, but on the other, and more troublingly, that Peace must be "hailed" in order to become our guest. A true stranger could never of course be "Hailed," because their very unfamiliarity would render them unrecognizable. Yet the speaker seems to lean upon her prior knowledge of this Stranger, electing to accommodate Peace specifically on the basis of its "gentle" nature. Yet Peace, as world traveler, is described in the somewhat menacing language of empire: Peace says Richardson, will "wider still extend / Thy boundless sway" (H, ll. 1.50–51). By presenting Peace as a foreign visitor in need of our recognition and acknowledgment, Richardson imagines England on the receiving end of Peace's global conquest, thereby effectively negating England's central purpose in the nineteenth-century world, and activates the strange temporalities that tend to interfere with hospitality.

The very trope that would present Peace as a "Stranger" in need of our recognition and hospitality generates temporalities of its own. The Stranger's revelation as "Peace" redoubles the allegorical work here: an allegorical figure is being re-allegorized as a Stranger, only to have the second layer stripped away. These layers of figuration obscure the alterity of this visitor. As Paul de Man says, Romantic poetry tends not to employ allegory because allegory leaves no interpretive residue.[100] The material is used up in the interpretation and cannot ramify further except as self-citation. Richardson's layered tropes control the strangeness of the Stranger within known and knowable discursive frameworks. Even the role of "stranger"—a name for alterity and unfamiliarity itself—becomes converted into the familiar role Stranger. The speaker hails Peace not only because it is recognized in advance as "gentle" but also because it is recognized in advance as the figuration for Peace, and therefore as peacefulness itself—even if the arrival of Peace *qua* allegorical figure takes the shape of a metaphorical foreign invasion and offers no guarantee beyond the allegory of its actual peacefulness. These allegories generate alternative temporalities as they accrue. De Man's sense is that allegory depends upon time because it depends upon repetition, as it cites precedents through its repeating chains of signification. As allegory confronts its failed attempts at repetition, it dialectically "establishes its language in the void of this temporal difference." "In the world of allegory," de Man explains, "time is the originary constitutive category."[101] Yet the allegory simply displaces onto one temporal plane the unpredictability of another, and of the other.

In this way, the tropes themselves ordain the intersubjective structure of hospitality, which presses hospitality to open toward the future. In the same way that " 'making time' is equivalent in Hebrew to 'inviting,' " says Anne Dufourmantelle to Derrida, with hospitality: "in order to produce time there have to be two of you, or rather there has to be some otherness. The future is given as being what comes to us from the other, from what is absolutely surprising."[102] In the poem, the unexpected arrival of a Stranger named Peace destabilizes the future of the nation. This future is what is allegorized as harvest time and extended, as its own scene of hospitality, at Harvest-Home. And because harvest is as much a set of labor practices as it is an allegory, Richardson comes up against the own orientation toward the future implicit in her vehicle: Harvest is something accomplished here and now that was always imagined; it belongs to the contemporary moment only in the sense that that represents the future moment of the past. And all of this before we begin to track the temporalities emerging from its figural processes. As Richardson explains: "The Plowman turns the soil, and careful strews / The seeds of future Harvest. . . . So shall the fruitful Earth / Yield her abundant increase; and the joys / Of universal Plenty bless our Land" (H, ll. 1.329–333). To harvest is to experience already the future of agriculture.

Melville shows through an analysis of Rousseau that Romantic hospitality opens up the future because it must always be awaited. Such scenes, he says, produce "temporal complexity" because awaiting one future ensures that we will miss another.[103] Richardson is open to such contingency, but, as we have seen, she also complicates matters considerably further. Richardson's willingness to welcome Peace as a "Stranger," for instance, invokes futurity in three different registers: in Dufourmantelle's sense that hailing the other is "making time"; in Derrida's sense that Harvest festivities mark an enforced, but only partially successful, cessation of national mourning;

FUTURE POETRY

and, in de Man's sense, through the repetitive mechanisms of the tropes themselves. And things get yet again more complicated when this entire suite of temporalities, taken in omnibus fashion, then repeats and repeats again in *Harvest* with the arrival of the second and third Strangers, each one amplifying this inaugural act of hospitality, retroactively establishing it as the original, and treating the others as its aftereffects. Frederick secures his meaning through the previous encounter with Peace, just as Harvest-Home becomes hospitable in reference to the reunion of Frederick's family. It becomes impossible to say which of these events comes first in a poem in which consequences routinely precede their causes, as with the work of its echoes, or when time is said to stop temporarily, as at Harvest-Home. *Harvest: A Poem* opens an unusual set of temporalities through its guarded willingness to welcome the Stranger, yet fails in that endeavor because its defenses are always up.

Felicia Hemans, Between Psychosis and Perversion

"Mrs. Hemans," as she was known, once seemed a marshal of morality, a docent of decency, and a paragon of patriotism; it will perhaps seem strange to situate her between psychosis and perversion. In recent decades, though, we have learned to see Hemans as an ironic, subversive, and ambivalent poet, who worked by "repetition, omission and moments of ungraspable affective intensity."[104] Not that there is anything especially subversive about perversion, either: if anything, it can be considered a zealous devotion to the status quo. "The perverse subject obeys orders," Kristin Hyldgaard observes, because:

> as far as the pervert is concerned, desire is an imperative that cannot be refused no matter whether he is an otherwise model citizen with all the highest and best moral standards. It is an imperative that comes from somewhere else; he is remote-controlled by something.[105]

While this description may especially bring Hemans's "Casabianca" to mind, I want to investigate how Hemans explores such an imperative in "An Evening Prayer at a Girls' School," her frequently anthologized poem from the 1826 literary annual *Forget Me Not*.[106] The poem is built around a series of imperatives from the speaker to the reader, which direct the reader's gaze toward some schoolgirls as they pray before bed. There is a perverse pleasure at the heart of these injunctions—the more perverse because the enjoyment is extracted from the spectacle of the girls' future destruction: "Gaze on—'tis lovely!"[107] If apostrophe, to borrow Culler's definition, is how we treat objects like subjects in order to fortify the speaker's will, we could say that apostrophe necessarily fosters a perverse relation.[108] A pervert, in Lacanian terms, is someone who objectifies themselves so as to fill in the lack in the other, and so produce the Other's enjoyment. Psychosis is a very different arrangement, and an incompatible one: it involves abolishing (or "excising") the big Other, so there is no difference between symbolic and real. What is interesting about "An Evening Prayer at a Girls' School" is how the repetition of its perverse apostrophes actually collapses any boundary between the girls and the reader. The reader, forced to explore the perversion of symbolizing the Real and the psychosis of realizing the symbolic, is relied upon to hold these pathways together, and thus functions, in a precise sense, as a sinthome.

Perversion, as Lacan warns, is not a break between the imaginary, real, and symbolic—after all, they are already separate—but the tie that holds these three elements together, embodying the obstacle to subjectivity.[109] Yet, to the extent that "the symptom subsists in so far as it is hooked onto language,"[110] Hemans can push the reader into a psychotic relation through her exploitation of literary language, including apostrophe, refrain, and rhyme. What emerges through this double inscription is a chronological torsion: doubly inscribed through the speaker's injunctions, the reader begins to experience time from the future, the better to glean enjoyment from the girls' deferred suffering here and now, in "this calm vesper time" (EP, l. 37). Although psychosis and perversion should be incompatible, in Hemans's poem the one arrangement continues into the other, as with a Moebius strip, and the reader is called upon to tie these disjunctive registers together.[111] In such a way, Hemans inculcates in the reader a mode of asynchronous being that, I will suggest, becomes a form of "women's writing" and feminism—with the Woman written as barred.

"Evening Prayer" is a poem about the future of patriarchal oppression. The concept "Woman," in "Evening Prayer," designates the moment when the future is stitched into the present. Susan Wolfson was the first to contrast the wholesomeness of the evening scene with the "bleak apprehensions" that follow: the reader is enjoined to see the "joyous creatures" as the unhappy and then dead people of the future, "what grief must nurture for the sky, / What death must fashion for eternity!"

FUTURE POETRY

(EP, ll. 11–12).[112] By encouraging the reader to watch school-aged girls from the perspective of their future destruction, Hemans formulates an untimely response to the masculinism of her contemporary moment and imagines ~~the woman~~ as a site of political transformation to come within that moment. In this way, the poem contributes to Hemans's longstanding poetic experiment with time.

The poem, written in Venus and Adonis stanzas, is built around a repeating set of injunctions to the reader: first "Hush!," and then "gaze on" and "gaze" (EP, ll. 1, 7, 9). The instruction to "Gaze on" precedes the instruction to "Gaze," meaning that the reader is commanded to do the thing they are already doing, or must continue with their voyeurism before they can take that pleasure for the first time. In the movement from "hush" to "gaze," the reader is relocated from the verbal register into the visual, and from reprimand to encouragement to an incitement to pleasure: "Gaze on—'tis lovely! . . . Gaze—yet what seest thou . . . ?" (EP, ll. 7–9). This is an example of what Lacan calls the "centrifugal dynamic" of the gaze in relation to time: "It starts off from the *instant of seeing*, and maintains it as its prop. Indeed, the eye beholds *instantaneously*."[113] The gaze, as a partial drive, collapses timelines, transforming them into moments. The fact that this gaze is summoned through apostrophe entrenches its temporal effects, as apostrophe itself, as Culler explains, resists temporality and narrative, enforcing only "a timeless present," regardless of its content.[114]

The addendum "Yet what seest thou?" indicates that, despite all appearances, our gaze has not been directed toward an object. The speaker hails our gaze as "lovely" in its own right: the poem sexualizes the gaze itself, not the thing it beholds. The object of this gaze will only later come into being, and so we are left to enjoy the repetition of the injunction to "gaze," and it is in this sense that our experience is "sexual." In its repetition, it fixates on death: as Alenka Zupančič has indicated, "death is what lurks in the very midst of sexual drives."[115] The presence of death in this poem links jouissance to deferment, our gaze being the mechanism through which we can glean the enjoyments to come already this evening: we look at "bright young heads . . . untouch'd by care," but enjoy the deferred unhappiness and deaths of these schoolgirls (EP, ll. 4–5). Similarly, the praying girls "make idols, and . . . find them clay" and so will learn to "bewail that worship" (EP, ll. 29–30). The reader is instructed to gaze not at the girls, but at their "true heart of hope, though hope be vain" (EP, l. 34). The speaker's injunction to the girls, "therefore pray!," expresses the logic perfectly: pray, not because things may improve, but because they will not—we want to anticipate your hopes being dashed and savor the dramatic irony (EP, l. 30).

The perverse logic depends upon a firm separation between the girls and the reader, each of whom the speaker apostrophizes commandingly. Yet as this distinction breaks down, the arrangement becomes psychotic. The girls, by making idols and finding them clay, are being encouraged to "love their delusion as they love themselves"—a sentence from Freud's letters that Lacan seizes upon in *Seminar III* to epitomize psychosis.[116] That is, the girls are hoping without hoping for anything, as a mode of ethical training and self-care. Samuel Taylor Coleridge had noted, earlier that year, that "hope without an object cannot live."[117] Exactly so: the girls, trained to hope without an object, become a positivized void, or what Singer calls "internalization without content."[118] They "cannot live," being disappointed women who do not yet exist—and the reader is looking on.

The poem, perversely, calls this "hope"—a term that, as we have seen in the discussion of *Beachy Head* above, can refer to the awaiting of something that has been deferred. Here, though, hope, being always already "vain," refers to the experience of the future in the present moment; it is a negation positivized as a "true heart"—the ineffable object *petit a*—that the reader can drill into as a wellspring of enjoyment for the speaker. "Hope" in this poem has a preservative function; it is "a sweet dew to keep your souls from blight." The speaker's repeated injunctions for us to gaze at this objectified negation generates enjoyment for the speaker ("'Tis lovely") as the reader learns to gaze at a hope that aspires only to be dashed. This is the "'pragmatic' double constraint" that arises when, as Derrida explains in an analysis of Marx, "contradiction and secret inhabit the injunction."[119] Yet the reader also becomes the objectified negation as the poem forces us to stand in the position of the girls: in gazing at nothing as nothing hopes for nothing, the reader becomes the object of their own gaze and thus becomes negativized within the scene. We are experiencing what Lacan would call a "temporal abyss," namely, psychosis, an experience with an "extra-temporal character": because "all of the symbolic is real" for the psychotic, the condition can be a "temporal funnel" leading outside of "ordinary time."[120] Hemans creates that funnel in the moment of the poem's enunciation, through the poem's repeated injunctions to the reader. The reader is caught, in the impossible deferment of hope and pleasure stitched back into the scene, between perversion and psychosis, getting the Other off on the love of its own delusion. I am speaking, here, of "ordinary psychosis," meaning a flattened relation to language.[121] It is a way of defying the patriarchal law of the signifier.[122]

The poem's first two stanzas are organized around two oppositions: on the one hand, the voyeuristic reader and the naïvely hopeful girls, and on the other, this evening's "joyous" girls and the dead women they will become. Hence everything is destabilized, even deconstructed, with the apostrophe "joyous creatures! that will sink to rest," which, in its *Hamlet*-like double valences of sleep and death, makes impossible any distinction between now and the future and between the reader and girls: the girls are readying themselves for bed, and so will immediately "sink to rest," but this only amplifies our sense that they *will* sink to rest permanently before too long (EP, l. 13). These girls are being asked to live their future sorrow already, and so thus, contradictorily, they should be happy while it lasts. The girls, in the speaker's instructions, are to "lift up your hearts! though yet no sorrow lies" within them—their future unhappiness is called upon to cancel out their current unhappiness, as if they are already tasting the affect of future lives and thus can retroactively experience as happiness the deferment of their unhappiness. So too, in our gaze their "woman's tenderness" should already be perceptible in "childhood's lip and cheek" (EP, l. 17). We can see these "fragile things" only either as they await their existence or after they have died—and this from a poet known for a "preoccupation with infanticide."[123] One sees a woman either too early or too late, as in Zeno's paradox, and so the reader is enjoined to fill in for this absence, to help it function—in a very real sense, "Her lot is on you" (EP, l. 25). "Woman's tenderness" is something that exists neither now, nor in the future, but can be generated retroactively by the perceptual movement between futurity and our current "holy hour" at the moment of enunciation (EP, ll. 24, 1). The reader alone has access to this vantage point, which is how the reader has to tie these temporalities together; in that sense, the reader is necessarily the woman who the poem awaits. The girls are the reader, and they coexist in the room asynchronously. At the "instant of seeing" the reader beholds themselves as a void that "cannot live," recognizing themselves only as an advance on jouissance given over to the Other: "'tis lovely."

Hence, in the lines: "to be found untired, / Watching the stars out by the bed of pain," we cannot know whether it is the reader or the girls who are "to be found untired," nor who is said to be "finding" them (EP, ll. 31–32). There is no longer any way to distinguish the girl from the woman or the reader from the girl-woman; it is precisely through this ambiguity, and the girls' propensity to be "found untired," and thus discovered by the reader in a moment of disobedience, that the poem lures us into the "bed of pain" that becomes a site of prurient fascination

192   Fracture Feminism

in this poem. Because the girls are compared to "birds, with slumber's honey-dew opprest, . . . at set of sun," they can next be apostrophized as "that," rather than "who" (EP, ll. 15–16). The "that," in turn, is what justifies their being called "creatures" in the tenor of the simile. That is, in the moment of the poem's enunciation ("evening" being synonymous with "at set of sun"), the vehicle of the simile returns as its own tenor, and so the speaker has foreclosed the usual gap between signifier and signified, between language and meaning. The simile enacts not a projection or displacement, but a "return from without" that links the Real to the symbolic through the reader as sinthome.[124] This is, essentially, ordinary psychosis, which depends on the collapse of metaphor and metonymy.[125]

The poem concludes with a final imperative for the reader, its most ambiguous of all: "Take the thought of this calm vesper time." In this bewildering injunction, everything depends on whether we understand it to be directed at the reader, or at the girls. In one reading, we are asked to "take" the thought of this time "on through the dark days fading from their prime," which is psychotic: it treats a symbolic construct, time, as an absence that might orient our desire, as we endeavor to "take" or appropriate it (EP, ll. 37–39). In another reading, we learn to enjoy the "sweet dew" of time's progress "through the dark days" as a preservative from "blight," which requires a perverted structure: we are turning ourselves into a machine for the production of the Other's enjoyment, a "sweet dew" always awaited, as if time were an example of prayer (EP, ll. 39–40). The tension between these incommensurate meanings is what makes possible a third reading, in which we can recollect the present, as if we were living in the future. That is, the ambiguity in the sentence, between the reader and the girls, and between psychosis and perversion, is how the poem envisions future-oriented vesper temporalities.

Hence the strange temporality of the poem's concluding couplet, which focuses on happiness: "Earth will forsake—O! happy to have given / The unbroken heart's first fragrance unto Heaven" (EP, ll. 41–42). Happiness comes from being caught between the future tense ("will forsake") and the past perfect ("to have given"), and so a girl's heart is always only "unbroken": heartbreak isn't something that ruins their innocence; rather, we are born with a heart that exists only to await its future breaking. Most crucially of all, it is a non sequitur, and so it is never clear why we are suddenly talking about Earth, nor what it is that Earth will forsake. We are left, it seems, "forsaking without an object," an activity that defines psychosis: forsaking nothingness itself, the void that structures meaning around it, rather than

FUTURE POETRY 193

repressing that material. Hence, we know that we will be "happy" only when we can retroactively anticipate that we will have given away the "first" of presumably many of the heart's "fragrances"—something that the heart, broken or unbroken, never had. Happiness is impossible, then, now and in the future, but still arises from the movement between one time and the other. The poem is exploiting an impossible temporality to generate its own surplus enjoyment, one without a referent anywhere but in its own mechanisms, and the reader can give *that* positivized absence "unto Heaven," in the pervert's manner.

Hemans has moved from perversion to psychosis, but only to take a pervert's pleasure from a psychotic relation to language. This is part of a general tendency in Hemans's work, to be "concerned with how the caprices of language and text instantiate socially anodyne performances of woman," as Singer and Sweet have put it.[126] Psychotically incorporating the reader into the figural work of the poem, Hemans compels us to experience perverse jouissance in a flattened way, thus inculcating a mode of being-in-time that, I have suggested, becomes a mode of "women's writing" specifically. In imagining "woman" as an impossible experience to come, and so here already, it also ensures that the girls' futures, however disappointing, will be tied to this moment. It achieves, then, a perverted goal, effectively freezing the trajectory of their lives at the apex of the Other's jouissance.

Byronic Destinerrance in "A Spirit's Return"

By 1830, when Hemans published the collection *Songs of the Affections*, she had supplanted the late Lord Byron as the most popular poet in Britain (along with Laetitia Elizabeth Landon). "Hemans' ascent and Byron's fall are a natural pairing," argues Jason S. Rudy, in the popular imagination of the time.[127] A new, "embryonic, or half-shaped" era of British poetry, one "dominated, or so it seemed, by female poets," was underway.[128] Poets of the later 1820s became fixated on the issue of their future reception, and, more generally, "how . . . their age [would] look from the perspective of the future."[129] These are poets who, says Andrew Bennett, "articulate most vividly a certain convention of female irony or resistance toward the possibility of posterity as a redemptive supplement to life."[130] Several poets of the era would experiment with advance hindsight by thinking about ghosts and a life beyond the grave, much as Byron had done in *Manfred*.

"Apparitions have a special charge for poets in this period because they mirror the dubious acts of reading they anticipated for their own poems, which might, perhaps, appear before future readers," explains David Stewart.[131] Yet ghost imagery, when used as a figure of the future, tends to emphasize the incompleteness of the present moment. That is because, as Jacques Khalip says:

> the future mobilizes the ghosts of the dead as portending figures for the ambiguities of living and being in a state of between-ness that challenges the very continuity of those claims, rendering them inadequate or unfinished. Put another way, the ghosts of the dead remind us that our ambitions are on shaky ground, nothing more than open graves.[132]

Ghost imagery, I would suggest, extrapolating on these claims, could serve as a figure for a reading to come, for being read and re-read, and for reading and re-reading. In serving in this capacity such imagery could splice the future into the present as its incomplete or impossible extimate point. This happens most prominently in the opening poem from *Songs of the Affections*, "A Spirit's Return."

The speaker of "A Spirit's Return" addresses the present with knowledge from the future: "shall not I, too, be, / My spirit-love! upborne to dwell with thee? / Yes!" (ASR, ll. 255–257). This is the Derridean yes, the Joycean yes: an affirmation of the intimacy to come even at the moment of its foreclosure, affirming its nonreferral to the center.[133] It is a self-addressed answer, addressed to its past self in the present, carrying repetition within itself. As Derrida explains: "The yes can only state itself by promising itself its own memory. The affirmation of the yes is the affirmation of memory. Yes must preserve itself, and thus reiterate itself, archive its voice in order to allow it once again to be heard."[134] But if "yes," in this case, is addressed to the speaker herself, "With thee" is addressed to the other. It functions as a sign of solidarity in the key of what Derrida elsewhere calls "destinerrance." Destinerrance is a neologism that marks the fusion of Derrida's own work with that of Lacan: it combines his own earlier neologism, "différance" with an "a," with the Lacanian suggestion that letters will always reach their destinations—which was famously a point of contention between the two thinkers.[135] Derrida, reflecting at last on the legacy of Lacan, revives his neologism "destinerrance" in tribute to his late rival. He offers it as a sign of intimacy: "to hear someone say 'we'

FUTURE POETRY   195

when speaking all alone after the death of the other," marks "an internal
drift" in the address, he suggests.[136] That is because

> "We" [like Hemans's "with thee"] is always said by a sole per-
> son. . . . it is always an "I" who utters "we," supposing thereby, in
> effect, in the asymmetrical structure of the utterance, the other
> to be absent, dead . . . or even arriving too late to object. . . . If
> there is some "we" in being-with, it is because there is always
> one who speaks all alone in the name of the other, from the
> other; there is always one who lives more, lives longer. I will
> not hasten to call this one the "subject."[137]

Hemans says, in effect, *yes* to this destinerrance, to herself as ex-sisting
in the other. She highlights that same asymmetry, inherent in a union
marked by, first, the sexual nonrelation, and second, the impossible temporal demands of speaking to the dead.

The bereaved speaker finds that, in death, her lover "became / Unto
my thoughts another, yet the same."[138] In its critical examination of deferred
sameness within difference, "A Spirit's Return" can be understood as a
repetition of *Manfred*, something encouraged by its playful title and Byron
epigraph. Byron was, and remains, a Romantic-era figure of deconstruction:
the effort "to achieve some kind of completion, to reconcile the various
contradictions" in Byron's work, says Jerome J. McGann, "only seems to
install them more deeply and more firmly."[139] Byron must thus be read as
one of Romanticism's "figures of failure," who "made it possible to begin
writing histories that would be multiple and self-contradictory."[140] Dino
Franco Felluga finds that "Byron's method can be said to be the defamil-
iarizing and antagonizing of the present" through hauntological means.[141]
His oeuvre has been called "a poetics of the Real" and a "deconstruction
of posterity."[142] Given Byron's investments in fracture and failure, we could
say that Hemans's return to Byron in "A Spirit's Return," by also being a
return to Manfred's return to Astarte, voices the echo of an echo of an echo.

"A Spirit's Return" echoes *Manfred*, and in so doing, deforms it,
demonstrating Susan Wolfson's point that Byronism "was a mystique in
which women collaborated."[143] Even in life, Byron was already a figure of
imaginary pastness, "a nostalgia for a place not Christian, not English, and
not the present," and a writer who refused to let the future retroactively
give meaning to the "rich multiplicity of present possibilities."[144] Hemans
invokes him to claim a utopian moment, yet only once she has accessed

196   FRACTURE FEMINISM

it from an alternative temporal direction. She transforms Byron into a
future site of women's writing in the present.

Hemans incorporates literary interpretation into the work of mourning as a way of thinking utopia temporally, through repetition. Her return
to Byron is an act of displacement particular to mourning: it conjures a void
or absence at, and as, the "center" of the text.[145] To this end, Derrida asks:

> Can one not affirm the nonreferral to the center, rather than
> bemoan the absence of the center? Why would one mourn
> for the center? Is not the center, the absence of play and dif-
> ference, another name for death? The death which reassures
> and appeases, but also, with its hole, creates anguish and puts
> at stake?[146]

That deathly void that we affirm with a Hemansian "yes!" ensures that texts
do not repeat themselves when re-read; the trajectory of one's reading is
pulled askew through metonymic procedures as one confronts the aporia of
the text. "A Spirit's Return" explores this problem. At the critical moment
of revelation, the speaker even cries out: "A void! A chain!," to imply that
the world as we know it is constructed around a foundational void now
apparent to her in the aftermath of her encounter (ASR, l. 225). Here at
the absence of play, a void inflects the metonymic chain as it begins its
swerve, exposing the poem's acts of mourning to the perils of différance.

David L. Clark observes that "both Derrida and romanticism are
peculiarly preoccupied with the problem of life, death, and living-on, as
well as the work of mourning and the irreducible remainder."[147] Mourning
is an uncanny and ambivalent process in "A Spirit's Return," characterizing
both the speaker's desire to be reunited with her lover and Hemans's own
engagements with Byron's work. "A Spirit's Return" gives one the sense of
reading *Manfred* inside-out: Hemans's speaker is patient, not grandiose;
her tone is of ennui, not desolation. While Manfred is haunted by the
past, seeking to revisit traumatic scenes, the speaker of "A Spirit's Return"
explores more paradoxical temporalities. While *Manfred* begins with an
epigraph from *Hamlet* about the risks of giving hospitality to specters,
"A Spirit's Return" begins with an epigraph from *Manfred* about the risks
seen from the other ghostly side. As with "Ithuriel" and *Harvest*, its time
is spectral time propelled by a ghostly jouissance. In effect, "A Spirit's
Return" enacts a Lacanian quarter-turn on Byron's discourse. Manfred had
addressed the ghost of Astarte through what Lacan would call the discourse

FUTURE POETRY 197

of the hysteric, using his own brokenness to address an unplumbable master signifier, in the hopes of generating knowledge. But Hemans allows excess jouissance to speak directly to the lack in her lover, with the hope of producing something towering and sublime.[148] Essentially, Hemans's poem, much like Barbauld's "On the Uses of History," opens the past to the analyst's discourse, to produce multiple future-oriented temporalities within it. As Lacan explains: "the analyst depends on the not-all."[149] Hence "A Spirit's Return" adapts *Manfred* for fracture feminism.

We see evidence of the discursive quarter-turn in the poem's epigraph, which the text attributes to Manfred. In Byron's text, it is a spirit, not actually the character Manfred, who says: "This is to be a mortal, / And seek the things beyond mortality!"[150] Hemans is putting a spirit's words in Manfred's mouth. Like Manfred, Hemans's speaker fights for the chance to have a supernatural conversation with her deceased lover, who is also apparently her sibling, in which they come momentarily "face to face" (ASR, ll. 127, 175). But, while Manfred is reckoning with a shameful and distressing past, Hemans's speaker, coming at it from the analyst's side, is oriented toward the future. Even more than is the case in *Manfred*, everything about her "communion with the dead" involves waiting, without guarantees, for the intimacy to come. There is alienation instead of regret, guilt, or despair. Her "communion with eternity" is paradoxically bounded, as implied by its position within an inset narrative: only at the moment of its finish, when "like a knell / Swept o'er my sense its closing words, 'Farewell!,'" does the speaker recognize the moment to have been everlasting (ASR, ll. 214–216). She can retrieve the moment of intimacy through acts of memory or narration, but at a cost: the present must be vacated of meaning, such that she awaits deliverance into an intimacy that she will already have experienced and found inadequate.

Her fleeting communion, bounded by duration, memory, and narrative, and retroactively confined into heroic couplets, will have been made to signify "eternity." In the intimacy to come, her lover will have been "for ever and ever mine" (ASR, l. 262). That the normative cultural ideal of monogamy must, in order to be plausible here, so directly confront its own paradoxes and, ironically, take a basically Byronic, incestuous shape, reveals the perverse kernel of sexual ideology within late Romanticism. The speaker, through a brief "glimpse" of her lover, comes to grasp the permanence of his situation. This paradox, when considered alongside the fact that the poem abruptly ends here, suggests the unsustainability of sexual rapport; worse, the fidelity to come seems only to remind the speaker, in the here and now that she is struggling to re-experience, that her imprisonment comes from "within me" (ASR, l. 249). Her only solace from this interpellation is through further and further interpellation, the reassurance that death welcomes only the worthy to its gated community, and that she may well be worthy despite her "struggles": it "summons *me* to go" (ASR, ll. 251, 242).

Pressing the universe for a chance to speak to her lover, the speaker says that, in an "imploring accent," she "taught one sound / Unto a thousand echoes—'Awake, appear, reply!' " (ASR, ll. 151–154). The pedagogical aspiration of this line is striking: to teach echoes to reverberate no longer is to teach them not to echo. Saying "taught" in the past tense, she presents an impossible task as an accomplished achievement. Yet the speaker's project of unification (i.e., the quest for "one sound") is soon, ironically, joined by other similarly unified sounds, such as her "one profound / Imploring accent," and "One prayer." Together, these phrases denote the failure of univocality at the moment when it seemed to have been definitively achieved. One cannot teach echoes not to echo, it appears. The pedagogical aspiration makes sense only if we learn to see the speaker as the object of her own lesson: she is the one learning to hear "a thousand echoes" as "one sound," which implies that she has learned to conflate various moments into one simultaneous experience. A deferment gained through the play of difference manages to collapse the present and future into one, which is how, very backhandedly, the poem achieves its goal of coherence. The "binding together" (*relier*) involves dispersion (*relire*), paradoxically.

"To teach unto" is a strange expression, ambiguous enough to make the direction of the teaching uncertain. Syntactically speaking, there remains the possibility that "one sound" is supposed to be learning about echoes, not the other way around. This would be, basically, an aural mirror stage collecting fragments under the banner "subject." These are lines, after all, marked by hard caesura and with intense enjambment, and the line break after "profound" suggests fracture or dispersal. The "one sound" is emphatically three: "Awake, appear, reply!" While the speaker may seem to demand a three-phase sequence—first awake, then appear, then reply—that sequence is compromised by each demand being impossible to fulfill. One cannot successfully command someone who is asleep, as they must be alert to understand the injunction; one cannot ask someone to appear if they are not already present to hear the call; one cannot demand that an echo reply, as echoes cannot speak for themselves—demanding a reply from an echo would be, in effect, to subject oneself to a ceaseless loop of similar demands to and from the other. The three impossible injunctions, then, cannot so easily form a sequence, as each depends on an unfulfillable condition. This is the death drive at work.

Hemans may have been aware of these difficulties: after all, the poem really emphasizes the difficulty of making echoes answer. The speaker admits that loving her late partner has not been easy, given how her heart has "but fateful music to bestow, / Echoes of harp-strings broken long ago" (ASR, ll. 21–22). Love, then, is a type of nostalgia arriving by destinerrance and characterized by what Michael O'Neill calls "the serene heartache of an endless yearning."[151] In this spirit, we should read the three terms not as a sequence but as a proliferation, a polyphony of conflicting demands. The speaker begins a strikingly Wordsworthian meditation on her lost pleasures, her joy "in all wild scenes" in her younger years (ASR, l. 32). Her thoughts, she explains, at that time "burst forth as a gale that swells . . . and from the leaves / Shakes out response" (ASR, ll. 43–45). The response was violently yet passively solicited. It moves uneasily from the past perfect to the present tenses as soon as it begins speaking figuratively. The line break after "leaves" and the caesura after "response" make the response from the leaves seem all the less assured, the leaves all the less cooperative. Especially so as the leaves merely stand in, metonymically, for the respondent, rather than responding directly themselves. In "A Spirit's Return," the speaker acknowledges that "each tone that broke / From the wood-arches . . . [would make] my quick soul vibrate as a lyre" (ASR, ll. 37–39). It is a play of obedience, between the wind's involuntary vibrations of the soul and its violent demand for a response.

The situation pointedly recalls Gayatri Chakravorty Spivak's meditations on the Ovidian character of Echo, who is said to guard the "difference between question and response."[152] Spivak appreciates Echo because her utterances are of "absolute chance rather than an obstinate choice."[153] The Romantic-era metaphor for this is of course the Aeolian harp, a correspondent breeze that Hemans liked to exploit, including in the lines quoted above. Hilariously, the involuntary response actually comes: the line complies with the request to "break" through its line break after "broke," fulfilling the speaker's request in a way that is grimly self-referential and that suggests, somewhat backhandedly, the inadvertent violence of the performative demand.

Hemans offers a contrast between two temporalities and two impossible sounds: the silently echoing harp-strings of the present are on offer as abundant recompense, in a manner of speaking, for the "perilous delight" of years past (ASR, l. 35). Hemans seems to draw a playful contrast between the present "harp-strings" and the past heartstrings (as in, "the fulness of a heart that burned / For the deep sympathies of mind, . . . Making my quick soul vibrate as a lyre") (ASR, ll. 22–39). These temporalities become independent but concurrent; the past is not earlier than the present. In the past, her heart poured out love with a violence that made a genuine connection impossible; now, her heart is worn out by questing, and the music it has to offer is merely an echo of old broken harp-strings. What the heart has to give are echoes of broken old harp-strings—the echo of the memory of a sound, the echo from broken strings. It is a sound that would be no sound, because broken strings do not resonate. The lover is being offered a positivized void, located between two impossible temporalities: a present in which the speaker can remembers back when intimacy would fail to work, running up against a "curtained world," and a present in which her heart works by activating the memory of when things were broken, from which we can imagine how them might have been. The speaker presents her lover with the void at the center of her poem: she is, in mourning, affirming the nonreferral to the center, rather than bemoaning the absence of the center. Or, in Lacanian terms, she will have been giving something she will never have had to someone who will never have wanted it.[154] It is to receive a gift, called love, from Time, "the beautifier of the dead," like Byron's Childe Harold at the Colosseum.[155]

The echo of the broken harp-strings, already an imitation of the wounded heartstrings, becomes a figure for contretemps, in the sense that her present offerings are the echo of an absence from the past. This is a fracture feminist perspective as viewed in verso from the "curtained world of spirits" (ASR, l. 46): the narrative present is a glimpse of a past event that never happened and couldn't happen. As the speaker explains a bit later in the poem: "an undertone / Was given to Nature's harp, for me alone" (ASR, ll. 81–82). The harp has gained its "undertone," a sup-plement, which is grief; it adds precisely nothing to the mix but makes that absence ramify into the future, where a radical intimacy to come will or would have been thinkable. It activates a split between the speaker of the poem and the speaker-as-character-in-the-poem, making us think of these levels as subject to separate concurrent temporalities—another form of "the I altered" that we have traced already through Barbauld and Smith. The alteration is amplified by the speaker's request to, in effect, *make me a lyre* by playing the broken harp-strings. Through the homophones of "lyre" and "liar," Hemans points us toward a sort of liar's paradox—a mechanism

FUTURE POETRY   201

that is said to evince the splitting of the subject.[156] In Hemans's version of the classic paradox, fidelity to the immediate real world would make one a lyre/liar; truth, on the other hand, would be an impossible experience to come. It is as if Hemans's speaker has recognized that melancholia is the deferred and displaced version of mourning; as the loss becomes unconscious it becomes increasingly prone to delay and dissemination, undercutting attempts at meaning or signification.

Although it mostly tracks the speaker's experience in the present—especially her affective detachment from the community around her—it includes, and juxtaposes, two scenes of memory, one Wordsworthian, the other Byronic, that are crucial to its sense of time. The echo becomes an important motif in both cases. Ovid's Echo stopped short, in Spivak's analysis, of producing "the impossible experience of identity as wound" and "the a-venir of a history not written."[157] Hemans's speaker can be said to achieve the impossible. While the poem's rhetoric of "glimpses" and "light" imply that mourning is a matter of vision, still the poem stages an impasse between sound and vision and actually privileges sound over vision as the preferred modality of reading. This is significant for the ways that it enables Hemans to imagine *différance* in ways alien to Derrida's theory. Re-reading, for Derrida, is a practice of mourning; in making this case, he seems to privilege the visual over the aural as the proper mode of mourning, as Vivian Nun Halloran notes.[158] Hemans's poem, through its unusual relationship to Byron's work and its emphasis on the echo, brings back the sonic element of re-reading and asks us to think about echo as the voice of melancholia. In this way, "A Spirit's Return" records its speaker's memories of the future. Prioritizing sound over vision and repetition over inauguration, Hemans's echoes challenge us to rethink deconstructive approaches to mourning and/as re-reading. She models a way of remembering how to remember, and repeating Manfred's acts of remembering even as she stages her own very different encounters with a present now dead and buried. To live with one foot in a future permeably walled off from the present, yet contained within it, may be a feminist survival strategy for a chronophilic era. It is even a temporal form of utopianism—what I have been calling contretempopianism.

The poems taken up in this chapter—even in their moments of hope for conviviality, as in *Beachy Head* or *Harvest*—pursue a bitter utopianism that upends the very connotations of utopia in its bleakness. Theirs is not even a progressivist "utopia limited" of the kind described by Nersessian, or a paradoxically boundless engulfing of boundaries, as described by Neyrat. In Nersessian's model, poets would make the best of a world of scarcity, by learning to love boundaries; in Neyrat's, they love an untouchable space beyond the boundaries of an "immunological drive."[159] The four poets featured here each summon a different kind of impossible utopia. They despair for their culture thoroughly enough to create new temporal possibilities in the here and now, without ever cultivating an enthusiasm for austerity or a drive to regulate, but remain free from, contagion. As if they were Žižeks from a previous century, they attune the reader to events "not discernible from any neutral 'objective' study of history, but only from an engaged position."[160] Their utopian future is already here but "visible only to believers," who are asked to respect the subtlety of the event as it opens time to new coordinates.[161] In this spirit, they use hermits as figures for collective life, psychotic structures to measure the time of girls' education, and extend hospitality in a moment of heightened nationalism. At root, the difference between their work and a "utopia, limited" is to be found in their different approach to lack. For Barbauld, Smith, Richardson, and Hemans, it is not that women have been deprived of something desirable; rather, they fashion the lack in themselves into the thing of which the culture at large has been deprived. It is the difference between standing *in* the political/social world, finding it wanting, and learning to make do in a radical new way (as Nersessian's study describes), or to embody that lack as a way of opening a hole in a world into which one cannot assimilate. It is to propose lack itself as a political cause, without asking for what remains to be redistributed or become the basis of a collectivity, and to insist on its present insusceptibility to the given political order. Essentially, these poets, as poets of the contemporary future, ex-sist on the obverse side of the limited utopia championed, in Nersessian's analysis, by poets like William Blake, John Keats, and Percy Shelley.

The innovative element in these four poets' work—that is, what makes it contretempopian in orientation—is that each imagines utopia as a time rather than as a place, and that, although the time of that utopia is something still to come, it is also already here *within* the horrifying world of the present without becoming *part* of it. They take the concept of "utopia" so literally as to ensure that it cannot be considered a place at all. Rather, they claim as a positive virtue the lack intrinsic but inassimilable to the political/social field. For Barbauld, Smith, Richardson, and Hemans, the awaited future is not a cultivated love of the obstacle or the shortfall, which is what Nersessian's study salutes, or a rhizomatic movement, as Neyrat's seeks, but a love of the lack that breaks open a lacking world, and a willingness to analyze politics from that nonexistent perspective.[162]

Chapter 5

Gulzara and *The Last Man*

Worldwide-izing the *Roman à Clef*

The Regency novel *Gulzara, the Princess of Persia, or, The Virgin Queen* (1816) and Mary Shelley's *The Last Man* (1826) are feminist *romans à clef* of the contemporary future.[1] The *roman à clef*, as a genre, would seem to be a particularly well-adapted host for fracture feminism, exploring the space between the factual and fictional, reality and hyperreality, the quotidian and satirical, the indicative and subjunctive: it would seem to be a form given to explore those aspects of contemporary life that will not be wholly contemporary. Yet, if the *roman à clef* is a novel that, in refusing to be fully fictional, is never quite a novel, these two *romans à clef* are never quite *romans à clef*, either. Being not all *roman à clef*, they become not-all *romans à clef* (I mean, in the Lacanian sense)—and therein lies their even stronger link to fracture feminism. *Gulzara*, written anonymously, features Orientalized versions of Princess Charlotte, the Prince Regent, and an array of prominent literary and political figures. *The Last Man* offers a fictionalized account of Shelley's late family and friends, many of whom also happened to be eminent poets, as if they were "social distancing" during a pandemic. Both novels combine attributes of the *roman à clef* with formal and temporal ambiguities drawn from the fracture feminist tradition, so as to find themselves discussing political systems at large, certainly in Britain but concomitantly on a worldwide scale, rather than lampooning a small circle of well-known personages.

Since the beginnings of prose fiction, the *roman à clef* has been an important tool for women writers as they have sought to confront powerful figures, starting with Madeline de Scudéry's incredibly long *Artamène, or the Great Cyrus* (1648–1653), of which *Gulzara* seems like a distant descendent, and Delarivier Manley's *The New Atalantis* (1709), which, in its dystopian focus on the invisibility of women, provides a template for *The Last Man*, despite its Tory partisanship. *Gulzara* and *The Last Man* are both equally, though, self-aware about their place in a British Romantic tradition of writing the contemporary future. *The Last Man*, for instance, rewrites a key passage from *Eighteen Hundred and Eleven* to re-summon Barbauld's depopulated London of the future, as a bleak commentary on the depopulated Shelley household of the author's present; *Gulzara* praises *Eighteen Hundred and Eleven* directly, in a long footnote. Wollstonecraftian arguments, too, arise throughout both novels. By adapting this Wollstonecraftian-Barbauldian feminist tradition to the subgenre of the *roman à clef*, these novels make possible new and more uncertain forms of political commentary.

Romans à clef are novels whose characters are thinly veiled versions of public figures, which comment, often satirically, upon actual people while taking refuge in the plausible deniability of the fiction. They are known especially for their capacity to stir up scandal and test the boundaries of what is legally permissible in print, but also for their tendency to confound accepted modes of literary interpretation. They blur the boundaries between novel and society page. To read a *roman à clef*, one has to unlearn how to read a novel. For Sean Latham, the form's mightiest defender, "the roman à clef, however, is not just an ancestor to the novel that long ago withered on the genealogical tree; it is instead a creative and stubbornly persistent counter-form to the novel"—a form with "disruptive powers."[2] Complicating matters is that before the mid–eighteenth century, as Catherine Gallagher has shown, the novel as a genre was presumed to be nonfictional: the veracity of the account was always a topic of consideration. The novel came to be recognized as a fictional construct—that is, as "nobody's story"—through tense cultural engagement with lack often ascribed to eighteenth-century female authorship. Gallagher places Manley, and thus implicitly the *roman à clef*, at the heart of this fraught cultural negotiation.[3] By the end of the eighteenth century, novel readers, even of realist novels, were expected to know that the narratives are fictional, and that the literary characters, however lifelike, are not real people. The *roman à clef* is, in this sense, a throwback to an earlier moment in the history of women's writing. It depends on a seemingly unskilled reader—though obviously this is a skill in itself—who can accept that the fictional characters *are* (in a basic way) real people. The form was especially popular in the 1890s and through modernism, but had an important presence in the Regency—most notoriously, with Lady Caroline Lamb's scathing portrait of Lord Byron in *Glenarvon* (1816). Other well-known examples from the period include John Polidori's "The Vampyre" (1816) (if one can speak of a short story *à clef*), which satirizes Lord Byron as an undead, roving leech, and Thomas Love Peacock's *Nightmare Abbey* (1818), which traps an assortment of famous poets, thinly veiled, in a mouldering mansion.

Both *Gulzara* and *The Last Man* eschew certain aspects of the traditional *roman à clef*, in ways that allow them to address the contemporary future. First, their elaborate narrative frames refuse to find easy analogues in the real world, and are difficult storyworlds to understand temporally either in relation to the "real world" or the main narrative. Second, they include characters who seem neither to be representative of real-world personages nor straightforwardly fictional, frustrating the reader's attempts to interpret these novels as *romans à clef*. Third, both novels end with extreme indeterminacy and ambiguity, ensuring that any attempt to fix a meaning through the two layers of the *roman à clef* will fail. Fourth, both novels undergo an unusual "generic transition" midway through, a swerve in tone and plot that, in the case of Shelley's novel, has been said to indicate "the eruption of the Real into the novel's Symbolic order."[4] Fifth, they take on a worldwide scale that is unusual, if not unprecedented, in the history of the subgenre. The *roman à clef* is most often used to skewer small social elites, which has meant that its scale is, quite often, sharply confined. While *Gulzara* and *The Last Man* do depict small, insular cadres, they construe their satire across a wide world much larger than England or even Europe. They should be seen as part of a wider tendency in Romantic-era writing, identified by Evan Gottlieb, for texts to challenge the ongoing hegemony of European empire-building—despite them being nineteenth-century British novels and thus complicit in that process.[5]

Gulzara and *The Last Man* use the strategies of writing the contemporary future that we have seen elsewhere in this study, but situate that fracture in temporality within a slippery international setting that, in the end, proves to be worldwide-izing. The spatializing discourses of these novels—their eagerness to travel and cross borders while remaining *romans à clef*—are part of what makes possible a narrative "torsion" that "heralds a new time," as Alain Badiou would say.[6] Much as we saw with Helen Maria Williams's translation of *Paul et Virginie*, *Gulzara* and *The*

Last Man combine a worldwide scale, unusually intrusive narrators, and narrative frames that collapse into the diegesis. These texts are, in effect, narrative cross-caps or Klein bottles, impossible structures that open into their own internal apertures. The torsion makes possible unusual temporalities that seem to depend upon knowledge from the future.

Novels like *Gulzara* and *The Last Man* indicate that a deconstructive reckoning with reason itself was underway in the Romantic period and was pursued as a way of undermining European hegemony worldwide. This is not to say that they openly challenge the project of empire; both texts could easily be accused of abetting European expansion. Yet the supplementary features of the work—such as the willingness of these novels to engage with national and international politics, imagine new systems of government, think comparatively, denaturalize power, attribute things that are obviously false to a fictional "Editor" in charge of producing the text, resist the one-to-one correlations that typify the *roman à clef*, develop elaborate nested structures of narration, and careen between things staggeringly ambiguous and things utterly unambiguous—tend to falter at key points, effectively worldwide-izing Europe's relation to points East and South, in much the same way that Barbauld had done in "On the Uses of History."

The Temporality of *Gulzara*

The year 1816 saw the publication of *Gulzara; Princess of Persia; or the Virgin Queen*, a satirical *roman à clef*, written anonymously, and replete with Orientalist imagery. It was published by John Souter, a prominent London publisher. It is likely that the author of *Gulzara*, still unidentified, was British and a woman. Souter, after all, was best known as the founding editor of *The British Lady's Magazine*, a liberal publication that made it its mission to offer writing for and by women "exclusively," as an expression of Souter's "firm conviction" that intellectual women, as readers and writers, were transforming "every department of civilized life."[7] Souter saw it as his professional purpose to offer publication opportunities for emerging women writers, sometimes without publishing their names, in works that would engage with central questions of gender and culture. In this way, regardless of who actually wrote *Gulzara*—Stephen C. Behrendt wonders if it may have been Souter himself, given the extent to which the topics explored in the novel so closely overlap with the concerns of the magazine—we can see it as a novel that would have been marketed and received as women's writing, and that engaged with questions of politics and culture from what was supposed to reflect a woman's perspective. Anonymous authorship was not unusual during this time, especially for women writers—a fact that has led Jennie Batchelor to warn that, in scholarship on the history of women's writing, "we leave Anon behind at our peril . . . even if she may sometimes turn out to be a he."[8] *Gulzara* places a female character—the eponymous princess—at the center of the story of modern British foreign and domestic politics, and adapts that story into domestic fiction, such that a woman's right to select her own partner, and for the right reasons, becomes the crux of it.

To a Regency reader, the premise of the novel would have seemed, let us say, familiar: when Abbas, the King of Persia, falls into a deep trance, his son, the Prince Ali—a figure of excess and vicious dullness—takes over the government on an interim basis. Ali's daughter, the eponymous princess Gulzara, suffers her father's cruelties, including the risk of an arranged marriage. The royal drama is set in the immediate aftermath of the second military defeat of the enchanter Noureddin, who, we are told, emerged as a leader in post-revolutionary Tartary and had captured territory all over Asia; Noureddin, in the early chapters, is defeated by the Persian general Selim and sent for a second time into exile, ending thirty years of war between Persia and Tartary. All of this conspicuously recalls the real-world situation of Princess Charlotte Augusta of Wales, daughter of the British Prince Regent and heir to the throne, in the aftermath of the Battle of Waterloo. In the words of Alan Rauch and Behrendt (the only two scholars to yet write on this novel, to my knowledge), *Gulzara* is a "thinly veiled roman à clef," the satire of which was "too obvious for the reader of the day to miss."[9] In 1816 Charlotte was, as Behrendt puts it, the great "hope of the Whigs," a figure easily lionized in contrast to George III and his son, the Prince Regent.[10] Charlotte was already a figure associated with "a variety of political tensions" and "a paradoxical politics," prone to carry "political undertones"—features of her public function that would become all the more pronounced the following year, upon her death in childbirth.[11] The novel brings these subtexts into contact with a whole other set of political subtexts associated with eighteenth-century "feminist Orientalism," a tradition recently traced by Samara Anne Cahill and associated, after the 1790s, with Mary Wollstonecraft. Specifically, *Gulzara* turns Princess Charlotte into what Cahill (following Miriam Cooke) calls a "Muslimwoman," a silent figure capable of serving in English fantasy

208   FRACTURE FEMINISM

as "the ultimate victim," but then also makes her the heroine of a typical
Regency marriage plot.[12]

Gulzara has yet to be hailed as a masterpiece. Behrendt, conceding
its want of "literary skill" and "sustained wit," and determining that the
author "seems to have no clear sense of what to do with Gulzara," sees
the novel merely as "a useful and revealing artifact of culture," given that
"its literary merit is negligible."[13] Yet, precisely because Gulzara fulfills the
mandate of a novel so poorly, it is, formally speaking, strange enough to
be worthwhile. Much of its strangeness is temporal. The novel carries the
present of British politics into the future, and then aborts that project
inexplicably. Although Behrendt claims of Gulzara that "satire of the sort
undertaken here is far less effective a tool for speculating about the future
than it is for commenting on the past and present," the novel actually
works quite hard to subvert the relation between the future and present.[14]
Present, future, and past are no longer plotted along a timeline here, which
makes Gulzara a transmission from the contemporary future. In thinking
British politics through what it calls an "appeal to—POSTERITY" that
would apply only to the immediate political present, Gulzara speaks to
its British reader from the contemporary future (G 248).

Much of the novel's temporal complexity derives from its dual
narrative frames. The first ten pages of Gulzara are addressed "To the
British Public" by the fictional editor, called such "for he can scarcely be
denominated the Translator" (G v). One becomes an editor, it appears, by
failing to meet the criteria for being a translator, as if editing were only the
failure of translation. This criterion would make Helen Maria Williams the
"editor," rather than translator, of Paul and Virginia, given the important
material that she adds and subtracts to and from Bernardin's text. In the
case of Gulzara, our "Editor," so-called, neither translates nor edits; he is
a character and narrator. In the outermost frame narrative, he narrates
his travels to Calcutta, where he meets Saleb, a "lively Persian, who had
been employed in the recent embassy of Sir Gore Ousely" (sic, G v). The
Editor, embroiled in a discussion of politics with Saleb, supposes that
Persians "would scarcely comprehend the propriety of female domination"
(G v). Saleb corrects this misimpression, offering the Editor a fifty-year-old
manuscript by a writer by the name of Hussein—a novel or a history, it
does not specify—in which Persia, too, had been governed by a Queen.
But the Editor cannot read "the languages of the East," so depends on
Saleb, a classic native informant, to read the manuscript aloud to him.
This would seem to make Saleb a translator, yet he is also, in effect, an

GULZARA AND *THE LAST MAN*   209

editor. Saleb agrees to read only "the meaning" of the narrative, rather
than translate word for word. He promises to "write from the Persian's
dictation . . . and dress it up afterwards" (*G* ix). The veracity of the history is never part of the discussion, so there are no assurances that the
narrative isn't fictional from the start. We are actually informed that "the
facts . . . of the little history," including the dates, "could not be made to
agree with other historians"; meanwhile, Saleb assures the Editor that "if
our historians invent both [time and circumstance], so much the more
ingenious are they" (*G* vi). All of which is to say that the novel goes out
of its way to layer uncertainty upon uncertainty, to the point where the
main emphasis is on how counterfactual the story seems to be. Only
through such means will the Editor glean a lesson in female governance.

Saleb assures the Editor that people experience time differently in
Persia: "In Persia we trouble ourselves very little upon points of chronology"; at the same time, it is certain that Hussein "certainly flourished
about fifty years ago" (*G* vi). The Editor, then, concludes that "on the
score of Chronology, no satisfaction was to be obtained," yet he "amused
himself with the facts of the Persian author" (*G* vii). From there, the
English Editor "resolves merely to make himself master of the facts, and
to marshal them in English in his own style" (*G* viii). Yet the Editor, we
are told, is neither translator nor author of this text: "he entertains few
of the usual apprehensions of authorship" (*G* ix). These reflections are
stamped with a specific time and place: "London, January 1, 1816," suggesting that some significant time has passed between the reading aloud
of the tale in Calcutta and the composing of the notice "To the British
Public." To make matters more confusing, this set of reflections leads into
a second narrative frame, "The Persian Dedication," signed by "Hussein,
the Son of Ahmed" at "Ispahan; in the year of the Hejira, 1143." We are
thus assured that 1143 in Ispahan is "certainly" fifty years before 1816 in
London. Just one page prior, Saleb had assured the narrator-editor that
Persians have no interest in specific times or dates; yet now Hussein, son
of Ahmed, the inset frame narrator, reports finding his own historical
document, on which it was "written that in the nine hundredth year of
the Hejira, on the tenth day of the fifth month, at the hour of noon, the
venerable Abbas, King of Persia, one of the greatest monarchs in Asia,
fell into a trance" (*G* 13). The extreme specificity of this temporal reference, and of Hussein's care in dating his preface to the day and hour
of its composition, suggests that Saleb's carelessness has been a personal
trait, not a cultural trait—already striking a blow against the stereotype

210   FRACTURE FEMINISM

of the Orient as timeless and ahistorical. Yet, it should also be noted that
a document from the year 900 has been rediscovered by the same person
243 years later, and conveyed, after a delay of only fifty years, to 1815
Calcutta, where it was paraphrased aloud by someone hoping to convey
only the general outline of the story without regard for accuracy, to an
English Editor who writes down, upon his return to London, his sense
of "the facts" despite finding none of them historically verifiable. The
English Editor finds, in the story, confirmation that Persians understand
female domination as well as anyone, such that the story might "shew
men to be the same in every quarter of the world" (vii). These humanist
aspirations seek to guarantee the regularity of time at the very moment
when time's fictitiousness becomes most apparent. (Derrida has noted as
much of humanist discourses generally.)[15] The Editor, meanwhile, three
times addresses the reader as "ladies and gentlemen," further underscoring
a gender division that had already been presented as the occasion for the
delivery of the manuscript (vii, ix, x).

    The reference to Ouseley as Saleb's employer is important because
the name heralds the resumption of diplomacy between Britain and Persia after some 200 years. In 1810, Ouseley was appointed the first British
ambassador to Persia since 1627–1628, when Dodmore Cotton's efforts
with King Abbas I of Persia (i.e., *Gulzara*'s proxy for George III) led to
disastrous and fatal results for the English delegation.[16] Ouseley, in contrast
to his ill-fated predecessor, had become at the time of *Gulzara*'s composition a celebrated figure in Britain for brokering the Treaty of Gulistan
between Russia and Persia in 1813, which ended ten years of war between
those nations by ceding considerable territory to Russia. There is some
indeterminacy in *Gulzara* regarding whether Saleb is supposed to have
worked for Ouseley in India or Persia, given that Ouseley, who was Irish
by birth, excelled as a textile trader and factory owner in Calcutta from
1787 to 1795, when he would move to Lucknow and began his diplomatic
career.[17] Be it in this earlier period or, more likely, in Persia quite recently,
the narrative frame of *Gulzara* would have us believe that Ouseley's office
has been employing Persians to generate histories of Abbas, as if to insist
that Britain's latest diplomatic triumphs remain haunted by previous failed
efforts. Because the novel's main narrative has supposedly been generated
out of Ouseley's office, *Gulzara* may be considered a fictional diplomatic
effort in its own right. Although the story seems to arise directly out of
a diplomatic effort, negotiated in 1813 by Britain, between Russia and
Persia, it focuses on the court of the seventeenth-century King Abbas I,

who was disappointed with English diplomatic efforts. Yet Abbas's court, as fictionalized in *Gulzara*, is conspicuously similar to the European world immediately following the 1815 Congress of Vienna—another even more recent scene of Anglo-Russian diplomacy. The novel thus finds its footing between two recent hallmarks of British diplomacy on the global stage— the Treaty of Gulistan and the Congress of Vienna—by treating them as concurrent with the collapse of British diplomacy in 1627–1628. As the novel, through its layers of framed narration, collapses and twists the historical timelines, Persia's immediate present becomes Britain's immediate present as placed in Persia's distant history, and the events of 1815 are said to precede the events of 1813. Placed in a tangle of atemporal diplomacy in which Europe's borders are redrawn implicitly, the novel would seem eager to find armistice in a worldwide-izing manner; the brief reference to Ouseley ensures that Metternich is not, in the space of this novel's allegory, the world's main powerbroker, even while it leaves Britain at the center of the world political order.

Rauch calls *Gulzara* "a poignant allegory of the Regency," for it expresses "anxiety and fear about the political state of England, couched (for safety's sake) in complicated structures of ambiguity and anonymity."[18] It is true that *Gulzara* was published in "the high period of state repression" leading up to Peterloo, an era defined in its censorship efforts by the *Treasonable and Seditious Practices Act* of 1795; many radical writers of this period, such as Leigh Hunt, Lord Byron, William Hone, and William Cobbett, wrote in clandestine fashion so as to avoid libel charges.[19] Yet I want to push back a bit on this analysis, because, in truth, the main allegory of *Gulzara* is not especially complicated, ambiguous, or couched. The equivalences are spelled out so directly—with no reference to any aspect of Persian history except for the use of some historical Persian names— that the novel would never have escaped the censorship offices of one of Britain's historically most repressive governments. The American edition of the novel, published that same year, takes the *roman à clef* concept quite literally, providing, as an appendix, a two-page "Key" that openly declares the European equivalent for each character: it assures the reader that Abbas is really George III; Ali, the Prince Regent; Gulzara, Princess Charlotte; Noureddin, Napoleon Bonaparte; Selim, Wellington; and so on.[20] Such a key would have been unnecessary for a British reader; the novel does very little to disguise the objects of its political analysis. The novel would have been left alone by the government because, despite its peculiar structure, it articulates a mainstream Whig perspective on Princess Charlotte and the Regency. Its fantasy of eventual rule by Princess Charlotte was a common Whig indulgence, and the novel even urges support for George III: Abbas, after all, was "the honest monarch" who "neither deserved this extreme of censure or of praise," but was simply misunderstood and let down by world-historical transformations in France and some unreliable ministers (G 74–75). Ali, albeit with some irony, is praised as "a prince of great precision and decorum," though possessed of other shortcomings (G 4). Souter, as a well-known liberal publisher, routinely printed political commentary of a similar moderate perspective without any fear of reprisal. Meanwhile Regency-era texts that were far subtler, yet more radical, faced government reprisal in a very real way.

Where there is ambiguity in *Gulzara*, it arises through matters of form, such as the novel's noticeable shifts in tone that correspond to shifts in genre, from the novel's mysteriously abrupt conclusion, or the way that the plot begins to exceed, temporally speaking, the politics and personages attributable to the Key. Part of this is endemic to the *roman à clef* as a form. As Latham explains, "To learn the key is to encounter a different text, one in which matters of form, character, and symbol give way to questions about motive, veracity, and revenge. Neither quite fiction nor nonfiction, it tests the self-sufficiency of these categories and thereby undermines the modernist novel's ability to construct 'a world elsewhere.' "[21] Yet the feminist Orientalism of *Gulzara*, which has been, at times, part of the *roman à clef* tradition since de Scudéry, demands stability from "a world elsewhere." In *Gulzara*, the mere presence of Hussein as a narrator compromises its Orientalism, given how Orientalist tableaux face "a constant pressure" from narrative: "If any Oriental detail can be shown to move, or to develop, diachrony is introduced into the system," Edward W. Said observes.[22] One wonders if the easy-to-crack code might be an avenue to readerly pleasure rather than a source of plausible deniability. Such is Slavoj Žižek's take on Bertolt Brecht's *Me-Ti*, which, through a similarly simple code, displaces European revolutionary movements into an imagined China. The transmutation, argues Žižek, "makes the text much more pleasurable," as now the reader gets "the additional pleasure provided by the very formal detours" to pleasure.[23] Like *Me-Ti*, the code in *Gulzara* is so straightforward as to make the text politically titillating, once a sense of danger "is retroactively constituted through secondary detours."[24] These formal elements of the novel, taken together, are a source of real literary power: far from being interesting merely as a cultural artifact, *Gulzara* appears to purposefully employ a number of highly destabilizing deconstructive techniques, many of them manipulations of narrative time, that would seem to align it with the wider discourse of fracture feminism.

Gulzara is quite aware of the tradition of Romantic atemporal feminist writing and openly aspires to be part of it. It quotes Anna Letitia Barbauld's *Eighteen Hundred and Eleven* in a long and pivotal footnote, in order to pit "Mrs. Barbauld" against the narrator Hussein on the questions of secularism and time.[25] The novel invokes Barbauld just as Hussein is explaining the Reign of Terror in France, saying that the "Angel of Mutation" had cast his eyes on Tartary, and had endeavored to help them reform, but had unfortunately "blew a little too strong" for the Tartars' especially light heads. The Angel, in explaining his rationale, proposes that "they are intoxicated for the present, but their ideas will settle, and all will be right."[26] Such a perspective, Hussein explains, is only possible because "the angel spoke like a being who looked only to the days of years that were yet in the womb of futurity" (*G* 13–14). To this, the fictional Editor attaches a footnote, quoting some of Barbauld's decisive lines about time: "Measuring, in lofty thought, the march of time; / Sudden he calls—'Tis now the hour,' he cries" (quoted on *G* 14). The novel, like those lines from Barbauld, pits two temporalities against each other, finding "the hour," specifically "now," to be dangerously shortsighted, yet "the womb of futurity" too destabilizing. It offers no way to reconcile these two very dangerous perspectives, demanding instead that we experience them in parallax. The Editor merely speculates, in the same footnote, about the origins of the "Angel of Mutation," explaining that, although "to decide is difficult," he "probably" sides with Hussein, rather than Barbauld, in thinking that the Angel is legitimately "celestial" (*G* 14).

As we can see in moments like this, *Gulzara* inherits an epistemic fracture, East and West, from the Orientalist tradition, but repositions that fracture as a difference between now and the future, distributed equally in places East and West. Thus, it presents the future as something internal to the now. Because it relocates the epistemological fault line in this way, *Gulzara*, like many Romantic-era texts engaging the Islamic world, eschews a "clash of civilizations" paradigm.[27] If anything, it locates barbarism in Europe, through the presentation of France as Tartary: as Eric B. Song has argued, "Tartars embody a violent threat on the border between East and West" in the Western European imagination and were frequently invoked in earlier English literature as "living relics of the barbarism at the heart of all nations."[28] France becomes, in this sense, both the wellspring of rights and the excluded interior of a democracy to come—that is, its own parergon. *Gulzara* likewise turns the discourse of Orientalism against the British, a gesture that cuts both ways. On the one hand, the Orientalist sheen defamilarizes and thus makes available for critical analysis the processes of British politics; the Regent's opulent lifestyle seems especially outlandish when Orientalized, validating the prevailing Whig view. On the other hand, the novel's emphatic Orientalism suggests that, despite the stereotypes, the exotic mysteries of Persia are really no stranger than anything that happens these days in Britain. The novel builds solidarity with Persia even through the violence of its Orientalist discourse—a possibility familiar from a wider radical Orientalist tradition.[29]

This multiply atemporal framing brings us back to Said's celebrated analysis of Orientalism. In eighteenth-century Orientalist texts, he argues, there was actually a tendency for texts, working comparatively, to highlight similarities between Eastern and Western cultures. They eschewed rather than fetishized exoticism. It sought to work by "sympathetic identification" in service of a broad humanism. This tended to contribute to a historicist worldview, in which a foreign power could penetrate others and thus find "a magnanimous form of humanity" in the Orient, by selectively collapsing cultural difference.[30] Yet, Said stresses, this more magnanimous form of Orientalism was not actually an alternative to exoticizing Orientalist discourses but contributory to them.[31] Events in these texts, Said notes, "are always symmetrical to, and yet diametrically inferior to, a European equivalent." In this way, supposes Said counterintuitively, Orientalist fiction might be seen as "a form of radical realism."[32] This offers us another way to understand the thinness of *Gulzara*'s satire: it is not a bewildering flaw in the text but a feature. Read in such a way, we can see in *Gulzara*'s transparent Orientalism an attempt to shape the reader's response to European politics, by means of what Jeffrey Einboden has called, in his reading of Percy Shelley, an expression of "indebtedness to Islam."[33] *Gulzara* pits its interest in intercultural sympathy (e.g., "shew men to be the same in every quarter") against its "modern" investments in historicism. It eagerly allows its layers of narration to refute each other, challenge each other, and cancel each other out, and in this it becomes worldwide-izing and future-oriented.

As the novel builds an elaborate analogy between Britain and Persia, it triangulates that story by way of Calcutta, another site of British colonial domination. Kolkata, readers are reminded, has its own long history of settlement by Persians, prior to and independent of the British Empire. *Gulzara* presents Persian writing as a remnant of Bengal's colonial past rather than of Britain's colonizing present, such that, even as we remain beholden to an East/West epistemic framework, Persia now functions as the West to the Bengali East, and has politics separate from, if highly redolent of, British political interests. It is a difference that emerges from an exact similarity, through the force of its atemporal repetition. In this counter-allochronic logic, Britain is the place now living out a timeless ancient political structure, while Persia, through the very fact of its Orientalization, gets to be modern and chronotopic.

Through this temporal irony, the novel begins to explore the contemporary future. It begins by tracing recent British politics through an Orientalizing veneer, but pursues that analogy right into what would be the British future. In chapter 6, Gulzara becomes Queen. She escapes the tragic death that would await the real Princess Charlotte, unbeknownst to the author, one year after the publication of *Gulzara*. That is, the novel does not stop narrating when it runs out of contemporary political material—it simply carries on into the future without an air of prediction. Yet the author resists the temptation to imagine progressive alternative futures, confining their aspirations to more responsible government and gradual reforms.

Perhaps because it is already writing the future, the novel ends very strangely, without resolving its plot. *Gulzara* abruptly ends once Almanzor, a minor character who seems like an ideal partner for Gulzara, gets introduced into the novel. He makes his first appearance about three quarters of the way through, but never becomes a major character, until he suddenly, in the novel's last pages, seems to attract Gulzara's attention as an alternative to her other more strategic political-erotic options. The two jostle about politics privately in her library, as Almanzor argues that to be a courtier is the same as being a patriot, because the monarch and the nation are one and the same being. Gulzara replies, with an air of mystery worthy of *Citizen Kane*, "Almanzor—," after which the novel offers five asterisks and a paragraph-length apology from the Editor, saying that he lost the rest of the manuscript. The novel ends literally mid-sentence. Why does it end so suddenly, without pursuing its own storyline or even finishing its sentence? Should the novel be considered a fragment? It would seem so, yet Souter saw fit to publish it without any explanatory note to that effect. There is no sense, say, that the author has died, or had to abandon the manuscript. The "Editor," who is of course an invention of the author and a character in the novel, acknowledges the "pause," essentially writing *aaaaaargh* on the wall of the cave, as in *Monty Python and the Holy Grail*.

Can a manuscript be lost by one of the characters *in* that manuscript? The novel's failure to sustain itself in narrative terms seems to be a consequence of a wider strategy of rethinking contemporary politics from the perspective of the future. Gulzara, here styled "the embryo queen," spends the novel in wait, "treasuring up particular convictions for future use" (*G* 154); it is "as if the English author of *Gulzara* stared into the telescope pointed at the future" and began to write in a " 'future-studies' mode."[34] Even the fact that she survives to that point in the narrative is already a significant challenge to the norms of nineteenth-century British Orientalist writing.[35] Accordingly, we are presented with a "complete" text that stops mid-sentence, and without any resolution of the plot, just as soon as Gulzara speaks her suitor's name.

Amidst the confusion, the Editor takes the opportunity to consider the reader's pleasure. The reader, the Editor explains in a smaller font, will have enjoyed this novel. The Editor merely wonders *which* reader it will be, the reader of 1816 or of "posterity":

> This unwilling pause the editor wishes to convert into an useful one, He is amazingly entertained himself with the reign of Gulzara; but will other people be so? Say *yes*,—her destiny will be unfolded in a second volume; *no*,—and he has only to rail at the depravity of taste; and, according to ancient and consolatory usage, appeal to—POSTERITY." (*G* 248)

As no further adventures of Gulzara and Almanzor were ever published, one can infer that "posterity" has taken the day. It is a novel apparently written for the approval of the future, not even needing to exist yet; yet it is seeking to make sense of its contemporary political moment, here styled as ancient Persian past, and is unwilling to imagine the deeper trajectory of Charlotte's political career.

What does "posterity" mean in this context? Much as Wollstonecraft had called for a "revolution in female manners" for which "we much wait," *Gulzara*'s eponymous protagonist uses her connubial present to open the political future.[36] The novel pins its political hopes on the matter of an egalitarian and future-oriented system of female education. The chapters on Gulzara's education distinctly channel Wollstonecraft: they suggest that women are enfeebled by the substandard education they receive, no matter how naturally smart and perceptive they may be, and that any man with a similar education, such as Ali, would struggle similarly. Yet sexual difference is, in this novel, defined by one's relation to lack. At Gulzara's birth, the astrologer-royal advises, in foreseeing her political future, that "there is a recess in the heart," an "aching void" that nothing can fulfill. The men of the court nod knowingly at this advice, recognizing themselves in it, while the women declare that "if this were the language of the stars, it was impossible to understand it" (G 6–7). That impossible kernel of the Real begins to shape the novel's marriage plot, such as it is, and even dismantles it from within. Gulzara's approach to courtship, we are told, is the consequence of a "mental scar" suffered from her severely patriarchal upbringing by Ali without a mother figure present (G 58). Meanwhile, the people of Persia love their female leader only in terms of her potential, using her orientation to the future as a reason to one day dismiss her: "So much for the future: as to the present, they wished not their future queen, at her tender and ductile age, to catch the hauteur and stiffness of the rajahs of India; to reign over them in the spirit of a drill sergeant; and to exhibit herself at court in the form and manner of wax-work," the narrator explains (G 67). The novel, then, creates a gap in temporality both in the reception of Gulzara and in her own thoughts; that gap is said to stem from her gender, which is itself an effect of the constant expectation that she "exhibit herself"; the gap is then transmuted into the gap of cultural difference, as the Editor, Saleb, and Hussein inhabit incongruous temporalities for the English "ladies and gentlemen." (One pictures, per Lacan, two children pulling up to a train platform and wondering if they have arrived at "ladies" or "gentlemen.")[37] The temporal gap, as it negotiates the "aching void" at the heart of the prophecy, becomes a matter of female education and, in the novel's parlance, "female domination." We might say that *Gulzara*'s Orientalism, in and through its self-conscious textuality and impossible temporalities, allows the author to place gender at the heart of British politics without wishing away the problems of patriarchal tyranny. With "Almanzor—," the author signals that she would rather have the narrative become untenable, or reach an intractable aporia, than to wish away the problem of gender as it relates to the contemporary future.

Almanzor is the only character in the *roman à clef* who does not appear to represent a real-world personage: the Key lists him, uniquely, as "unknown." He seems to be named after the tenth-century Al-Andalus military leader and chancellor of the Umayyad caliphate, known especially for his campaigns against Christians in what is now Spain. In a decade when Orientalist fiction had been rapidly modernizing, largely in response to Napoleon's administrative needs, developing new, more secular imagery, delighting to classify, catalogue, accumulate, and aiming to explore deeper historical connections across the epistemic fracture of East and West[38]—the name "Almanzor" seems to reconstitute a much older and openly violent mode of relation between Christianity and Islam. Such an allusion would seem to undermine an Orientalist novel's "capacity for dealing histori- cally . . . with non-European and non-Judeo-Christian cultures," marking instead its aspiration to chart "unreachable temporal and cultural fron- tiers."[39] Almanzor, for instance, in a feat of historical hysteron proteron, is offered to the reader as a possible successor to Abbas, despite there being 550 years and a continent separating their historical namesakes. As far as the novel's allegory of the Regency is concerned, Behrendt proffers a number of hypotheses as to Almanzor's identity, finding no conclusive fit: "In the final analysis, Almanzor's identity must necessarily remain a dead-end."[40] This dead-end, I will suggest, should be treated as such—as an excessive remainder or aporia of the allegory, which renders the novel unsustainable in political and narrative terms. He fulfills the prophecy of the "aching void"; this is perhaps why the men in the court immediately recognize it, while the women find it incomprehensible. The fulfillment of such nonsense, in a way that remains excessive and supplementary to the *roman à clef*, strains the narrative up to and including the point where it apparently breaks. Almanzor, then, is the crucial figure in this novel for the way that he exceeds and escapes the dictates of the *roman à clef* and thus deactivates its system of one-to-one equivalences. In a novel replete with formal parerga, he is a parergon unto himself—an extraordinary supplement attached to the lack found in its structure.

The frustration of narrative in Orientalist texts (like Byron's *Lara*) can be understood, argues Andrew Warren, as a critique of Orientalism itself.[41] Almanzor might be read in a similar way. Once Almanzor arrives into the novel, what had begun as a gentle satire of the Regency with Orientalist ornamentation suddenly shifts into the mode of domestic fiction. That is, the novel begins to focus on whom Gulzara should marry. The shift is sudden and disquieting, even uncanny: the standard elements of domestic fiction (i.e., the genre quintessentially near, pertaining to the home and all that is close to it) distinctly clash with the elements of Orientalist fiction (i.e., the genre quintessentially far, pertaining to the exotic and foreign), to give the impression of something too close to home and unexpectedly alien. We are left with the impression that something is not right with the author's narrative performance. We are left to ask: is *Gulzara* even a novel? It contains very little that is fictional, preferring simply to give new names to things as they actually exist in Britain and Europe; it has no real plot, and seems to end before it begins; it has no characters in any meaningful literary sense; it doesn't observe generic rules very well.

It is in this uncanny way that the novel's Orientalist trappings become significant. What had seemed a mere ornamentation—a way, perhaps, to generate the pleasures of the recognition and thus to retroactively render the text pointedly "political"—becomes, within its immediate literary context, a form of resistance to clock time. Writing of Percy Shelley and the broader era of the Napoleonic Wars, Makdisi argues that "the arrival of Europe in the Orient [during this era] thus suddenly and even suddenly wrenches the latter into 'the' stream of history."[42] Said offers the broader context for this chronotopia, arguing that, when Britons wrote about the Orient after the Napoleonic Wars, they inevitably exerted a political will to expansion.[43] English writers of the nineteenth century would turn to Orientalism as a way to confront political realities beyond their own fantasies, to gain access to "a set of imposing resistances" provided by the concept of the "Orient"; nevertheless, finds Said, the Orient exists, in these writings, to give the European subject the illusion of control over himself.[44] Gottlieb approaches the situation somewhat differently, but shares the sense that British writing of points East reached a turning point with Waterloo: France having been defeated, explains Gottlieb, "Britain began to grapple with the possible repercussions of its newfound global authority."[45] It did so, he explains, not with proto-Victorian arrogance but often with a measure of unexpected humility: rather than approaching the rest of the world through a "clash of civilizations" paradigm, literary texts were formulating "a macropolitics" that acknowledged the interdependence of Britain with the rest of the world, and sometimes "such relations could be conceived as cooperative and egalitarian rather than competitive and hierarchical."[46] Of course, just because this sort of writing "could be conceived as cooperative and egalitarian" does not negate Said's crucial point, that European Orientalist writings were always and irreducibly contributing to the project of Empire, even when they had good intentions, relatively speaking. But it means—as Said also recognizes—that the Orient (so-called) would have to become subjected to history and, therefore, chronology, in a way parallel with developments in Europe.

Does the mere invocation of the name "Almanzor"—enough, apparently, to stop the novel in its tracks—mark a note of resistance to this modern, administrative Orientalist modality? Marilyn Butler warns that, "whatever the East came afterward to represent as an abstraction, . . . in English culture in the Napoleonic war period . . . the place of a poem's setting always means what it says, and the time is always in some sense the present."[47] In a superficial way, *Gulzara* seems to embody this principle, as it highlights, through its references to Abbas I and Ouseley, the depth of Anglo-Persian relations as they weigh upon and shape British politics after the Congress of Vienna. Yet in no sense is the time of *Gulzara* "the present," despite its completely up-to-date description of Regency politics. *Gulzara* is emphatically a work of the future, not merely for the way that it imagines next steps for the political career of Princess Charlotte but for the way that it presents a kernel of futurity embedded in its vision of the contemporary European order. *Gulzara* reminds us that there was no "contemporary" Orient, or rather that Orientalism is a discourse that cannot understand the "contemporary";[48] by extension, though, it also vacates the contemporariness of Europe, through its *roman à clef* structure. Although this situation depends on asymmetrical power relations between Europe and the Middle East, it also exploits a temporal fracture that could pull European politics into otherwise impossible political arrangements.

That situation is significant, given how, behind *Gulzara*'s experiments with the politics of time, we find its recognition of an emergent capitalist economy and concern about the displacement and invisibility of labor. The novel shows Persia transforming, tragically, into "one large and fluctuating workshop, rather tended to create a pauper population than to assist one"; the country's systems of international trade break down, once "a disposition to work for themselves became increasingly prevalent" across Asia (*G* 92–93). Even royal pageantry is, here, shown to be a product of hidden labor: Ali is presented as a vain and silly man, devoted only to his appearance and to the planning of parties, but also as one who, with his mother's help, "worked night and day at the plan for three months" (*G* 12). *Gulzara* is, then, directly a novel of globalization, but which imagines, through the abortive disturbance called Almanzor, a way out of those impasses by embracing the meaningless lack at the heart of the system. This strategy is its most profound link to Williams's *Paul and Virginia*. Both *Gulzara* and *Paul and Virginia* see "globalization" in the Derridean manner: as a Janus-faced fantasy of life without work, which, at one and the same time, renders work invisible through its displacement elsewhere, and grimly fulfills that fantasy through mass joblessness.[49] *The Last Man* will do the same, as we will soon see. In response, all three texts ask their reader to tarry with the "aching void" at the heart of such a structure, and to indulge the narrative disruptions that result. Thus, they welcome a worldwide future into the globalizing present.

"Hours Passed—Centuries": The Future Orientation of *The Last Man*

Shelley's *The Last Man* is a novel about loss and mourning but also survival, and the capacity to think flexibly about time is the most valuable survival skill it teaches. Its author had just repatriated to a nation that had, over the preceding century, as we have seen, regularized clock time and aggressively codified approaches to history. "In *The Last Man*," argues Timothy Ruppert, "Shelley overturns artificially kept time and chronological history, thereby undermining two basic props of both conventional English literature and the British worldview in the years following the Napoleonic Wars."[50] It is a novel set in the future and that theorizes futurity; at the same time, its political concerns—the possible restoration of the monarchy, the emergence of development of parliamentary institutions, the fading relevance of the aristocracy—appear emphatically to be those of the early nineteenth century, making it easy to read this novel more as a satirical *roman à clef* than as groundbreaking speculative fiction.[51] Yet if its political imagination seems unexpectedly fainthearted at first, this is only so Shelley can set the stage for the fictional pandemic, which soon begins to reshape government in dangerously metaphorical ways. The catastrophic pandemic, which first appears immediately after Lionel Verney makes a heartfelt defense of nobility, Lords, and aristocracy (S 222–223), eventually remakes Europe's social and political institutions into smaller, more equal political units on a post-national scale and focuses the novel's attention on a small cadre of survivors. We begin to see, much as Mary L. Mullen has recently proposed, that a literary focus on institutions of government may backhandedly indicate that certain futures, barely restrained and held in check, lie in wait residually; even the form of the novel, Mullen suggests, may "allow multiple historical temporalities within the present to be brought onto a shared singular path."[52] Through the timescales made possible by the pandemic, the novel can be said to resuscitate revolutionary politics, however ambivalently, for the conservative 1820s, and to think about the effects of the plague in relation to the British Romantic literary tradition. The circle of survivors is based, after all, in the style of a *roman à clef*, on the small circle of Romantic writers who constituted the author's circle of family and friends.

222   FRACTURE FEMINISM

Instead of using the far-distant future setting or fictional destruction
of humankind as opportunities to renovate politics through wish fulfillment,
The Last Man seeks out the ways that political life becomes enmeshed
with time, enabling it to imagine electoral reform in the mode of "to
come." Lionel Verney makes a statement to this effect early in the novel
as he befriends Adrian, his onetime nemesis and proxy for the author's
late husband, Percy Bysshe Shelley: "What has been, though sweet, is
gone; the present is good only because it is about to change, and *the to
come is all my own*" (S 37, emphasis mine). Having cast "the to come" as
a mode of being in the present, one that can be his own personal private
property, Lionel seeks to protect it at all costs throughout the novel. He
explains to Idris, his wife, that "we are so formed, that we must love life,
and cling to it; . . . Let us not, through security in hereafter, neglect the
present. This present moment, short as it is, is a part of eternity, and the
dearest part, since it is our own unalienably. Thou, the hope of my futurity,
art my present joy" (S 340). There may appear to be a gap between the
first quotation, in which it is the "to come" that is "all my own," and the
second, in which it is the "present moment" that is "our own unalienably."
But there is no inconsistency here, because present joy is "the hope of my
futurity," a gesture that brings the present into the future synchronically: *In
the future*, the novel is saying, *I will hope for happiness in today's present*,
which doesn't make sense, and conversely and equally paradoxically, *I am
already adjusting to the unpredictable*. The two quotations use the language
of ownership quite resolutely, yet what appears to be an emphasis on ownership may instead be a claim to singularity. *The Last Man* is, as the title
suggests, a novel that finds isolation rather than coalition—an outgrowth
of its asymptotic orientation toward the future. Its emphasis on singular
experience, as made possible through the impossible act of conjoining
the future with the present, dares to approach politics through intimacy
and love, even in the face of certain death. What makes the present "our
own" is a shared and ferocious orientation toward "hope" and "futurity."
Lionel even calls it "the hope of my futurity," a term that suggests a ripple
effect, through which one's immediate orientation toward the future might
perhaps, one hopes, extend itself across time eternally. It is a paradox,
describing something not just fictional but impossible; yet Lionel claims
it unrelentingly. By attaching "this present moment" to "eternity," Lionel
can experience future joys today—and one of those joys is "hope," a word
with its own orientation to the future. Yet the novel tends to describe

GULZARA AND *THE LAST MAN*   223

such a commitment in the past perfect rather than imperfect, tense, as if enacting the impossible were an accomplished fact.

Although the novel is filled with, and framed by, prophets and prophecies, Lionel's orientation toward the future occurs in a different register: he remains open to the impossible as it appears, however conditionally or tenuously, in actual fact and immediately. This is not a prediction but an affirmation of the immediacy of the Real: "Posterity is no more" (S 322). Its approach to politics and erotics has enabled the novel to generate several important deconstructive analyses, including Betty Bennett's, Barbara Johnson's, Judith Butler's, and Elizabeth Effinger's.[53] Bennett even elevates this aspect to the novel to the level of an allegory, maintaining that "Verney . . . represents deconstruction, in fact, his life is a *bildungsroman* played out in a series of deconstructions in a macabre world."[54] Throughout this study, I have tried to suggest that there was, within Romanticism, a literary history of this sort of future-oriented historiography of the contemporary. Calling history "the ocean of forgotten time" (S 408), Shelley recalls Helen Maria Williams's "ocean of futurity" and a previous generation's often-fictionalized feminist historiography; calling "futurity" a property "all my own" recalls Felicia Dorothea Browne's experiments in political temporality in "War and Peace."[55] As Orianne Smith indicates, "Shelley was firmly convinced that she was a visionary writer, the last female prophet in a matrilineal genealogy of visionary discourse."[56] Shelley styled herself as "a prophetic orphan in a world [that] had become increasingly more hostile to female visionary discourse."[57] As I have argued throughout this book, feminist writers such as Williams, Browne, Barbauld, and Wollstonecraft knew that the contemporary political upheavals of their day would make sense only in hindsight. Yet, having asserted the impossibility of predicting what contemporary politics would be, they would go on to explain matter-of-factly what the future's judgment was going to be. They adopted a perspective on politics that was by their own admission impossible, as though they were visitors from the future operating as a cut in the field of politics. Shelley revives this tradition of women's writing in *The Last Man*, reactivating a previous generation's discourse about revolution and war in the post-Waterloo era.

A substantial line of scholarship has read *The Last Man* as a meditation on hope and prophecy, and indeed the novel is filled with prophecies and is itself a prophecy of sorts.[58] The Cumaean Sibyl presents a narratological paradox to readers, as Christopher Bundock points out: the narrative frame depends on "a mind that can be both before and after the end of consciousness," because "in order to *represent* the lastness of humanity, Shelley's text has to be on both sides of 'the end.' "[59] Washington similarly argues that the experience would, temporally speaking, be unknowable and ever uncertain for Lionel.[60] Ruppert, focusing on the frame narrative and the novel's epigraph from Milton, maintains that Shelley's focus is more on *what may happen* than *what will happen*. The device of the Sibylline leaves connects Shelley quite directly to the tradition of writing the contemporary future as an act of feminist resistance, given how, as Smith has argued, "the sibyl is a representation of Shelley's mother, a literary mother whose visionary works have been ignored and misunderstood."[61] Yet for all its investment in prophecy, the novel is quite wary of that discourse. The epigraph, drawn from Milton, advises us to "Let no man seek / Henceforth to be foretold what shall befall / Him or his children" (S 1). The novel features a cult leader known as the Impostor, for instance, who assures his followers that they will flourish in the afterlife if they do his bidding. The novel contrasts its many figures of prophecy against a different kind of orientation to futurity, one that seeks to build the future into the narrative present. Johnson, noting this, calls it "the strange temporality at the end of man," which she says pervades the novel everywhere.[62] The novel seems to be caught between two contrasting historical discourses, of singularity and of fate, a tension that gives way to "the conception of reflexiveness that first opens up a space for action."[63]

The novel's first figure for such an orientation is "The Englishwoman," as she has sometimes been known, the narrator of the frame story and the novel's most obvious figure for the author as she imagines herself in her roles as European traveler, legatee, and editor. Shelley seems to know that such an orientation would be impossible, and she doesn't suggest that it isn't impossible. Nevertheless, she accomplishes the impossible rhetorically. Bundock, paraphrasing Maurice Blanchot's philosophy, suggests that "for prophecy to be meaningful . . . it must 'predict' something radically unexpected, something that is, strictly, *impossible* given the prevailing frame of social, intellectual and political life."[64] Read in that way, the frame story in *The Last Man* seems like the least prophetic part of the novel: the story it proffers seems, for several hundred pages, merely an extension of, or satire upon, modern British politics, until the plague as plot device authorizes the novel to broaden the scope of the possible, or to pursue the impossible future already. Because the novel's orientation to the future mostly plays out at the level of language, it affects merely the characters' experience of catastrophe, not the catastrophe itself. It does not remake the government or save the world from plague. But Lionel's experience, like the Englishwoman's, shows us how to differentiate between the brazenly political of the current moment and a contemporary future that always remains open as a rupture within it.

Shelley's characters learn to think time across a parallax gap. One scene about halfway through the novel illustrates the parallax and its relevance to the catastrophe. Shelley's England of the future is a republic, and there is an election for Lord Protector. One particularly strange facet of Book I of the novel is how familiar the imaginary political system is, despite the abdication of the king: there is an elected government but still a whole system of aristocracy and gentry, and Raymond, the Byron-like character, is supposed to be admirable because of his proposal to restore the monarchy. Raymond's opponent in the election, and indeed more generally his nemesis, is Ryland, "the leader of the popular party" (S 55). In a novel purportedly transcribed from the collation of Sibylline leaves, it is interesting how Ryland, out on the stump, uses the rhetoric of prophecy to make his case to voters: "When love is no longer akin to hate, then brotherhood will exist: we are very far from that stage at present," he says (S 220). An objection emerges from the crowd, in the voice of a "little old astronomer" named Merrival. Merrival is foolish because, like Robert Merry in reverse, he thinks in such long-term ways as to entirely disregard the immediate crisis. Merrival objects to Ryland's message, saying, "[We are] not so far [from that stage] as you may suppose. . . . The poles precede slowly, but securely; in an hundred thousand years—." Interrupting, Ryland retorts that "we shall all be underground" (S 220). Yet Merrival won't back down. In a hundred thousand years, he says, "the pole of the earth will coincide with the pole of the ecliptic," and so "an universal spring will be produced, and earth become a paradise." Ryland sarcastically and "contemptuously" says, "And we shall of course enjoy the benefit of the change" (S 220). The exchange makes Ryland seem obnoxious and Merrival quaintly misguided. Yet while they may seem to be disagreeing, they are actually expressing merely a difference of historical vision, not of opinion: neither thinks that cooperation could be possible "at present." They are disagreeing only on whether a hundred thousand years is an appropriate scale for political thinking. The novel does not have an easy answer for the question of scale and seems to side with neither character. Yet the dispute, which has been marked by interruptions, is itself interrupted by Lionel's arrival with news from Greece—a juxtaposition that brings the discussion of timescale into the politics of pandemic, specifically. "We have strange news here," he says. The Greeks have toppled Constantinople and have begun to rebuild it, but they also, upon entering the city, have fallen victim to a novel virus. While this is bad news from a public health perspective, it is good news politically: Lionel has shown that the Greeks are perfectly capable, already today, of achieving great things together. What had seemed impossible a moment before has arrived as news: the principles of brotherhood and collaboration are alive and well, even if, given the plague, the brother-collaborators cannot be either thing for very long. Lionel focuses the crowd's attention on the dire situation at hand; no one any longer contemplates with Merrival a "paradise" of the distant future (S 220). Instead of endorsing either Ryland's pessimism or Merrival's optimism, Lionel somehow sews the futuristic utopian principle of brotherhood into the here and now of modern politics. He does not make political progress actually possible, but he does insist upon the potential for the impossible to happen anytime. He is thinking about politics in the realm of contretempopia.

Later in the novel, unfortunately, the Impostor incarcerates Lionel for several months in a dungeon. The situation, thoroughly Radcliffean, shakes Lionel's experience of time. A parallax gap emerges between his timeframes. "Hours passed—centuries," Lionel says, as "to-morrow the ruffian had declared that I should die. When would to-morrow come? Was it not already here?" (S 391). Fans of the musical *Annie* will know how paradoxical this question is: tomorrow is by its nature never "already here." Note the disorganized syntax of the statement, which creates what might be considered a Freudian slip: Lionel does not say that "the ruffian had declared that I should die to-morrow," but rather, "to-morrow the ruffian had declared that I should die," as if the accomplished fact of "had declared" were a thing that would happen soon. Something scheduled for tomorrow is being described in the past perfect tense. We see something similar happening to Idris earlier in the novel: "I have discovered—to-morrow—that is, to-day—already the to-morrow is come—before dawn, foreigners, Austrians, my mother's hirelings, are to carry me off to Germany, to prison, to marriage" (S 85). Here too, tomorrow is understood as a contemporary event in the context of imprisonment. Through such passages, *The Last Man* stitches events from the future into the present of the narrative. For Idris, "to-day" and "tomorrow" coincide through the collision of different narrative timelines, much as, for Lionel, "hours" and "centuries" can run at the same rate. Lionel's parallax perspective enables him to situate the near future (tomorrow) and the distant future (centuries) each within the present moment—if only possibly, and by a rhetorical question. Idris's utterance, given seemingly just past midnight, describes "to-morrow" as "before dawn" of "today." If Lionel can measure his own fate in hours and the earth's in centuries, he can find the two futures to be coextensive yet irreconcilable. Here, we see the ways in which Shelley has been influenced by texts such as *Beachy Head* and "Ode to Folly." Like the speakers of those earlier poems, and also like Idris, Lionel wonders if either form of future, or maybe even both, may actually be here already.

The statement "hours passed—centuries" presents a counterpoint to a moment much earlier in the novel, in which Lionel, describing his happiness, says that "years passed thus—even years" (S 92). Whereas in the dungeon we have two very different units of time, hours and centuries, running coextensively, here Lionel is differentiating between "years" and "years," which would seem to be identical units. The statement suggests that the first "years" is less emphatic than its equal measure, or perhaps that the first "years" should be taken figuratively and the second literally, given "the progress of time." In an oddly offhand way, Lionel says, "in progress of time, I also became a father" (S 92); he is delighted that the children all grow and play together, though this is ominous, given the novel's emphasis on Sophoclean tragedy and the disastrously irresponsible fathers found in Shelley's earlier fiction, especially *Frankenstein* and *Mathilda*.

When Lionel's son Alfred turns nine, he is sent off to Eton to be educated. Although Alfred is "proportionably pleased" to be taking "the primary step toward manhood," it is Lionel, primarily, who is amazed by the scene:

> Here were the future governors of England; . . . Here were the beings who were to carry on the vast machine of society; here were the lovers, husbands, fathers; here the landlord, the politician, the soldier; some fancied that they were even now ready to appear on the stage, eager to make one among the dramatis personae of active life. (S 227)

This meditation is deeply conventional, performing exactly the sort of ideological work that Lee Edelman takes to task in *No Future*: the students are presumed to embody a future that merely replicates and justifies the political present.[65] Even on Alfred's first day of school, Lionel looks at Eton with hindsight, astounded not merely at the promise and potential of the pupils, but with what they will have accomplished, personally and professionally, in due course. At Eton, one experiences the future of England already, in the mode of reproductive futurism. Not only does this fantasy make visiting Eton a moving experience for the parents, but it also seems to inform the mindset of the students, who are eager to step into their professional lives. Their future is available now, even in the ambiguity of Lionel's iterations of the verb "to be": the "were" of "here were" jostles against the were of "were to carry," working ambiguously within the past perfect tense and the hypothetical, until "were," opening in past and future directions alternatingly, gives way to the outlandishly present-oriented pastness of "were even now." There is something deeply ironic about Lionel's satisfaction here, given that the pandemic has already begun to spread, a fact that significantly delimits the prospects for these children. The looming extinction event, much as Kate Singer suggests, stimulates the "transversal energy" of queer resistance—something further activated by the text's citational practices, which, it has been said, produce "the anachronistic inversion of present and past" in a way that would obliterate Lionel's fantasy of the students' future vocations.[66]

Later in the novel, Lionel finds a vocation of his own: "It was my task each day to visit the various families assembled in our town, and when the weather permitted, I was glad to prolong my ride, and to muse in solitude over every changeful appearance of our destiny, endeavoring to gather lessons for the future from the experience of the past" (S 310). This reverses the ideological tractor beam of the previously quoted passage: what Lionel didn't realize, when he first looked upon the children of Eton, was that he himself was the one who would later, in those children, find his own vocation—when the weather permitted. He would perform these services even when weather did not permit! He explains that "often, pushing my way with difficulty through the narrow snow-blocked town, I crossed the bridge and passed through Eton. No youthful congregation of gallant-hearted boys thronged the portal of the college; sad silence pervaded the busy school-room and noisy playground" (S 310). Lionel is understandably disturbed by the silence at Eton, which comes to stand metonymically for a generation of dead children and their unrealized potential. Yet the silence of Eton in winter reminds the reader that the earlier Edelmanian moment wasn't ever a tragically naive prediction, but rather an imaginative act of futurity in the present. Lionel had emphasized the children's capacity for "fancy" and compared the situation to theatre. In this double act of imagination, whereby the children imagine themselves "ready for the stage," Lionel is bringing a future, that plainly will never happen, into the here and now of Eton today. At the time of Alfred's enrollment, the sun had just turned black and the tale of populations dying had begun to circulate in England. Lionel offers no medical solution to this problem, but had decided that "we were by nature a poetical people, a nation easily duped by words, ready to array clouds in splendor, and bestow honour on the dust" (S 222). The silence of Eton was already envisioned and predicted; Lionel counteracts this likely catastrophe by "bestowing honour on the dust," insisting that although the future would never happen, it was already happening. This is one way that "creative thought inspires and sustains new sociopolitical paradigms" in this novel, as Ruppert has maintained.[67]

Imaginative acts by "poetical people" cannot flatten the curve, so to speak, even in a fictional space like Shelley's. But they might reorient subjects toward catastrophe; they can make pestilence not something to be endured but to work within and through. As Lionel explains, "pestilence had become a part of our future, our existence; it was to be guarded against, like the flooding of rivers." The simile of the river gives meaning to an otherwise impossible temporality: Lionel is positing a collective future, "our future," that has already confronted and incorporated pestilence, enabling the future to be something that "had become" *qua* accomplished fact. Meanwhile, the phrase "to be guarded against" demands that the past and future fuse together in the present moment, which threatens to stretch out eternally through the use of the infinitive. Moreover, the river simile makes the plague something figuratively manageable with vigilance, viaducts, and sandbags.

Although these are characters imagining their futures, or lack of futures, from the twenty-first century, the question of politics in the nineteenth century remains at stake. Morton Paley has argued that Shelley's bleak novel undercuts the Romantic emphasis on imagination. Bennett and Ruppert have each argued otherwise, maintaining that Shelley's work enlists imagination to remake political structures.[68] I suppose I would agree with Bennett and Ruppert, but in a limited and qualified way. In my view, it is the plague itself that remakes politics in good and bad ways in Shelley's novel, but imaginative acts, and especially acts of language, make catastrophe livable if not survivable. The situation at hand hasn't changed—everyone is doomed—but the characters learn to imagine lifespans differently. *The Last Man* is a novel that, through the power of language and especially figurative language, transmutes Shelley's mourning

230 FRACTURE FEMINISM

into global catastrophe, and then manages that catastrophe by learning to accommodate the global impossible in individual terms, rhetorically. By finding and exploiting a parallax gap between temporalities, Shelley continues a previous generation's model of feminist historiography even as she imagines the extinction of human life completely.

Learning to Count:
My Three Brothers Paul, Lionel Verney, and Me

Romans à clef often excavate "the still unstable gap between novel and biography";[69] *The Last Man* goes another step further, through its ambivalent autobiographical elements. While *The Last Man* is a spectacularly imaginative novel, it is also a memoir of sorts, an act of mourning for deceased family and friends. Although it is Shelley's most personal novel, really an elegy, it feels strangely detached from its author because we receive the narrative through a protagonist who is male, cautious, conservative, and resentful—basically everything that Mary Shelley was not. Colin Carman has argued that this is a source of the novel's queer power.[70] It is a novel about the Shelley Circle without any easily corollary for (arguably) its main character, Mary Shelley herself. The author is everywhere in this text, but in no particular place: Shelley appears in the acts of memorialization of Percy Bysshe Shelley, Lord Byron, and Claire Claremont; in the editorial work of the Englishwoman; in Lionel's experience as an orphan and in his teenage fascination with Adrian that turns to idealizing love. Yet none of these figures equate with Mary Shelley in so direct a way as we see with Raymond (Byron), Perdita (Claremont), or Adrian (P.B. Shelley). In this way, Mary Shelley is noticeably absent from this narrative, even as she crosses the three registers of author/frame narrator/protagonist, and so the novel can be seen as an elaborate structure built around, and to create, a hole. In that hole, like flowers placed in a vase, is Lionel Verney. Mary Shelley lingers throughout the story as *The Last Man*'s Almanzor, the incomprehensible excess to what otherwise would have been a *roman à clef*.

Lionel is from the start a figure from the future. The novel opens with a spelunking frame narrator, who forces her way through mysterious forbidden passages into Sibyl's cave in 1818 Naples. There, the frame narrator discovers, along with an ominous goat skeleton, writings on leaves and bark in many ancient and modern languages. Ancient and modern prophecies are intermingled together, it seems, at least judging by the languages used. The frame narrator makes many trips to the cave to retrieve further writings; the text of *The Last Man* is the translated result of the project. How a long, multilingual narrative depicting the late twenty-first century has found its way into a cave in 1818, and how many leaves would be necessary to contain this rather long novel, is hard to know or understand—one can only assume that this narrative is a prophecy of Sibyl, detailing "relations of events but lately passed" (S 5). Ruppert has argued about the frame of this novel that "Shelley's Romantic traveler thus finds an image of the future in a place of the past and presents it to the eyes of the present. This seemingly vertiginous narrative experiment allows Shelley to unsettle hierarchical, linear understandings of human temporality and so to present history as founded indecisively on disrupted time."[71] Already, here, and even beyond the normal parameters of prophecy, the temporality of the scene is all askew: these events are "but lately passed" to the frame narrator in 1818, describing events from the late twenty-first century, and published by Shelley in 1826. The distinction between future and past has been rendered meaningless already, just in the first few pages. Moreover, if it has been written by the oracle Sibyl, it takes a rather strange form: the tone of the novel is not predictive, but nostalgic and reflective, and tracks the very subjective and limited viewpoint of Lionel Verney. Moreover, the novel allegorizes the lives of Percy Shelley, Lord Byron, and Claire Claremont, and in this sense it consigns its author's tragic recent past to the distant future.

The novel is filled with figures of prophecy, from Sibyl to Evadne, and also subjects of prophecy, as in the novel's frequent comparisons of Lionel and Oedipus (e.g., S 78). As Lionel sends Alfred to Eton for school, he reflects, "when my boy shall have obtained the place I now hold, I shall have tottered into a grey-headed, wrinkled old man. Strange system! riddle of the Sphinx, most awe-striking!" (S 228). Lionel, however, was not to enjoy the luxury of a dotage after all. After a while, he begins to confront the implications of the plague through the figure of Oedipus: "Why talk of infancy, manhood, and old age? We all stood equal sharers of the last throes of time-warn nature. Arrived at the same point of the world's age—there was no difference in us; the name of parent and child had lost their meaning; young boys and girls were level now with men" (S 318). Later yet, he turns for comfort to *Oedipus at Colonus* and *Antigone*, with the hope of understanding what it means to live on in the aftermath of a disastrous prophecy fulfilled (S 372). Such figures connect Shelley's novel to the question of psychoanalytic interpretation and the intellectual

232   FRACTURE FEMINISM

legacy of Lacan, given how, for the Lacan of *L'Étourdit*, the Freudian word "interpretation" is, in essence, "oracular" and "apophantic": the word, Lacan argues, connects psychoanalysis to the practice of the "former masters of truth," those of ancient Greece, whose writings were likewise "scattered."[72]

The first two hundred or so pages of the novel are spent in praise of Raymond and Adrian, figures for Lord Byron and Percy Bysshe Shelley. With and through Lionel, we learn to look at them with wonder and gratitude, just as we learn to feel their vulnerabilities. The big shift happens at the start of chapter 19, after what we are told is "a long interval" from chapter 18: Lionel begins to regret "this tedious dwelling on the sorrows of others, while my own were only in apprehension" (S 267). His own sorrows must no longer be in apprehension, or apprehended by the reader, or apprehended only; he will henceforth include himself in the story. He does so, it seems, because he finally can: "Time and experience have placed me on a height from which I can comprehend the past as a whole," he says, so even "in the lonely state of singleness which hems me in," nevertheless, "in this way I must describe it" (S 267). The topological metaphor is interesting. He is presenting this new perspective as a "height" rather than a "situation" or a "time," and imagining that this new way of proceeding will be better than doing as he had been doing before, which he says was a matter of "glowing with hope" and using "history as an opiate." What is being negotiated, then, from this "height," is actually a relation to time, to historicity. It is a contretempopic discourse. Lionel associates "history" with "hope," thus linking the past and future, while "experience" is associated with "height," a vantage from which one can "comprehend the past" synthetically. Yet the topological metaphor will not deactivate temporality, for the height represents a turning away from the present: he is now, he says, "able to escape from the mosaic of circumstance, by perceiving and reflecting back the grouping and combined colouring of the past" (S 268). Lionel, in this formulation, has become a mirror up to history, which he will manipulate by "disposing light and shade so as to form a picture in whose very darkness there will be harmony" (S 267). A mirror, then, directing light away from the scene, to create just the proper amount of shade, to create, through synesthesia, "harmony." Shelley's late husband is famous for supposing that poets are "the *mirrors* of the gigantic shadows which *futurity* casts upon the present."[73] Here, Lionel claims to be a mirror casting shadows *away* from the present: he is a glass from the future that features the colors of the past, and the present, a disappointing mosaic, is better left unseen and has nothing to do with it. Yet the effect of the resolution is entirely unclear: we are to stop apprehending his sorrows, it seems, unless we are to stop *merely* apprehending his sorrows. No clue is given as to how to understand the word "apprehension," given its three quite divergent meanings. Is Lionel dreading, apprehensively, the arrival of future sorrows? He really appears to have sorrows already, but perhaps he feels he has mentioned only his future despair, or perhaps his future despair is already inside his despair right now. Unless he is saying that his sorrows have been too *easily apprehended by the reader's mind*, and therefore need muddying? Or have his sorrows been "apprehended," as by the police, arrested or stopped in their tracks? We have, after all, heard tell of a mysterious "interval." Despite this and seemingly because of it, Lionel says that, "I am again impelled by the restless spirit within me to continue my narration," he says, even if "I must alter the mode which I have hitherto adopted." What he means by "continue" in this context is quite unclear.

Lionel's decision to include his own sorrows in the narrative recalls an inordinately charming anecdote featured in Jacques Lacan's psychoanalytic seminars, once in 1954 and again in 1964. Lacan was both times discussing a question from the Binet-Simon intelligence test, which asks children to parse an "absurd sentence"—that is, "I have three brothers, Paul, Ernest, and me"—as a way to test their mental acuity.[74] Lacan objects to this question as a means of measuring mental development, calling the error in the sentence "quite natural": there are indeed three brothers, but there is also an entirely separate level at which one is expected to exempt oneself from one's count or one's account.[75] Consciousness, Lacan argues, is "not transparent to itself," as he tries to explain through reference to Kant and Descartes. Returning to this example ten years later, Lacan explains that subjectivity comes into being only through systems of signification from which one is expected to exempt oneself. Says Lacan: "before any formulation of the subject, of a subject who thinks, . . . [there is] a level at which there is counting, things are counted, and in this counting he who counts is already included. It is only later that the subject has to recognize himself as such, recognize himself as he who counts."[76] First, one has to count, and in doing so one must learn to count oneself; only subsequently can there be "I at the level at which I am to reflect the first I, that is to say, the I who counts." Lacan takes this as evidence for the existence of the unconscious, which is a gap fundamental to the subject around which the system of signification can develop. As Lorenzo Chiesa has shown, the issue then becomes the basis of sexual difference, in Lacan's

234   FRACTURE FEMINISM

thought, as only the phallic side of the sexuation chart qualifies as "one."[77] Hence also the ambiguity of phrases such as "the I who counts," which only confuses matters further by proving applicable to both *the I who is included in the tally* and *the I who is doing the tallying, and therefore must not be included.* And with this ambiguity, suggestive of "the radical originality of the subject," as Lacan says, we confront the fact that this is really a Romantic-era political question. In her lifetime, Shelley had confronted the French Revolution, the invention of the national census, and the violent repression of democratic reform. All three are directly matters of learning "who counts," and in the novel the question of who and what "counts" is of central importance, as its apocalyptic universe transitions from a basically stable aristocratic republican government to a situation in which surviving humans, themselves constantly being tallied, become, despite and through their dwindling numbers, "equal sharers of the last throes of time-worn nature" (S 318). The word "equal" is important here, as it implies an equivalence that can found a bleak necro-democracy; the alternative to such an arrangement, as Jacques Rancière has argued, would be dissensus, of the sort valorized by fracture feminism. Death, then, marks for Shelley what Rancière would call "the opening of an interval for political subjectivization."[78] In *The Last Man*, the question of politics is always a question of time, of timeworn nature, and especially of *who counts*; yet, as Lacan reminds us, the question of who counts requires the simultaneous operation of several temporalities and a willingness to exempt oneself from one's narrative.

All of this brings us back to Lionel's resolution to be a mirror, "reflecting back the grouping and combined colouring of the past." The claim is significant, I think, because of several prior encounters with mirrors in this novel, each concerning Lionel's sister Perdita as she confronts her self-loathing and finds strategies for self-erasure. When Perdita, after hosting a large gala, begins to suspect that her husband Lord Raymond is in love with the princess Evadne, and that he soon will be giving up his political career, she locks herself in her room. Worried about her dim prospects, she "stood before a large mirror—she gazed on her reflected image" to take stock of herself and think about time (S 135). "All proceeds, changes, and dies," she says, identifying with the image in the mirror but only insofar as it can mark a space within time. She is gazing on herself as if from the future, taking melancholy solace in the temporariness of her privilege. "Vase am I," she says, "never again will you see yourself thus" (S 135). Opening up, then, a temporal gap between "I," who is definitively a vase, and "you," who is looking into the mirror, and "me," who is recognized in the mirror, Perdita begins to become alienated from her own paltry pleasures. "Vase am I," which is effectively an expression of what has been called Perdita's "monomaniacal sympathy,"[79] asserts a capacity to be objectified, turned into an aesthetic object, but also a useful object. Quickly the issue becomes the meaning of such an object. One thinks of Lacan's disagreement with Heidegger about the meaning of vases. For Heidegger, vases show that human processes can unite the earth and sky, as they take flowers from the earth but open toward the sky. Lacan sees vases quite differently, and rather more as Perdita does. He sees vases as the instrument through which "emptiness and fullness as such enter the world," in the sense that vases create a void, or an absence, where before there was merely nothing. But making a little house for a void, a void that cannot be filled even by flowers "because in the first place in its essence it is empty," a vase reveals that even the most concrete things are always already figurative, and that signification, like macaroni he says, depends on "the introduction of a gap or a hole" through which structures of meaning can be built. The Real, in this way, is the basis of the symbolic, yet the Real, like the hollow of the vase, cannot exist without the structure built around it. That is Perdita, right there, after her party, confronting the future—indeed, looking at her present self, the "me," through a "you" who is me looking as a way to distance herself from the "I" who is a vase.[80] Now that is using one's noodle!

When Perdita looks into a mirror, far from her feeling artificially whole and secure, what happens is a radical tripartite splitting of the subject—she has the customary Lacanian splitting between I and me, but then, by calling her image "you" instead of "me," she disavows this identification. Time is the factor that intervenes to create this second order of separation. She is looking at herself from the future, such that the woman who hosted the gala, beautifully dressed and socially successful, can already be gone. Consequently, Perdita begins to erase herself from her husband's experience. Raymond feels compelled to be cheerful around her, finding that she is "as a mirror, [and] changed as he changed" (S 185). After the gala, she had disavowed her image, calling it "you"; now we have a second level of disavowal, where she begins to identify not as a different person, but with the very instrument of reflection.

Lacan, for such a celebrated theorist of subjectivity and mirror effects, never directly considers the option of identifying with the mirror. Simone de Beauvoir, however, briefly does. Although *The Second Sex* is a book characterized by antipathy for psychoanalysis, Beauvoir cites Lacan one time, in a footnote, and does so favorably. She concedes that there is a mirror stage, and that it inaugurates children into subjectivity. Beauvoir concludes that the mirror stage must happen coequally for each gender, yet warns, later in the book, that although girls experience a mirror stage like anyone else, they then must also take a further step and begin to identify with the mirror itself.[81] Perdita, mirror-like, embodies this predicament, willfully destroying her own subjectivity in further and further forms of negation until she arrives at her *passage à l'acte*. Basically, she moves from embodying the Real to making a hole in the Real. It is the same progression that Lacan describes in *Seminar X*, in his bleak account of women's jouissance: first, one becomes an image; second, one becomes a void; third, one burrows a hole directly in the Real.[82] Such a progression, advises Lacan, is what makes woman "much more real and much truer than man, in that she knows the worth of the yardstick of what she is dealing with in desire" and refuses to disdain this multiply self-negating route, having taken it on deliberately as a matter of protest.[83]

This brings us back to Lionel's resolution. It depends on a split enacted between Lionel the subject of the story and Lionel the story-teller, yet the resolution is no sooner made than it fails. When Lionel and Adrian report, as they ride through London for the last time in a re-enactment of Barbauld's *Eighteen Hundred and Eleven*, that "no human step was heard, nor human form discerned," it is obvious that they are not including themselves in the tally. They are the ones who count other people, but they themselves are apparently not ones who count. It is exactly the opposite of Perdita's gesture. They are present, and are even talking to each other, yet they feel quite confident that no humans are anywhere present. They search for human life by listening for "human steps," without considering that their own steps would be undetectable by this method, given how, riding horseback, their steps would sound like hooves. Searching for human life, they are shocked and horrified to discover that the city is filled with non-human animals: "Troops of dogs, deserted of their masters, passed us; and now and then a horse, unbridled and unsaddled, trotted toward us" (S 332). Oxen are living in deserted houses in "luxurious accommodation." Although *The Last Man* has been compellingly discussed as a fiction of biopolitics, such a reading is complicated by the fact that the plague, far from reducing all organisms to the minimalist category of bare life, seems to have very carefully delimited human from non-human animals.[84] And this division, so interesting to a wave of recent scholars of the novel, ensures that the surveyors "inscribe the count of the uncounted as a supplement," as Rancière would say.[85]

In a kind of reversal of *The Twilight Zone*, which, in its inaugural episode, explores the visceral horror of walking through an empty town, Shelley shows the city fully populated, but with other species. Shelley has been praised in recent scholarship for, in one account, imagining sovereignty without human beings, and, in another, developing a cosmopolitan notion of freedom and truth through models of animal existence.[86] Basically, it seems the non-human animals have finally inherited the earth. Yet as night falls they hear "a voice, a human voice, strange now to hear," one that belongs to "a little girl," perhaps ten years old, but dressed "in glittering robes and shawls fit for a woman," and playing with her Newfoundland dog, named Lion (S 333). In this Swiftian satire on human and non-human civilization, the dog has a name and the girl does not. It is a metaphorical name, one that, like the encounter with horses unbridled, seems designed to further locate primal wildness in a domesticated animal; it is also a metonymic name, in that it performs a double geographical displacement, treating a creature in London first as a creature from Newfoundland and next as a creature from Africa; it is also a synecdochic name, because Lion is an abbreviation of Lionel, and in this sense it is a scene of self-discovery. Lionel thought he would be discovering himself in the girl, but found her to be dressed as a woman; he found his avatar in the dog. Through an elaborate chain of associations, Lionel has finally found a way to include himself in his own narrative—although only a child would be foolish enough to make that error, according to Binet and Simon. Yet if this chain of replacements, involving horses and oxen, dogs and troops, Newfoundlands and Lions, girls and women, seems elaborate, we should acknowledge that most scenes of self-discovery work through metonymic replacement and disavowal. That is indeed why it is difficult, very often, to include oneself in one's account: "the subject arises as exclusion from the very field that it [i.e., the signifier] determines, being then neither the one who is designated, nor the one who designates."[87] Lionel, following this script, discovers himself and, having done so, reports what he has discovered as if he had not been there.

Lionel's resolution to include his own sufferings in his narrative was supposedly made possible "by time and experience," and it is a commitment that is supposed to enable him to look upon his present moment as part of "the past as a whole," paradoxical as that may sound. He has become able to examine his current situation as if from a temporal remove, until he can narrate by "perceiving and reflecting back the grouping and combined colouring of the past." Yet of course things are not that simple, when we will recall that Lionel's resolution followed "a long interval." The interval is itself a part of the narrative, although it is paradoxically not: the reader wouldn't know of any interval except that Lionel has narrated it to us, because otherwise we can see right across the page to the end of chapter 18. What lurks there at the end of chapter 18 is a poem by Schiller as translated by Coleridge, which ends, "so often do the spirits / Of great events stride on before the events, / And in to-day already walks tomorrow" (S 266). The lines, in the context of the novel, are densely ironic, as they reverse almost completely the narrative developments. The poem maintains that the present is ever filled with potentiality, to the extent that we can find the future embedded in the present. But the lines seem to have produced an "interval," and on the other side of it Lionel seems to be suggesting that he has learned, during that interval, to "reflect back" on things from the past. Just as Perdita feels disgust at finding, in her loveliness as captured by the mirror, an inverse vision of the bleakness to come, and so she disavows image to identify with the mirror instead, so too does Lionel read German poetry until the lines produce "an interval," a hole or void, around which he, vase-like, can assemble a new narrative structure, one characterized by taking the poem inversely and "reflecting back" upon things happening all around him. He, like Perdita, is seeing the present from the future, rather than, as Schiller recommends, seeing the potentiality embedded in the present. "Soon the present hours would join those past," he says, as "shadows of future ones rose dark and menacing from the womb of time" (S 257–258). It is perhaps "the womb of time" that makes Lionel say that "so effeminate a horror ran through my frame." Lionel, though, has no frame, but rather is a frame—he is a vase, not a mosaic. Far from inhabiting a "third sex," as Johnson has maintained, we can see here that Lionel is becoming-woman: he is learning to identify with the mirror, as Beauvoir cautions against.[88] He aspires to become the spirit of a great event, striding on before the event. Instead of harboring "hope," as he used to, he will henceforth situate himself in the future, disavowing what he sees, until he has managed to speak with the voice of time itself. He will begin to include himself in his narrative, "impelled," as he says, "by the restless spirit within me to continue."

Lionel's "restless spirit within me" directly echoes Schiller's claim about spirits that stride on before the events. For Schiller, an event and its spirit are not experienced simultaneously: the spirit strides "before the events." For those of us living in the present, this makes the "event" an impossible horizon, which must be awaited with all messianicity, until such time as the event comes and we will know that we have then missed the spirit. To claim "a restless spirit within me" is to disregard this paradox quite aggressively. Lionel is a man who strides ahead of his own times. If, as Schiller says, "in to-day already walks tomorrow," then someone like Lionel, present and not present at every scene, can speak for the future even as it remains a part of, and takes up residence within, the here and now. Lionel has found the spirit of the catastrophe "within me," which suggests that he is visiting from the future, present now but yet uncounted like the brother of Paul and Ernest.

Ernst Bloch observes that an orientation to the future begets a feeling of aloneness: "Here we are left alone with ourselves, then: indeed, no longer protected by anything outside or above, in fact. . . . We are lonesome, and stand in the dark of an infinite, merely asymptotic convergence toward the goal."[89] Yet, in this convergence without convergence, Bloch stresses, the impulse toward the future "must be unselfish and communal" even as its work is isolating.[90] *The Last Man* imagines extreme isolation to be the foundation of a collective, worldwide experience. The novel does not seek to cure or heal, as Brittany Pladek notes, but to pare down and reimagine.[91] This, in the end, may be a hallmark of fracture feminism. This study has shown that, again and again—with Paul, separated from Virginia, or the hermit of Smith's *Beachy Head*, or the depopulated London of *Eighteen Hundred and Eleven* and *The Last Man*, or the quietness of Hemans's "Girls' School," the strandedness that epitomizes the Siege of Gibraltar for Merry, or the pivotal "nor you alone" of Richardson's *Harvest*—thinking about the future would seem to require a stillness and isolation that is both antisocial yet transformative. *Gulzara* shows life at the royal court to be isolating in this same way, while *The Last Man* pushes the sentiment to a bleak extreme by literalizing it as an extinction event. Bloch supposes that isolation can enable our thinking from the future during a moment of immediate crisis. But the "our" in question is the very thing in jeopardy in this model. Certainly, it would appear that fracture feminism complicates a person's claim to social belonging. Shelley and the author of *Gulzara* put themselves at odds with the present when they conjure fictional spaces of isolation. In such a state, it becomes an open question, the extent to which their writings were contemporary with the authors' own moment. Žižek warns, in a moment of optimism: "All we can be certain of is that the existing system cannot reproduce itself indefinitely: whatever will come

240 FRACTURE FEMINISM

after will not be 'our future.' "[92] The question then becomes: whose future is summoned by these atemporal texts? Does the act of exempting oneself from "our future," by positing a future of one's own, *depend* upon a space of radical isolation, even hermitage, as epitomized by what we have been calling the "fracture"? And would that diminish its political purchase? These are the questions that we shall turn to next, by way of conclusion.

Conclusion

Fracture feminism is difficult to evaluate as a political movement because it emerged especially from a quite rarified club of female "philosophers," self-styled, and its stock in trade was imagined scenes of extreme isolation. It was not an especially populist movement, nor in any way affirmational. Could fracture feminism, which seems to depend on setting oneself apart from others, have any political purchase in a world in which political movements tend to be associated with collectives? It is telling that so many of these texts—Barbauld's, Merry's, Smith's, Hays's, Shelley's, Richardson's, Hemans's, Williams's—invest so powerfully in the figure of the hermit or the radically solitary traveler. It is further telling that the fracture feminists experimented with time rather than affirming the dignity of female lives or demanding rights for women. Certainly, they engaged with broad questions of social history and objected to structural forms of gender-based violence, physical and epistemological. Yet none of these texts are optimistic in the slightest, despite pinning their hopes on Hope, Bliss, and Fancy. One leaves these texts astonished by the depth, subtlety, and range of the fracture feminists' thought, and the audacity of their experiments in language, but with little confidence that women's lives, or society in general, were about to be improved.

It may not be clear why someone would abandon all hope, on the one hand, but preserve a libidinal investment in the future, on the other, and specifically for hope's sake. Nor why—if the future were indeed so attractive—such a person would opt for the contemporary future rather than the future to come. But such concerns only point to a limitation in our use of the concept of hope: we tend to start with a relatively secure "I" and extrapolate hopes outward from there, instead of using the figure of hope to cast the "I" into an abyss of doubt. For instance: in recent years, the notion of "hope without hope" has emerged within Romantic studies in ways that have been tremendously generative. "Hope," explicitly or implicitly "without hope," has been discussed as a feature of apocalyptic or post-apocalyptic thought in the period; as the name for a wish, especially in Percy Shelley's poetry, to be integrated into nature; or as a feature of poetic thought that ought to be renounced in favor of desire.[1] Like the fracture feminists' work, the purveyors of these semi-hopeful modalities would seem to be committed to the present in the absence of a future. Yet the fracture feminists claim the future specifically as a place from which to be in the present: in essence, when they hope they hope from a present without the present, rather than cultivating hope without hope *in* the present. They claim an alien presence within the social order, call this place "hope," and treat it as the object of utopian longing. Such hope refuses to call for a transformation in the existing social order, and may even thwart existing calls. We have such hope expressed variously in Wollstonecraft, Robinson, Browne, Smith, and Shelley. To call such a modality "the future," as the fracture feminists do, is to contest the very parameters of social participation, and effectively to imagine one's own removal without removal from the body politic. It is to imagine oneself radically heterogenous to the social order and yet there imperceptibly within it. To sustain such a wish is different than to focus on matters of life and death, because the death drive is the mechanism, not the goal, of such a poetics—and through such a mechanism, the very idea of a goal, of a hoped-for object, is obliterated.

It is analogous to the way that Lacan, when challenged to answer the Kantian question of "what may I hope for?," insisted instead upon asking, "from where do you hope?"[2] This goes further than asserting a hope without hope, as it would seem to imply that identifying the particular wellspring of one's hoping—that is, the unconscious rather than a rational system—is more important than identifying hope's proper object, even if that object is to be found in negation. Instead of worrying about whether hope had any content, it would destabilize one's own place in relation to the community. "No chance for it to ex-sist except through good luck, by which I mean that hope won't change anything, which makes it futile, by not allowing that to happen," Lacan posits, without offering any indication as to what "it" or "that" might refer to or what "good luck" might imply.[3] No longer would we ask the question, *what should we dare to hope for, if anything, given current conditions*, nor even the Edelmanian *what do we instead desire?*—but rather: *where do I stand in relation to those around me?*

CONCLUSION   243

It is to implicate oneself, through locating one's own act of hoping, in the question of who belongs, and to claim that fracture in the body politic as the wellspring of one's aspirations. Yet, to ask "from where do you hope?" is the opposite of a populist gesture, and is even (to an alarming extent) an openly elitist one: the question, bypassing Kantian "ethical criteria," as it does, leads Lacan to say: "I think the analytic discourse should be withheld from the rabble."[4] The aim cannot be to position everyone in a fracture within the symbolic order, or to give them mastery of the unconscious; rather, it is to recognize the ways that one is partially aloof from the symbolic coordinates that constitute life and to claim a hope that would destroy itself.

A similar attitude is built into fracture feminism, I think, which is perhaps what gives the movement its ambiguously elitist feel. Fracture feminism certainly involves a significant quotient of what Julia Kristeva has called "feminine genius." It is not representative of the period's writing generally, by women or men. The contemporary future seems, then, strangely individualized—the unconscious place from which I hope—despite the fact that these writers often responded to one another's work and built, across decades, a literary tradition spanning genres. I would suggest, though, that fracture feminism does make a powerful cultural intervention, though never a spectacular or even discernable one. Kristeva understands such creativities well. Genius, according to Kristeva, tends to express itself through "subjective initiative" rather than collective action, and so exerts a decentralized and "highly personal force, tiny yet irreducible, on which depends the possibility of deconstructing any given 'condition.'"[5] Though it arises only in the uniqueness of each iteration, it is "*nevertheless* something that can be shared," insofar as "genius" consists in challenges to "the sociocultural conditions of . . . identity."[6] This is a good description of fracture feminism, I think, and effectively a re-statement of the question "from where do I hope?"

Kristeva's work is so interesting because the category of feminine genius is a vexed one, to say the least. It was especially fraught during the Romantic period. Scholars such as Ashley Cross have found it inadequate when dealing with Romantic-era feminist writing, given how the term implied a self-assurance and control that could be claimed only by men of privilege or, occasionally, women in exile.[7] Jacques Derrida observes that the concept of genius is such a masculine domain that francophones say "un génie" in the masculine, even when referring to a woman.[8] Yet wherever genius appears, Derrida says, it "brings about the absolute mutation

244 FRACTURE FEMINISM

and discontinuity of all others," be it in temporal, sequential, or generic terms.[9] One might say that it marks a fracture internal to clock time and invisible to it. Genius is, basically, Derrida's name for the Lacanian Real: in its silent form, he says, it "surpasses both the symbolic and the imaginary, it grapples with the impossible. Genius gives without knowing it, beyond knowledge."[10] It is exactly the feature that Wollstonecraft admires in Macaulay, that Robinson and Cowley admire in Merry, that Barbauld seeks to historicize, that Smith favors in her hermit, that Hays seeks to eroticize, and that the inductees of the period's literary feminist halls of fame, such as those in *A Letter to the Women of England* and "Ithuriel," are said to share. The tendency in genius toward discontinuity is what gives us the impression that these works have been written from the future, a future that had already arrived. Female "genius," as expressed within the fracture feminist tradition, would seem to reveal a world to come ex-sisting within the contemporary world.

The implicit question that motivates a number of these texts—I am thinking especially of *A Letter to the Women of England*, *Paul and Virginia*, *Eighteen Hundred and Eleven*, "Ode to Folly," *Beachy Head*, and *Gulzara*—is: "Of whom and of what are we contemporaries?" It is a question that philosophers today are still pursuing. "Of whom and of what are we contemporaries?," asks Giorgio Agamben directly, as he ponders to what extent a person can belong, or not belong, to their own times.[11] Equipped with a poet's taste for irony and a lifetime's engagement with the thought of Walter Benjamin, Agamben argues that

> Those who are truly contemporary, who truly belong to their time, are those who neither perfectly coincide with it nor adjust themselves to its demands. They are thus in this sense irrelevant. But precisely because of this condition, precisely through this disconnection and this anachronism, they are more capable than others of perceiving and grasping their own time.[12]

This study, I think, has offered similar arguments much less efficiently. The fracture feminists would comment upon the most pressing political questions of their time—including the Siege of Gibraltar, the French Revolution, the Napoleonic Wars, women's rights, the abolition of the slave trade, the reform at the ballot, the consolidation of sexual norms, girls' education, and the brutishness of capitalism—by situating themselves at once within their immediate historical moment and at an inassimilable

CONCLUSION   245

point of futurity extimate to it. They wrote the future into the present, as
though contesting clock time were a necessary first step toward challenging
the era's legal, military, and political superstructure. Their writing belonged
to an archive from the future, immediately accessible. They stripped the
present moment of even its capacity to cohere as a moment, arguably
rendering themselves "irrelevant" in the process. Being (per Agamben)
"on time for an appointment that one cannot but miss," they pried open
a "fracture" in time during an age of intense chrononormativity.[13] Yet
because these writers did not perceive themselves to "own" their historical moment, the era was resolutely never "their own time"—a fact that
changes the connotation of being-contemporary. Because women were
systematically excluded from discussions of public policy,[14] they tended
not to perceive themselves to be living in "*my* time," and so needed to find
other ways to introduce "a caesura" into official modes of timekeeping.[15]
It was actually their enforced inability to "own" the present that led these
writers to untether time from clock and calendar.

Reading Agamben in light of the fracture feminist tradition, one
wonders: did writers of the Romantic period in Britain, an era so unusually
invested in chrononormativity, negotiate this threat of disconnection in
any distinctive way? And was gender a factor in their collective attempt
to become "truly contemporary"? I would answer both questions affirma-
tively, in light of this study.

The former question (i.e., about historical distinctiveness) is important
because Agamben's present does not seem to be any particular historical
moment or place, just an ever-refreshed "now," which means that those
who are deemed "truly contemporary" would seem to be doing something
relatively universal and replicable, however rare. Agamben's text is punc-
tuated by only fleeting references to specific dates, such as September 11,
2001—a date which, in his text, could really be replaced by the date of any
significant event. Yet the fracture feminists emphatically, again and again,
ascribe their unusual perspective on time to their particular historical
conditions. Their reflections respond to immediate world-historical events,
like the French Revolution or the Battle of Waterloo; they also react to
broader historical transformations, such as the militarization of culture;
they commemorate more intimate losses, like the deaths of family and
friends. In each case, though, fracture feminists tend to write as if they
were encountering a gap in temporality caused by circumstance; they do
not tend to describe themselves as innately gifted seers. The tone is more
of reportage, on the model, say, of Williams's *Letters Written in France*:

they are seeking to make an accurate account of a future that they already inhabit. This separates the fracture feminists from Agamben's model and from the eighteenth-century prophetic tradition as well.

The second question (i.e., about sexual difference) is important because Agamben so emphatically attributes "contemporariness" to visionary men. It is the domain of "an intelligent man."[16] "The contemporary is he who firmly holds his gaze on his own time," Agamben claims, adding that the contemporary is, "the one whose eyes are struck by the beam of darkness that comes from his own time."[17] In doing so, he risks fetishizing a coterie of visionary, male geniuses—effectively a Bloomian pose that, over the decades, has especially stultified the study of British Romanticism.[18] It is a particularly masculinist model for literary analysis, and one that especially plagued academic studies of British Romanticism over the twentieth century. Indeed, it was precisely the recovery and canonization of the era's women writers that finally allowed the field to get beyond, and even repudiate, this model. In this context, it may seem counterproductive to suggest, as I have perhaps been doing, that women writers were the ones whose eyes were struck by the "dark rays" of the late eighteenth and early nineteenth centuries. But I would suggest that understanding the connection between women's writing and "the contemporary" requires us to rethink the status of the visionary artist through the refraction produced by sexual difference.

Universalism of Agamben's sort is a symptom of an ideology that, Kristeva elsewhere argues, has long kept women in a "diagonal" relation with time.[19] That is, by assuming that what is meant by "the present" is a relatively stable affair, and that those lucky few who are "contemporary" might share common traits across the centuries, Agamben enables himself to think of being-contemporary as a masculine prerogative. My two questions arising from Agamben's text, then, turn out to be mutually constituting to the extent that they are really aspects of the same question. The challenge as outlined by Elizabeth Freeman is to develop an analysis of "*temporal* transitivity that does not leave feminism, femininity, or other so-called anachronisms behind."[20]

Radical women's writing of the Romantic period tends to work through particulars. Patricia A. Matthew has highlighted how important the biographies of individual women were, even when displaced and fictionalized, for the feminist discourse of the period.[21] Yet women were, meanwhile, being semi-excluded from the realm of biography. Gina Luria Walker asks, with regard to literary biography: "how we can deploy female

CONCLUSION   247

biography as an accurate gauge of a woman's place in posterity in the absence of comprehensive, almost always incomplete, information?"[22] I would propose that we could learn to take those absences seriously as an authorizing condition for fracture feminism. It is not really a matter of recovering lost information about these women and their writings, so much as learning to perceive the constitutive gap or fracture that *made* their writing "women's writing" even within their immediate historical moment. The Real did inflect the era's "cultural symptomology," and fracture feminists were responding to that.[23] Their writing is not-whole and should not be made whole retroactively. This means that ways of reading are needed that can factor in the swerve of the Real and the endless loops occasioned by its impossible presence. A universalizing approach, even one like Agamben's, which is so fascinated with temporal gaps and fractures, proves inadequate to this literary tradition.

I have tried to surmount this impasse by using a psychoanalytic and deconstructive approach—not to blend those approaches, but to find the zone conducive to both. Psychoanalysis teaches us that time and sexual difference are produced together, such that there can be no study of temporality without taking seriously sexual difference and vice versa, too. Joan Copjec has articulated this best. In a close reading of Freud, she explains that

> neither term—time or sex—has priority over the other. The two are co-originary. The subject is sexuated inasmuch as she is finite, subject to time. Or: sex belongs not to the essence of the subject but to her historicity; it defines her life of pleasure/unpleasure inasmuch as she is finite, subject to time's vicissitudes.[24]

Yet, because this pleasure/unpleasure dichotomy quickly, so often in literature as in life, becomes prone to cycles of repetition, I have been especially drawn to think about the literary history of time and sex in relation to the death drive, or what Derrida would call an anarchive drive. This is where deconstruction and psychoanalysis, despite their ongoing differences, converge, to form what we have variously called "echo" or "destinerrance" or "Derridanalysis."

The writers studied in this book were not exactly excluded from political discussions, and neither were they included; they located aporias in dominant political discourse and commandeered them as a way to ex-sist, as Lacan would have said, in the ideological gaps and fissures of their moment. They were neither straightforwardly insiders nor outsiders: as Bruce Fink would say, "we can discern a place for [such writing] within our symbolic order, and even name it, but it nevertheless remains ineffable, unspeakable."[25] These authors, adopting a feminist perspective both paradoxical and impossible, were writing the contemporary future. It is experimental, speculative, philosophical political thought—the very sort of thought for which female Romantic writers seldom get credit, as Kate Singer has noticed and done much to rectify.[26] The fracture made possible a politics of the not-all (or not-whole, if you prefer), spoken from a perspective that is internal to but not quite "present" in the body politic. The future is not, in their work, awaited; it is experienced directly within the immediate political context of the moment. They speak for and from the contemporary future, a time that ex-sists in the writings of British Romanticism.

Art historians say that the contemporary necessarily "signifies multiple ways of being with, in, and out of time, separately and at once, with others and without them," such that it is forever menaced by "the threat of unregulated and multiple claims of interpretive authority."[27] In literary writing of the Romantic period, the fracture feminists' interpretive claims were multiple but certainly regulated: the Della Cruscans were mocked in *The Baviad* and reproached in the Preface to *Lyrical Ballads*; Barbauld did not publish poetry again after *Eighteen Hundred and Eleven*, and, like Smith, had to wait until after her death to publish her indictment of the present; Richardson had to self-publish; Hemans and Shelley had to become the saintly "Mrs. Hemans" and "Mrs. Shelley" in order to find a readership; Williams was actually jailed. Yet they did not write as marginalized figures or cultural outsiders. Instead, they wrote of time "through detachment and mediation," by the "jostling of edges or propinquities," as Jacques Khalip and Forest Pyle say of the contemporary. "Contemporariness," they explain, "marks a relation to sameness that can be intimately known through its estrangement."[28] The key concept here (for my purposes) is difference through intimacy, exploring a sameness without sameness, internally fractured by and parergonal with the broader British culture's increasingly zealous fetishization of sexual difference.

The matrix of sexual difference—a relatively new construction during this period—was being ever more severely enforced as the revolutionary era gave way to the Regency.[29] The fracture feminists, across their decades of activity, always acutely registered sexual difference as a major factor in their thinking, and often described sexual difference as a difference internal to sameness, as if it were the effect of a drive's perpetual deferment. Sexual difference, in this feminist tradition, arises through a gap caused and sustained by desire, which is why these texts are so often "overtly hostile to the myth of female desirelessness," as Morgan Rooney has said of *A Letter to the Women of England*.[30]

Charlotte Caroline Richardson's poem "To-Morrow" exemplifies this tendency clearly. In two crisp octaves telling of "Anna" and "Edward," Richardson warns that, even as the peace brings men home to England, it will also send many a woman "far distant from her peaceful dwelling," in search of intimacy with lovers who had been killed in the war.[31] Richardson uses the past and present tenses for Edward and the future tense for Anna, to describe activities that they are doing concurrently and together. Richardson offers a vision, then, of England's men and women living at separate times—men now, and women "to-morrow"—which makes any attempt at sexual union an act of future mourning and necrophilia, "pillow'd on his clay-cold breast."[32] Similarly, Felicia Hemans, in "A Thought of the Future," describes a void called "love" that forces lovers into different temporalities in endless loops of delay and dispersal: "that power, the dweller of thy secret breast . . . Finding no place of rest . . . And winning no reply."[33] In both poems, women live in a future that is already here, leading them to miss out, endlessly, on rapport between the sexes and participation in national celebrations. In both poems, the women resolve to move into a wider, cosmopolitan frame, beyond the national borders, effectively worldwide-izing their erotic experience.

Kristeva suggests that the roles assigned to women in the popular European imagination, especially with regard to maternity, and including the very category "women," have given women an uneasy relation to time. "Female subjectivity as it gives itself up to intuition becomes a problem with respect to a certain conception of time," argues Kristeva, given how women, forced into a "diagonal" relation to their dominant cultures, enable "temporality [to] render explicit a rupture, an expectation, or an anguish which other temporalities work to conceal."[34] Richardson and Hemans, in the examples given above, make explicit this rupture and its attendant anguish; other writers discussed in this study are often doing the same thing. But they do this not by the mere fact of being women, but by being, precisely, ~~philosophers~~—that is, by pursuing speculative thought through the limitations of the signifier, so as to keep contemporary history not-whole. In this sense, I suspect that fracture feminism, if read as an ongoing engagement with the contemporary future, may end up challenging both Kristeva's theory of women's time and Agamben's theory of the contemporary. Although the fracture feminists were indeed "introducing into time an essential dishomogeneity," as Agamben would appreciate, that very dishomogeneity is what prevented them from universalizing their observations, and thus speaking in a way that would be broadly relevant.[35] Fracture feminism, though, also offers a different way than Kristeva's to think about women's alienation from, or resistance to, clock time as a political factor—one based more in analysis interminable and feats of figuration than in "intuition." These writers develop histories, to quote Anne C. McCarthy, of "what arises outside of the temporalities and signifying processes of so-called ordinary life."[36] Yet theirs are not voices from the margins in any straightforward manner. True to the logic of the parergon, they find the outside of ordinary life somewhere interior to it, making, in effect, Klein bottles out of time and signification.

Bertolt Brecht urged artists to engage with their own time, even if they did so critically or indirectly. Using the quintessentially Romantic symbol of the wind, he encouraged radical artists to embrace the immediate moment: "I believe that an artist, even if he sits in strictest seclusion in the traditional garret working for future generations, is unlikely to produce anything without some wind in his sails. And this wind has to be the wind prevailing in his own period, and not some future wind."[37] There are a number of ways that such sailboats might be steered, because "the only impossibility is to sail with no wind at all or with tomorrow's wind."[38] The fracture feminists take what is essentially the opposite tack, yet somehow also follow this advice perversely to the letter. They sail with tomorrow's wind, which is no wind at all—in the sense of a negative wind, rather than the absence of wind—and so begin to activate impossibilities. Their contretempopian visions are not world-building but time-protecting, and await only the despair of the current moment. They produce nothing, rather than "anything," but a nothing that inheres within the hegemonic discourses of the nation, invisibly warping flows of capital, libido, and history. The nothing confounds attempts to count or be counted, to claim rights or build coalitions; it is not-sum future wind.

Notes

Introduction

1. Taylor, "Felicia Hemans," 10.

2. Colley, *Britons: Forging the Nation 1707–1837*, 1–3; Behrendt, *British Women Poets*, 82; Hurl-Eamon, *Marriage and the British Army*, 4.

3. Taylor, "Felicia Hemans," 20.

4. Browne, "War and Peace," ll. 1–14.

5. Reno, *Amorous Aesthetics*, 181; Najarian, "Sexual Politics," 522.

6. Behrendt, *British Women Poets*, 12.

7. Macaulay, *Observations*, 34–35.

8. Weiss, *The Female Philosopher*.

9. Miller, *The Invention*; Rohrbach, *Modernity's Mist*; Faflak, *Marking Time*.

10. Balfour, *The Rhetoric*; Smith, *Romantic Women Writers*; Bundock, *Romantic Prophecy*.

11. Crimmins, *The Romantic Historicism*; Sachs, "The Glimmer."

12. Quoted in Behrendt, "Mary Shelley," 86.

13. Derrida, *Paper Machine*, 41–43.

14. Kingstone, *Victorian Narratives of the Recent Past*.

15. François, *Open Secrets*, 81–94; Levinson, "Notes and Queries"; McLane, "Afterword: Emergent."

16. Lacan, *Seminar XX*. For discussion of the difficulty in translating this term into English, see Tyrer, *Out of the Past*, 115–117.

17. Lacan, *Seminar XX*, 72–73.

18. Zupančič, *What Is Sex?*, 36–37.

19. McDayter, *Untrodden Regions of the Mind*; Mandell, "The First"; Faflak, *Romantic Psychoanalysis*; Carman, *Radical Ecology*; Collings, *Disastrous Subjectivities*; Sigler, "Lacan's Romanticism."

20. de Man, "Shelley Disfigured," 67; Rajan, *Dark Interpreter*, 19–20; Bode, "Romanticism and Deconstruction"; Christensen, *Romanticism at the End*, 2–3; Clark, "Lost and Found," 167; Wang, *Romantic Sobriety*, 36–40.

21. Garofalo, *Women, Love*; Sigler, *Sexual Enjoyment*.
22. Rancière, "Who Is the Subject," 304.
23. Caruth, *Literature in the Ashes*, 88. Emphasis in the original.
24. Butler, "Further Reflections on Conversations of Our Time," 13.
25. Chandler, *England in 1819*, 100; de Groote, "Old Familiar Faces," 78.
26. Thompson, "Time," 61.
27. Favret, *War at a Distance*, 52.
28. Koselleck, *Futures Past*, xxiv.
29. Koselleck, 253.
30. Bundock, *Romantic Prophecy*, 11.
31. Chandler, *England in 1819*, 5; Sachs, "1816," 89; Faflak, *Marking Time*.
32. Sharma, "Biopolitical Economy," 441.
33. Fabian, *Time and the Other*, 31–36.
34. Freeman, *Time Binds*. See especially Freeman's analysis of *Frankenstein*, 96–136.
35. Mullen, "Two Clocks," 67.
36. Tomalin, *Telling the Time*, 46, 48.
37. Krapp, "Female Romanticism," 73.
38. Paulson, "Present, Period, Crisis," 167.
39. Zupančič, *Shortest*, 177; Derrida, *Without Alibi*, 234. Emphasis Derrida's.
40. As per the film by Jarmusch, *The Dead Don't Die*.
41. Badiou, *Lacan*, 198–99.
42. Lacan, *Autre Écrits*, 425; Badiou, *Lacan*, 147.
43. Badiou, *Lacan*, 169.
44. Soler, *What Lacan Said*, 46.
45. Derrida, *Aporias*, 34.
46. Browne, "War and Peace," ll. 35–36. Emphasis mine.
47. Browne, l. 32.
48. Derrida, *Rogues*, 121.
49. von Clausewitz, *On War*, 87.
50. Browne, "War and Peace," ll. 2, 99.
51. Derrida, *Politics*, 16.
52. Derrida, *Archive Fever*, 68.
53. Caputo, "The Messianic," 162.
54. Lacan, *Seminar XX*, 80.
55. Hemans, *The Works*, 7:289.
56. Rohrbach, *Modernity's Mist*, 1–3. Emphasis in the original.
57. Derrida, *Spurs*, 51.
58. McCarthy, *Awful Parenthesis*, 17, 19, 94.
59. Said, *Orientalism*, 118.
60. Labbe, *Romantic Visualities*; Curran, "Romantic Poetry," 192.
61. Freud, *SE*, 23:129–132, 267–269.

NOTES TO CHAPTER 1

62. Freud, 22:135.

63. Freud, 22:135.

64. Christensen, *Romanticism at the End*.

65. Bundock, *Romantic Prophecy*, 10.

66. Percy Bysshe Shelley, "A Defence of Poetry," in *Shelley's Poetry and Prose*, ed. Donald H. Reiman and Neil Fraistat, 2nd ed. (New York: Norton, 2002), 535; for an analysis of this quotation in light of futurity, see Chris Washington, *Romantic Revelations*, 30.

67. Behrendt, *British Women Poets*, 40.

68. Behrendt, 45.

69. Behrendt, 41.

70. Freud, *SE*, 22:134.

71. Cornell, "Derrida's Negotiations as a Technique of Liberation," 197.

72. Lacan, *Seminar XX*, 80.

73. By this, I mean "women" in the Lacanian sense, of anyone who "get[s] the idea or sense that there must be a jouissance that is beyond" the limitations of the phallus. See Lacan, *Seminar XX*, 76.

74. Lacan, *Seminar XX*, 44.

75. Lacan, *Seminar X*, 284.

76. Lacan, 284. I am grateful to Celiese Lypka for her time spent thinking about this passage with me.

77. Krapp, "Female Romanticism," 73.

78. Hadley, "Back to the Future," 1039.

79. Derrida, *Resistances*, 40.

80. Freud, *SE*, 23:107.

81. Derrida, *Archive Fever*, 56.

82. Cixous, *Insister*, 159.

83. Cixous, 123.

84. Cixous, 124.

85. Cixous, 162.

86. Lacan, *Écrits*, 161–175.

87. Robinson, "Letter," 2.

88. Lake, "History Writing," 90.

89. Zupančič, *The Odd One*, 131–132.

90. Lacan, *Seminar XX*, 60–61.

Chapter 1

1. Hofkosh, "Introduction," paras. 2–3.

2. Derrida, *Archive Fever*, 70.

3. Carlson, *England's First Family*, 39.

4. Weiss, *The Female Philosopher*.

5. Wollstonecraft, "Rights of Woman," 122–123n5. Further references to this text will be given parenthetically, with VRW.

6. Bradshaw, "The Limits," 28, 32, 35n2.

7. McCarthy, "Why Anna Letitia Barbauld," 363.

8. Clery, *Eighteen Hundred and Eleven: Poetry, Protest, and Economic Crisis*, 4–5.

9. Lacan, *Seminar XX*, 63, 73.

10. Lacan, 145.

11. Cross, *Robinson and the Genesis*, 139.

12. Juengel, "Mary Wollstonecraft's Perpetual Disaster," para. 19.

13. Hofkosh, "Introduction," para. 5.

14. Collings, *Disastrous Subjectivities*, 34.

15. For the deconstructive legacy of this Leninist question, see Nancy, "What Is to Be Done?"

16. Wollstonecraft, "Letters Written in Sweden," 294–295.

17. Keane, *Women Writers*, 129–130.

18. Freeman, *Time Binds*, xxii.

19. Woolf, *A Room of One's Own*.

20. Foucault, *Discipline and Punish*, 31.

21. Derrida, *Archive Fever*, 76.

22. Mandell, "The First," 78.

23. Wollstonecraft, "Rights of Woman," 175.

24. Wollstonecraft, 174.

25. Looser, "Ithuriel," 81. Further references to this text will be given parenthetically, with I.

26. Looser, "Mary Wollstonecraft, 'Ithuriel,' " 70.

27. Looser, 71–72.

28. Derrida, *Archive Fever*, 80.

29. Derrida, 74.

30. Rancière, *Figures of History*, 62.

31. Rancière, 61–62.

32. Rancière, 66.

33. Rancière, 69–70.

34. Lacan, *Seminar XX*, 70.

35. Lacan, 76, 73.

36. Looser, "Mary Wollstonecraft, 'Ithuriel,' " 90nn1–2.

37. Bennington and Derrida, *Jacques Derrida*, 8.

38. Looser, "Mary Wollstonecraft, 'Ithuriel,' " 90–91n4.

39. Derrida, *Archive Fever*, 80.

40. Lacan, *Seminar XX*, 8.

41. Lacan, 66.

NOTES TO CHAPTER 1

42. Lacan, 73–74.

43. Cross, *Robinson and the Genesis*, 148.

44. Singer, *Romantic Vacancy*, 36–37.

45. Rooney, "Belonging to No/Body," 364.

46. Agamben, *What Is an Apparatus?*, 47.

47. Agamben, 41.

48. Robinson, "Letter," 27–28. Further references to this text will be given parenthetically, with L.

49. Žižek, *Parallax*, 4.

50. Vernooy-Epp, "Teaching Mary Darby Robinson," 20; Cross, *Robinson and the Genesis*, 151.

51. Cross, *Robinson and the Genesis*, 150.

52. Žižek, *Incontinence*, 137–138.

53. Wallraven, *A Writing Halfway*, 80.

54. Kristeva, "Women's Time," 13–14.

55. Lacan, *Écrits*, 17, 30.

56. Vernooy-Epp, "Teaching Mary Darby Robinson," 20–21.

57. Hodson, "Women Write the Rights."

58. Copjec, *Read My Desire*, 235.

59. Copjec, 234.

60. Lacan, *Écrits*, 6, 554.

61. Lacan, *Seminar XXIII*, 10.

62. "Intuition, n.," sec. 5.a.

63. Lupton, *Reading*, 145.

64. Mallarmé, *The Poems*, 44–47; Lacan, *Seminar I*, 157.

65. Agamben, *What Is an Apparatus?*, 46.

66. Derrida, *Without Alibi*, 202.

67. Derrida, 206.

68. Derrida, 204–205.

69. Lupton, *Reading*, 151.

70. Derrida, "Signature Event Context," 313.

71. Derrida, 315.

72. Derrida, 316.

73. Craciun et al., "Letter," para. 3; Vernooy-Epp, "Teaching Mary Darby Robinson," 15–16.

74. Lacan, *Seminar XI*, 20–21.

75. Derrida, *Archive Fever*, 85.

76. Kamuf, *Signature Pieces*, 23–41.

77. Derrida, "Signature Event Context," 328.

78. Derrida, 311.

79. Derrida, 309.

80. Cross, *Robinson and the Genesis*, 148.

256 NOTES TO CHAPTER 1

81. Lacan, *Seminar XVII*, 87.

82. Lacan, 145–146.

83. Chandler, *England in 1819*, 114–120; Rosenbaum, "A Thing Unknown," 393; Rohrbach, "Barbauld's History"; Favret, "Field of History," para. 28.

84. Barbauld, "On the Uses," 417; McCarthy, *Anna Letitia Barbauld*, 492. Further references to "On the Uses of History" will be given parenthetically, with U.

85. Lacan, "Seminar IX," sec. 16.5.62.

86. Rancière, *Figures of History*, 61–70.

87. Lacan, *Écrits*, 273; Derrida, "Geopsychoanalysis."

88. Lacan, *Écrits*, 273.

89. Lacan, 273.

90. Lacan, 273–274.

91. Looser, *British Women Writers*, 16.

92. Looser, 20.

93. McInnes, *Wollstonecraft's Ghost*, 100.

94. Chandler, *England in 1819*, 114–117.

95. Clery, *Eighteen Hundred and Eleven: Poetry, Protest, and Economic Crisis*, 1–4.

96. Derrida, "A Time for Farewells," xiii.

97. Lacan, "On a Reform in Its Hole," 20.

98. Gallop, *The Deaths of the Author*, 120.

99. Gottlieb, *Romantic Globalism*; Hogan, *Other Englands*, 1–26; Alliez and Lazzarato, *Wars and Capital*.

100. See Peggy Kamuf's gloss on this term in Derrida, *Without Alibi*, 303n2.

101. Derrida, "Faith and Knowledge," 29–30; Derrida, *Paper Machine*, 112–120; Li, "Elliptical Interruptions."

102. Gustafson, "Abolition, Phallocentrism," 133.

103. Barbauld, "Eighteen Hundred," ll. 165–166.

104. Deleuze and Guattari, *Anti-Oedipus: Capitalism and Schizophrenia*, 8.

105. Barbauld, "Eighteen Hundred," l. 158.

106. Barbauld, ll. 170–171.

107. Derrida, *On Cosmopolitanism*, 38.

108. Sachs, *Poetics of Decline*, 124.

109. Crimmins, *The Romantic Historicism*, 3.

110. Derrida, "A Time for Farewells," vii.

111. Shelley, "Valerius," 333.

112. Shelley, 334.

113. Barbauld, "Eighteen Hundred," ll. 211–214.

114. Sachs, "Future! Decline," 361; Reeder, "A World," 579; Rohrbach, "Barbauld's History," 179.

115. Barbauld, "Eighteen Hundred," ll. 159–162.

116. Barbauld, ll. 205–208.

NOTES TO CHAPTER 2

117. Derrida, "Psychoanalysis Searches," 269.

118. Lacan, *Écrits*, 681.

119. Withers, *Placing the Enlightenment*, 149.

120. Derrida and Roudinesco, *For What Tomorrow*, 185–186; Derrida, "Psychoanalysis Searches," 245, 267.

121. Withers, *Placing the Enlightenment*, 179.

122. Bauman, *Liquid Modernity*, 8.

123. Vukanović and Grmuša, "Introduction," 2–3.

124. Favret, "Field of History," para. 28.

125. Koselleck, *Futures Past*, xxiv.

126. Koselleck, 130.

127. Derrida, "Geopsychoanalysis," 335.

128. Phillips, *On Historical Distance*, 95.

129. Derrida, "Geopsychoanalysis," 319.

130. Lacan, *Seminar XX*, 81.

131. Derrida, "Psychoanalysis Searches," 238–239.

132. Freud, *SE*, 21:125–126, 21:136–138.

133. Lacan, *Écrits*, 291.

134. Lacan, *Seminar XVII*, 38.

135. Sachs, *Poetics of Decline*, 107.

136. Here I am drawing upon the discussion of femaleness in Lacan, *Seminar XX*, 73.

137. Looser, *British Women Writers*, 7, 8.

138. Looser, 1–2.

139. Lacan, *Seminar XI*, 25; Lacan, *Seminar XVII*, 15.

Chapter 2

1. Prasad, *Colonialism*, 44.

2. Prasad, 63.

3. Walker, "Adoption, Narrative, and Nation, 1800–1850," 963.

4. Walker, 963.

5. Lacan, *Seminar VII*, 23–24.

6. Bernardin de Saint Pierre, *Paul and Virginia*, 2004, 84. Further references to this text will be given parenthetically, with W. References to Bernardin's French text and to other translations of the novel will be given in the notes.

7. Mellor, *Romanticism and Gender*, 82.

8. Ferrier, *Marriage*, 284.

9. Richardson, "Rethinking Romantic Incest," 554.

10. Crisman, "Now Misery."

11. Schechter, "Psychoanalytic Theory," 696, 701, 704.

12. Lacan, "Seminar IX," sec. 6.12.61 (p. 7); Coles, *The Importance*, 59–65.

13. Smith, "The Suffering Hero," 637–639.

14. Wollstonecraft, "French Revolution," 112.

15. Agamben, *The End of the Poem*, 8.

16. Lacan, *Seminar VII*, 309.

17. Freud, *SE*, 4:262.

18. Derrida, *Politics*, 149.

19. Hara, "Deconstructing," 148. Emphasis in the original.

20. Gottlieb, *Romantic Globalism*, 15–16.

21. Derrida, *Politics*, 236.

22. Calè, "Sympathy in Translation," para. 2.

23. Calè, para. 2; Pucci, "Snapshots," 94.

24. Bernardin de Saint Pierre, *Paul and Virginia*, 2004, 6–7; Kennedy, *Helen Maria Williams*, 124.

25. Coleman, "Global Context," 135–136.

26. Pauk, "Promoting Feminism."

27. Wright, *British Women Writers*, xv.

28. Wollstonecraft, "Rights of Woman," 67–68.

29. Sinanan, "Maroon Resistance," para. 7.

30. Sinanan, para. 7.

31. Ty, *Unsex'd Revolutionaries*, 73, 84; Williams, *Letters Containing a Sketch*, 1.7.

32. Derrida, *Rogues*, 58; Cheah and Guerlac, "Introduction," 9.

33. Williams, *Letters Written in France*, 69; Kennedy, *Helen Maria Williams*, 52–89; Craciun, *British Women Writers*, 98–114.

34. Calè, "Sympathy in Translation," para. 14.

35. Derrida, *Beast & Sovereign II*, 9.

36. Miège, *Indentured Labour*, 4.

37. Vaughan, *Creating the Creole Island*, 2.

38. Vaughan, 2–3, 206.

39. Derrida, *Monolingualism*, 40.

40. Berman, *Creole Crossings*, 200–201n2.

41. Kitson, *Romantic Literature*, 11.

42. Derrida, *Politics*, 28–29, 42–44.

43. Gordon, *Creolizing Political Theory*; Gordon and Roberts, *Creolizing Rousseau*.

44. Kapor, "Shifting Edenic Codes," 226; Ravi, "Indo-Mauritians," 34.

45. Cassity, "Caught by the Throat."

46. Rancière, "The Politics of Literature," 15; Vaughan, *Creating the Creole Island*, 164.

47. Kapor, "Shifting Edenic Codes," 218.

48. Neill, "The Sentimental Novel," 37.

NOTES TO CHAPTER 2   259

49. Kennedy, *Helen Maria Williams*, 41–46.

50. Vaughan, *Creating the Creole Island*, 255–258.

51. Allen, "Satisfying the 'Want for Labouring People,'" 64; Jung, "Outlawing 'Coolies,'" 678.

52. Labio, "Reading," 676.

53. Baucom, *Specters of the Atlantic*, 24.

54. Neill, "The Sentimental Novel," 43.

55. Bernardin de Saint Pierre, *Paul et Virginie*, 168; Bernardin de Saint Pierre, *Paul and Virginia*, 2004, 113; Pucci, "Snapshots," 115n25.

56. Bernardin de Saint-Pierre, *A Voyage*, 101.

57. Cassity has persuasively outlined the abolitionist resonance of Bernardin's decision to designate the woman as a "Maroon," explicitly, in the context of the French colonial imagination. See Cassity, 100.

58. Derrida, *Of Grammatology*, 226.

59. Derrida, "'Relevant' Translation," 178–179.

60. Derrida, *Beast & Sovereign II*, 61; Derrida, "'Relevant' Translation," 174.

61. Calè, "Sympathy in Translation," para. 2.

62. Derrida, *Truth*, 57–61.

63. Duro, "What Is a Parergon?"

64. Williams, *Letters Written in France*, 241.

65. Rohrbach, *Modernity's Mist*, 50. Emphasis in the original.

66. Kennedy, *Helen Maria Williams*, 107–112.

67. Derrida, *Politics*, 7–8.

68. Derrida, 7.

69. Derrida, 302. Emphasis in the original.

70. Derrida, *Aporias*, 12.

71. Bernardin de Saint Pierre, *Paul and Virginia*, 1989, 72; Bernardin de Saint Pierre, *Paul and Virginia*, 2004, 54.

72. Derrida, *Without Alibi*, 228.

73. Bernardin de Saint Pierre, *Paul et Virginie*, 110–125; Bernardin de Saint Pierre, *Paul and Virginia*, 1989, 101–114.

74. Calè, "Sympathy in Translation."

75. Cohen, "Sentimental Communities," 106.

76. Derrida, *Politics*, 1.

77. Derrida, 16.

78. Cassity, "Caught," 100.

79. Egerton, "Changing Concepts," 338.

80. Qtd. in Egerton, 338.

81. Derrida, *Of Grammatology*, 222.

82. Duquette, "Dissenting Cosmopolitanism," 92.

83. Zytaruk, "Take Care Some Seeds."

84. Derrida, *Specters of Marx*, 11.

260   NOTES TO CHAPTER 2

85. Berman, *Creole Crossings*, 75.

86. Cohen, "Sentimental Communities," 111–112.

87. Derrida, *Of Grammatology*, 179–180.

88. Derrida, *Specters of Marx*, 23.

89. Derrida hints in this direction in Derrida and Rottenberg, *Negotiations*, 44; Derrida, *Without Alibi*, 227.

90. Derrida, "Enlightenment Past."

91. Derrida, *DP1*, 30.

92. London, "Clock Time and Utopia's Time in Novels of the 1790s," 542.

93. Walker, "I Sought," 143.

94. Wallace, *Revolutionary Subjects in the English "Jacobin" Novel, 1790–1805*, 120.

95. Rajan, *Romantic Narrative*, 82–116; Weiss, *The Female Philosopher*, 88–89.

96. Wallace, 121, 123.

97. Hays, *The Victim*, 45. Further citations will be given parenthetically, with H.

98. Pollak, *Incest and the English Novel*, 49, 173–177.

99. Pollak, 101.

100. Eleanor Ty, "Editor's Introduction," in *The Victim of Prejudice*, by Mary Hays, ed. Eleanor Ty (Peterborough: Broadview, 1994), vii–xxxvii; Toni Bowers, "Clarissa's Darkness," in *Women, Gender, and Print Culture in Eighteenth-Century Britain: Essays in Memory of Betty Rizzo*, ed. Temma Berg and Sonia Kane (Bethlehem, PA: Lehigh University Press, 2013), 17; Patricia Meyer Spacks highlights the differences between *The Victim of Prejudice* and *Clarissa* in their representation of consciousness, but accepts that they share the same plot: see *Novel Beginnings: Experiments in Eighteenth-Century English Fiction* (New Haven, CT: Yale University Press, 2006), 253.

101. Ulmer, "William Wordsworth and Philosophical Necessity."

102. Ty, "Editor's Introduction," xxiii.

103. Lacan, *Seminar V*, 2017.

104. Lacan, 179.

105. Lacan, 157.

106. Lacan, 179.

107. Lacan, 179.

108. Lacan, 179.

109. Lacan, 177–178.

110. Lacan, 179.

111. Lacan, 158–159.

112. Lacan, 168.

113. Lacan, 154.

114. Lacan, 155.

NOTES TO CHAPTER 3

115. Lacan, 179.

116. Lacan, 150.

117. Lacan, 157.

118. Derrida, *DP2*.

119. George, *Botany, Sexuality*.

120. Lacan, *Seminar V*, 2017, 152.

121. Godwin, *Political Justice*, 1:199, 1:196.

122. Adams, "Mary Hays, Disciple of William Godwin"; Rajan, *Romantic Narrative*, 84–93.

123. Bloch, *Principle*, 27.

124. Lacan, *Seminar XX*, 94.

125. Lacan, 25.

126. Shelley, *Frankenstein*, 121.

127. Lacan, *Seminar XI*, 211.

128. Lacan, *Seminar V*, 2017, 147.

129. Bernardin de Saint Pierre, *Paul and Virginia*, 1989; Bernardin de Saint Pierre, *Paul and Virginia*, 2004.

130. Walker, *Site Unscene*.

131. Wollstonecraft, "Rights of Woman," 122.

132. George, *Botany, Sexuality*.

133. Lacan, *Seminar V*, 2017, 145.

134. Brooks, "Chastity Renegotiated," 22.

135. Ty, *Unsex'd Revolutionaries*, 62.

136. Kristeva, "Feminine Genius?," 502.

137. Ty, "Editor's Introduction," xxi.

138. Lacan, *Seminar V*, 2017, 178.

139. Lacan, "Seminar V," n.d., 139. Here I have opted for Cormac Gallagher's unpublished translation rather than Grigg's, so as to highlight the words "title-deeds" and "future." The Grigg translation reads: "the child has all the titles in his pocket for later use" (179).

140. Lacan, *Seminar V*, 2017, 476.

141. Freud, *SE*, 19:173.

142. Ty, *Unsex'd Revolutionaries*, 61.

143. Golightly, *The Family, Marriage, and Radicalism*, 18–24.

Chapter 3

1. Morgan, *Narrative Means, Lyric Ends*, 9; Culler, *Pursuit of Signs*, 148–149; McCarthy, *Awful Parenthesis*, 11. McCarthy quotes these same passages from Morgan and Culler.

2. Derrida, *Archive Fever*, 10–11.

3. Lacan, *Seminar X*, 55, 260.

4. Bostetter, "The Original Della Cruscans and the Florence Miscellany."

5. Lacan, *Seminar XX*, 44, 36–37. Joyce's work, interestingly, is Lacan's primary example of women's writing.

6. Lacan, 37, 139–142.

7. Gamer, *Romanticism, Self-Canonization*, 100.

8. Knowles, "Della Cruscanism," 582.

9. Cowley, "To Della Crusca. The Pen."

10. Derrida, *Archive Fever*, 11.

11. Lacan, *Seminar XX*, 22, 38.

12. Finberg, "Introduction," xxxvi–xlvii.

13. Wanko, "Celebrity Studies," 355.

14. McCarthy, "The Repression of Hester Lynch Piozzi; or, How We Forgot a Revolution in Authorship," 101.

15. Longaker, *The Della Cruscans*, 3.

16. Robinson, "Mary Robinson and the Della Crusca Network," 117.

17. Robinson, 117.

18. Gamer, *Romanticism, Self-Canonization*, 101.

19. Derrida, *Archive Fever*, 84.

20. Freeman, *Time Binds*, xxiii.

21. Freeman, 62.

22. Labbe, "Anthologised Romance," para. 1.

23. Labbe, para. 5.

24. Robinson, "Della Crusca," 170.

25. Pascoe, *Romantic Theatricality*, 3.

26. McGann, *The Poetics of Sensibility*, 75.

27. Robinson, *The Poetry of Mary Robinson*, 86–87.

28. Freeman, *Time Binds*.

29. Freeman, 3.

30. Robinson, *Memoirs of Mary Robinson, "Perdita," from the Edition Edited by Her Daughter*, 194.

31. Robinson, "*Ainsi*," 15.

32. Freeman, *Time Binds*, 95.

33. de Man, "Rhetoric of Temporality."

34. Robinson, "*Ainsi*," 15.

35. Robinson, 15.

36. Robinson, 16.

37. Robinson, 8.

38. Spivak, "Echo."

39. Robinson, "*Ainsi*," 16.

40. Freeman, *Time Binds*, 104.

41. Robinson, "*Ainsi*," 11.

NOTES TO CHAPTER 3   263

42. Robinson, 15.

43. Robinson, 9.

44. Robinson, 10.

45. Robinson, 12. Charlotte Smith would later use this same technique in *Beachy Head*, when the speaker appraises an ocean pearl through the hidden labor and violence that have allowed for the pearl's commodification.

46. Robinson, 14.

47. Kuiken, *Imagined Sovereignties*, 8–9.

48. Collings, *Disastrous Subjectivities*, 8.

49. Lacan, *Seminar XX*, 56–60.

50. Lacan, "Seminar on 'The Purloined Letter,'" 39.

51. For a discussion of a similar phenomenon in Wordsworth's poetry, see Kuiken, *Imagined Sovereignties*, 165.

52. Robinson, "*Ainsi*," 14.

53. Robinson, 12.

54. Robinson, 13.

55. Butler, *Gender Trouble*; Sedgwick, *Epistemology of the Closet*.

56. Edelman, *No Future*.

57. Knowles, "Della Cruscanism," 593.

58. Robinson, *The Poetry of Mary Robinson*, 87.

59. Derrida, *Politics*, 24.

60. Robinson, "*Ainsi*," 1.

61. Robinson, 2.

62. Robinson, 7.

63. Robinson, 2.

64. Lacan, *Seminar VII*, 298–300.

65. Derrida, *Politics*, 24.

66. Merry, *Laurel*, 9.

67. Merry, 17.

68. Merry, "To Anna Matilda [Oct. 28, 1788]," ll. 51, 30; Cowley, "To Della Crusca [February 26, 1789]."

69. Merry, "To Anna Matilda [Oct. 28, 1788]," 136; Cowley, "To Della Crusca [June 19, 1789]"; Merry, *Laurel*, 9.

70. Cowley, "To Della Crusca [February 26, 1789]," ll. 58–59.

71. Merry, *Laurel*, 9.

72. Merry, "To Anna Matilda [Oct. 28, 1788]," l. 51.

73. Jameson, *Allegory and Ideology*, 2–3.

74. Merry, *Laurel*, 9. Emphasis in the original.

75. Koselleck, *Futures Past*, 56.

76. Merry, *Laurel*, 29.

77. Koselleck, *Futures Past*, 115.

78. Merry, *Laurel*, 10.

79. Merry, 10.
80. Merry, 10.
81. Merry, 11.
82. Žižek, *Incontinence*, 105.
83. Merry, *Laurel*, 13.
84. Merry, 13.
85. Žižek, *Incontinence*, 113.
86. Žižek, 112–113.
87. Žižek, 46.
88. Merry, *Laurel*, vi. Emphasis in the original.
89. Žižek, *Incontinence*, 50.
90. Muñoz, *Cruising Utopia*, 56.
91. Merry, *Laurel*, 18.
92. Merry, 20–21.
93. Merry, 21. Emphasis in the original.
94. Cowley, "To Della Crusca [May 20, 1788]," ll. 17–22.
95. Cowley, ll. 55–56.
96. Cowley, ll. 1–2; Merry, "The Adieu," l. 1.
97. Cowley, "To Della Crusca [May 20, 1788]," l. 9.
98. Cowley, l. 23.
99. Lacan, *Seminar XVII*, 54, 147–148.
100. Cowley, "To Della Crusca [May 20, 1788]," ll. 59–66.
101. Cowley, ll. 60–64.
102. Cowley, "To Della Crusca [Aug. 4, 1787]," ll. 2–3.
103. Cowley, "To Della Crusca [May 20, 1788]," ll. 98–100.
104. Robinson, *The Poetry of Mary Robinson*, 52–56.
105. Cowley, "To Della Crusca [February 26, 1789]," ll. 39–40.
106. Labbe, "Anthologised Romance," para. 16.
107. Labbe, *The Romantic Paradox*, 53.
108. Cowley, "To Della Crusca [February 26, 1789]," ll. 87–88.
109. Labbe, "Anthologised Romance."
110. Cowley, "To Della Crusca [February 26, 1789]," l. 93.
111. Cowley, ll. 64–65.
112. Cowley, l. 66.
113. "Bower, n.1."
114. Cowley, "To Della Crusca [February 26, 1789]," ll. 69–70.
115. Cowley, l. 70.
116. Cowley, l. 93.
117. Cowley, l. 98.
118. Cowley, ll. 91–93.
119. Cowley, l. 55.
120. Cowley, ll. 83–86.

Notes to Chapter 3   265

121. Cowley, ll. 77–80.

122. Cowley, l. 75.

123. Cowley, "To Somebody." I am indebted to Michael Gamer's archival work here, as I would have had no access to this poem had he not featured it on his Della Cruscan webpage: www.english.upenn.edu/~mgamer/Etexts/dellacrusca.html

124. Cowley, ll. 1–8. Emphasis in the original.

125. Cowley, ll. 9, 17–19, 22.

126. Cowley, l. 17.

127. Labbe, *The Romantic Paradox*, 55.

128. Gamer, *Romanticism, Self-Canonization*, 100.

129. Poovey, *The Proper Lady*, 203; Walker, *Marriage, Writing*, 70.

130. Robinson, "Della Crusca," 171.

131. Labbe, "Anthologised Romance," para. 5.

132. Merry, "The Adieu," ll. 1–5, 39–41.

133. Merry, l. 44.

134. Derrida, *Archive Fever*, 79. Emphasis in the original.

135. Merry, "The Adieu," l. 37.

136. Merry, l. 44.

137. Merry, ll. 34–36.

138. Merry, ll. 12–13, 30.

139. Merry, l. 25.

140. Merry, ll. 2–13.

141. Barnard, "Tongues," 184.

142. Lacan, *Seminar XX*, 70.

143. Merry, "The Adieu," ll. 12–14.

144. Lacan, *Seminar XX*, 45.

145. Merry, "The Adieu," l. 37.

146. Merry, "Tranquillity," ll. 31–32.

147. Merry, ll. 11–14.

148. Merry, ll. 27, 23.

149. Lacan, *Seminar XXIII*, 9.

150. Freeman, *Time Binds*, xxi.

151. Merry, "Folly," ll. 33–34, 47.

152. Merry, ll. 71–72, 60.

153. Merry, 68–70.

154. Sargent, "Citation," 316.

155. Washington, *Romantic Revelations*.

156. Labbe, *The Romantic Paradox*, 54.

157. Merry, "Folly," l. 46.

158. Brown, "Seashells on Mountaintops"; Thomas, "Living Fossils."

159. Cutler, *The Seashell on the Mountaintop*; Rowland, "Thomas Jefferson," 227–228.

160. Cutler, 202.

161. Sachs, "1816."

162. White, *New Chapters in the Warfare of Science*, 20.

163. Jefferson, *Notes on the State of Virginia*, 49; Rowland, 228.

164. Agamben, *What Is an Apparatus?*, 52.

165. Merry, "Folly," ll. 49, 54.

166. Merry, ll. 52, 59–60.

167. Merry, l. 55.

168. Merry, ll. 60–64.

169. Merry, ll. 37–42.

170. Merry, ll. 65–66.

171. Merry, ll. 67–72.

172. Merry, l. 73.

173. Merry, ll. 74–78.

174. Kristeva, "Women's Time," 12.

175. Lacan, *Seminar XX*, 145.

176. Lacan, 145.

177. Merry, "Folly," ll. 55–60.

178. Washington, *Romantic Revelations*, 5.

179. Derrida, *Archive Fever*, 94.

180. Freeman, *Time Binds*, 62.

181. McGann, *The Poetics of Sensibility*, 96.

Chapter 4

1. Wollstonecraft, "Hints," 274.

2. Shelley, "Defence," 535.

3. Wollstonecraft, "French Revolution," 79, 96; Nagra, "Look," l. 12.

4. Gerrard, "Poems on Politics," 302.

5. Rancière, *The Politics of Aesthetics*, 36.

6. Redfield, *The Politics of Aesthetics*, 34–35.

7. Redfield, 37.

8. Nagle, *Sexuality*, 50–67; Wolfson, *Romantic Interactions*, 113–140, 211–252.

9. Wolfson, *Borderlines*, 47.

10. Behrendt, "Poetry," 13.

11. Vanheule, "Ordinary Psychosis."

12. Culler, *Theory of the Lyric*, 294.

13. Turner and Pöppel, "Metered Poetry, the Brain, and Time"; Morgan, *Narrative Means, Lyric Ends*; Culler, *Theory of the Lyric*, 294.

NOTES TO CHAPTER 4 267

14. Ricoeur, *Time and Narrative*, 1:3.

15. McHale, "Beginning," 16–18.

16. For the implications of Barbauld's discussing laundry as an event, see Hofkosh, "Materiality."

17. Žižek, *The Year*, 128.

18. Žižek, 128.

19. Lacan, *Seminar VII*, 139.

20. Lupton, *Reading*, 5.

21. Rancière, *The Politics of Aesthetics*, 24.

22. Barbauld, "Love and Time." Further citations to this poem will be given parenthetically, with LT.

23. Burroughs, "Prescott, Robert."

24. Behrendt, *British Women Poets*, 75.

25. Favret, *War at a Distance*, 49.

26. Merry, "To Anna Matilda [Aug. 21, 1787]," ll. 3–4.

27. Looser, *Women Writers and Old Age*, 120–137.

28. Brewer, *The Sinews of Power*, xvii; Behrendt, *British Women Poets*, 82–83; Hurl-Eamon, *Marriage and the British Army*, 4.

29. Cox, *Romanticism in the Shadow*, 1, 3; Favret, *War at a Distance*.

30. Favret, *War at a Distance*, 51, 49.

31. Mulso Chapone, "To Stella," l. 62.

32. Mulso Chapone, ll. 25, 13, 35; Barbauld, "Love and Time," l. 11.

33. de Man, "Autobiography," 76.

34. de Man, 70–71.

35. de Man, 76, 70.

36. Ragland and Milovanovic, "Introduction," xv. Emphasis in original.

37. Lacan, *Seminar XX*, 4.

38. Lacan, 4.

39. Lacan, *Seminar XI*, 26.

40. Irigaray, *This Sex*.

41. Barbauld, "Love and Time," l. 34; Lacan, *Seminar XX*, 145.

42. Lacan, *Seminar XX*, 144.

43. Barbauld, "Washing Day," l. 33. Further citations to this poem will be given parenthetically, with WD.

44. Colebrook, "Images Without Worlds," 11.

45. Gibbs-Smith, "I—Notes on the History of Ballooning."

46. Trévien, "The Spectacle," 49.

47. Lacan, *Seminar XI*, 203–215.

48. Curran, "Romantic Poetry," 203.

49. Lacan, *Seminar X*, 276.

50. Bloch, *Principle*, 98.

268 NOTES TO CHAPTER 4

51. Smith, "Beachy Head," ll. 564–567. Further citations to this poem will be given parenthetically, with S.

52. Singer, *Romantic Vacancy*, 4, 8.

53. Potkay, "Wordsworth's Hope," 266, 276; Washington, *Romantic Revelations*, 4, 95.

54. Bloch, *Principle*; Muñoz, *Cruising Utopia*, 55–56.

55. Carlson, *England's First Family*, 134.

56. Wollstonecraft, "Rights of Woman," 186.

57. Goodman, "Conjectures"; Kelley, "Romantic Histories."

58. Goodman, "Conjectures," 986.

59. Heringman, *Romantic Rocks*, 276–277.

60. Hunter, "The No-Prospect Poem," 145.

61. Canuel, *Justice, Dissent*, 102.

62. Sachs, "1816," 96.

63. Freeman, *Time Binds*, xi.

64. Derrida, "*Geschlecht* II," 171.

65. Derrida, 180–182.

66. Derrida, 172–175.

67. Derrida, *The Post Card*, 9–10.

68. Capuano, *Changing Hands*, 1, 3.

69. Labbe, *Writing Romanticism*, 130.

70. Bloch, *Principle*, 690.

71. Bloch, 959. Emphasis in the original.

72. Freud, *SE*, 5:539.

73. Nersessian, *Utopia*.

74. Neyrat, *Atopias*, 7, 65–70.

75. Lacan, *Seminar VII*, 272.

76. Labbe, *Charlotte Smith: Romanticism, Poetry and the Culture of Gender*, 10.

77. Lacan, *Seminar XX*, 72–73.

78. Bloch, *Principle*, 927.

79. Butler, *Frames of War*, 101.

80. Benjamin, *Illuminations*, 261.

81. Jameson, *The Political Unconscious*, 278, 290.

82. de Jackson, *Romantic Poetry by Women: A Bibliography, 1770–1835*, 239; Sigler, "On Reading Charlotte Caroline Richardson's 'On Hearing a Friend Play on the Psaltery' with Coleridge's 'The Eolian Harp,'" 229–230.

83. Behrendt, *British Women Poets*, 96–97.

84. Robinson, "Harvest Home," l. 51; Keats, "Ode to a Nightingale," l. 33.

85. Cross, *Robinson and the Genesis*, 241.

86. Robinson, "Harvest Home," ll. 24, 32, 69.

87. Robinson, ll. 56, 58, 10.

NOTES TO CHAPTER 4   269

88. Robinson, ll. 14–15, 20.

89. Richardson, "Harvest," ll. 2.24–28. Further citations to this poem will be given parenthetically, with H.

90. Derrida, *Archive Fever*, 86.

91. Packham, "Wollstonecraft's Cottage Economics," 455.

92. Derrida, "Hostipitality," 3.

93. Derrida, 3.

94. Derrida, 14.

95. Simpson, *Romanticism*, 12.

96. Melville, *Romantic Hospitality*, 8.

97. Derrida and Dufourmantelle, *Of Hospitality*, 125.

98. Austen, *Persuasion*.

99. Derrida and Dufourmantelle, 93.

100. de Man, "Rhetoric of Temporality," 189–190.

101. de Man, 207.

102. Derrida and Dufourmantelle, 76.

103. Melville, *Romantic Hospitality*, 36.

104. Singer and Sweet, "Beyond Domesticity," 2.

105. Hyldgaard, "Conformity."

106. Though the poem is usually given a 1826 date, Susan J. Wolfson reminds us that the 1826 *Forget Me Not* was published in late 1825. See "Editing Felicia Hemans for the Twenty-First Century," *Romanticism on the Net*, no. 19 (2000), doi.org/10.7202/005931ar

107. Hemans, "Evening Prayer," l. 7. Further references to this poem will be given parenthetically, with EP.

108. Culler, *Pursuit of Signs*, 135–140.

109. Lacan, *Seminar XXIII*, 26.

110. Lacan, 28.

111. Hence when people ask: "have you read 'An Evening Prayer at a Girls' School'?," you can say: "I'm a frayed knot."

112. Wolfson, "Domestic Affections," 145.

113. Lacan, *Seminar XXIII*, 70.

114. Culler, *Pursuit of Signs*, 149.

115. Zupančič, *What Is Sex?*, 101.

116. Lacan, *Seminar III*, 214–215.

117. Coleridge, "Work Without Hope," l. 14.

118. Singer, *Romantic Vacancy*, xiv.

119. Derrida, *Specters of Marx*, 191, 213.

120. Lacan, *Écrits*, 326–327.

121. Vanheule, "Ordinary Psychosis."

122. McGowan, "The Psychosis of Freedom," 48.

123. McGuire, "I Leave Thee Not," 125.

124. Lacan, *Seminar III*, 46–47.

125. Lacan, 214–230.

126. Singer and Sweet, "Beyond Domesticity," 2.

127. Rudy, "Hemans' Passion," 546.

128. Stewart, *The Form of Poetry*, 3, 5.

129. Stewart, 7.

130. Bennett, *Romantic Poets*, 75.

131. Stewart, *The Form of Poetry*, 131.

132. Khalip, *Anonymous Life*, 116.

133. Derrida, "Ulysses Gramophone."

134. Derrida, 276.

135. Muller and Richardson, *The Purloined Poe*; Derrida, "No Apocalypse," 29–30.

136. Derrida, *Resistances*, 42.

137. Derrida, 43.

138. Hemans, "A Spirit's Return," l. 124. Further citations to this poem will be given parenthetically, with ASR.

139. McGann, *Byron and Romanticism*, 89.

140. McGann, 291.

141. Felluga, *The Perversity of Poetry*, 74.

142. Collings, *Disastrous Subjectivities*, 26; Bennett, *Romantic Poets*, 199.

143. Wolfson, *Romantic Interactions*, 268.

144. Lew, "The Necessary Orientalist?," 183; Rohrbach, *Modernity's Mist*, 134.

145. Derrida, *Writing and Difference*, 297.

146. Derrida, 297.

147. Clark, "Lost and Found," 163.

148. Lacan, *Seminar XVII*, 39.

149. Lacan, "Italian," 2.

150. Byron, "*Manfred*," ll. 2.4.133–134.

151. O'Neill, "'A Deeper,'" 5.

152. Spivak, "Echo," 26.

153. Spivak, 27.

154. Lacan, *Écrits*, 516; Lacan, *Seminar VIII*, 34.

155. Byron, "Childe Harold," ll. 4.1162–1170. My thanks to Clara Tuite for suggesting this connection to me.

156. Lacan, *Seminar XI*, 139–141.

157. Spivak, "Echo," 25.

158. Halloran, "Performative Mourning."

159. Nersessian, *Utopia*; Neyrat, *Atopias*, 16.

160. Žižek, *The Year*, 129.

161. Žižek, 130.

162. Nersessian, *Utopia*, 16–19.

Chapter 5

1. *Gulzara*, 1816; Shelley, *The Last Man*. Further citations to these novels will be given parenthetically, with *G* or *S*.

2. Latham, *The Art of Scandal: Modernism, Libel Law, and the Roman à Clef*, 25, 10.

3. Gallagher, *Nobody's Story*, 88–144.

4. Gottlieb, "*Jouissance*," 170.

5. Gottlieb, *Romantic Globalism*, 10–11.

6. Badiou, *Lacan*, 199.

7. Behrendt, *Royal Mourning*, 61–63.

8. Batchelor, "Anon, Pseud," 80.

9. Rauch, *Useful Knowledge*, 73; Behrendt, *Royal Mourning*, 64.

10. Behrendt, *Royal Mourning*, 77.

11. Schor, *Bearing*, 198–200.

12. Cahill, *Intelligent Souls?*, 3.

13. Behrendt, *Royal Mourning*, 72–73.

14. Behrendt, 72.

15. Derrida, *Without Alibi*, 228.

16. Herbert, *Travels in Persia*, xv–xxxvii, 200–222; Childs, "The Evolution of British Diplomatic Representation in the Middle East."

17. Avery, "Ouseley, Gore."

18. Rauch, *Useful Knowledge*, 74.

19. Moody, "Thomas Brown [Alias Thomas Moore], Censorship and Regency Cryptography"; Tuite, "Not Guilty."

20. *Gulzara*, 1816.

21. Latham, *The Art of Scandal: Modernism, Libel Law, and the Roman à Clef*, 9.

22. Said, *Orientalism*, 240.

23. Žižek, *Incontinence*, 151.

24. Žižek, 151.

25. The novel's allegory, as the Key spells out, incorporates large swaths of Regency literary culture, with the minor characters of Salid, Khaled, Amru, Mirza Osmin, and Adhim representing Walter Scott, Robert Southey, Lord Byron, Samuel Taylor Coleridge, and William Wordsworth respectively. Yet Barbauld is singled out for special attention by appearing, without Orientalist transposition, in the prominent footnote. Unlike the others, she is not a character in the novel but cited as an intellectual source precisely for her engagement with the future.

26. *Gulzara*, 1816, 25.

27. Gottlieb, *Romantic Globalism*, 98–99.

28. Song, *Dominion Undeserved*, 18, 19.

29. Cohen-Vrignaud, *Radical Orientalism*, 5.

30. Said, *Orientalism*, 118.

272   NOTES TO CHAPTER 5

31. Said, 118.
32. Said, 72.
33. Einboden, *Islam and Romanticism*, 135–136.
34. Behrendt, *Royal Mourning*, 68–69.
35. Lew, "The Necessary Orientalist?," 172–173.
36. Wollstonecraft, "Rights of Woman," 114, 91.
37. Lacan, *Écrits*, 416–417.
38. Said, *Orientalism*, 120–123.
39. Said, 120.
40. Behrendt, *Royal Mourning*, 75.
41. Warren, *The Orient*, 97.
42. Makdisi, "Versions of the East," 228.
43. Said, *Orientalism*, 169.
44. Said, 193.
45. Gottlieb, *Romantic Globalism*, 97.
46. Gottlieb, 98–99, 148.
47. Butler, "The Orientalism," 78.
48. Said, *Orientalism*, 98.
49. Derrida, *Without Alibi*, 224–227.
50. Ruppert, "Time and the Sibyl," 153.
51. Cox, *Romanticism in the Shadow*, 156–158.
52. Mullen, *Novel Institutions*, 2.
53. Bennett, "Radical Imaginings"; Johnson, *A Life with Mary Shelley*; Effinger, "A Clandestine Catastrophe."
54. Bennett, "Radical Imaginings."
55. Bernardin de Saint Pierre, *Paul and Virginia*, 2004, 89; Browne, "War and Peace."
56. Smith, *Romantic Women Writers*, 190.
57. Smith, 191.
58. See, for instance: Kucich, "The Last Man and the New History"; Hutchings, "A Dark Image"; Ruppert, "Time and the Sibyl"; Wang, "We Must Live Elsewhere"; Smith, *Romantic Women Writers*, 190–217; Bundock, *Romantic Prophecy*, 214–222; Washington, *Romantic Revelations*, 66–99.
59. Bundock, *Romantic Prophecy*, 221.
60. Washington, *Romantic Revelations*, 68–69.
61. Smith, *Romantic Women Writers*, 217.
62. Johnson, *A Life with Mary Shelley*, 4.
63. Koselleck, *Futures Past*, 202.
64. Bundock, *Romantic Prophecy*, 123.
65. Edelman, *No Future*.
66. Singer, "It's the End," 221; Sargent, "Citation," 321.
67. Ruppert, "Time and the Sibyl," 142.

NOTES TO CONCLUSION 273

68. Bennett, "Radical Imaginings"; Ruppert, "Time and the Sibyl."

69. Latham, *The Art of Scandal: Modernism, Libel Law, and the Roman à Clef*, 35.

70. Carman, *Radical Ecology*, 162–163.

71. Ruppert, "Time and the Sibyl," 144.

72. Gilet-Le Bon, "L'interprétation," 5; Lacan, "L'Étourdit."

73. Shelley, "Defence," 535. Emphasis mine.

74. Lacan, *Seminar II*, 56.

75. Lacan, *Seminar XI*, 20.

76. Lacan, 20.

77. Chiesa, *The Not-Two*, 105–179.

78. Rancière, "Who Is the Subject," 304.

79. Jones Square, "The 'Victim,'" 68.

80. Lacan, *Seminar VII*, 120–121.

81. Beauvoir, *The Second Sex*, 269, 338–339.

82. Lacan, *Seminar X*, 184–186.

83. Lacan, 191.

84. Chatterjee, "Our Bodies."

85. Strang, "Common Life"; Haslanger, "The Last Animal"; Washington, *Romantic Revelations*, 88–90; Rancière, "Who Is the Subject," 305.

86. Washington, *Romantic Revelations*, 82, 88–89; Haslanger, "The Last Animal," 661.

87. Lacan, "Seminar IX," sec. 9.5.62 (p. 6).

88. Johnson, *A Life with Mary Shelley*, 8; Beauvoir, *The Second Sex*, part 3, chap. 11.

89. Bloch, *The Spirit*, 177.

90. Bloch, 203.

91. Pladek, *The Poetics of Palliation*, 143.

92. Žižek, *The Year*, 134–135.

Conclusion

1. Washington, *Romantic Revelations*, 6; Khalip, "Contretemps," 629; Gottlieb, *Romantic Realities*, 156; Edelman, "The Pathology," 42–43.

2. Lacan, *Television*, 35, 43.

3. Lacan, 44.

4. Lacan, 43.

5. Kristeva, "Feminine Genius?," 496.

6. Kristeva, 503–504.

7. Cross, *Robinson and the Genesis*, 167–171.

8. Derrida, *Geneses*, 5.

9. Derrida, 70.
10. Derrida, 75.
11. Agamben, *What Is an Apparatus?*, 39.
12. Agamben, 40.
13. Agamben, 42, 46.
14. McInnes, *Wollstonecraft's Ghost*, 14–19.
15. Agamben, *What Is an Apparatus?*, 52. Emphasis in original.
16. Agamben, 41.
17. Agamben, 44–45.
18. Bloom, *Visionary Company*.
19. Kristeva, "Women's Time," 15.
20. Freeman, *Time Binds*, 63. Emphasis in original.
21. Matthew, "Biography and Mary Wollstonecraft."
22. Walker, "I Sought," 143.
23. Collings, *Disastrous Subjectivities*, 7.
24. Copjec, "The Sexual Compact," 37.
25. Fink, *The Lacanian Subject: Between Language and Jouissance*, 122.
26. Singer, *Romantic Vacancy*, xvi.
27. Smith, "Questionnaire," 48; Kester, "Questionnaire," 8.
28. Khalip and Pyle, "Introduction," 3.
29. Laqueur, *Making Sex*; Sigler, *Sexual Enjoyment*.
30. Rooney, "Belonging to No/Body," 361.
31. Richardson, "To-Morrow," l. 12.
32. Richardson, ll. 15–16.
33. Hemans, "A Thought," ll. 6–12.
34. Kristeva, "Women's Time," 17.
35. Agamben, *What Is an Apparatus?*, 52.
36. McCarthy, *Awful Parenthesis*, 5.
37. Brecht, "Emphasis on Sport," 184.
38. Brecht, 184.

Works Cited

Adams, M. Ray. "Mary Hays, Disciple of William Godwin." *PMLA* 55, no. 2 (1940): 472–483. doi.org/10.2307/458457

Agamben, Giorgio. *The End of the Poem: Studies in Poetics*. Translated by Daniel Heller-Roazen. Stanford, CA: Stanford University Press, 1999.

———. *What Is an Apparatus?: And Other Essays*. Translated by David Kishik and Stefan Pedatella. Stanford, CA: Stanford University Press, 2009.

Allen, Richard B. "Satisfying the 'Want for Labouring People': European Slave Trading in the Indian Ocean, 1500–1850." *Journal of World History* 21, no. 1 (2010): 45–73.

Alliez, Éric, and Maurizio Lazzarato. *Wars and Capital*. Cambridge, MA: MIT Press, 2018.

Austen, Jane. *Persuasion*. Edited by Janet Todd and Antje Blank. The Cambridge Edition of the Works of Jane Austen. Cambridge: Cambridge University Press, 2006.

Avery, Peter. "Ouseley, Gore." In *Encyclopædia Iranica*, 2004. www.iranicaonline. org/articles/ouseley-sir-gore

Badiou, Alain. *Lacan*. Translated by Kenneth Reinhard and Susan Spitzer. The Seminars of Alain Badiou. New York: Columbia University Press, 2018.

Balfour, Ian. *The Rhetoric of Romantic Prophecy*. Stanford, CA: Stanford University Press, 2002.

Barbauld, Anna Letitia. "Eighteen Hundred and Eleven." In *Selected Poetry and Poems*, edited by William McCarthy and Elizabeth Kraft, 160–173. Peterborough: Broadview Press, 2001.

———. "Love and Time: To Mrs. Mulso." In *Selected Poetry and Poems*, edited by William McCarthy and Elizabeth Kraft, 105–107. Peterborough: Broadview, 2001.

———. "On the Uses of History." In *A Selection from the Poems and Prose Writings of Mrs. Anna Letitia Barbauld*, edited by Grace A. Ellis, 393–426. Boston: Osgood, 1874.

———. "Washing Day." In *Selected Poetry and Poems*, edited by William McCarthy and Elizabeth Kraft, 145–147. Peterborough: Broadview, 2001.

Barnard, Suzanne. "Tongues of Angels: Feminine Structure and Other Jouissance." In *Reading Seminar XX: Lacan's Major Work on Love, Knowledge, and Feminine Sexuality*, edited by Suzanne Barnard and Bruce Fink, 171–185. Albany, NY: SUNY Press, 2002.

Batchelor, Jennie. "Anon, Pseud, and 'By a Lady': The Spectre of Anonymity in Women's Literary History." In *Women's Writing, 1660-1830: Feminisms and Futures*, edited by Jennie Batchelor and Gillian Dow, 79–96. London: Palgrave Macmillan, 2016.

Baucom, Ian. *Specters of the Atlantic: Finance Capital, Slavery, and the Philosophy of History*. Durham, NC: Duke University Press, 2005.

Bauman, Zygmunt. *Liquid Modernity*. Cambridge, UK: Polity, 2000.

Beauvoir, Simone de. *The Second Sex*. Translated by H.M. Parshley. New York: Vintage, 1952.

Behrendt, Stephen C. *British Women Poets and the Romantic Writing Community*. Baltimore: Johns Hopkins University Press, 2009.

———. "Mary Shelley, *Frankenstein*, and the Woman Writer's Fate." In *Romantic Women Writers: Voices and Countervoices*, edited by Paula R. Feldman and Theresa M. Kelley, 69–87. Hanover, NH: University Press of New England, 1995.

———. "Poetry." In *The Cambridge Companion to Women's Writing in the Romantic Period*, edited by Devoney Looser, 1–15. Cambridge: Cambridge University Press, 2015.

———. *Royal Mourning and Regency Culture: Elegies and Memorials of Princess Charlotte*. New York: Palgrave Macmillan, 1997.

Benjamin, Walter. *Illuminations*. Edited by Hannah Arendt. Translated by Harry Zohn. New York: Schocken Books, 1986.

Bennett, Andrew. *Romantic Poets and the Culture of Posterity*. Cambridge: Cambridge University Press, 1999.

Bennett, Betty T. "Radical Imaginings," October 1, 1997. www.rc.umd.edu/editions/mws/lastman/bennett.htm

Bennington, Geoffrey, and Jacques Derrida. *Jacques Derrida*. Translated by Geoffrey Bennington. Chicago: University of Chicago Press, 1993.

Berman, Carolyn Vellenga. *Creole Crossings: Domestic Fiction and the Reform of Colonial Slavery*. Ithaca, NY: Cornell University Press, 2006.

Bernardin de Saint Pierre, Jacques-Henri. *Paul and Virginia*. Translated by John Donovan. London: Penguin, 1989.

———. *Paul and Virginia*. Translated by Helen Maria Williams. Doylestown, PA: Wildside Press, 2004.

———. *Paul et Virginie*. London: Machell Stace, 1795.

WORKS CITED 277

———. *A Voyage to the Island of Mauritius, (or, Isle of France) the Isle of Bourbon, the Cape of Good-Hope, &c. With Observations and Reflections upon Nature and Mankind. By a French Officer.* Translated by John Parish. London: W. Griffin, 1775.

Bloch, Ernst. *The Principle of Hope.* Translated by Neville Plaice, Stephen Plaice, and Paul Knight. 3 vols. Cambridge, MA: MIT Press, 1986.

———. *The Spirit of Utopia.* Translated by Anthony A. Nassar. Stanford, CA: Stanford University Press, 2000.

Bloom, Harold. *The Visionary Company: A Reading of English Romantic Poetry.* Revised and enlarged edition. Ithaca, NY: Cornell University Press, 1971.

Bode, Christoph. "Romanticism and Deconstruction: Distant Relations and Elective Affinities." In *Romantic Continuities: Papers Delivered at the Symposium of the "Gesellschaft Für Englische Romantik" Held at the Catholic University of Eichstätt (October 1990)*, edited by Günther Blaicher and Michael Gassenmeier, 131–159. Essen: Verlag Die Blaue Eule, 1992.

Bostetter, Edward E. "The Original Della Cruscans and the Florence Miscellany." *Huntington Library Quarterly* 19, no. 3 (1956): 277–300. doi.org/10.2307/3816310

"Bower, n.1." In *OED Online.* Oxford: Oxford University Press, June 2020.

Bowers, Toni. "Clarissa's Darkness." In *Women, Gender, and Print Culture in Eighteenth-Century Britain: Essays in Memory of Betty Rizzo*, edited by Temma Berg and Sonia Kane, 3–24. Bethlehem, PA: Lehigh University Press, 2013.

Bradshaw, Penny. "The Limits of Barbauld's Feminism: Re-reading 'The Rights of Woman.'" *European Romantic Review* 16, no. 1 (2005): 23–37. doi.org/10.1080/1050958042000338534

Brecht, Bertolt. "Emphasis on Sport." In *Cultural Resistance Reader*, edited by Stephen Duncombe, translated by John Willett, 183–185. London: Verso, 2002.

Brewer, John. *The Sinews of Power: War, Money, and the English State, 1688–1783.* Cambridge, MA: Harvard University Press, 1990.

Brooks, Marilyn L. "Mary Hays's *The Victim of Prejudice*: Chastity Renegotiated." *Women's Writing*, no. 15 (2008): 13–31.

Brown, Walt. "In the Beginning: Compelling Evidence for Creation and the Flood—129. Seashells on Mountaintops." Center for Scientific Creation, February 27, 2020. www.creationscience.com/onlinebook/EarthSciences15.html

Browne, Felicia Dorothea. "War and Peace." In *The Domestic Affections, and Other Poems*, 89–124. London: T. Cadell and W. Davies, 1812.

Bundock, Christopher M. *Romantic Prophecy and the Resistance to Historicism.* Toronto: University of Toronto Press, 2016.

Burroughs, Peter. "Prescott, Robert." In *Dictionary of Canadian Biography.* Vol. 5. University of Toronto / Université Laval, 1983. www.biographi.ca/en/bio/prescott_robert_5E.html

278 WORKS CITED

Butler, Judith. *Frames of War: When Is Life Grievable?* London: Verso, 2009.

———. "Further Reflections on Conversations of Our Time." *Diacritics* 27, no. 1 (1997): 13–15.

———. *Gender Trouble: Feminism and the Subversion of Identity.* 10th Anniversary Edition. New York: Routledge, 1999.

Butler, Marilyn. "The Orientalism of Byron's *Giaour.*" In *Byron and the Limits of Fiction*, edited by Bernard Beatty and Vincent Newey. Totowa, NJ: Barnes and Noble, 1988.

Byron, George Gordon (Lord). "*Childe Harold's Pilgrimage.*" In *The Complete Poetical Works*, edited by Jerome J. McGann, 2:174. Oxford: Clarendon Press, 1980.

———. "*Manfred.*" In *The Complete Poetical Works*, edited by Jerome J. McGann, 4:51–102. Oxford: Clarendon Press, 1986.

Cahill, Samara Anne. *Intelligent Souls?: Feminist Orientalism in Eighteenth-Century English Literature.* Lewisburg: Bucknell University Press, 2019.

Calè, Luisa. "Sympathy in Translation: Paul et Virginie on the London Stage." *Romanticism on the Net*, no. 46 (2007). id.erudit.org/iderudit/016135ar

Canuel, Mark. *Justice, Dissent, and the Sublime.* Baltimore: Johns Hopkins University Press, 2012.

Capuano, Peter. *Changing Hands: Industry, Evolution, and the Reconfiguration of the Victorian Body.* Ann Arbor: University of Michigan Press, 2015.

Caputo, John D. "The Messianic: Waiting for the Future." In *Deconstruction in a Nutshell: A Conversation with Jacques Derrida*, 156–180. New York: Fordham University Press, 1997.

Carlson, Julie A. *England's First Family of Writers: Mary Wollstonecraft, William Godwin, Mary Shelley.* Baltimore: Johns Hopkins University Press, 2006.

Carman, Colin. *The Radical Ecology of the Shelleys: Eros and Environment.* New York: Routledge, 2018.

Caruth, Cathy. *Literature in the Ashes of History.* Baltimore: Johns Hopkins University Press, 2013.

Cassity, Conny. "Caught by the Throat: Anti-Slavery Assemblages in *Paul et Virginie* and *Belinda.*" *Eighteenth-Century Fiction* 31, no. 1 (2018): 99–115. doi.org/10.3138/ecf.31.1.99

Chandler, James. *England in 1819: The Politics of Literary Culture and the Case of Romantic Historicism.* Chicago: University of Chicago Press, 1999.

Chatterjee, Ranita. "Our Bodies, Our Catastrophes: Biopolitics in Mary Shelley's *The Last Man.*" *European Romantic Review* 25, no. 1 (2014): 35–49. doi.org /10.1080/10509585.2013.863494

Cheah, Pheng, and Suzanne Guerlac. "Introduction: Derrida and the Time of the Political." In *Derrida and the Time of the Political*, edited by Pheng Cheah and Suzanne Guerlac, 1–37. Durham, NC: Duke University Press, 2009.

Chiesa, Lorenzo. *The Not-Two: Logic and God in Lacan.* Cambridge, MA: MIT Press, 2016.

WORKS CITED 279

Childs, J. Rives. "The Evolution of British Diplomatic Representation in the Middle
East." *Journal of The Royal Central Asian Society* 26, no. 4 (1939): 634–647.
doi.org/10.1080/03068373908730936

Christensen, Jerome. *Romanticism at the End of History*. Baltimore: Johns Hopkins
University Press, 2004.

Cixous, Hélène. *Insister of Jacques Derrida*. Translated by Peggy Kamuf. Stanford,
CA: Stanford University Press, 2007.

Clark, David L. "Lost and Found in Translation: Romanticism and the Legacies
of Jacques Derrida." *Studies in Romanticism* 46, no. 2 (2007): 161–182.

Clausewitz, Carl von. *On War*. Translated by Michael Howard and Peter Paret.
Indexed ed. Princeton, NJ: Princeton University Press, 1984.

Clery, E.J. *Eighteen Hundred and Eleven: Poetry, Protest, and Economic Crisis*.
Cambridge: Cambridge University Press, 2017.

Cohen, Margaret. "Sentimental Communities." In *The Literary Channel: The
Inter-National Invention of the Novel*, edited by Margaret Cohen and Carolyn
Dever, 106–132. Princeton, NJ: Princeton University Press, 2002.

Cohen-Vrignaud, Gerard. *Radical Orientalism: Rights, Reform, and Romanticism*.
Cambridge: Cambridge University Press, 2015.

Colebrook, Claire. "Images Without Worlds." In *Fragmentation of the Photographic
Image in the Digital Age*, edited by Daniel Rubinstein, 11–27. New York:
Routledge, 2020.

Coleman, Deirdre. "The Global Context." In *The Cambridge Companion to Wom-
en's Writing in the Romantic Period*, edited by Devoney Looser, 129–144.
Cambridge: Cambridge University Press, 2015.

Coleridge, Samuel Taylor. "Work Without Hope." In *The Poetical Works of S. T.
Coleridge: Including the Dramas of* Wallenstein, Remorse, *and* Zapolya, 2:81.
London: W. Pickering, 1828.

Coles, Prophecy. *The Importance of Sibling Relationships in Psychoanalysis*. Abing-
don: Routledge, 2018.

Colley, Linda. *Britons: Forging the Nation 1707–1837*. New Pimlico ed. London:
Pimlico, 2003.

Collings, David. *Disastrous Subjectivities: Romanticism, Modernity, and the Real*.
Toronto: University of Toronto Press, 2019.

Copjec, Joan. *Read My Desire: Lacan against the Historicists*. Cambridge, MA:
MIT Press, 1994.

———. "The Sexual Compact." *Angelaki* 17, no. 2 (2012): 31–48. doi.org/10.10
80/0969725X.2012.701047

Cornell, Drucilla. "Derrida's Negotiations as a Technique of Liberation." *Discourse:
Journal for Theoretical Studies in Media & Culture* 39, no. 2 (Spring 2017):
195–215. doi.org/10.13110/discourse.39.2.0195

Cowley, Hannah. "To Della Crusca [Aug. 4, 1787]." In *The British Album*, 1:8–9.
London: John Bell, 1790.

280   WORKS CITED

———. "To Della Crusca [February 26, 1789]." In *The British Album*, 2:144–148. London: John Bell, 1790.

———. "To Della Crusca [June 19, 1789]." In *The British Album*, 2:169–172. John Bell, 1790.

———. "To Della Crusca [May 20, 1788]." In *The British Album*, 1:101–105. London: John Bell, 1790.

———. "To Della Crusca. The Pen." In *The British Album*, 2nd ed., 1:3–4. London: John Bell, 1790.

———. "To Somebody at Margate." *The World*, September 15, 1787. www.english. upenn.edu/~mgamer/Etexts/dellacrusca.html#margate

Cox, Jeffrey N. *Romanticism in the Shadow of War: Literary Culture in the Napoleonic War Years.* Cambridge: Cambridge University Press, 2014.

Craciun, Adriana. *British Women Writers and the French Revolution: Citizens of the World.* Houndmills, UK: Palgrave Macmillan, 2005.

Craciun, Adriana, Anne Irman Close, Megan Musgrave, and Orianne Smith. "Introduction and Note on the Texts (*A Letter to the Women of England on the Injustice of Mental Subordination, with Anecdotes*)." Romantic Circles, May 1998. romantic-circles.org/editions/robinson/mrletterfrst.htm

Crimmins, Jonathan. *The Romantic Historicism to Come.* New York: Bloomsbury, 2019.

Crisman, William. " 'Now Misery Has Come Home': Sibling Rivalry in Mary Shelley's *Frankenstein.*" *Studies in Romanticism* 36, no. 1 (1997): 27–41. doi. org/10.2307/25601210

Cross, Ashley. *Mary Robinson and the Genesis of Romanticism: Literary Dialogues and Debts, 1784–1821.* New York: Routledge, 2017.

Culler, Jonathan. *The Pursuit of Signs: Semiotics, Literature, Deconstruction.* Ithaca, NY: Cornell University Press, 1981.

———. *Theory of the Lyric.* Cambridge, MA: Harvard University Press, 2015.

Curran, Stuart. "Romantic Poetry: The I Altered." In *Romanticism and Feminism*, edited by Anne K. Mellor, 185–207. Bloomington: Indiana University Press, 1988.

Cutler, Alan. *The Seashell on the Mountaintop.* New York: Plume, 2004.

Deleuze, Gilles, and Félix Guattari. *Anti-Oedipus: Capitalism and Schizophrenia.* Translated by Robert Hurley, Mark Seem, and Helen R. Lane. Minneapolis: University of Minnesota Press, 1983.

Derrida, Jacques. *Aporias.* Translated by Thomas Dutoit. Palo Alto, CA: Stanford University Press, 1993.

———. *Archive Fever: A Freudian Impression.* Translated by Eric Prenowitz. Chicago: University of Chicago Press, 1995.

———. "Enlightenment Past and to Come." Le Monde diplomatique, November 1, 2004. mondediplo.com/2004/11/06derrida

WORKS CITED   281

———. "Faith and Knowledge: The Two Sources of 'Religion' at the Limits of Reason Alone." In *Religion*, edited by Jacques Derrida and Gianni Vattimo, 1–78. Stanford, CA: Stanford University Press, 1998.

———. *Geneses, Genealogies, Genres, & Genius: The Secrets of the Archive*. Translated by Beverley Bie Brahic. New York: Columbia University Press, 2006.

———. "Geopsychoanalysis 'and the Rest of the World.'" In *Psyche: Inventions of the Other*, edited by Peggy Kamuf and Elizabeth Rottenberg, translated by Peggy Kamuf, 1:318–343. Stanford, CA: Stanford University Press, 2007.

———. *"Geschlecht* II: Heidegger's Hand." In *Deconstruction and Philosophy: The Texts of Jacques Derrida*, edited by John Sallis, translated by John P. Leavey, 161–196. Chicago: University of Chicago Press, 1987.

———. "Hostipitality." Translated by Barry Stocker and Forbes Morlock. *Angelaki* 5, no. 3 (2000): 3–18.

———. *Monolingualism of the Other, or, The Prosthesis of Origin*. Translated by Patrick Mensah. Stanford, CA: Stanford University Press, 1998.

———. "No Apocalypse, Not Now (Full Speed Ahead, Seven Missiles, Seven Missives)." Translated by Catherine Porter and Philip Lewis. *Diacritics* 14, no. 2 (1984): 20–31.

———. *Of Grammatology*. Translated by Gayatri Chakravorty Spivak. Corrected ed. Baltimore: Johns Hopkins University Press, 1997.

———. *On Cosmopolitanism and Forgiveness*. Translated by Mark Dooley and Michael Hughes. Thinking in Action. London: Routledge, 2001.

———. *Paper Machine*. Translated by Rachel Bowlby. Stanford, CA: Stanford University Press, 2005.

———. *Politics of Friendship*. Translated by George Collins. London: Verso, 1997.

———. "Preface by Jacques Derrida: A Time for Farewells: Heidegger (Read by) Hegel (Read by) Malabou." In *The Future of Hegel: Plasticity, Temporality, and Dialectic*, by Catherine Malabou. London: Routledge, 2004.

———. "Psychoanalysis Searches the States of Its Soul: The Impossible Beyond of a Sovereign Cruelty (Address to the States General of Psychoanalysis)." In *Without Alibi*, edited and translated by Peggy Kamuf, 238–280. Stanford, CA: Stanford University Press, 2002.

———. *Resistances of Psychoanalysis*. Translated by Peggy Kamuf, Pascale-Anne Brault, and Michael Naas. Stanford, CA: Stanford University Press, 1998.

———. *Rogues: Two Essays on Reason*. Translated by Pascale-Anne Brault and Michael Naas. Stanford, CA: Stanford University Press, 2005.

———. "Signature Event Context." In *Margins of Philosophy*, translated by Alan Bass, 307–330. Chicago: University of Chicago Press, 1982.

———. *Specters of Marx: The State of the Debt, The Work of Mourning, and the New International*. Translated by Peggy Kamuf. New York: Routledge, 1994.

282   WORKS CITED

———. *Spurs: Nietzsche's Styles/Éperons: Les Styles de Nietzsche.* Translated by Barbara Harlow. Chicago: University of Chicago Press, 1978.

———. *The Beast & the Sovereign, Volume II.* Translated by Geoffrey Bennington. The Seminars of Jacques Derrida. Chicago: University of Chicago Press, 2011.

———. *The Death Penalty, Vol. 1.* Translated by Peggy Kamuf. The Seminars of Jacques Derrida. Chicago: University of Chicago Press, 2012.

———. *The Death Penalty, Vol. 2.* Translated by Elizabeth Rottenberg. The Seminars of Jacques Derrida. Chicago: University of Chicago Press, 2017.

———. *The Post Card: From Socrates to Freud and Beyond.* Translated by Alan Bass. Chicago: University of Chicago Press, 1987.

———. *The Truth in Painting.* Translated by Geoff Bennington and Ian McLeod. Chicago: University of Chicago Press, 1987.

———. "Ulysses Gramophone: Hear Say Yes in Joyce." In *Acts of Literature*, edited by Derek Attridge, translated by Tina Kendall and Shari Benstock, 253–309. New York: Routledge, 1992.

———. "What Is a 'Relevant' Translation?" Translated by Lawrence Venuti. *Critical Inquiry* 27, no. 1 (2001): 174–200.

———. *Without Alibi.* Translated by Peggy Kamuf. Stanford, CA: Stanford University Press, 2002.

———. *Writing and Difference.* Translated by Alan Bass. Chicago: University of Chicago Press, 1978.

Derrida, Jacques, and Anne Dufourmantelle. *Of Hospitality.* Translated by Rachel Bowlby. Stanford, CA: Stanford University Press, 2000.

Derrida, Jacques, and Elizabeth Rottenberg. *Negotiations: Interventions and Interviews, 1971–2001.* Stanford, CA: Stanford University Press, 2002.

Derrida, Jacques, and Élisabeth Roudinesco. *For What Tomorrow . . . A Dialogue.* Translated by Jeff Fort. Stanford, CA: Stanford University Press, 2004.

Duquette, Natasha. "Dissenting Cosmopolitanism and Helen Maria Williams's Prison Verse." *Women's Writing* 27, no. 1 (2020): 80–96. doi.org/10.1080/09699082.2019.1654175

Duro, Paul. "What Is a Parergon?" *The Journal of Aesthetics and Art Criticism* 77, no. 1 (2019): 23–33. doi.org/10.1111/jaac.12619

Edelman, Lee. *No Future: Queer Theory and the Death Drive.* Durham, NC: Duke University Press, 2004.

———. "The Pathology of the Future; or, the Endless Triumphs of Life." In *Constellations of a Contemporary Romanticism*, edited by Jacques Khalip and Forest Pyle, 35–46. New York: Fordham University Press, 2016.

Effinger, Elizabeth. "A Clandestine Catastrophe: Disciplinary Dissolution in Mary Shelley's *The Last Man.*" *European Romantic Review* 25, no. 1 (2014): 19–34. doi.org/10.1080/10509585.2013.863493

Egerton, Frank N. "Changing Concepts of the Balance of Nature." *Quarterly Review of Biology* 48, no. 2 (1973): 332–350.

WORKS CITED   283

Einboden, Jeffrey. *Islam and Romanticism: Muslim Currents from Goethe to Emerson*. London: Oneworld Publications, 2014.

Fabian, Johannes. *Time and the Other: How Anthropology Makes Its Object*. New York: Columbia University Press, 2014.

Faflak, Joel, ed. *Marking Time: Romanticism and Evolution*. Toronto: University of Toronto Press, 2017.

———. *Romantic Psychoanalysis: The Burden of the Mystery*. Albany, NY: SUNY Press, 2008.

Favret, Mary A. "Field of History, Field of Battle." In *Romantic Frictions*, edited by Theresa M. Kelley. Romantic Circles Praxis Series. Romantic Circles, 2011. www.rc.umd.edu/praxis/frictions/HTML/praxis.2011.favret.html

———. *War at a Distance: Romanticism and the Making of Modern Warfare*. Princeton, NJ: Princeton University Press, 2010.

Felluga, Dino Franco. *The Perversity of Poetry: Romantic Ideology and the Popular Male Poet of Genius*. Albany, NY: SUNY Press, 2005.

Ferrier, Susan Edmonstone. *Marriage*. Boston: Little, Brown and Company, 1893.

Finberg, Melinda C. "Introduction." In *Eighteenth-Century Women Dramatists*, edited by Melinda C. Finberg. Oxford: Oxford University Press, 2001.

Fink, Bruce. *The Lacanian Subject: Between Language and Jouissance*. Princeton, NJ: Princeton University Press, 1995.

Foucault, Michel. *Discipline and Punish: The Birth of the Prison*. Translated by Alan Sheridan. New York: Vintage, 1977.

François, Anne-Lise. *Open Secrets: The Literature of Uncounted Experience*. Stanford, CA: Stanford University Press, 2008.

Freeman, Elizabeth. *Time Binds: Queer Temporalities, Queer Histories*. Durham, NC: Duke University Press, 2010.

Freud, Sigmund. *The Standard Edition of the Complete Psychological Works of Sigmund Freud*. Translated by James Strachey. 24 vols. London: Hogarth Press, 1964.

Gallagher, Catherine. *Nobody's Story: The Vanishing Act of Women Writers in the Marketplace, 1670–1820*. Berkeley: University of California Press, 1994.

Gallop, Jane. *The Deaths of the Author: Reading and Writing in Time*. Durham, NC: Duke University Press, 2011.

Gamer, Michael. *Romanticism, Self-Canonization, and the Business of Poetry*. Cambridge: Cambridge University Press, 2017.

Garofalo, Daniela. *Women, Love, and Commodity Culture in British Romanticism*. Farnham, UK: Ashgate, 2012.

George, Sam. *Botany, Sexuality and Women's Writing, 1760–1830: From Modest Shoot to Forward Plant*. Manchester: Manchester University Press, 2007.

Gerrard, Christine. "Poems on Politics." In *The Oxford Handbook of British Poetry, 1660–1800*, edited by Jack Lynch and John T. Lynch, 286–302. Oxford: Oxford University Press, 2016.

Gibbs-Smith, C. H. "I—Notes on the History of Ballooning." *The Journal of Navigation* 10, no. 1 (January 1957): 63–67. doi.org/10.1017/S03734633000 16350

Gilet-Le Bon, Stéphanie. "L'interprétation: <<apophantique>> et <<oraculaire>>." Translated by Richard G. Klein. *La Lettre Mensuelle* 138 (1995): 5–8.

Godwin, William. *Enquiry Concerning Political Justice, and Its Influence on Morals and Happiness.* 3rd ed. 2 vols. London: G.G. and J. Robinson, 1798.

Golightly, Jennifer. *The Family, Marriage, and Radicalism in British Women's Novels of the 1790s: Public Affection and Private Affliction.* Lewisburg, PA: Bucknell University Press, 2012.

Goodman, Kevis. "Conjectures on *Beachy Head*: Charlotte Smith's Geological Poetics and the Ground of the Present." *ELH* 81, no. 3 (2014): 983–1006.

Gordon, Jane Anna. *Creolizing Political Theory: Reading Rousseau through Fanon.* New York: Fordham University Press, 2014.

Gordon, Jane Anna, and Neil Roberts, eds. *Creolizing Rousseau.* London: Rowman & Littlefield, 2015.

Gottlieb, Evan. "*Jouissance*, Obscene Undersides, and Utopian/Dystopian Formations in Sarah Scott's *Millenium Hall* and Mary Shelley's *The Last Man*." In *Lacan and Romanticism*, edited by Daniela Garofalo and David Sigler, 157–176. Albany, NY: SUNY Press, 2019.

———. *Romantic Globalism: British Literature and Modern World Order, 1750–1830.* Columbus: The Ohio State University Press, 2014.

———. *Romantic Realities: Speculative Realism and British Romanticism.* Edinburgh, UK: Edinburgh University Press, 2016.

Groote, Brecht de. "'Old Familiar Faces': *Frankenstein*, Anachronism, and Late Style." *Litteraria Pragensia* 28, no. 56 (2018): 71–82.

Gulzara, Princess of Persia; or, The Virgin Queen. London: John Souter, 1816.

Gulzara, Princess of Persia; or, The Virgin Queen. US edition. Philadelphia: M. Carey, 1816.

Gustafson, Ryan. "Abolition, Phallocentrism, and the Mondialisation of Psychoanalysis: A Review of Derrida's Psychoanalytic Argument in *The Death Penalty: Volume II*." *The Undecidable Unconscious: A Journal of Deconstruction and Psychoanalysis* 4 (2017): 129–140. doi.org/10.1353/ujd.2017.0005

Hadley, Karen. "'Back to the Future?': The Narrative of Allegory in Recent Critical Accounts of Romanticism." *ELH* 69, no. 4 (2002): 1029–1045.

Halloran, Vivian Nun. "Performative Mourning: Remembering Derrida through (Re)Reading." *Postmodern Culture* 15, no. 3 (2005). doi.org/10.1353/pmc.2005.0021

Hara, Kazuyuki. "Deconstructing the Oedipus Complex: Kenzaburo Ôe and Hakuri Murakami on the Way to a Theory of Global Culture." In *Knots: Literature and Psychoanalysis After Lacan*, edited by Jean-Michel Rabaté, 147–163. New York: Routledge, 2020.

Haslanger, Andrea. "The Last Animal: Cosmopolitanism in *The Last Man.*" *European Romantic Review* 27, no. 5 (2016): 659–678. doi.org/10.1080/105095 85.2016.1211009

Hays, Mary. *The Victim of Prejudice.* Edited by Eleanor Ty. Peterborough, UK: Broadview, 1994.

Hemans, Felicia. "A Spirit's Return." In *Songs of the Affections, with Other Poems,* 3–17. Edinburgh, UK: William Blackwood and T. Cadell, 1830.

———. "A Thought of the Future." In *The Works of Mrs. Hemans with A Memoir by Her Sister,* 6:200–201. Philadelphia: Lea and Blanchard, 1840.

———. "Evening Prayer at a Girls' School." In *The Forest Sanctuary: With Other Poems,* 2nd ed., 273–275. Edinburgh, UK: William Blackwood and T. Cadell, 1829.

———. *The Works: With a Memoir of Her Life by Her Sister.* Vol. 7. 7 vols. London: Blackwood, 1839.

Herbert, Thomas. *Travels in Persia, 1627–1629.* Edited by William Foster. The Broadway Travellers. New York: RoutledgeCurzon, 1928.

Heringman, Noah. *Romantic Rocks, Aesthetic Geology.* Ithaca, NY: Cornell University Press, 2004.

Hodson, Jane. "Women Write the Rights of Woman: The Sexual Politics of the Personal Pronoun in the 1790s." *Language and Literature: Journal of the Poetics and Linguistics Association* 16, no. 3 (2007): 281–304. doi. org/10.1177/0963947007079113

Hofkosh, Sonia. "Introduction: Mary Wollstonecraft Even Now." In *Mary Wollstonecraft Even Now.* Romantic Circles Praxis Series. Romantic Circles, 2019. romantic-circles.org/praxis/wollstonecraft/praxis.2019.wollstonecraft. hofkosh.html

———. "Materiality, Affect, Event: Barbauld's Poetics of the Everyday." In *Anna Letitia Barbauld: New Perspectives,* edited by William McCarthy and Olivia Murphy, 80–102. Lewisburg: Bucknell University Press, 2014.

Hogan, Sarah. *Other Englands: Utopia, Capital, and Empire in an Age of Transition.* Stanford, CA: Stanford University Press, 2018.

Hunter, Walt. "The No-Prospect Poem: Lyric Finality in Prynne, Awoonor, and Trethewey." *The Minnesota Review* 2015, no. 85 (2015): 144–152. doi. org/10.1215/00265667-3144702

Hurl-Eamon, Jennine. *Marriage and the British Army in the Long Eighteenth Century: "The Girl I Left Behind Me."* Oxford: Oxford University Press, 2014.

Hutchings, Kevin. " 'A Dark Image in a Phantasmagoria': Pastoral Idealism, Prophecy, and Materiality in Mary Shelley's *The Last Man.*" *Romanticism* 10, no. 2 (2004): 228–244. doi.org/10.3366/rom.2004.10.2.228

Hyldgaard, Kirsten. "The Conformity of Perversion." *The Symptom* 5 (Winter 2004). www.lacan.com/conformperf.htm

"Intuition, n." In *OED Online*. Oxford University Press. Accessed February 14, 2020. www.oed.com/view/Entry/98794

Irigaray, Luce. *This Sex Which Is Not One*. Translated by Catherine Porter and Carolyn Burke. Ithaca, NY: Cornell University Press, 1985.

Jackson, J.R. de. *Romantic Poetry by Women: A Bibliography, 1770–1835*. Oxford: Clarendon Press, 1993.

Jameson, Fredric. *Allegory and Ideology*. New York: Verso Books, 2019.

———. *The Political Unconscious: Narrative as a Socially Symbolic Act*. New York: Routledge, 2013.

Jarmusch, Jim. *The Dead Don't Die*. [Film.] Focus Features, 2019.

Jefferson, Thomas. *Notes on the State of Virginia*. London: John Stockdale, 1787.

Johnson, Barbara. *A Life with Mary Shelley*. Edited by Shoshana Felman and Judith Butler. Stanford, CA: Stanford University Press, 2014.

Jones Square, Shoshannah Bryn. "The 'Victim of Too Much Loving': Perdita Verney's Self-Destructive Sympathy in Mary Shelley's *The Last Man*." *Studies in the Literary Imagination* 51, no. 1 (2018): 61–78.

Juengel, Scott J. "Mary Wollstonecraft's Perpetual Disaster." In *Romanticism and Disaster*, edited by Jacques Khalip and David Collings. Romantic Circles Praxis Series. Romantic Circles, 2012. www.rc.umd.edu/praxis/disaster/HTML/praxis.2012.juengel.html

Jung, Moon-Ho. "Outlawing 'Coolies': Race, Nation, and Empire in the Age of Emancipation." *American Quarterly* 57, no. 3 (2005): 677–701.

Kamuf, Peggy. *Signature Pieces: On the Institution of Authorship*. Ithaca, NY: Cornell University Press, 2018.

Kapor, Vladimir. "Shifting Edenic Codes: On Two Exotic Visions of the Golden Age in the Late Eighteenth Century." *Eighteenth-Century Studies* 41, no. 2 (2008): 217–230.

Keane, Angela. *Women Writers and the English Nation in the 1790s: Romantic Belongings*. Cambridge: Cambridge University Press, 2001.

Keats, John. "Ode to a Nightingale." Edited by Ernest de Sélincourt, 191–194. New York: Dodd, Mead & Company, 1905.

Kelley, Theresa M. "Romantic Histories: Charlotte Smith and Beachy Head." *Nineteenth-Century Literature* 59, no. 3 (2004): 281–314.

Kennedy, Deborah. *Helen Maria Williams and the Age of Revolution*. Lewisburg, PA: Bucknell University Press, 2002.

Kester, Grant. "Questionnaire on 'The Contemporary.'" *October*, no. 130 (2009): 7–9.

Khalip, Jacques. *Anonymous Life: Romanticism and Dispossession*. Stanford, CA: Stanford University Press, 2008.

———. "Contretemps: Of Extinction and Romanticism." *Literature Compass* 13, no. 10 (2016): 628–636. doi.org/10.1111/lic3.12343

Khalip, Jacques, and Forest Pyle. "Introduction: The Present Darkness of Romanticism." In *Constellations of a Contemporary Romanticism*, edited by Jacques Khalip and Forest Pyle, 1–15. New York: Fordham University Press, 2016.

Kingstone, Helen. *Victorian Narratives of the Recent Past: Memory, History, Fiction.* Houndmills: Palgrave Macmillan, 2017.

Kitson, Peter J. *Romantic Literature, Race, and Colonial Encounter.* New York: Palgrave Macmillan, 2007.

Knowles, Claire. "Della Cruscanism and Newspaper Poetics: Reading the Letters of Simkin and Simon in *The World.*" *Studies in Romanticism* 57, no. 4 (2018): 581–600.

Koselleck, Reinhart. *Futures Past: On the Semantics of Historical Time.* Translated by Keith Tribe. Cambridge, MA: MIT Press, 1985.

Krapp, John. "Female Romanticism at the End of History." *Texas Studies in Literature and Language* 46, no. 1 (2004): 73–91. doi.org/10.1353/tsl.2004.0003

Kristeva, Julia. "Is There a Feminine Genius?" Translated by Julia Kristeva. *Critical Inquiry* 30, no. 3 (2004): 493–504. doi.org/10.1086/421159

———. "Women's Time." Translated by Alice Jardine and Harry Blake. *Signs* 7, no. 1 (1981): 13–35.

Kucich, Greg. "The Last Man and the New History." Romantic Circles, September 13, 1997. romantic-circles.org/sites/default/files/RCOldSite/www/villa/vc97/kucich.html

Kuiken, Kir. *Imagined Sovereignties: Toward a New Political Romanticism.* Oxford: Oxford University Press, 2014.

Labbe, Jacqueline M. *Charlotte Smith: Romanticism, Poetry and the Culture of Gender.* Manchester: Manchester University Press, 2003.

———. *Romantic Visualities: Landscape, Gender, and Romanticism.* Houndmills, UK: Palgrave Macmillan, 1998.

———. "The Anthologised Romance of Della Crusca and Anna Matilda." *Romanticism on the Net*, no. 18 (2000). www.erudit.org/en/journals/ron/1900-v1-n1-ron430/005916ar

———. *The Romantic Paradox: Love, Violence and the Uses of Romance, 1760–1830.* Houndmills, UK: Macmillan, 2000.

———. *Writing Romanticism: Charlotte Smith and William Wordsworth, 1784–1807.* New York: Palgrave Macmillan, 2011.

Labio, Catherine. "Reading by the Gold and Black Clock; Or, the Recasting of Bernardin de Saint-Pierre's *Paul et Virginie.*" *Eighteenth-Century Fiction* 16, no. 4 (2004): 671–694.

Lacan, Jacques. *Autre Écrits.* Edited by Jacques-Alain Miller. Paris: Seuil, 2001.

———. *Écrits: The First Complete Edition in English.* Translated by Bruce Fink. New York: Norton, 2006.

———. "Italian Note [1973]." Translated by Cormac Gallagher, May 2009.

———. "L'Étourdit." Translated by Cormac Gallagher. *The Letter*, no. 41 (2009): 31–80.

———. "On a Reform in Its Hole." Translated by John Holland. *S: Journal of the Circle for Lacanian Ideology Critique* 8 (2015): 14–21.

———. "Seminar on 'The Purloined Letter.'" In *The Purloined Poe: Lacan, Derrida, and Psychoanalytic Reading*, edited by John P. Muller and William J. Richardson, translated by Jeffrey Mehlman, 28–54. Baltimore: Johns Hopkins University Press, 1988.

———. *Television: A Challenge to the Psychoanalytic Establishment*. Edited by Joan Copjec. Translated by Denis Hollier, Rosalind Krauss, Annette Michelson, and Jeffrey Mehlman. New York: Norton, 1990.

———. *The Seminar of Jacques Lacan, Book I: Freud's Papers on Technique, 1953-1954*. Edited by Jacques-Alain Miller. Translated by John Forrester. New York: Norton, 1988.

———. *The Seminar of Jacques Lacan, Book II: The Ego in Freud's Theory and in the Technique of Psychoanalysis, 1954-1955*. Edited by Jacques-Alain Miller. Translated by Sylvana Tomaselli. New York: Norton, 1988.

———. *The Seminar of Jacques Lacan, Book III: The Psychoses*. Edited by Jacques-Alain Miller. Translated by Russell Grigg. New York: Norton, 1993.

———. *The Seminar of Jacques Lacan, Book V: Formations of the Unconscious*. Edited by Jacques-Alain Miller. Translated by Russell Grigg. Cambridge, UK: Polity, 2017.

———. "The Seminar of Jacques Lacan, Book V: The Formations of the Unconscious, 1957-1958." Translated by Cormac Gallagher, n.d.

———. *The Seminar of Jacques Lacan, Book VII: The Ethics of Psychoanalysis, 1959-1960*. Edited by Jacques-Alain Miller. Translated by Dennis Porter. New York: Norton, 1992.

———. *The Seminar of Jacques Lacan, Book VIII: Transference, 1960-61*. Edited by Jacques-Alain Miller. Translated by Bruce Fink. Cambridge, UK: Polity, 2015.

———. "The Seminar of Jacques Lacan, Book IX: Identification, 1961–1962." Translated by Cormac Gallagher, n.d.

———. *The Seminar of Jacques Lacan, Book X: Anxiety, 1962-63*. Edited by Jacques-Alain Miller. Translated by A.R. Price. Cambridge, UK: Polity, 2015.

———. *The Seminar of Jacques Lacan, Book XI: The Four Fundamental Concepts of Psychoanalysis*. Edited by Jacques-Alain Miller. Translated by Alan Sheridan. New York: Norton, 1978.

———. *The Seminar of Jacques Lacan, Book XVII: The Other Side of Psychoanalysis*. Edited by Jacques-Alain Miller. Translated by Russell Grigg. New York: Norton, 2007.

———. *The Seminar of Jacques Lacan, Book XX: Encore: On Feminine Sexuality, the Limits of Love and Knowledge, 1972-1973*. Edited by Jacques-Alain Miller. Translated by Bruce Fink. New York: Norton, 1998.

———. *The Seminar of Jacques Lacan, Book XXIII: The Sinthome, 1975-76*. Edited by Jacques-Alain Miller. Translated by A.R. Price. Cambridge, UK: Polity, 2016.

Lake, Crystal B. "History Writing and Antiquarianism." In *The Cambridge Companion to Women's Writing in the Romantic Period*, edited by Devoney Looser, 88–100. Cambridge: Cambridge University Press, 2015.

Laqueur, Thomas. *Making Sex: Body and Gender from the Greeks to Freud*. Cambridge, MA: Harvard University Press, 1990.

Latham, Sean. *The Art of Scandal: Modernism, Libel Law, and the Roman à Clef*. Modernist Literature & Culture. Oxford: Oxford University Press, 2009.

Levinson, Marjorie. "Notes and Queries on Names and Numbers." *Romantic Circles*, Praxis Series, Romantic Numbers (2013). romantic-circles.org/praxis/numbers/HTML/praxis.2013.levinson

Lew, Joseph. "The Necessary Orientalist? *The Giaour* and Nineteenth-Century Imperialist Misogyny." In *Romanticism, Race, and Imperial Culture, 1780–1834*, edited by Alan Richardson and Sonia Hofkosh, 173–202. Bloomington: Indiana University Press, 1996.

Li, Victor. "Elliptical Interruptions: Or, Why Derrida Prefers Mondialisation to Globalization." *CR: The New Centennial Review* 7, no. 2 (December 24, 2007): 141–154. doi.org/10.1353/ncr.2007.0040

London, April. "Clock Time and Utopia's Time in Novels of the 1790s." *Studies in English Literature, 1500–1900* 40, no. 3 (2000): 539–560. doi.org/10.2307/1556260

Longaker, John Mark. *The Della Cruscans and William Gifford: The History of a Minor Movement in an Age of Literary Transition*. Philadelphia: University of Pennsylvania Press, 1924.

Looser, Devoney, ed. "APPENDIX. Ithuriel, the Angel of Truth, Thus Relateth an Event of the Heavens." *Tulsa Studies in Women's Literature* 35, no. 1 (2016): 81–91.

———. *British Women Writers and the Writing of History, 1670–1820*. Baltimore: Johns Hopkins University Press, 2000.

———. "Mary Wollstonecraft, 'Ithuriel,' and the Rise of the Feminist Author-Ghost." *Tulsa Studies in Women's Literature* 35, no. 1 (2016): 59–91.

———. *Women Writers and Old Age in Great Britain, 1750–1850*. Baltimore: Johns Hopkins University Press, 2010.

Lupton, Christina. *Reading and the Making of Time in the Eighteenth Century*. Baltimore: Johns Hopkins University Press, 2018.

Macaulay, Catherine. *Observations on the Reflections of the Right Hon. Edmund Burke, in a Letter to the Right Hon. Earl of Stanhope*. London: C. Dilly, 1790.

Makdisi, Saree. "Versions of the East: Byron, Shelley, and the Orient." In *Romanticism, Race, and Imperial Culture, 1780–1834*, edited by Alan Richardson and Sonia Hofkosh, 203–236. Bloomington: Indiana University Press, 1996.

Mallarmé, Stéphane. *The Poems*. Translated by Keith Bosley. Harmondsworth, UK: Penguin, 1977.

Man, Paul de. "Autobiography as De-Facement." In *The Rhetoric of Romanticism*, 67–81. New York: Columbia University Press, 1984.

———. "Shelley Disfigured." In *Deconstruction and Criticism*, edited by Harold Bloom et al, 39–73. New York: Continuum, 1979.

———. "The Rhetoric of Temporality." In *Blindness and Insight: Essays in the Rhetoric of Contemporary Criticism*, 2nd ed., 187–228. Theory and History of Literature 7. Minneapolis: University of Minnesota Press, 1983.

Mandell, Laura. "The First Women (Psycho)Analysts; or, The Friends of Feminist History." *MLQ: Modern Language Quarterly* 65, no. 1 (2004): 69–92.

Matthew, Patricia A. "Biography and Mary Wollstonecraft in *Adeline Mowbray* and *Valperga*." *Women's Writing* 14, no. 3 (2007): 382–398. doi.org/10.1080/096 99080701644915

McCarthy, Anne C. *Awful Parenthesis: Suspension and the Sublime in Romantic and Victorian Poetry*. Toronto: University of Toronto Press, 2018.

McCarthy, William. *Anna Letitia Barbauld: Voice of the Enlightenment*. Baltimore: Johns Hopkins University Press, 2008.

———. "The Repression of Hester Lynch Piozzi; or, How We Forgot a Revolution in Authorship." *Modern Language Studies* 18, no. 1 (1988): 99–111. doi.org/10.2307/3194704

———. "Why Anna Letitia Barbauld Refused to Head a Women's College: New Facts, New Story." *Nineteenth-Century Contexts* 23, no. 3 (2001): 349–379. doi.org/10.1080/08905490108583548

McDayter, Ghislaine, ed. *Untrodden Regions of the Mind: Romanticism and Psychoanalysis*. Lewisburg, PA: Bucknell University Press, 2002.

McGann, Jerome J. *Byron and Romanticism*. Cambridge: Cambridge University Press, 2002.

———. *The Poetics of Sensibility: A Revolution in Literary Style*. Oxford: Clarendon Press, 1996.

McGowan, Todd. "The Psychosis of Freedom: Law in Modernity." In *Lacan on Psychosis: From Theory to Praxis*, edited by Jon Mills and David L. Downing, 47–77. London: Routledge, 2019.

McGuire, Kelly. " 'I Leave Thee Not': Felicia Hemans and Maternal Suicide." *Studies in the Literary Imagination* 51, no. 1 (2018): 121–137.

McHale, Brian. "Beginning to Think about Narrative in Poetry." *Narrative* 17, no. 1 (2009): 11–27. doi.org/10.1353/nar.0.0014

McInnes, Andrew. *Wollstonecraft's Ghost: The Fate of the Female Philosopher in the Romantic Period*. London: Routledge, 2017.

McLane, Maureen. "Afterword: Emergent Complexity and 'The The': Making Romanticism Count." *Romantic Circles* Romantic Numbers (2013). romantic-circles.org/praxis/numbers/HTML/praxis.2013.mclane_response_set1

Mellor, Anne K. *Romanticism and Gender*. New York: Routledge, 1993.

WORKS CITED 291

Melville, Peter. *Romantic Hospitality and the Resistance to Accommodation*. Waterloo, ON: Wilfrid Laurier University Press, 2007.

Merry, Robert. "Ode to Folly." In *The British Album*, 2nd ed., 1:15–18. London: John Bell, 1790.

———. "Ode to Tranquillity." In *The Poetry of the World*, edited by Edward Topham, 1st ed., 1:18–20. London: John Bell, 1788.

———. "The Adieu and Recall to Love." In *The British Album*, 2nd ed., 1:1–2. London: John Bell, 1790.

———. *The Laurel of Liberty, A Poem*. London: John Bell, 1790.

———. "To Anna Matilda [Aug. 21, 1787]." In *The British Album*, 2nd ed., 1:10–13. London: John Bell, 1790.

———. "To Anna Matilda [Oct. 28, 1788]." In *The British Album*, 2:133–136. London: John Bell, 1790.

Miège, Jean-Louis. *Indentured Labour in the Indian Ocean and the Particular Case of Mauritius*. Leiden, Netherlands: Intercontinenta, 1986.

Miller, Christopher R. *The Invention of Evening: Perception and Time in Romantic Poetry*. Cambridge: Cambridge University Press, 2006.

Moody, Jane. "Thomas Brown [Alias Thomas Moore], Censorship and Regency Cryptography." *European Romantic Review* 18, no. 2 (2007): 187–194. doi. org/10.1080/10509580701297919

Morgan, Monique R. *Narrative Means, Lyric Ends: Temporality in the Nineteenth-Century British Long Poem*. Columbus: The Ohio State University Press, 2009.

Mullen, Mary. *Novel Institutions: Anachronism, Irish Novels and Nineteenth-Century Realism*. Edinburgh, UK: Edinburgh University Press, 2019.

———. "Two Clocks: *Aurora Leigh*, Poetic Form, and the Politics of Timeliness." *Victorian Poetry* 51, no. 1 (2013): 63–80.

Muller, John P., and William J. Richardson, eds. *The Purloined Poe: Lacan, Derrida & Psychoanalytic Reading*. Baltimore: Johns Hopkins University Press, 1988.

Mulso Chapone, Hester. "To Stella." In *Eighteenth Century Women Poets: An Oxford Anthology*, edited by Roger H. Lonsdale, 238–240. Oxford: Oxford University Press, 1990.

Muñoz, José Esteban. *Cruising Utopia: The Then and There of Queer Futurity*. New York: NYU Press, 2009.

Nagle, Christopher C. *Sexuality and the Culture of Sensibility in the British Romantic Era*. New York: Palgrave Macmillan, 2007.

Nagra, Daljit. "Look We Have Coming to Dover!" In *Look We Have Coming to Dover!*, 32. London: Faber and Faber, 2007.

Najarian, James. "Sexual Politics and the Performance of Gender in Romantic Poetry." In *A Companion to Romantic Poetry*, edited by Charles Mahoney, 521–537. Chichester, UK: Wiley-Blackwell, 2011.

Nancy, Jean-Luc. "What Is to Be Done?" Translated by Irving Goh. *Diacritics* 42, no. 2 (2014): 100–117.

Neill, Anna. "The Sentimental Novel and the Republican Imaginary: Slavery in *Paul and Virginia*." *Diacritics* 23, no. 3 (1993): 36–47.

Nersessian, Anahid. *Utopia, Limited: Romanticism and Adjustment.* Cambridge, MA: Harvard University Press, 2015.

Neyrat, Frédéric. *Atopias: Manifesto for a Radical Existentialism.* Translated by Walt Hunter and Lindsay Turner. New York: Fordham University Press, 2017.

O'Neill, Michael. "'A Deeper and Richer Music': Felicia Hemans in Dialogue with Wordsworth, Byron and Shelley." *Charles Lamb Bulletin*, 2009. search. proquest.com/mlaib/docview/814472394/4E364AAC168C4999PQ/9

Packham, Catherine. "Mary Wollstonecraft's Cottage Economics: Property, Political Economy, and the European Future." *ELH* 84, no. 2 (2017): 453–474. doi. org/10.1353/elh.2017.0018

Pascoe, Judith. *Romantic Theatricality: Gender, Poetry, and Spectatorship.* Ithaca, NY: Cornell University Press, 1997.

Pauk, Barbara. "Promoting Feminism and an International Community of Letters: Helen Maria Williams' *Paul and Virginia*." In *Literature as Translation/ Translation as Literature*, edited by Christopher Conti and James Gourley, 101–116. Newcastle upon Tyne, UK: Cambridge Scholars Publishing, 2014.

Paulson, Michael S. "Present, Period, Crisis: Desynchronization and Social Cohesion in Jane Austen." *Modern Philology* 116, no. 2 (October 15, 2018): 164–185. doi.org/10.1086/698716

Phillips, Mark Salber. *On Historical Distance.* Cumberland, RI: Yale University Press, 2013.

Pladek, Brittany. *The Poetics of Palliation: Romantic Literary Therapy, 1790–1850.* Oxford: Oxford University Press, 2019.

Pollak, Ellen. *Incest and the English Novel, 1684–1814.* Baltimore: Johns Hopkins University Press, 2003.

Poovey, Mary. *The Proper Lady and the Woman Writer: Ideology as Style in the Works of Mary Wollstonecraft, Mary Shelley, and Jane Austen.* Chicago: University of Chicago Press, 1985.

Potkay, Adam. "Wordsworth's Hope." *The Wordsworth Circle* 50, no. 3 (2019): 265–289. doi.org/10.1086/704523

Prasad, Pratima. *Colonialism, Race, and the French Romantic Imagination.* New York: Routledge, 2009.

Pucci, Suzanne R. "Snapshots of Family Intimacy in the French Eighteenth Century: The Case of *Paul et Virginie*." *Studies in Eighteenth-Century Culture*, no. 37 (2008): 89–118.

Ragland, Ellie, and Dragan Milovanovic. "Introduction: Topologically Speaking." In *Lacan: Topologically Speaking*, edited by Ellie Ragland and Dragan Milovanovic, xiii–xl. New York: Other Press, 2004.

Works Cited 293

Rajan, Tilottama. *Dark Interpreter: The Discourse of Romanticism*. Ithaca, NY: Cornell University Press, 1986.

———. *Romantic Narrative: Shelley, Hays, Godwin, Wollstonecraft*. Baltimore: Johns Hopkins University Press, 2010.

Rancière, Jacques. *Figures of History*. Translated by Julie Rose. Cambridge, UK: Polity, 2014.

———. *The Politics of Aesthetics*. London: Continuum, 2006.

———. "The Politics of Literature." *SubStance* 33, no. 1 [issue #103] (2004): 10–24.

———. "Who Is the Subject of the Rights of Man?" *South Atlantic Quarterly* 103, no. 2/3 (2004): 297–310.

Rauch, Alan. *Useful Knowledge: The Victorians, Morality, and the March of Intellect*. Durham, NC: Duke University Press, 2001.

Ravi, Srilata. "Indo-Mauritians: National and Postnational Identities." *L'Esprit Créateur* 50, no. 2 (2010): 29–45.

Redfield, Marc. *The Politics of Aesthetics: Nationalism, Gender, Romanticism*. Stanford, CA: Stanford University Press, 2003.

Reeder, Jessie. "A World without 'Dependant Kings': *Eighteen Hundred and Eleven* and the Forms of Informal Empire." *Studies in Romanticism* 53, no. 4 (2014): 561–590. doi.org/NA

Reno, Seth T. *Amorous Aesthetics: Intellectual Love in Romantic Poetry and Poetics, 1788–1853*. Liverpool, UK: Liverpool University Press, 2019.

Richardson, Alan. "Rethinking Romantic Incest: Human Universals, Literary Representation, and the Biology of Mind." *New Literary History* 31, no. 3 (2000): 553–572. doi.org/10.1353/nlh.2000.0038

Richardson, Charlotte Caroline. "Harvest. A Poem." In *Harvest, A Poem, in Two Parts: With Other Poetical Pieces*, 1–42. London: printed for the author by William Thorne, 1818.

———. "To-Morrow." In *Harvest, A Poem, in Two Parts: With Other Poetical Pieces*, 88–89. London: printed for the author by William Thorne, 1818.

Ricoeur, Paul. *Time and Narrative*. Translated by Kathleen McLaughlin and David Pellauer. Vol. 1. 3 vols. Chicago: University of Chicago Press, 1984.

Robinson, Daniel. "Della Crusca, Anna Matilda, and Ludic Sensibility." *The Wordsworth Circle* 42, no. 2 (2011): 170–174.

———. "Mary Robinson and the Della Crusca Network." In *Grasmere 2010: Selected Papers from the 40th Anniversary Wordsworth Summer Conference*, edited by Richard Gravil, 115–126. Tirril: Humanities-Ebooks, 2010.

———. *The Poetry of Mary Robinson: Form and Fame*. Palgrave Macmillan, 2011.

Robinson, Mary. "A Letter to the Women of England on the Injustice of Mental Subordination, with Anecdotes." Romantic Circles, May 1998. romantic-circles.org/editions/robinson/mrletterfrst.htm

———. "*Ainsi va Le Monde* (1790)." In *A Letter to the Women of England, on the Injustice of Mental Subordination*, edited by Adriana Craciun, Anne Irman

Close, Megan Musgrave, and Orianne Smith, 1998. romantic-circles.org/editions/robinson/mrainsi90frst.htm

———. "Harvest Home." In *Mary Robinson: Selected Poems*, edited by Judith Pascoe, 319–321. Peterborough, UK: Broadview Press, 1999.

———. *Memoirs of Mary Robinson, "Perdita," from the Edition Edited by Her Daughter*. Edited by J. Fitzgerald Molloy. Philadelphia: Gibbings and Company, 1895.

Rohrbach, Emily. "Anna Barbauld's History of the Future: A Deviant Way to Poetic Agency." *European Romantic Review* 17, no. 2 (2006): 179–187.

———. *Modernity's Mist: British Romanticism and the Poetics of Anticipation*. New York: Fordham University Press, 2016.

Rooney, Morgan. "'Belonging to No/Body': Mary Robinson, 'The Natural Daughter,' and Rewriting Feminine Identity." *Eighteenth Century Fiction* 18, no. 3 (Spring 2006): 355–372. doi.org/10.1353/ecf.2006.0048

Rosenbaum, Susan. "'A Thing Unknown, without a Name': Anna Laetitia Barbauld and the Illegible Signature." *Studies in Romanticism* 40, no. 3 (2001): 369–399.

Rowland, Stephen M. "Thomas Jefferson, Extinction, and the Evolving View of Earth History in the Late Eighteenth and Early Nineteenth Centuries." In *The Revolution in Geology from the Renaissance to the Enlightenment*, edited by Gary D. Rosenberg, 225–246. Boulder, CO: Geological Society of America, 2009.

Rudy, Jason R. "Hemans' Passion." *Studies in Romanticism* 45, no. 4 (2006): 543–562. doi.org/10.2307/25602072

Ruppert, Timothy. "Time and the Sibyl in Mary Shelley's *The Last Man*." *Studies in the Novel* 41, no. 2 (2009): 141–156. doi.org/10.1353/sdn.0.0054

Sachs, Jonathan. "1816: Romanticisms Quick and Slow." *Keats-Shelley Journal* 46 (2017): 88–98.

———. "Future! Decline." *Poetics Today* 37, no. 3 (2016): 355–368.

———. "The Glimmer of Futurity, 1811–1815." In *The Regency Revisited*, edited by Tim Fulford and Michael E. Sinatra, 17–30. New York: Palgrave Macmillan, 2016.

———. *The Poetics of Decline in British Romanticism*. Cambridge: Cambridge University Press, 2018.

Said, Edward W. *Orientalism*. New York: Vintage Books, 1979.

Sargent, Andrew. "Citation and the No Future of Romanticism in Mary Shelley's *The Last Man*." *European Romantic Review* 31, no. 3 (2020): 313–324.

Schechter, Marshall D. "Psychoanalytic Theory as It Relates to Adoption." *Journal of the American Psychoanalytic Association* 15, no. 3 (1967): 695–708.

Schor, Esther. *Bearing the Dead: The British Culture of Mourning from the Enlightenment to Victoria*. Princeton, NJ: Princeton University Press, 1994.

WORKS CITED

Sedgwick, Eve Kosofsky. *Epistemology of the Closet.* Updated. Berkeley: University of California Press, 2008.

Sharma, Sarah. "The Biopolitical Economy of Time." *Journal of Communication Inquiry* 35, no. 4 (2011): 439–444. doi.org/10.1177/0196859911417999

Shelley, Mary. *Frankenstein: The 1818 Text, Contexts, Criticism.* Edited by J. Paul Hunter. 2nd ed. Norton Critical Edition. New York: Norton, 2012.

———. *The Last Man.* Edited by Morton D. Paley. Oxford World's Classics. Oxford: Oxford University Press, 2008.

———. "Valerius, the Reanimated Roman." In *Mary Shelley: Collected Tales and Stories*, edited by Charles E. Robinson, 332–344. Baltimore: Johns Hopkins University Press, 1990.

Shelley, Percy Bysshe. "A Defence of Poetry." In *Shelley's Poetry and Prose*, edited by Donald H. Reiman and Neil Fraistat, 2nd ed., 509–535. New York: Norton, 2002.

Sigler, David. "Lacan's Romanticism." In *Knots: Literature and Psychoanalysis After Lacan*, edited by Jean-Michel Rabaté, 55–69. New York: Routledge, 2020.

———. "On Reading Charlotte Caroline Richardson's 'On Hearing a Friend Play on the Psaltery' with Coleridge's 'The Eolian Harp.'" *Women's Writing* 22, no. 2 (2015): 229–243. doi.org/10.1080/09699082.2015.1011840

———. *Sexual Enjoyment in British Romanticism: Gender and Psychoanalysis, 1753–1835.* Montreal: McGill-Queen's University Press, 2015.

Simpson, David. *Romanticism and the Question of the Stranger.* Chicago: University of Chicago Press, 2012.

Sinanan, Kerry. "Maroon Resistance, White Violence, and Romanticism's Envy of Black Freedom." *Romantic Circles Unbound* (blog), Summer 2020. romantic-circles.org/blog_rc/maroon-resistance-white-violence-and-romanticism%E2%80%99s-envy-black-freedom

Singer, Kate. "It's the End of the World as We Know It and I Feel Queer: Mary Shelley, Queer Affect, and Shapeshifting through *The Last Man*." In *Material Transgressions: Beyond Romantic Bodies, Genders, Things*, edited by Kate Singer, Ashley Cross, and Suzanne L. Barnett, 213–231. Liverpool, UK: Liverpool University Press, 2020.

———. *Romantic Vacancy: The Poetics of Gender, Affect, and Radical Speculation.* Albany, NY: SUNY Press, 2019.

Singer, Kate, and Nanora Sweet. "Beyond Domesticity: Felicia Hemans in the Wider World." *Women's Writing* 21, no. 1 (2014): 1–8.

Smith, Anthony D. "The Suffering Hero: Belisarius and Oedipus in Late 18th Century French and British Art." *RSA Journal* 137, no. 5398 (1989): 634–640.

Smith, Charlotte. "Beachy Head." In *The Poems of Charlotte Smith*, edited by Stuart Curran, 217–250. Oxford: Oxford University Press, 1993.

Smith, Orianne. *Romantic Women Writers, Revolution, and Prophecy: Rebellious Daughters, 1786–1826*. Cambridge: Cambridge University Press, 2013.

Smith, Terry. "Questionnaire on 'The Contemporary.'" *October*, no. 130 (2009): 46–54.

Soler, Colette. *What Lacan Said About Women: A Psychoanalytic Study*. Translated by John Holland. New York: Other Press, 2006.

Song, Eric B. *Dominion Undeserved: Milton and the Perils of Creation*. Ithaca, NY: Cornell University Press, 2013.

Spacks, Patricia Meyer. *Novel Beginnings: Experiments in Eighteenth-Century English Fiction*. New Haven, CT: Yale University Press, 2006.

Spivak, Gayatri Chakravorty. "Echo." *New Literary History* 24 (1993): 17–43.

Stewart, David. *The Form of Poetry in the 1820s and 1830s: A Period of Doubt*. Palgrave Studies in the Englightenment, Romanticism, and Cultures of Print. Cham, Switzerland: Palgrave Macmillan, 2018.

Strang, Hilary. "Common Life, Animal Life, Equality: *The Last Man*." *ELH* 78, no. 2 (2011): 409–431.

Taylor, Barbara D. "Felicia Hemans and *The Domestic Affections, and Other Poems*; or Mrs Browne's Publishing Project." *Women's Writing* 21, no. 1 (2014): 9–24. doi.org/10.1080/09699082.2014.881060

Thomas, Brian. "'Living Fossils' Point to Recent Creation." The Institute for Creation Research, September 21, 2015. www.icr.org/article/living-fossils-point-recent-creation

Thompson, E.P. "Time, Work-Discipline, and Industrial Capitalism." *Past & Present* 38 (1967): 56–97.

Tomalin, Marcus. *Telling the Time in British Literature, 1675–1830: Hours of Folly?* New York: Routledge, 2020.

Trévien, Claire. "The Spectacle of Science: The Art of Illusion in Prints of the French Revolution." *Rupkatha Journal on Interdisciplinary Studies in Humanities* 3, no. 1 (2011): 42–51.

Tuite, Clara. "Not Guilty: Negative Capability and the Trials of William Hone." In *Censorship and the Limits of the Literary: A Global View*, edited by Nicole Moore, 33–48. New York: Bloomsbury, 2015.

Turner, Frederick, and Ernst Pöppel. "Metered Poetry, the Brain, and Time." In *Beauty and the Brain: Biological Aspects of Aesthetics*, edited by Ingo Rentschler, Barbara Herzberger, and David Epstein, 71–90. Basel, Switzerland: Birkhäuser, 1988. doi.org/10.1007/978-3-0348-6350-6_4

Ty, Eleanor. "Editor's Introduction." In *The Victim of Prejudice*, by Mary Hays, vii–xxxvii. edited by Eleanor Ty. Peterborough: Broadview, 1994.

———. *Unsex'd Revolutionaries: Five Women Novelists of the 1790s*. Toronto: University of Toronto Press, 1993.

Tyrer, Ben. *Out of the Past: Lacan and Film Noir*. Cham, Switzerland: Springer, 2016.

Ulmer, William A. "William Wordsworth and Philosophical Necessity." *Studies in Philology* 110, no. 1 (2013): 168–198.

Vanheule, Stijn. "On Ordinary Psychosis." In *Lacan on Psychosis: From Theory to Praxis*, edited by Jon Mills and David L. Downing, 77–103. London: Routledge, 2019.

Vaughan, Megan. *Creating the Creole Island: Slavery in Eighteenth-Century Mauritius*. Durham, NC: Duke University Press, 2005.

Vernooy-Epp, Dawn M. "Teaching Mary Darby Robinson's Reading List: Romanticism, Recovery Work, and Reconsidering Anthologies." *Pedagogy* 9, no. 1 (2009): 13–34.

Vukanović, Marija Brala, and Lovorka Gruić Grmuša. "Introduction: Capturing Space and Time: Mission (Im)Possible." In *Space and Time in Language and Literature*, edited by Marija Brala Vukanović and Lovorka Gruić Grmuša, 1–20. Newcastle upon Tyne, UK: Cambridge Scholars Publishing, 2009.

Walker, Eric C. "Adoption, Narrative, and Nation, 1800–1850: The Case of William Austin." *Journal of British Studies* 53, no. 4 (2014): 960–991.

———. *Marriage, Writing, and Romanticism: Wordsworth and Austen after War*. Stanford, CA: Stanford University Press, 2009.

Walker, Gina Luria. "'I Sought & Made to Myself an Extraordinary Destiny.'" *Women's Writing* 25, no. 2 (2018): 124–149. doi.org/10.1080/09699082.2017.1387341

Walker, Jonathan. *Site Unscene: The Offstage in English Renaissance Drama*. Evanston, IL: Northwestern University Press, 2017.

Wallace, Miriam L. *Revolutionary Subjects in the English "Jacobin" Novel, 1790–1805*. Lewisburg, PA: Bucknell University Press, 2009.

Wallraven, Miriam. *A Writing Halfway Between Theory and Fiction: Mediating Feminism from the Seventeenth to the Twentieth Century*. Würzburg, Germany: Königshausen & Neumann, 2007.

Wang, Fuson. "We Must Live Elsewhere: The Social Construction of Natural Immunity in Mary Shelley's *The Last Man*." *European Romantic Review* 22, no. 2 (2011): 235–255. doi.org/10.1080/10509585.2011.544931

Wang, Orrin N. C. *Romantic Sobriety: Sensation, Revolution, Commodification, History*. Baltimore: Johns Hopkins University Press, 2011.

Wanko, Cheryl. "Celebrity Studies in the Long Eighteenth Century: An Interdisciplinary Overview." *Literature Compass* 8, no. 6 (2011): 351–362. doi.org/10.1111/j.1741-4113.2011.00806.x

Warren, Andrew. *The Orient and the Young Romantics*. Cambridge Studies in Romanticism 109. Cambridge: Cambridge University Press, 2014.

Washington, Chris. *Romantic Revelations: Visions of Post-Apocalyptic Life and Hope in the Anthropocene*. Toronto: University of Toronto Press, 2019.

Weiss, Deborah. *The Female Philosopher and Her Afterlives: Mary Wollstonecraft, the British Novel, and the Transformations of Feminism, 1796–1811*. Palgrave

Studies in the Enlightenment, Romanticism, and Cultures of Print. Cham, Switzerland: Palgrave Macmillan, 2017.

White, Andrew Dickson. *New Chapters in the Warfare of Science*. D. Appleton, 1888.

Williams, Helen Maria. *Letters Containing a Sketch of the Politics of France, from the Thirty-First of May 1793, till the Twenty-Eighth of July 1794, and Of the Scenes Which Have Passed in the Prisons of Paris*. 2 vols. London: G.G. and J. Robinson, 1795.

———. *Letters Written in France, in the Summer 1790, to a Friend in England; Containing Various Anecdotes Relative to the French Revolution*. Edited by Neil Fraistat and Susan S. Lanser. Peterborough, UK: Broadview, 2001.

Withers, Charles W.J. *Placing the Enlightenment: Thinking Geographically about the Age of Reason*. Chicago: University of Chicago Press, 2007.

Wolfson, Susan J. *Borderlines: The Shiftings of Gender in British Romanticism*. Stanford, CA: Stanford University Press, 2006.

———. "'Domestic Affections' and 'the Spear of Minerva': Felicia Hemans and the Dilemma of Gender." In *Re-Visioning Romanticism: British Women Writers, 1776–1837*, edited by Carol Shiner Wilson and Joel Haefner, 128–166. Philadelphia: University of Pennsylvania Press, 1994.

———. "Editing Felicia Hemans for the Twenty-First Century." *Romanticism on the Net*, no. 19 (2000). doi.org/10.7202/005931ar

———. *Romantic Interactions: Social Being and the Turns of Literary Action*. Baltimore: Johns Hopkins University Press, 2010.

Wollstonecraft, Mary. "*A Vindication of the Rights of Woman*." In *The Works of Mary Wollstonecraft*, edited by Janet Todd and Marilyn Butler, 5:61–266. London: William Pickering, 1989.

———. "*An Historical and Moral View of the French Revolution*." In *The Works of Mary Wollstonecraft*, edited by Janet Todd and Marilyn Butler, 6:1–235. London: William Pickering, 1989.

———. "Hints." In *The Works of Mary Wollstonecraft*, edited by Janet Todd and Marilyn Butler, 5:267–276. London: William Pickering, 1989.

———. "*Letters Written in Sweden, Norway, and Denmark*." In *The Works of Mary Wollstonecraft*, edited by Janet Todd and Marilyn Butler, 6:237–348. London: William Pickering, 1989.

Woolf, Virginia. *A Room of One's Own*. Edited by Susan Gubar. Orlando: Harvest Books, 2005.

Wright, Eamon. *British Women Writers and Race, 1788–1818: Narrations of Modernity*. Houndmills, UK: Palgrave Macmillan, 2005.

Žižek, Slavoj. *Incontinence of the Void: Economico-Philosophical Spandrels*. Cambridge, MA: MIT Press, 2017.

———. *The Parallax View*. Cambridge, MA: MIT Press, 2006.

———. *The Year of Dreaming Dangerously*. London: Verso, 2012.

Zupančič, Alenka. *The Odd One In: On Comedy*. Cambridge, MA: MIT Press, 2008.

———. *The Shortest Shadow: Nietzsche's Philosophy of the Two*. Cambridge, MA: MIT Press, 2003.

———. *What Is Sex?* Cambridge, MA: MIT Press, 2017.

Zytaruk, Maria. " 'Take Care Some Seeds in the Letter': Material and Textual Practices of Seed Exchange in the Long Eighteenth Century." *Lumen: Selected Proceedings from the Canadian Society for Eighteenth-Century Studies* 38 (2019): 179–199. doi.org/10.7202/1059279ar

Index

Abbas I, King of Persia, 207, 210–11, 220
  as proxy for George III in *Gulzara*, 210, 211, 212
Agamben, Giorgio, 20–21, 37, 42, 67, 148, 244, 245–46, 247, 250
Aikin, Lucy, 24
allegory. *See* Barbauld, Anna Letitia: "Love and Time: To Mrs. Mulso"; "Ithuriel"; Merry, Robert; Robinson, Mary Darby
Andrews, Charles, 33, 34
Antigone, 96, 176, 231
Austen, Jane, 8, 95
  Persuasion, 18, 184

Badiou, Alain, 9, 205
Baillie, Joanna, 38
Barbauld, Anna Letitia, 2, 20, 37, 38, 120, 146–47, 223, 248, 271n25
  Eighteen Hundred and Eleven (1812), 19, 47, 50–52, 53–56, 59, 63, 160, 204, 213, 236, 239, 244
  A Legacy for Young Ladies (1826), 46, 49
  "Love and Time: To Mrs. Mulso" (1825), 157, 159, 160–65, 169
  "On the Uses of History" (1826), 19, 24, 46–64, 135, 197, 206
  "The Rights of Woman" (1792), 24

"Washing Day" (1797), 156, 157, 165–68, 175
Batchelor, Jennie, 207
Battle of Waterloo. *See* Napoleonic Wars
Baucom, Ian, 74
Beachy Head (Smith), 20, 157, 159, 168–78, 239, 263n45
Beauvoir, Simone de, *The Second Sex*, 235–36, 238
Behrendt, Stephen C., 3, 15, 179, 206–7, 208, 218
Bell, John, 16, 117
Bennett, Andrew, 193
Bennett, Betty, 223, 229
Bennington, Geoffrey, 33
Berman, Carolyn Vellenga, 91
Bernardin de Saint Pierre, Jacques-Henri
  Paul et Virginie (1788), translation by Helen Maria Williams (*Paul and Virginia*) (1795), 15–16, 65–93, 95–96, 108
  Studies of Nature (1784), 73, 89
  Voyage to the Île de France (1773), 74
Blake, William, 202
Bloch, Ernst, 104, 168, 169, 173, 174, 177, 178, 239
Brecht, Bertolt, 212, 250

301

Brewer, John, 161
Browne, Felicia Dorothea. *See*
Hemans, Felicia
Bundock, Christopher M., 7, 15,
223–24
Burke, Edmund, *Reflections on the*
Revolution in France, 6
Butler, Judith, 7, 178, 223
Butler, Marilyn, 219–20
Byron, Lord, 157, 159, 200, 201, 205,
211
depiction of in Mary Shelley, *The*
Last Man, 230, 231, 232, 271n25
Lara, 218
Manfred, 157, 193, 195–97

Cahill, Samara Anne, 207–8
Calé, Luisa, 78
Canuel, Mark, 172
capitalism, 28, 46, 220, 244–45
Capuano, Peter, 172–73
Caputo, John D., 11
Carman, Colin, 230
Caruth, Cathy, 7
Cassity, Conny, 73, 88, 259n57
Celan, Paul, 71
Chandler, James, 50, 51, 63
Chapone, Hester Mulso
"To Stella" (1775), 159, 162
Charlotte Augusta, Princess of Wales,
203, 207–8, 211–12, 215, 216,
220
Chiesa, Lorenzo, 233–34
Christensen, Jerome, 15
chronology *vs.* geography, 58–59
chrononormativity, 8, 59, 64, 121,
141, 152, 245
literary resistance to, 121, 154,
166–67, 219
See also Barbauld, Anna Letitia:
"Love and Time: To Mrs. Mulso";

Cowley, Hannah; Merry, Robert:
"Ode to Folly"; Robinson, Mary:
Ainsi va le Monde
Cixous, Héléne, 17
Claremont, Claire, depiction of in
Mary Shelley, *The Last Man*, 230,
231
Clark, David L., 196
Clery, E.J., 24–25, 50
Colebrook, Claire, 165
Coleman, Deirdre, 69
Coleridge, Samuel Taylor, 190, 238
depiction of in Mary Shelley, *The*
Last Man, 271n25
Coles, Prophecy, 67
Collings, David, 26, 124
contemporariness, 37, 55, 62, 244–46,
248
contemporary future, definition of,
4–5, 11
contretempopia, definition of, 11–12,
20, 74, 132, 201, 202
Cooke, Miriam, 207
Copjec, Joan, 39, 247
Cowley, Hannah, 19, 20, 37, 38, 116–
17, 118, 171
The Runaway (1776), 118
"To Della Crusca" (poem series,
1789), 20, 117, 127–28, 132–39,
143
"To Somebody at Margate" (1787),
139–40
Cox, Jeffrey, 161
creolization, 71–72, 85, 88
Croker, John Wilson, review of
Barbauld's *Eighteen Hundred and*
Eleven, 50
Cross, Ashley, 25, 36, 45, 179, 243
Culler, Jonathan, 157, 188, 189
Curran, Stuart, 166–67
Cutler, Alan, 147–48

Dacre, Charlotte
  The Libertine (1807), 118
  Zofloya, or the Moor (1806), 118
de Man, Paul, 122, 162, 165, 185, 186,
  187
death drive, the, 81–82, 92, 126, 127,
  164, 198–99, 242
  Derrida on, 35, 142, 247
deconstructionism
  protocols and strategies of, 3, 15
  relationship to psychoanalysis, 11,
    17–18, 125, 247
  See also Derrida, Jacques; Spivak,
    Gayatri Chakravorty
Defoe, Daniel, 95
Della Cruscan poetic circle, 2, 20,
  115–54, 248
Derrida, Jacques, 8, 13, 23, 89, 117,
  210
  on adoption, 68, 70
  analysis of *Oedipus at Colonus*,
    184–85
  anarchive drive, 115
  and archive fever, 119
  and the author, 43, 44
  on the center, 196
  contretemps, 87
  criticism of rights, 99
  on death and friendship, 82
  and the death drive, 35, 92, 142,
    247
  on deconstruction, 84–85
  and destinerrance, 194–95, 247
  and différance, 194–95, 196, 201
  on the future, 11, 12, 29, 31, 50–51
  on genius, 243–44
  on hands, 172
  on hospitality, 180–81, 183
  and the parergon, 78
  and psychoanalysis, 17–18, 48, 56,
    57, 60, 61

on translation, 77
and the university, 42
on worldwide-ization, 11, 52–53,
  57, 71–72, 93, 220, 260n89
de Scudéry, Madeline, *Artamène, or
  the Great Cyrus* (1648-1653),
  204, 212
Dufourmantelle, Anne, 186
DuPlessis, Rachel Blau, 158
Duquette, Natasha, 90

echo, 14, 83, 90, 95, 122–123, 126–
  129, 145, 167, 179–181, 183–184,
  187, 195, 198–201, 247
Edelman, Lee, 126, 227–28, 242
Effinger, Elizabeth, 223
Egerton, Frank N., 89
Eighteen Hundred and Eleven (Barbauld),
  19, 47, 50–52, 53–56, 59, 63, 160,
  204, 213, 236, 239, 244
Einboden, Jeffrey, 214
Enlightenment, the, 57, 58, 59–60
  and rights discourses, 91, 93
erotohistory. *See* Robinson, Mary
  Darby, *Ainsi va le Monde* (1790)
"An Evening Prayer at a Girls' School"
  (Hemans), 20, 157, 159, 165,
  187–93, 239
ex-sistence, definition of, 39

Favret, Mary A., 59, 160–61
Felluga, Dino Franco, 195
female education. *See under* women
female philosopher, the, 3, 24, 28, 32,
  94
Ferrier, Susan, *Marriage* (1818), 66
Fink, Bruce, 248
fracture feminism, definition of, 1, 3,
  13, 16, 241, 243
Freeman, Elizabeth, 28, 119–20, 121,
  122, 123, 126, 146, 172, 246

French Revolution
  fracture feminists and, 17, 19–20,
    27, 64, 166, 244, 245
  Helen Maria Williams's support for,
    70, 81–82
  See also Burke, Edmund: *Reflections
    on the Revolution in France*;
    Merry, Robert: *The Laurel of
    Liberty*; Robinson, Mary: *Ainsi va
    le Monde*; Wollstonecraft, Mary:
    *An Historical and Moral View of
    the French Revolution*
Freud, Sigmund, 153, 184, 190, 232,
    247
  and the category of "woman,"
    14–15
  challenges to the ideas of, 17, 48
  and dreams, 173, 174
  and the Oedipus complex, 66–67,
    68, 97, 107, 111, 113–14
  and the superego, 61–62
future, the, definitions of, 8, 10, 11.
    See also contemporary future,
    definition of
futurity, definition of, 10–11

Gallagher, Catherine, 204
Gallagher, Cormac, 261n139
Gallop, Jane, 51
Gamer, Michael, 116, 119, 140
genius, feminine, 21, 110, 243–44
George, Sam, 109
George III, King, 207, 213
  King Abbas I of Persia as proxy for
    in *Gulzara*, 210, 211, 212
Godwin, William, 43, 94, 95, 104, 108
  *Memoirs of the Author of the
    Vindication of the Rights of
    Woman* (1798), 23–24
Golightly, Jennifer, 112
Goodman, Kevis, 170, 171, 173
Gottlieb, Evan, 68, 205, 219

Grey, Lady Jane, 30, 33
*Gulzara; Princess of Persia; or the
    Virgin Queen* (Anon., 1816), 203,
    206–21, 239, 271n25
Gustafson, Ryan, 52

Hadley, Karen, 17
Halloran, Vivian Nun, 201
Harvest: A Poem (Richardson), 20,
    157, 159, 179–87, 239
Hays, Mary, 2, 3, 37, 38, 104
  The Memoirs of Emma Courtney
    (1796), 94
  The Victim of Prejudice (1799), 19,
    66, 68, 93–114, 260n100
Heidegger, Martin, 235
Hemans, Felicia (Felicia Dorothea
    Browne), 12, 157–58, 159, 165,
    187–93, 242, 248, 249
  The Domestic Affections (1812), 1
  Forget Me Not (1825/1826), 269n106
  "An Evening Prayer at a Girls'
    School" (1825), 20, 157, 159, 165,
    187–93, 239
  Songs of the Affections (1830), 193,
    194
  "A Spirit's Return" (1828), 16, 20,
    157, 159, 193–202
  "A Thought of the Future" (1829),
    249
  "War and Peace" (1812), 1–2, 10–
    11, 14, 18, 223
history
  Anna Letitia Barbauld on, 46–64
  place of the French Revolution in,
    129–30
Hofkosh, Sonia, 23, 26
hope, 242–43. *See also* Hemans,
    Felicia; Robinson, Mary Darby;
    Shelley, Mary; Shelley, Percy
    Bysshe; Smith, Charlotte;
    Wollstonecraft, Mary

hospitality, 92, 157, 180–87
Hughes, John, 34
Hunter, Walt, 172
Hyldgaard, Kristin, 187

incest. *See* Hays, Mary: *The Victim of Prejudice*; Oedipus Complex; Williams, Helen Maria: *Paul and Virginia*
isolation. *See* Barbauld, Anna Letitia; Hays, Mary; Hemans, Felicia; Merry, Robert; Shelley, Mary; Smith, Charlotte; Richardson, Charlotte Caroline; Williams, Helen Maria
"Ithuriel" (Anon., 1798), 24, 30–36, 64

Jameson, Fredric, 129, 178
Jefferson, Thomas, *Notes on the State of Virginia* (1781/1787), 148
Johnson, Barbara, 223, 224, 238
jouissance, feminine, Lacan and, 25, 32–33, 35–36, 104–5, 116, 236, 253n73
Joyce, James, *Finnegans Wake*, 116, 262n5
Juengel, Scott, 25

Kant, Immanuel, 233, 242, 243
Keane, Angela, 28
Keats, John, 179, 202
Kelley, Theresa, 170
Khalip, Jacques, 194
    and Forest Pyle, 248
Klein, Melanie, 98
Koselleck, Reinhard, 7, 59–60, 129–30
Krapp, John, 8, 16
Kristeva, Julia, 39, 152, 246, 249–50
    on feminine genius, 21, 110, 243–44
    on the Oedipus complex, 110

Kuiken, Kir, 124

Labbe, Jacqueline M., 120, 135, 140, 141, 147, 173, 177
Lacan, Jacques, 115, 159, 166, 167, 262n5
    concept of the big Other, 9, 163–65, 177, 182, 188
    and the death drive, 35–36
    disagreement with Heidegger about the meaning of vases, 235
    discussion of Achilles and the tortoise, 35
    and ex-sistence, 39, 143–44
    and feminine jouissance, 25, 32–33, 35–36, 104–5, 116, 236, 253n73
    and the four discourses, 46, 48, 62–63, 134, 196–97
    on the future, 51
    and the gaze, 189
    and hope, 242–43
    on including oneself, 44, 233–34, 237
    on llanguage, 116, 117, 118, 122, 140–46, 153, 154
    and logical time, 18
    and the not-whole, 5, 11, 16, 25, 64, 124, 160, 177, 257n136
    and object *a*, 16, 46, 47, 64, 131, 141, 190
    on the Oedipus complex, 66, 67–68, 70, 96–99, 103, 107–8, 109, 111, 113, 261n139
    on perversion, 188
    on psychoanalysis, 18, 46, 48, 56, 66–67, 231–32, 233–34
    on psychosis, 190
    and the Real, 39, 167, 235–36, 244
    and sexual difference, 25, 233–34
    and subjectivity, 106, 233–34, 235–36
    on ~~The Woman~~ as not-whole, 5–6, 25, 177

Lake, Crystal B., 21
Lamb, Lady Caroline, *Glenarvon* (1816), 205
Landon, Laetitia Elizabeth, 193
The Last Man (Shelley), 16, 44–45, 59, 168, 203–6, 220–31, 234, 236, 239
Latham, Sean, 204, 212
London, April, 93
Looser, Devoney, 30, 31, 49, 64, 161
Lupton, Christina, 41, 43, 159

Macaulay, Catherine, 2, 3, 28–30, 37, 38, 64, 119, 244
Makdisi, Saree, 219
Mallarmé, Stéphane, 42
Manley, Delarivier, *The New Atalantis* (1709), 204
Marx, Karl, 27
Matthew, Patricia A., 246
McCarthy, Anne C., 13, 115, 250, 261n1
McCarthy, William, 24
McGann, Jerome J., 120, 154, 195
McHale, Brian, 158
Melville, Peter, 182, 186
Merry, Robert, 16, 19–20, 37, 116, 120, 135–36, 159
    "The Adieu and Recall to Love" (1787), 20, 116, 117, 133, 140–43
    The Laurel of Liberty (1790), 117, 121, 126–32, 147
    "Ode to Folly" (1787), 20, 116, 118, 146–54, 171–72, 176, 227, 239, 244
    "Ode to Tranquillity" (1787), 117, 135, 140–41, 144–45
Montgolfier brothers and their hot air balloon, 166, 167
Mullen, Mary L., 8, 221
Mulso, Mary Prescott, 160, 161–64
Muñoz, José Esteban, 131, 169

Nagra, Daljit, 156
Napoleonic Wars, 17, 69, 73, 179, 219, 244
    Battle of Waterloo, 17, 20, 179, 207, 219, 245
Neill, Anna, 73, 75
Nersessian, Anahid, 175, 201–2
Neyrat, Frédéric, 175, 201–2
not-whole, the, Lacan and, 5, 11, 16, 25, 124, 160, 177

Oedipus complex, 19, 66–68, 93–114
Oedipus at Colonus, 184, 231
Oedipus Rex, 67, 68, 106, 184
O'Neill, Michael, 199
Orientalism. See *Gulzara; Princess of Persia; or the Virgin Queen*
Ouseley, Sir Gore, 208, 210–11

Packham, Catherine, 180
Paley, Morton, 229
Paul and Virginia (Williams), 15–16, 19, 65–93, 95–96, 108–9, 114, 135, 175, 205–6, 208, 223, 239
Paulson, Michael S., 8
Peacock, Thomas Love, *Nightmare Abbey* (1818), 205
perversion, 187–202. See also Oedipus complex
Phillips, Mark Salber, 60
Piozzi, Hester Lynch, 119
    "Sonnet. On an Air Balloon" (1788), 156
Pladek, Brittany, 239
Polwhele, Richard, 31
Porter, Jane, 30, 33
Prasad, Pratima, 65
Prescott, Robert, 160, 162
psychoanalysis
    fracture feminism and the protocols of, 3
    relationship to deconstructionism, 11, 17–18, 125, 247

See also Derrida, Jacques; Freud, Sigmund; Lacan, Jacques
psychosis, 157, 187–202

Ragland, Ellie, and Dragan Milovanovic, 163, 167
Ranciére, Jacques, 6, 32, 47, 49, 58, 156, 160, 168, 234, 237
Rauch, Alan, 207, 211
Redfield, Marc, 157
Reeder, Jessie, 54
Rees, Thomas, 33, 34
Richardson, Charlotte Caroline, 2, 120, 146–47, 248
  Harvest: A Poem (1818), 20, 157, 159, 179–87, 239
  "To-Morrow" (1818), 249
  Waterloo: A Poem, on the Late Victory (1815), 179
Richardson, Samuel
  Clarissa (1747/1748), 16, 95, 109, 260n100
Rickards, Lydia, 47–48, 48–49, 51–52
Ricoeur, Paul, 158
Robinson, Daniel, 119, 120, 121, 141
Robinson, Mary Darby (pseudonym Mary Anne Randall), 116–17, 118, 159
  Ainsi va le Monde (1790), 19–20, 116, 117, 121–27, 132
  "Harvest Home" (1800), 179
  A Letter to the Women of England (1799), 3, 18–19, 24, 36–46, 51, 59, 64, 118, 168, 249, 253n87
  Lyrical Tales (1800), 118
  Sappho and Phaon (1796), 36, 118
  Walsingham (1797), 118, 121
Rohrbach, Emily, 12, 13, 54–55
romans à clef, nature of, 203–6, 230. See also *Gulzara; Princess of Persia; or the Virgin Queen*; Shelley, Mary: *The Last Man*

Rooney, Morgan, 249
Rousseau, Jean-Jacques, 44, 72, 86, 91, 186
Rudy, Jason S., 193
Ruppert, Timothy, 221, 224, 229, 231

Sachs, Jonathan, 53, 54, 63
Said, Edward W., 13, 212, 214, 219
Sappho, 30, 133
Sargent, Andrew, 147
Schiller, Friedrich von, as translated by Samuel Taylor Coleridge, 238–39
Scott, Walter, 15
  depiction of in Mary Shelley, *The Last Man*, 271n25
sexual difference, 6, 25, 120, 156–57, 233–34, 246, 247, 248–49. See also Robinson, Mary Darby: *A Letter to the Women of England*; Smith, Charlotte: *Beachy Head*; Wollstonecraft, Mary: *Vindication of the Rights of Woman*
sexual enjoyment, 33–34
Shelley, Mary, 3, 68, 248
  Frankenstein (1818), 65, 87, 123, 126, 227
  The Last Man (1826), 16, 44–45, 59, 168, 203–6, 220–31, 234, 236, 239
  Mathilda (1820, published 1959), 100, 227
  "Valerius, or the Reanimated Roman" (1819, published 1976), 19, 54, 62
Shelley, Percy Bysshe, 15, 202, 214, 219, 222, 232, 242
  depiction of in Mary Shelley, *The Last Man*, 230, 231
Siege of Gibraltar, 17, 19–20, 146–50, 153, 239, 244
Simpson, David, 182
Sinanan, Kerry, 70

Singer, Kate, 36, 169, 190, 193, 228, 248
  and Nanora Sweet, 193
slavery. *See* Williams, Helen Maria: *Paul and Virginia*
Smith, Charlotte, 2, 120, 146–47
  Beachy Head (1807), 20, 157, 159, 168–78, 239, 263n45
Smith, Orianne, 223, 224
Soler, Colette, 10
Song, Eric B., 213
Souter, John, publication of *Gulzara; Princess of Persia; or the Virgin Queen*, 16, 206–7, 212, 215
Southey, Robert, depiction of in Mary Shelley, *The Last Man*, 271n25
Spacks, Patricia Meyer, 260n100
Spivak, Gayatri Chakravorty, 12, 123, 199, 201
Steno, Nicolas, 147
Stewart, David, 194

Thompson, E.P., 7
Tomalin, Marcus, 8
Ty, Eleanor, 95, 110, 112

Vaughan, Megan, 71
The Victim of Prejudice (Hays), 19, 66, 68, 93–114, 260n100
Vindication of the Rights of Woman (Wollstonecraft), 24, 25–30, 38, 40, 69, 109
Voltaire, 148
Vukanović, Marija Brala, and Lovorka Gruić, 59

Walker, Eric C., 65
Walker, Gina Luria, 246–47
Walker, Jonathan, 109
Warren, Andrew, 218
Washington, Chris, 147, 153, 224

Waterloo, Battle of. *See under* Napoleonic Wars
Wilkes, John, as character in "Ithuriel," 34
Williams, Helen Maria, 2, 37, 65, 79, 120, 159, 248
  Julia (1790), 70–71
  Letters Written in France (1790), 245
  Paul and Virginia (1795), 15–16, 19, 65–93, 95–96, 108–9, 114, 135, 175, 205–6, 208, 223, 239
  Poem on the Bill Lately Passed for Regulating the Slave Trade (1788), 73
Withers, Charles W.J., 57
Wolfson, Susan, 188, 195, 269n106
Wollstonecraft, Mary, 2, 3, 5, 20, 146–47, 159, 223
  An Historical and Moral View of the French Revolution (1794), 46, 52, 64, 67, 113, 156
  on Anna Letitia Barbauld, 24–25
  "The Cave of Fancy," 170, 175
  centrality to fracture feminism, 18–19
  discussed in William Godwin, *Memoirs of the Author of the Vindication of the Rights of Woman* (1798), 23–24
  influence of on Anna Letitia Barbauld, "On the Uses of History," 24, 46–64
  influence of on "Ithuriel," 24, 30–36
  influence of on Mary Robinson, *A Letter to the Women of England*, 24, 36–46
  on poetry, 155–57
  Posthumous Works (1798), 23
  praise for Catherine Macaulay, 28–29

reception of, 23–24, 25

Vindication of the Rights of Woman (1792), 24, 25–30, 38, 40, 69, 109

woman, as not-whole, 5–6, 14–15, 25, 177, 188–89

women, education and rights of. See *Gulzara; Princess of Persia; or the Virgin Queen*; Hays, Mary: *The Victim of Prejudice*; Robinson, Mary Darby: *A Letter to the Women of England*; Wollstonecraft, Mary: *Vindication of the Rights of Woman*

Woolf, Virginia, 29, 31, 40

Wordsworth, William, 157, 159, 169, 176, 199, 201

depiction of in Mary Shelley, *The Last Man*, 271n25

Lyrical Ballads (1798), 120

"Ode: Intimations of Immortality" (1807), 8, 18

Xanthippe, 30, 34

Žižek, Slavoj, 37, 38, 130–31, 158–59, 202, 212, 239–40

Zupančič, Alenka, 6, 8, 21, 189

Zytaruk, Maria, 90

www.ingramcontent.com/pod-product-compliance
Lightning Source LLC
Chambersburg PA
CBHW022047230426
43672CB00008B/1091